So I'm a Spider, So What? 2

Art:
Asahiro Kakashi

Original Story:
Okina Baba

Character Design:
Tsukasa Kiryu

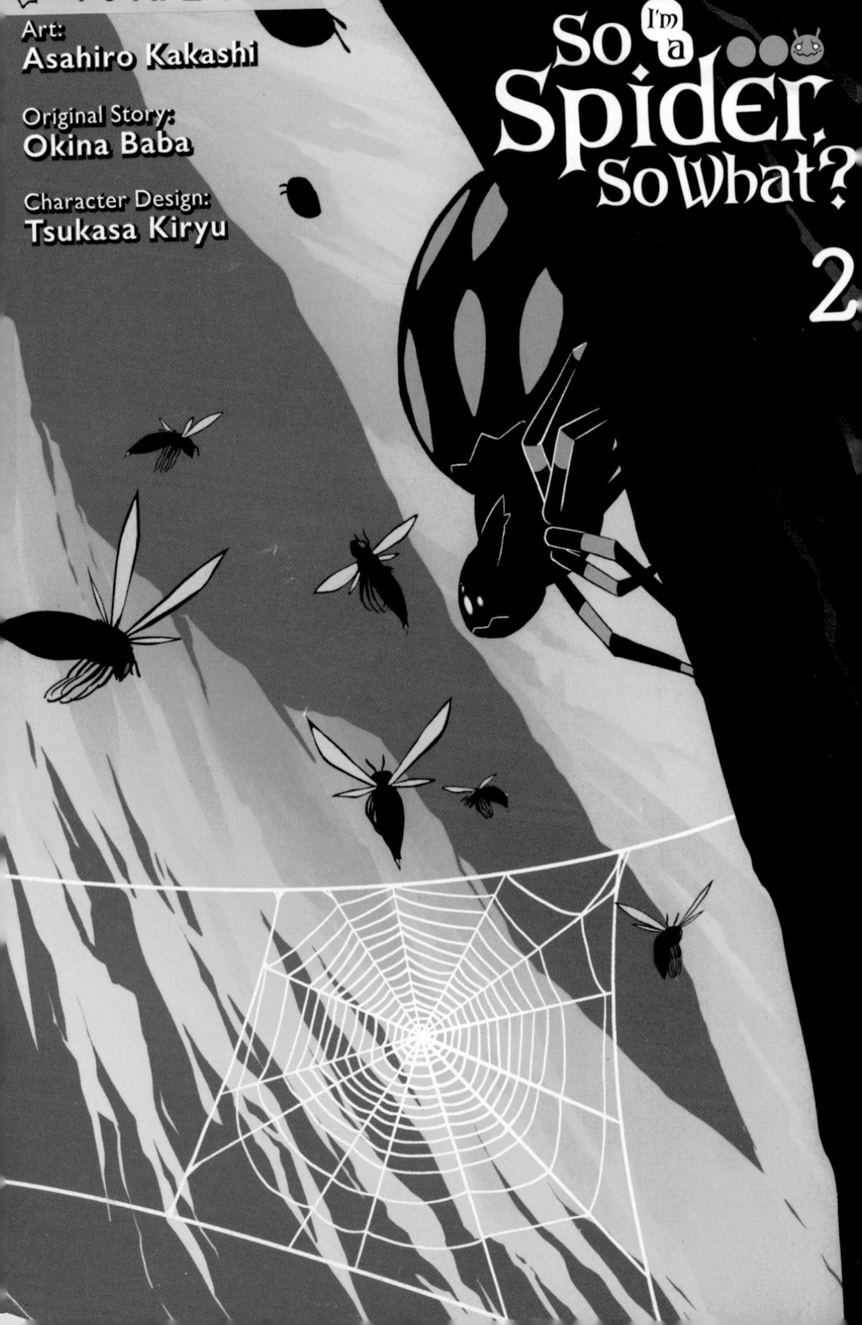

So I'm a Spider, So What?

CONTENTS

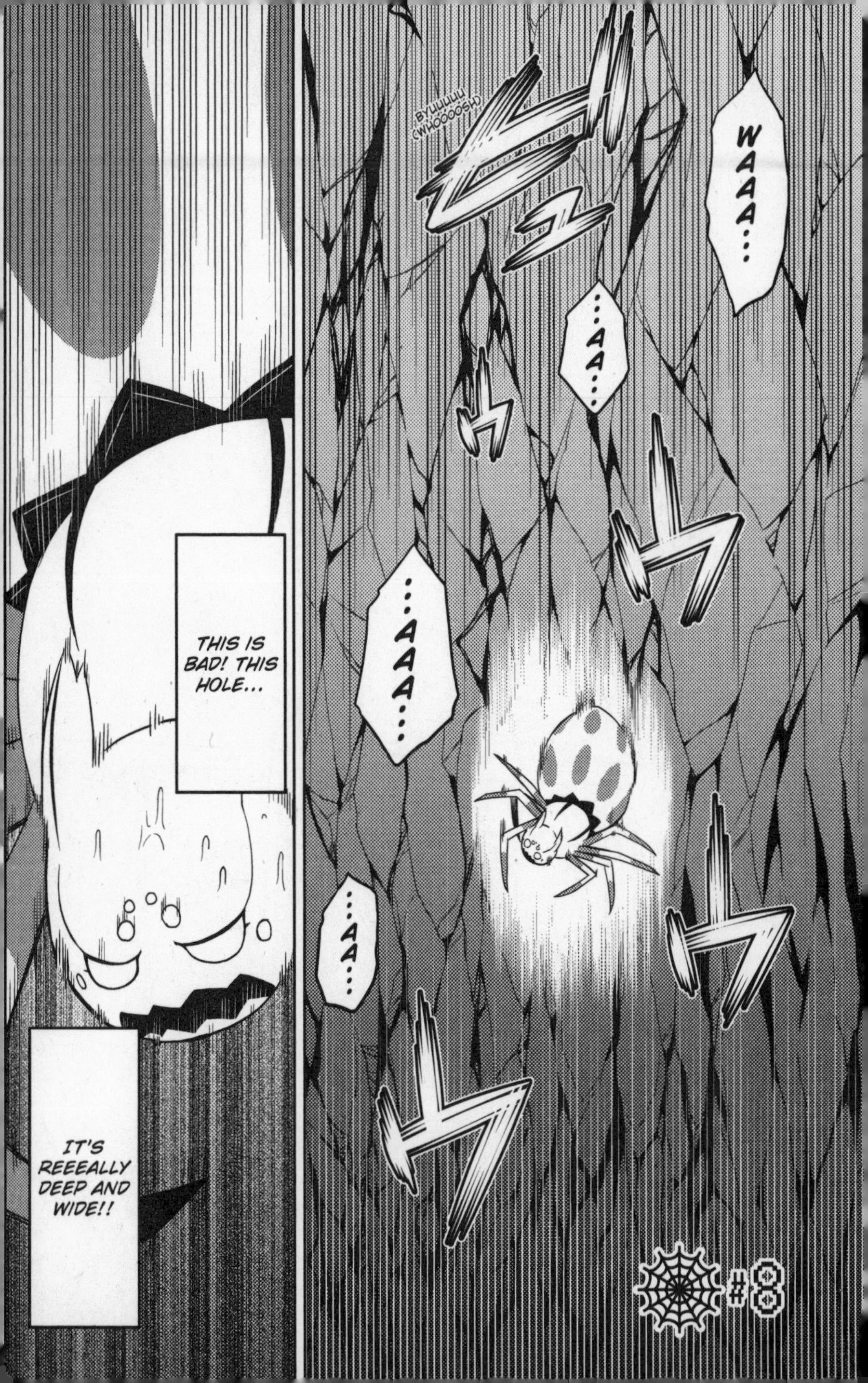
WAAAA...
BYUUUUU (WHOOOOSH)
...AA...
...AAA...
...AA...
#8
THIS IS BAD! THIS HOLE...
IT'S REEEALLY DEEP AND WIDE!!

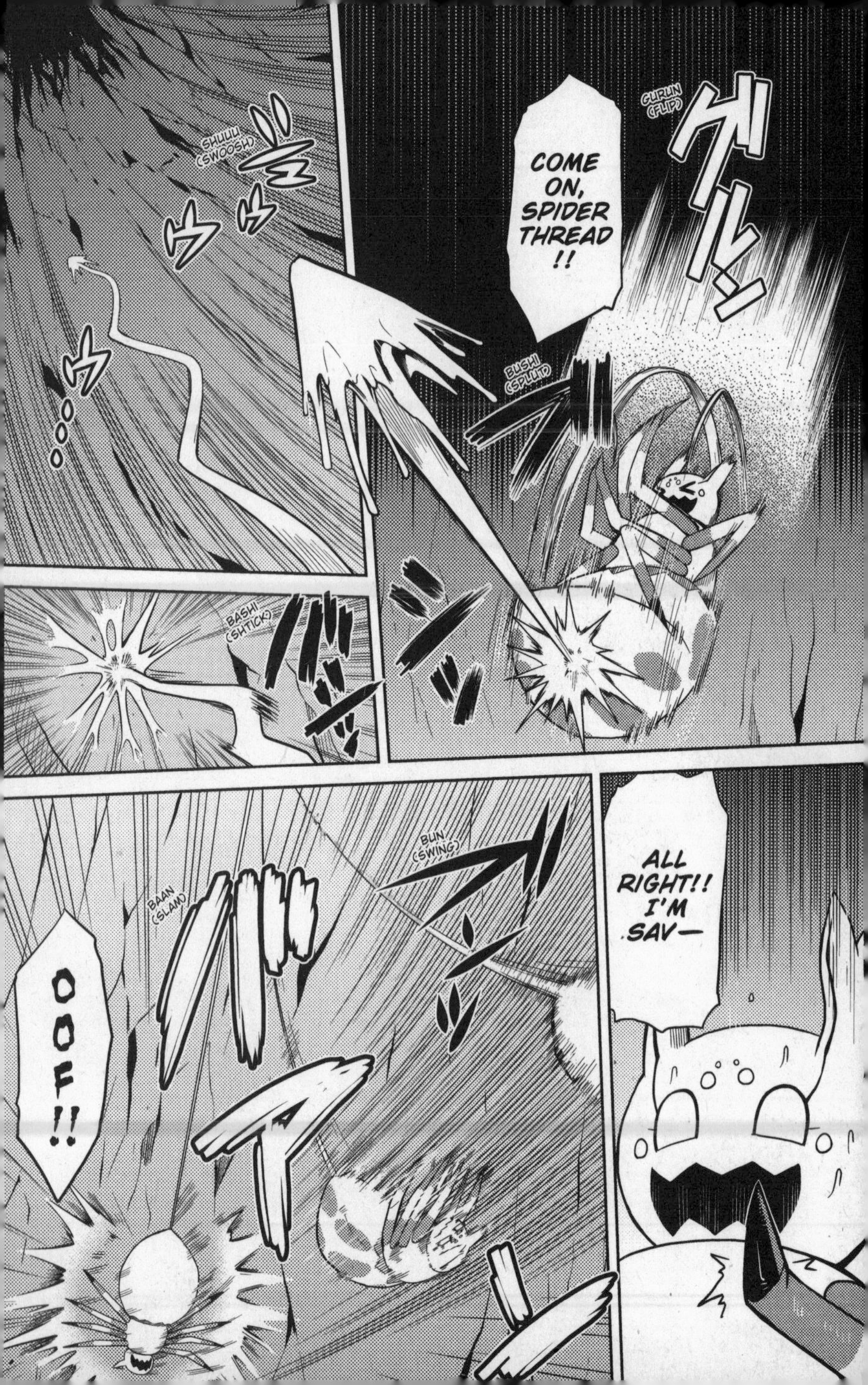
GURUN (FLIP)
COME ON, SPIDER THREAD!!
BUSHI (SPLUT)
SHUUU (SWOOSH)
BASHI (SHTICK)
ALL RIGHT!! I'M SAV—
BUN (SWING)
BAAN (SLAM)
OOF!!

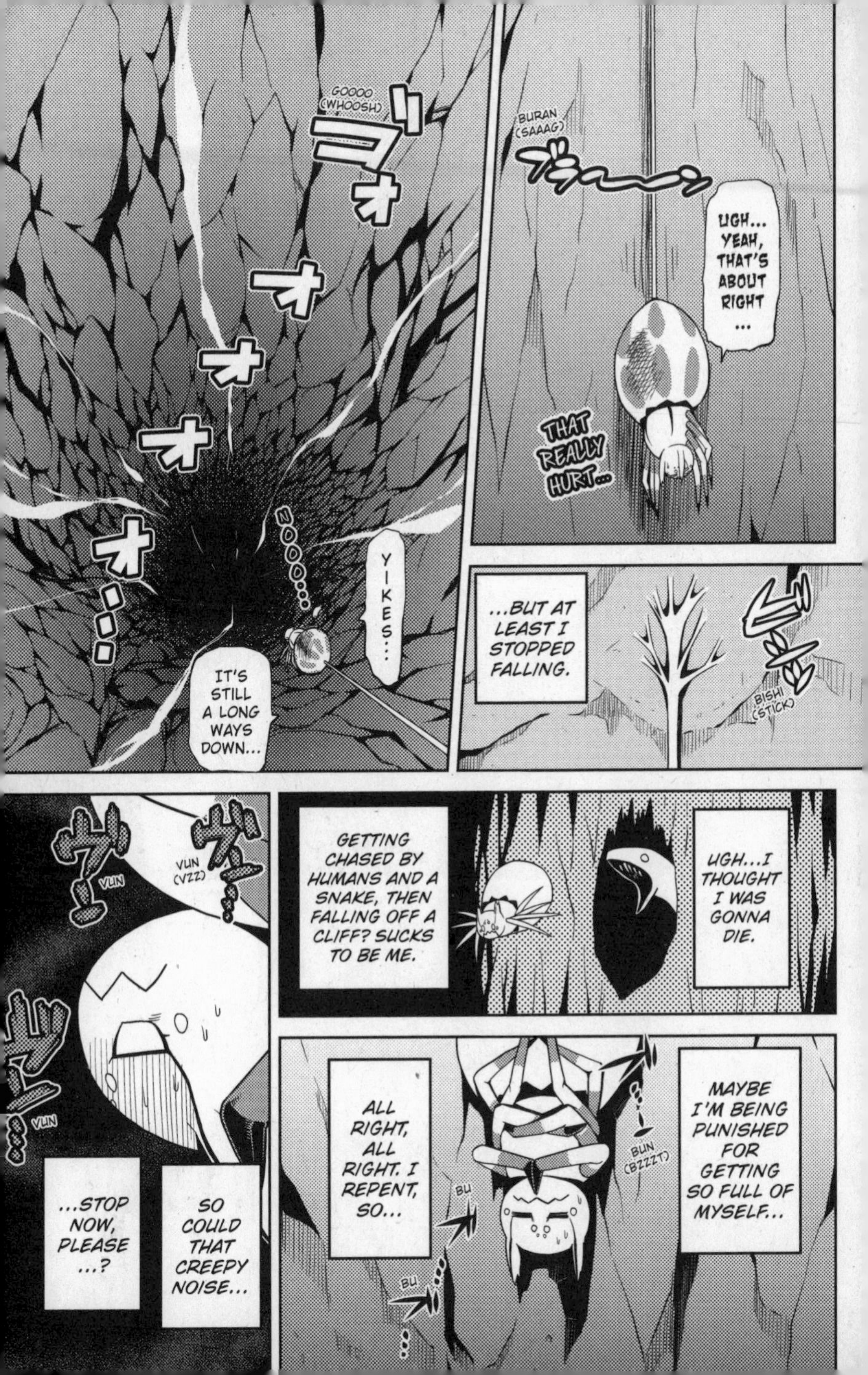
BURAN (SAAAG)
UGH... YEAH, THAT'S ABOUT RIGHT ...
THAT REALLY HURT...
...BUT AT LEAST I STOPPED FALLING.
BISHI (STICK)
GOOOO (WHOOSH)
NOOOO...
YIKES...
IT'S STILL A LONG WAYS DOWN...
UGH...I THOUGHT I WAS GONNA DIE.
GETTING CHASED BY HUMANS AND A SNAKE, THEN FALLING OFF A CLIFF? SUCKS TO BE ME.
MAYBE I'M BEING PUNISHED FOR GETTING SO FULL OF MYSELF...
BUN (BZZZT)
BU
ALL RIGHT, ALL RIGHT. I REPENT, SO...
BU
VUN (VZZ)
VUN
VUN
SO COULD THAT CREEPY NOISE...
...STOP NOW, PLEASE ...?

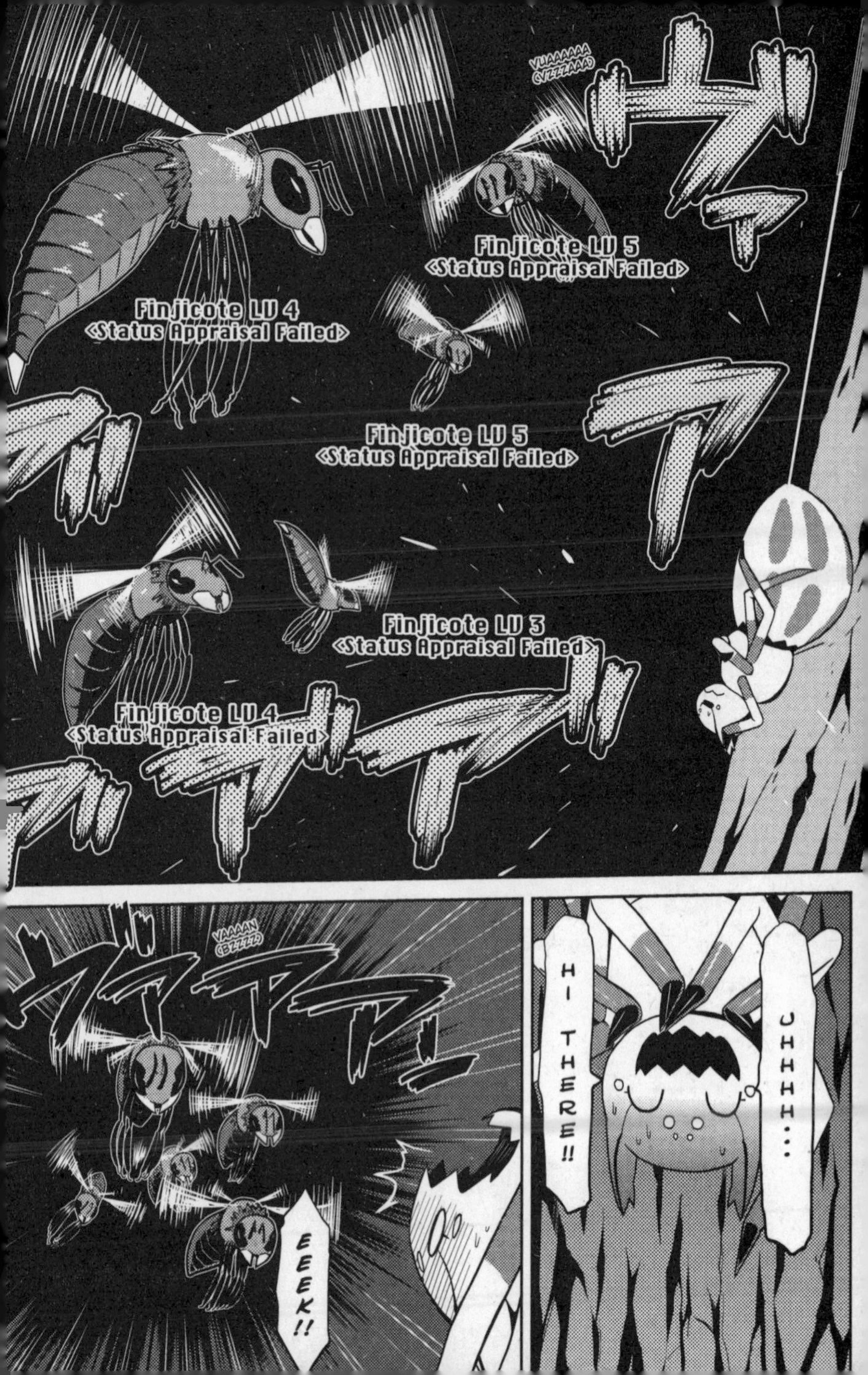
VUAAAAAA (VZZZAAA)
Finjicote LV 5
<Status Appraisal Failed>
Finjicote LV 4
<Status Appraisal Failed>
Finjicote LV 5
<Status Appraisal Failed>
Finjicote LV 3
<Status Appraisal Failed>
Finjicote LV 4
<Status Appraisal Failed>
UHHHH...
HI THERE!!
VAAAAN (BZZZZ)
EEEK!!

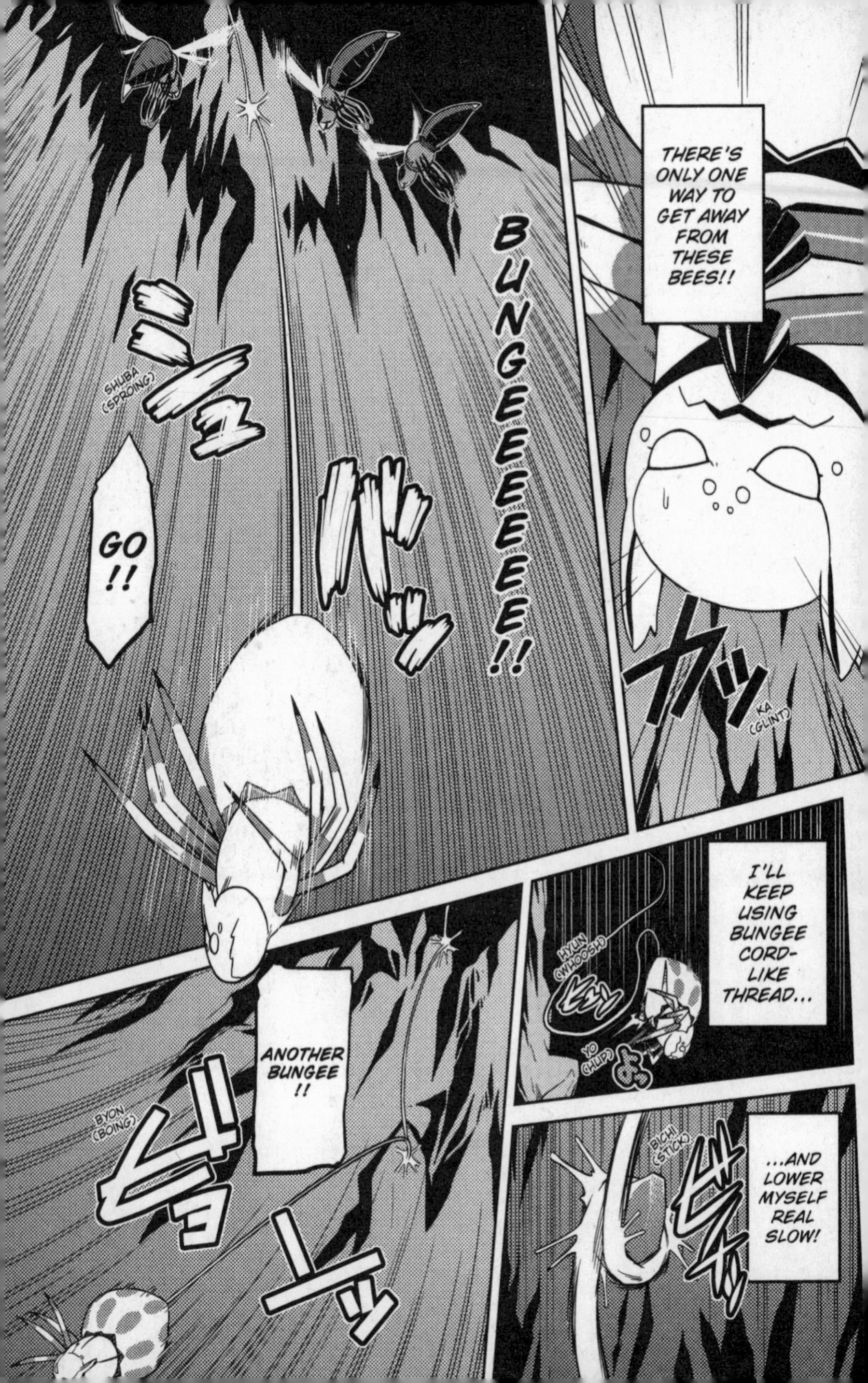
THERE'S ONLY ONE WAY TO GET AWAY FROM THESE BEES!!
KA (GLINT)
BUNGEEEEEEEE!!
SHUBA (SPROING)
GO!!
I'LL KEEP USING BUNGEE CORD-LIKE THREAD...
HYUN (WHOOSH)
YO (HUP)
...AND LOWER MYSELF REAL SLOW!
BICHI (STICK)
ANOTHER BUNGEE!!
BYON (BOING)

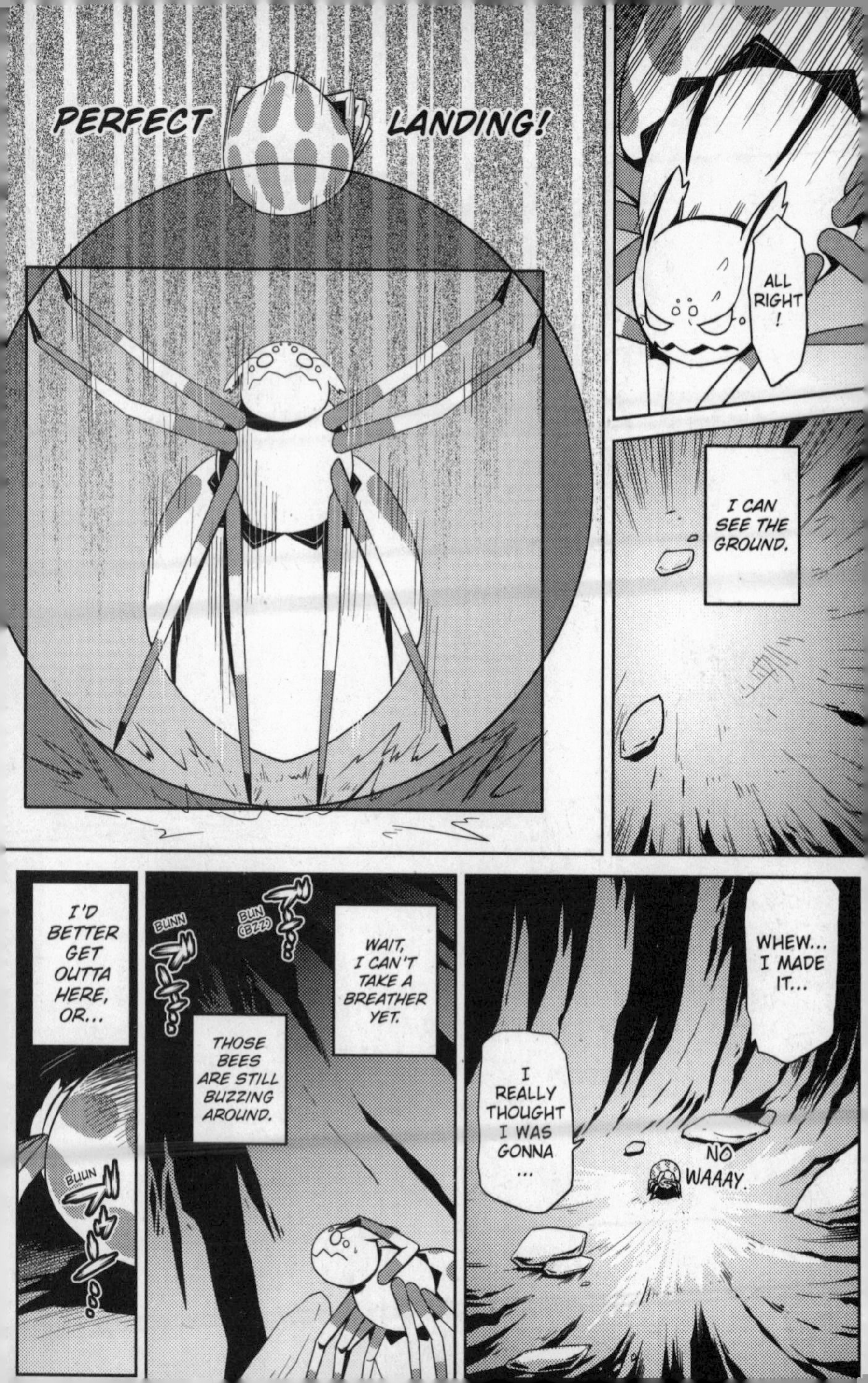
ALL RIGHT!
I CAN SEE THE GROUND.
PERFECT LANDING!
WHEW... I MADE IT...
I REALLY THOUGHT I WAS GONNA...
NO WAAAY.
WAIT, I CAN'T TAKE A BREATHER YET.
BUN (BZZZ)
BUNN
THOSE BEES ARE STILL BUZZING AROUND.
I'D BETTER GET OUTTA HERE, OR...
BUUN

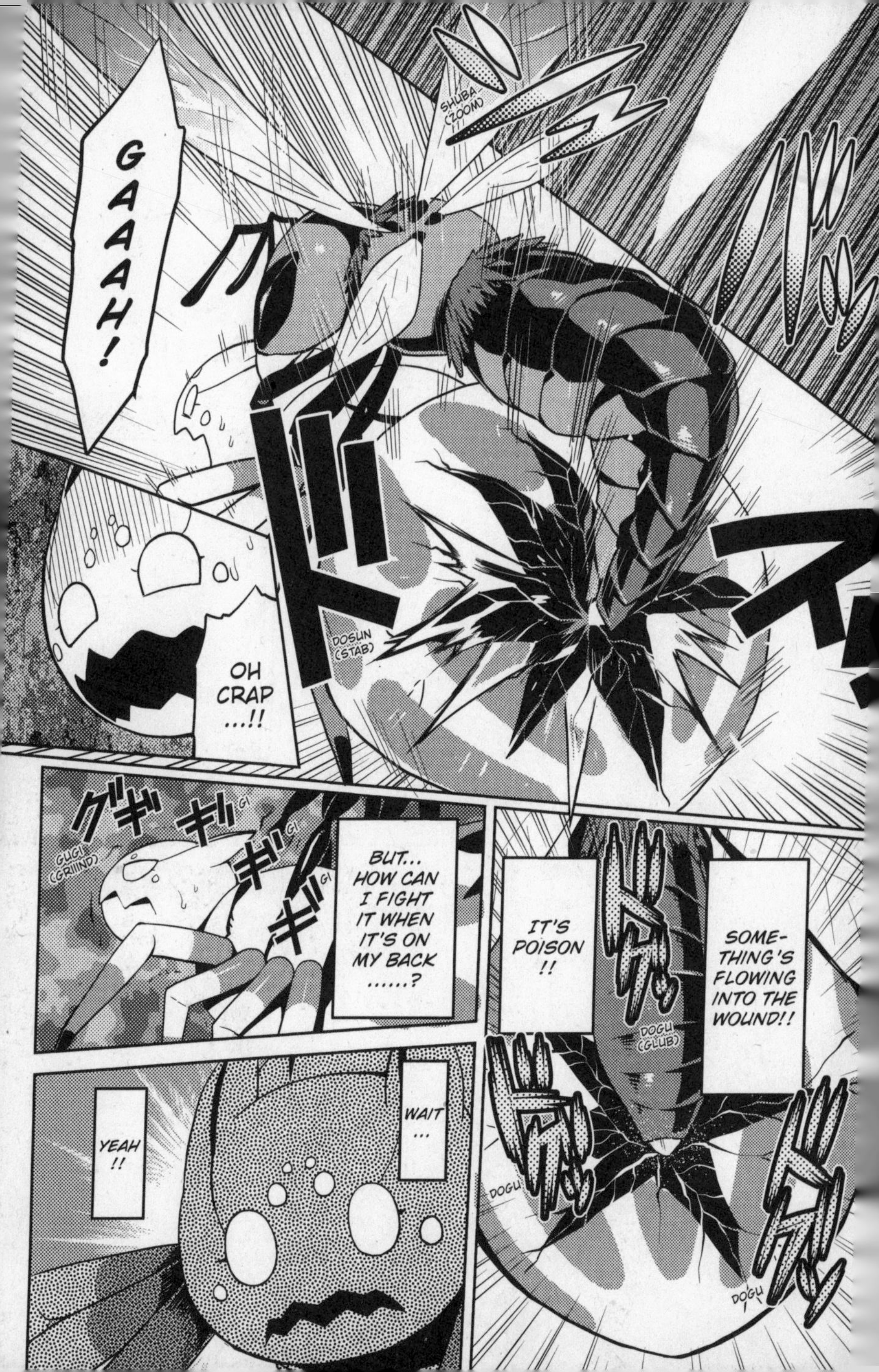
SHUBA (ZOOM)
GAAAAH!
DOSUN (STAB)
OH CRAP ...!!
SOME-THING'S FLOWING INTO THE WOUND!!
DOGU (GLUB)
IT'S POISON !!
DOGU
DOGU
BUT... HOW CAN I FIGHT IT WHEN IT'S ON MY BACK ......?
GI
GI
GUGI (GRIIIND)
WAIT ...
YEAH !!

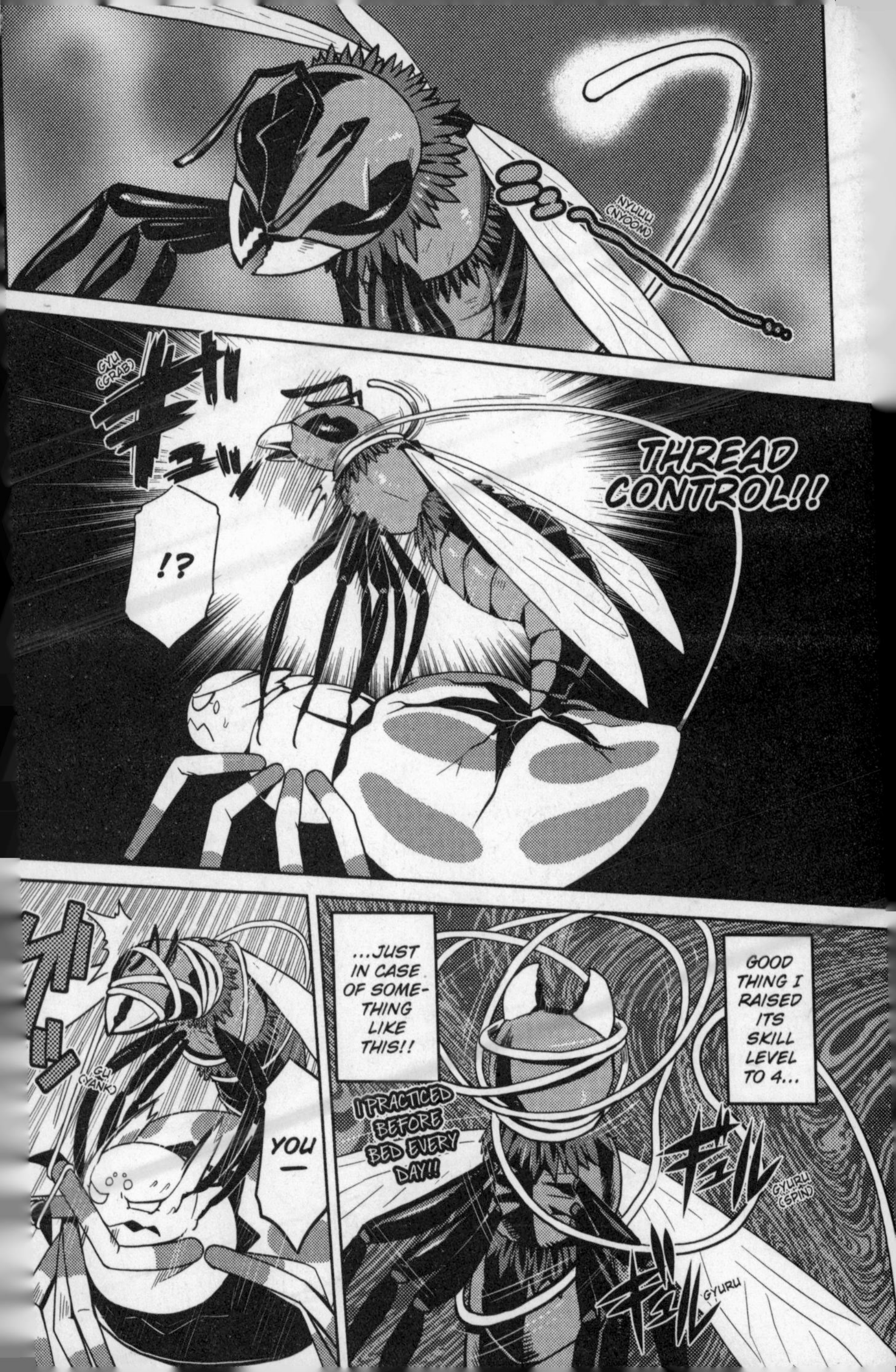
NYUUU (NYOOM)
THREAD CONTROL!!
GYU (GRAB)
!?
GOOD THING I RAISED ITS SKILL LEVEL TO 4...
...JUST IN CASE OF SOMETHING LIKE THIS!!
I PRACTICED BEFORE BED EVERY DAY!!
GYURU (SPIN)
GYURU
GU (YANK)
YOU—

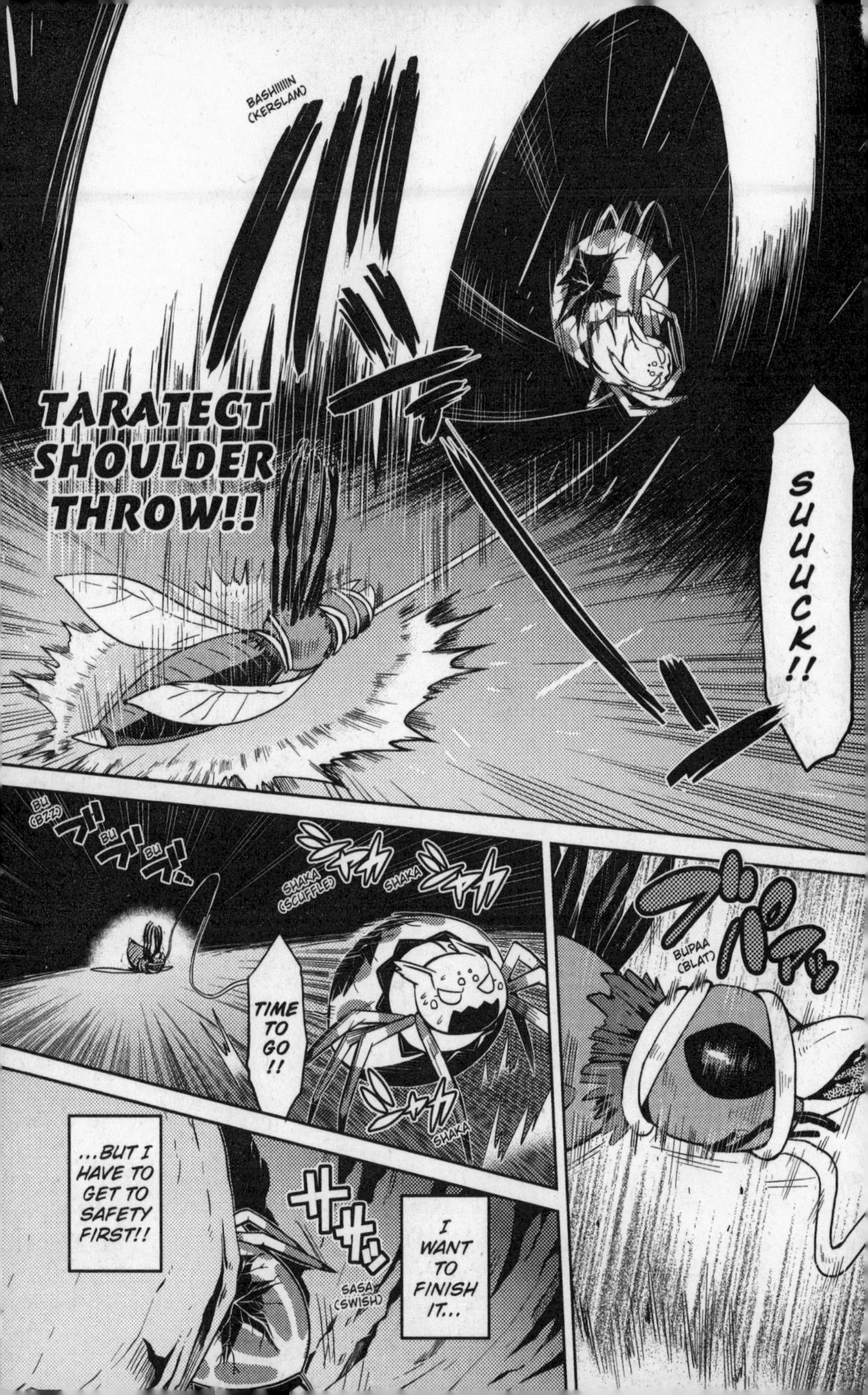
BASHIIIIIN (KERSLAM)
SUUUUCK!!
TARATECT SHOULDER THROW!!
BUPAA (BLAT)
SHAKA
SHAKA (SCUFFLE)
BU (BZZ) BU BU
TIME TO GO!!
SHAKA
I WANT TO FINISH IT...
SASA (SWISH)
...BUT I HAVE TO GET TO SAFETY FIRST!!

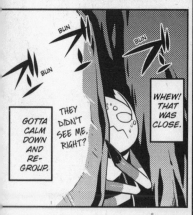

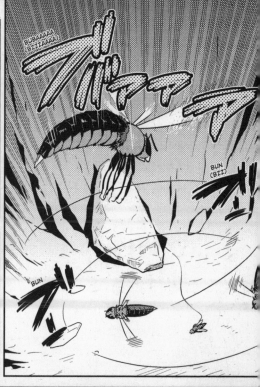

BUBAAAAA (BZZZAAAAA)
BUN (BZZ)
BUN
BUN
BUN
BUN
WHEW! THAT WAS CLOSE.
THEY DIDN'T SEE ME, RIGHT?
GOTTA CALM DOWN AND RE-GROUP.
POON (BING)
Small Taratect
LV 2
Nameless
HP: 6/36
MP: 33/36
SP: 11/36
9/36
OH GEEZ... I'M NEARLY DEAD!
THAT ONE ATTACK WIPED OUT MOST OF MY HP.
OWWW...
GOOD THING MY POISON RESISTANCE IS SO HIGH...
OTHERWISE, IT PROBABLY WOULD'VE KILLED ME.
I WANNA KILL THAT BEE FOR FOOD AND TO LEVEL UP AND RECOVER...
...BUT IT'D BE A BAD IDEA TO GO OUT THERE.
SA SA SA (SNEAK)
PIN (YANK)

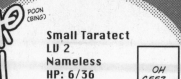

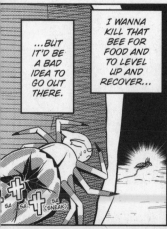

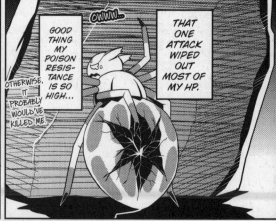

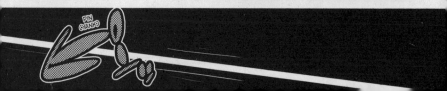

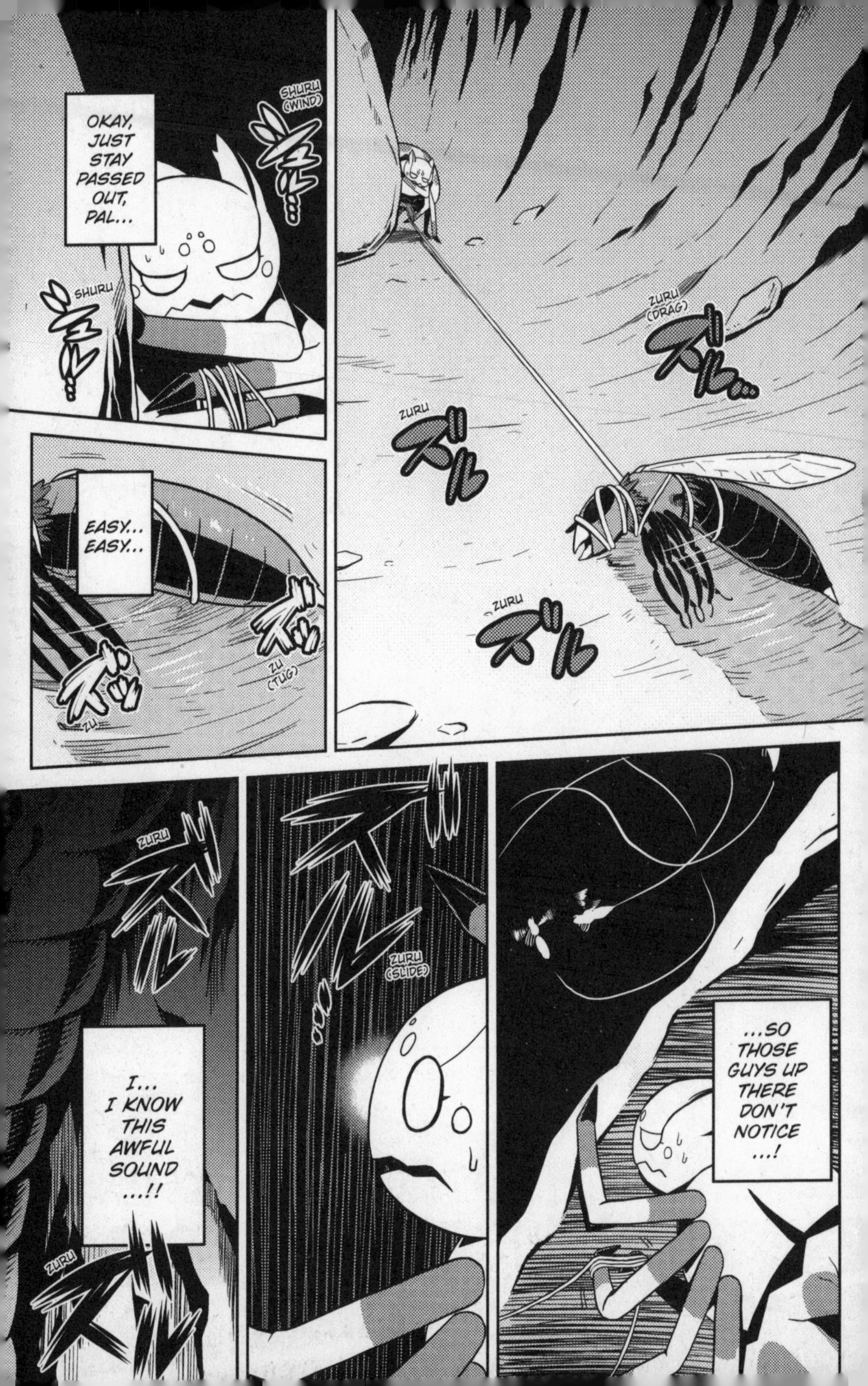
ZURU (DRAG)
ZURU
ZURU
SHURU (WIND)
OKAY, JUST STAY PASSED OUT, PAL...
SHURU
EASY... EASY...
ZU (TUG)
ZU
...SO THOSE GUYS UP THERE DON'T NOTICE ...!
ZURU (SLIDE)
ZURU
I... I KNOW THIS AWFUL SOUND ...!!
ZURU

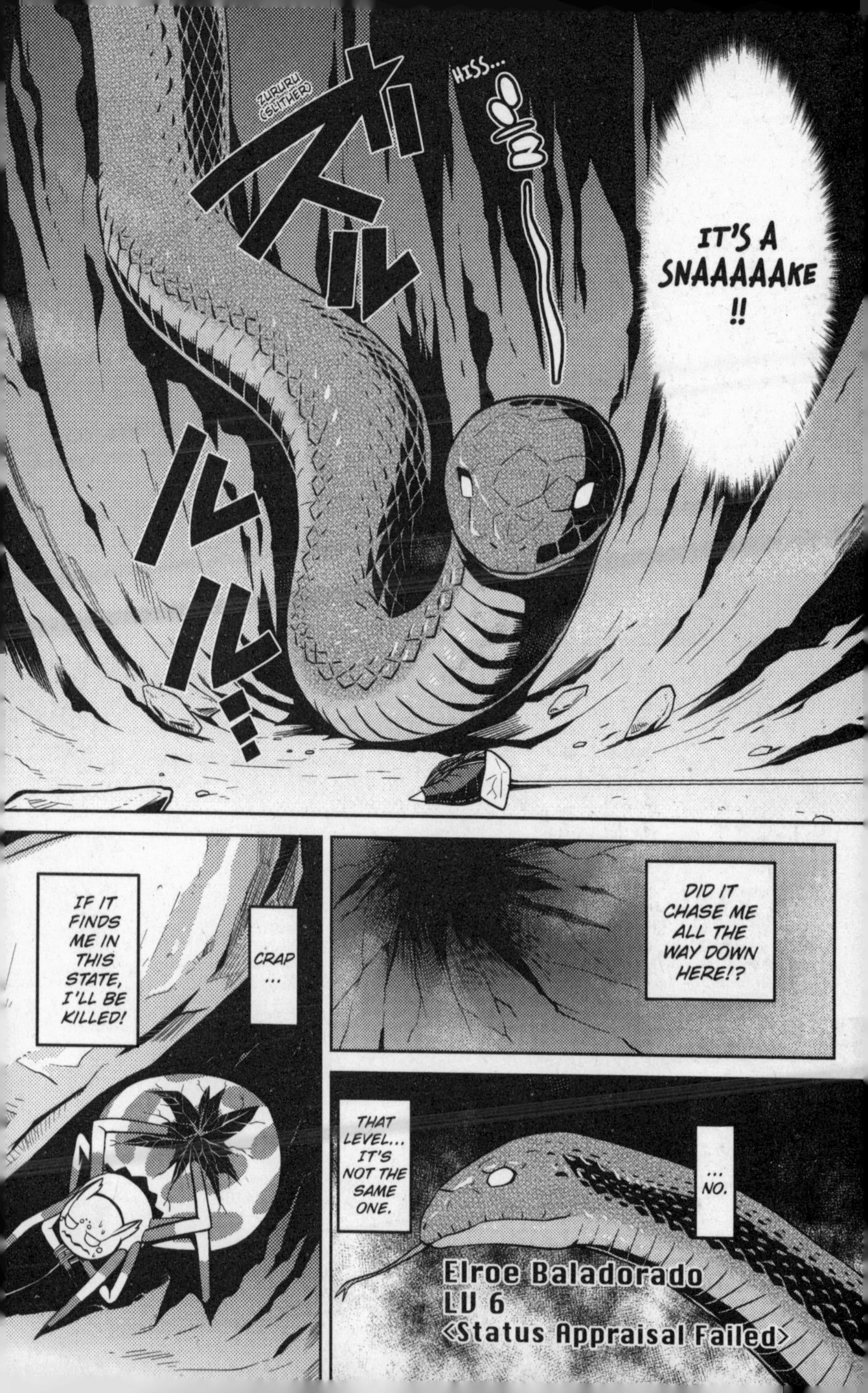
IT'S A SNAAAAAKE !!
HISS...
ZURURU (SLITHER)
DID IT CHASE ME ALL THE WAY DOWN HERE!?
... NO.
THAT LEVEL... IT'S NOT THE SAME ONE.
Elroe Baladorado
LV 6
«Status Appraisal Failed»
CRAP ...
IF IT FINDS ME IN THIS STATE, I'LL BE KILLED!

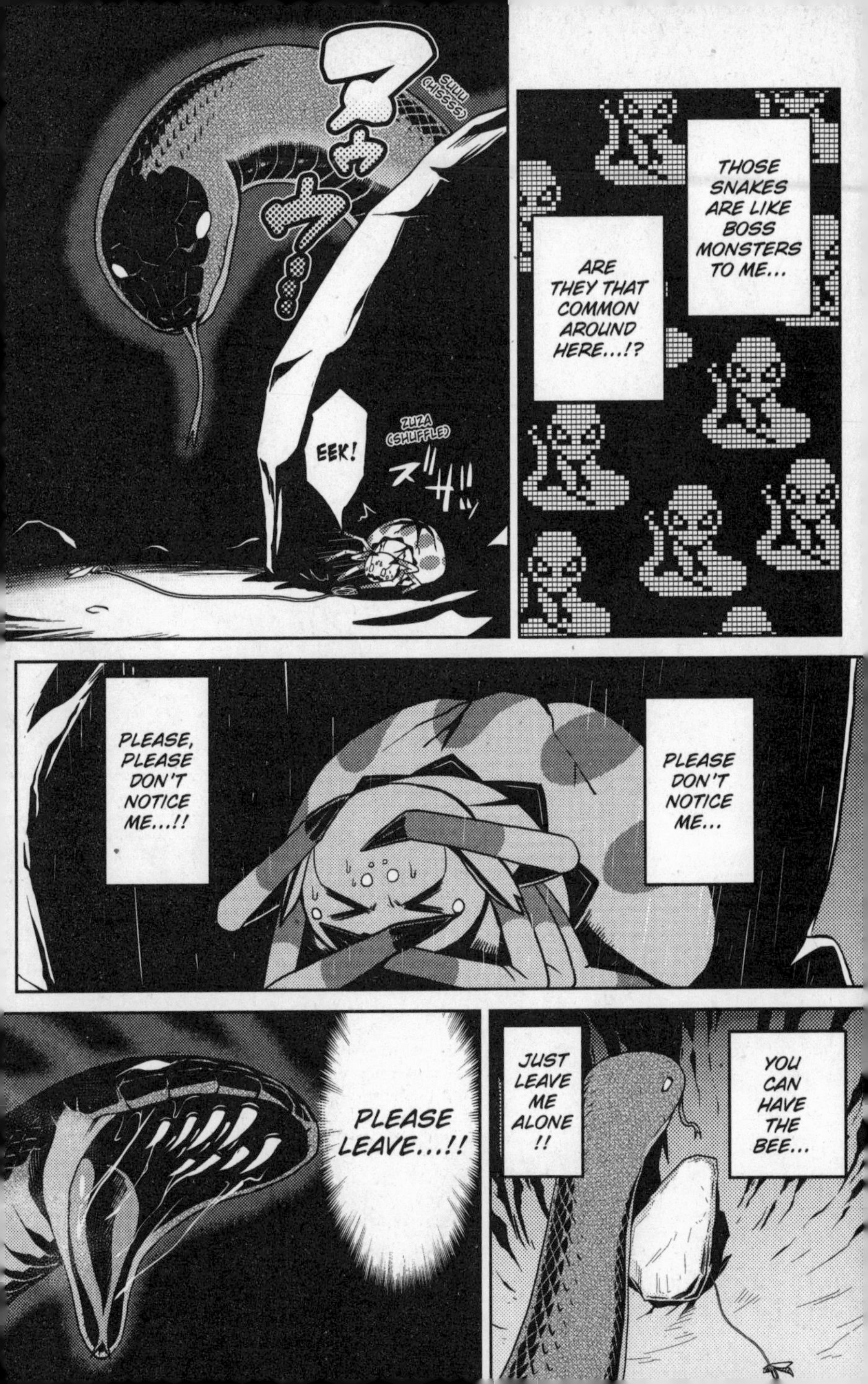
THOSE SNAKES ARE LIKE BOSS MONSTERS TO ME...
ARE THEY THAT COMMON AROUND HERE...!?
SUUU (HISSSS)
EEK!
ZUZA (SHUFFLE)
PLEASE DON'T NOTICE ME...
PLEASE, PLEASE DON'T NOTICE ME...!!
YOU CAN HAVE THE BEE...
JUST LEAVE ME ALONE !!
PLEASE LEAVE...!!

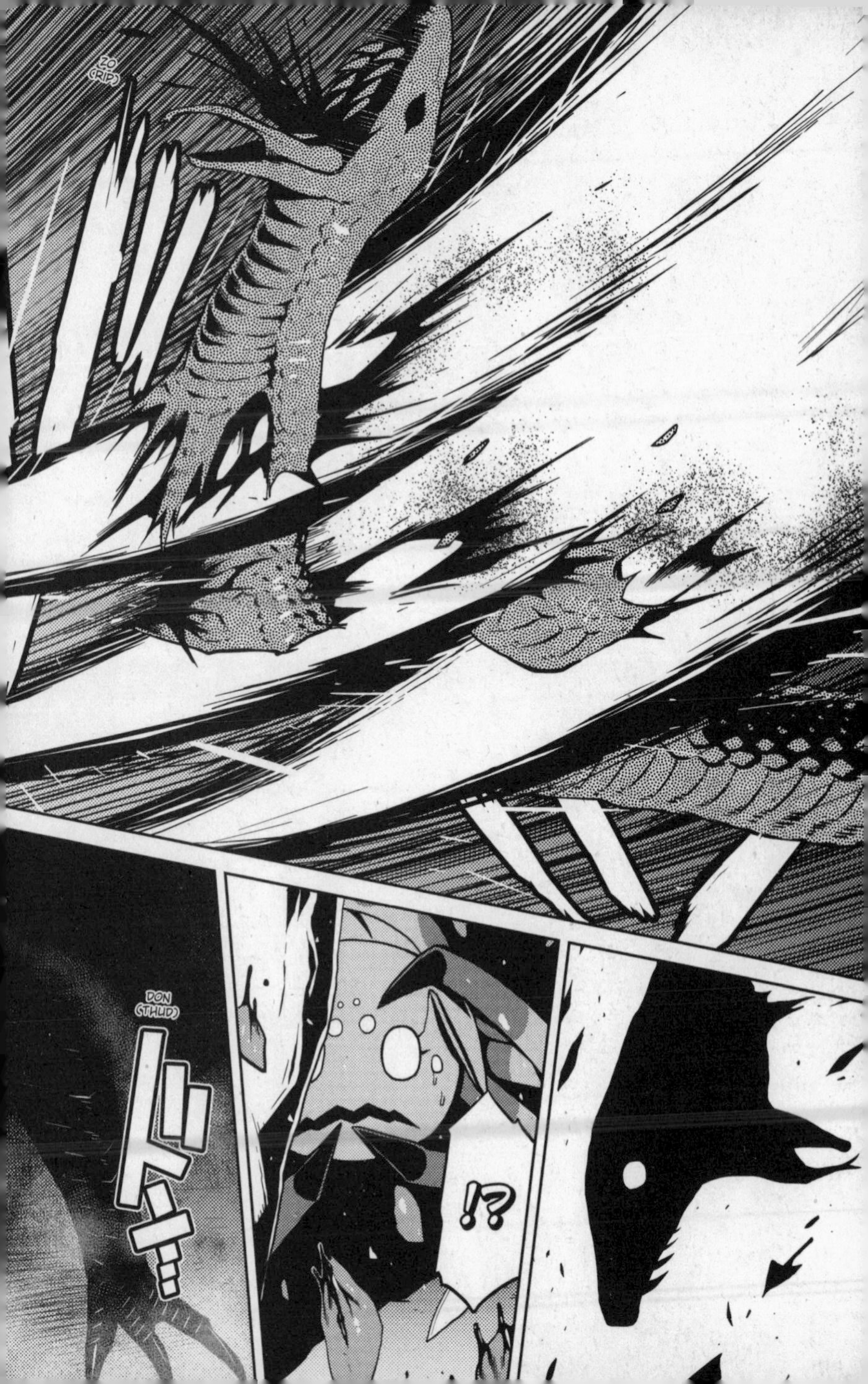
ZO (RIP)
!?
DON (THUD)

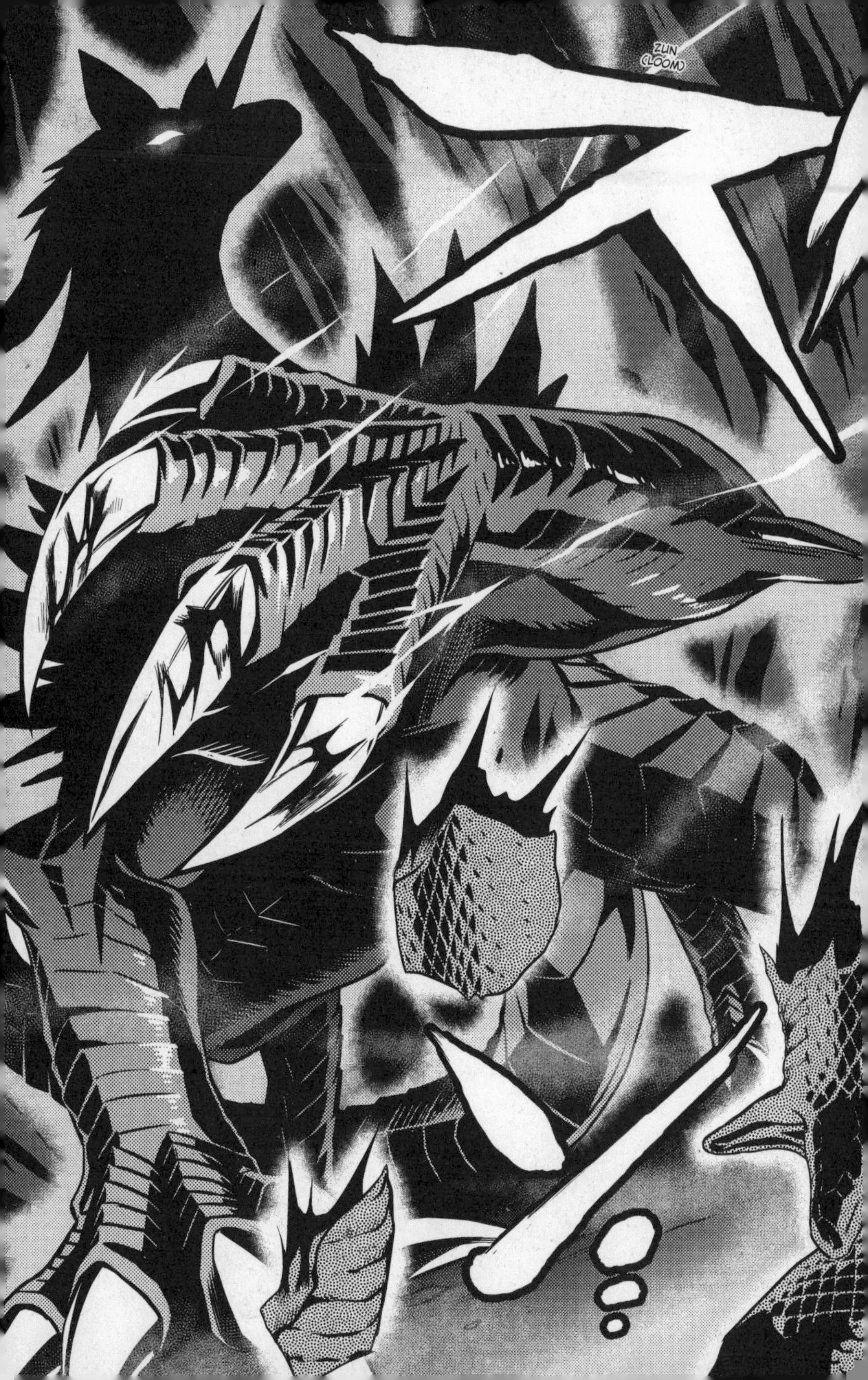
ZUN
(LOOM)

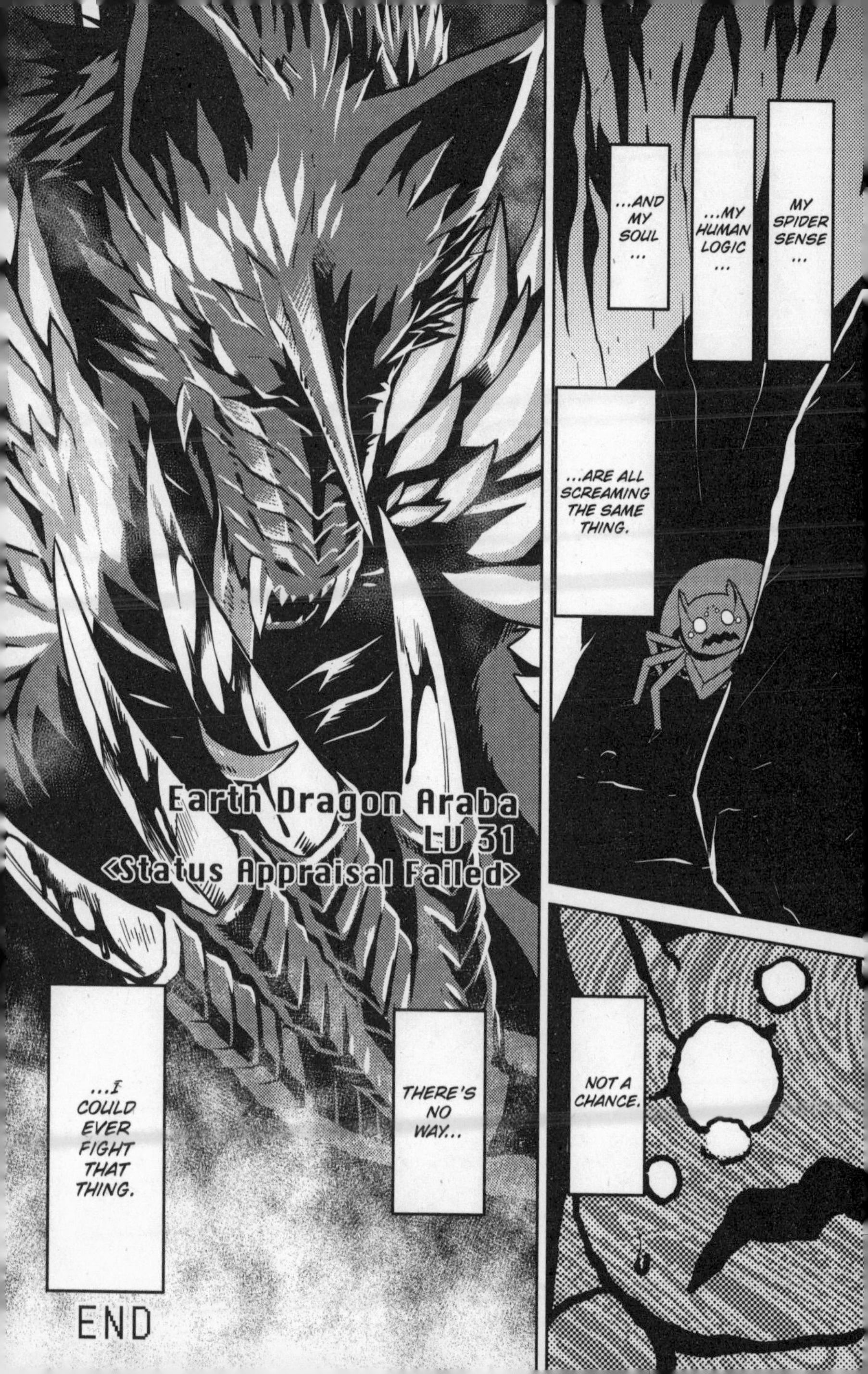
MY SPIDER SENSE...
...MY HUMAN LOGIC...
...AND MY SOUL...
...ARE ALL SCREAMING THE SAME THING.
NOT A CHANCE.
Earth Dragon Araba
LV 31
«Status Appraisal Failed»
THERE'S NO WAY...
...I COULD EVER FIGHT THAT THING.
END

So I'm a Spider, So What?

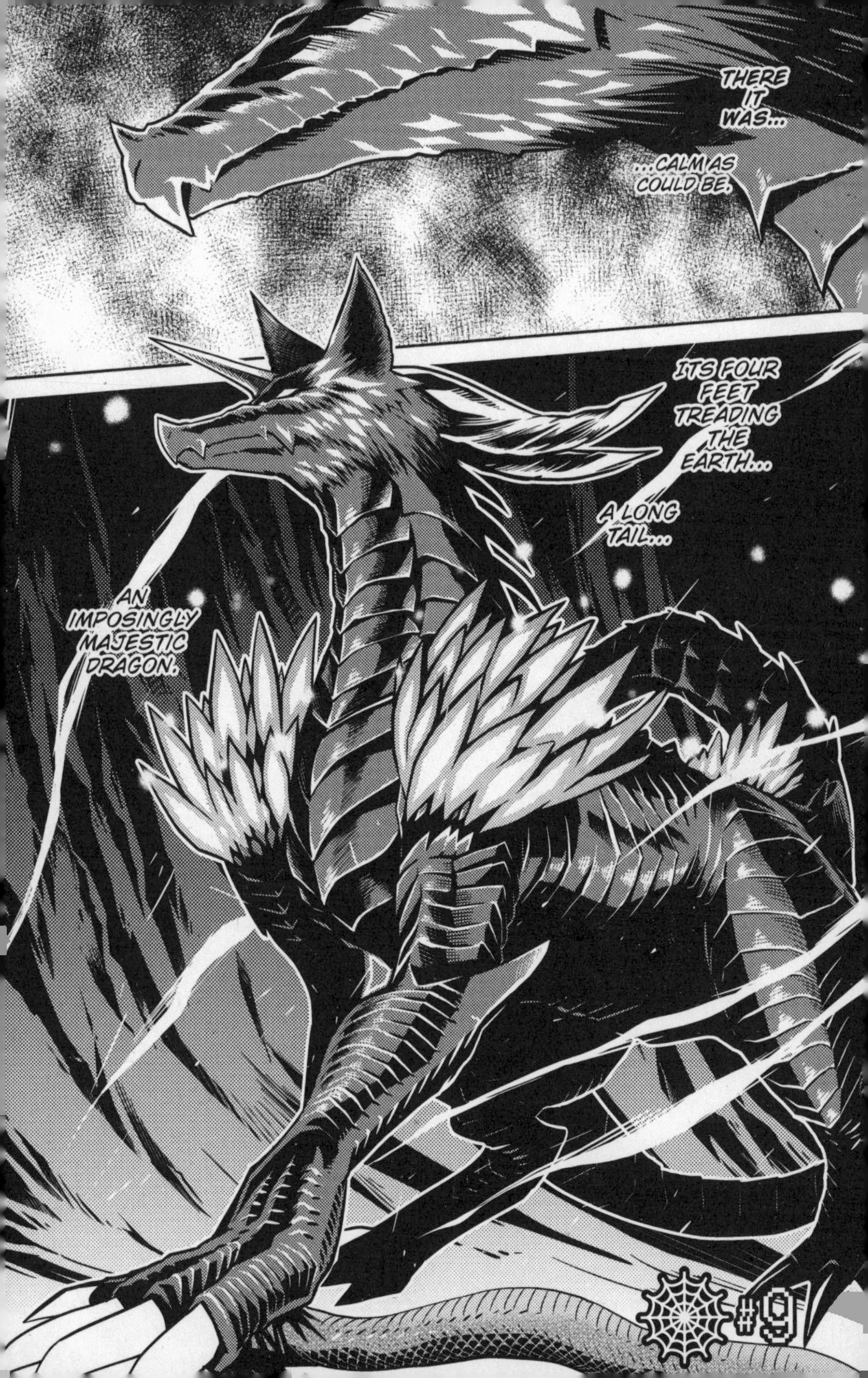
THERE IT WAS...
...CALM AS COULD BE.
ITS FOUR FEET TREADING THE EARTH...
A LONG TAIL...
AN IMPOSINGLY MAJESTIC DRAGON.
#9

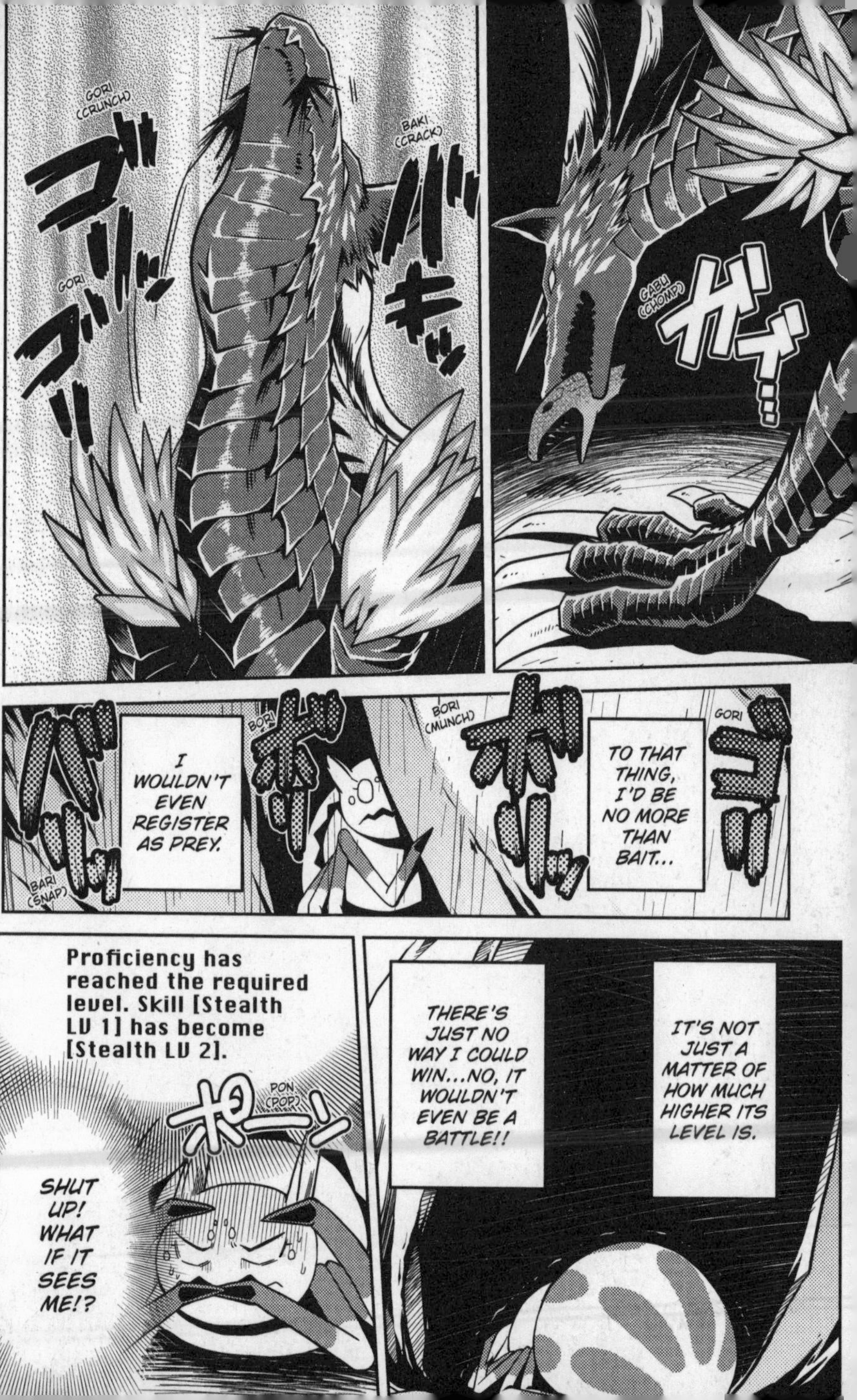
GABU (CHOMP)
BAKI (CRACK)
GORI (CRUNCH)
GORI
GORI
TO THAT THING, I'D BE NO MORE THAN BAIT...
BORI (MUNCH)
BORI
I WOULDN'T EVEN REGISTER AS PREY.
BARI (SNAP)
IT'S NOT JUST A MATTER OF HOW MUCH HIGHER ITS LEVEL IS.
THERE'S JUST NO WAY I COULD WIN...NO, IT WOULDN'T EVEN BE A BATTLE!!
Proficiency has reached the required level. Skill [Stealth LV 1] has become [Stealth LV 2].
PON (POP)
SHUT UP! WHAT IF IT SEES ME!?

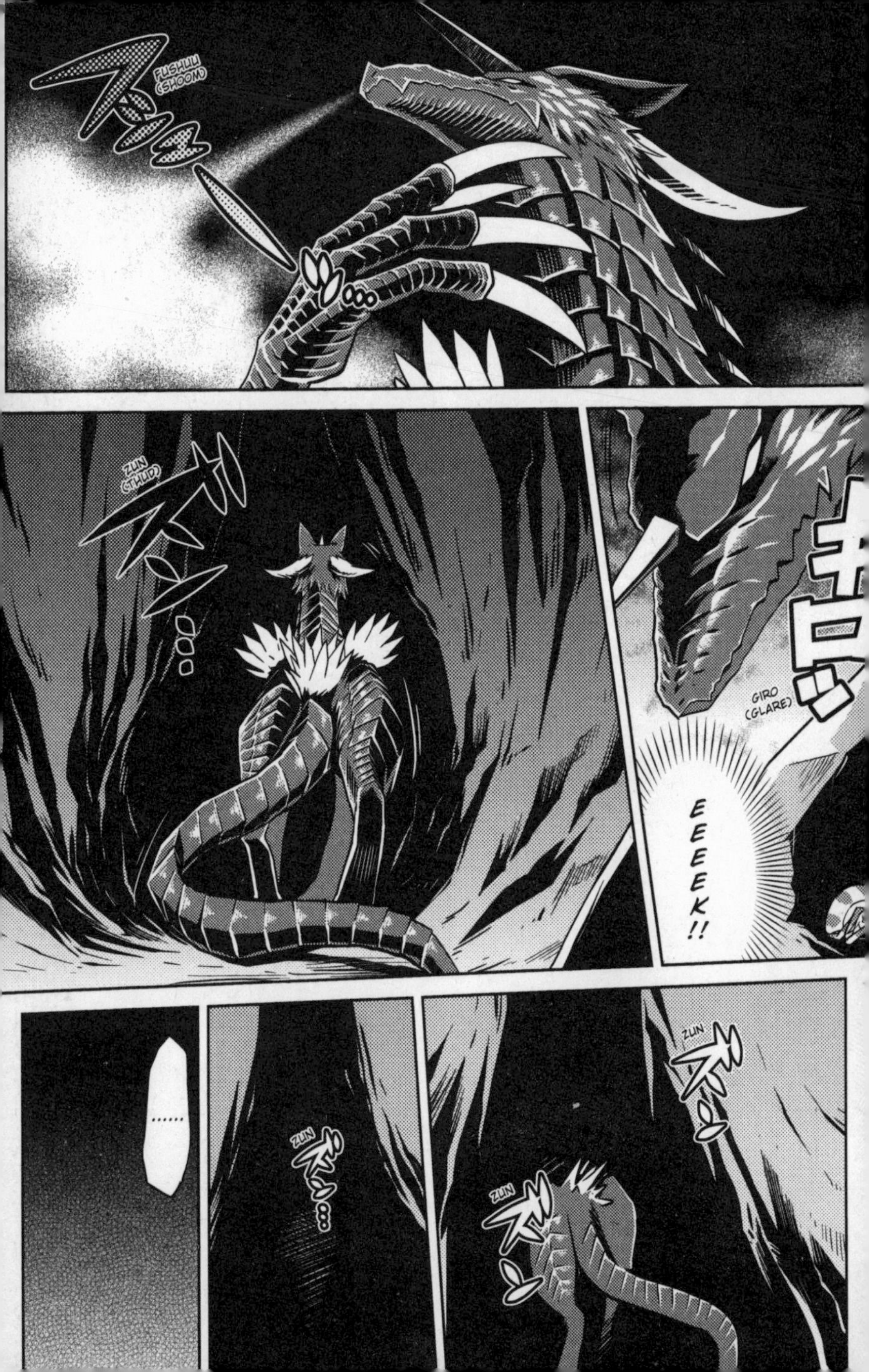
FUSHUU (SHOOM)
GIRO (GLARE)
EEEEEK!!
ZUN (THUD)
ZUN
ZUN
ZUN
......

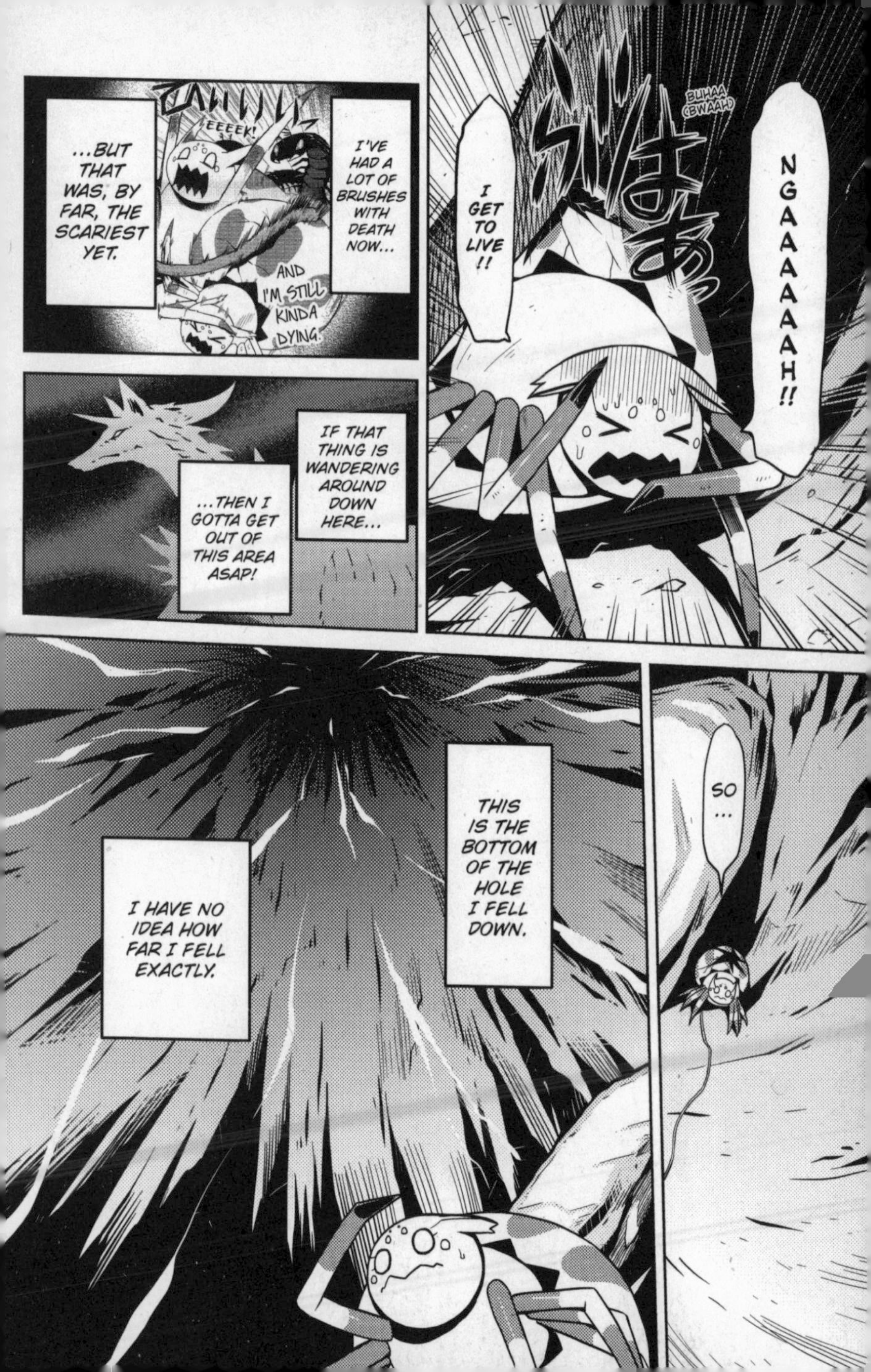
BUHAA (BWAAH)
NGAAAAAAAH!!
I GET TO LIVE!!
I'VE HAD A LOT OF BRUSHES WITH DEATH NOW...
...BUT THAT WAS, BY FAR, THE SCARIEST YET.
EEEEEK!
AND I'M STILL KINDA DYING.
IF THAT THING IS WANDERING AROUND DOWN HERE...
...THEN I GOTTA GET OUT OF THIS AREA ASAP!
SO...
THIS IS THE BOTTOM OF THE HOLE I FELL DOWN.
I HAVE NO IDEA HOW FAR I FELL EXACTLY.

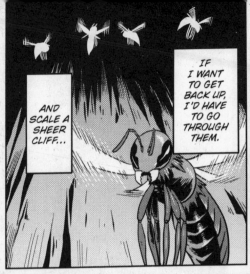

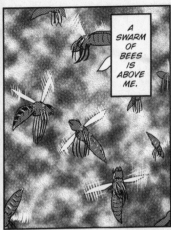

A SWARM OF BEES IS ABOVE ME.
IF I WANT TO GET BACK UP, I'D HAVE TO GO THROUGH THEM.
AND SCALE A SHEER CLIFF...
YEAH.
NOT GONNA HAPPEN.
I CAN'T MOVE QUICKLY WHILE I'M CLINGING TO A WALL...
...OR AIM MY THREAD VERY WELL.
GRRRR...
MY STRENGTH IS FIGHTING IN ENCLOSED SPACES.
BUT THOSE BEES CAN FLY AROUND FREELY...

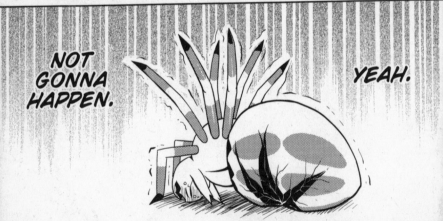

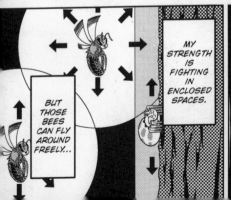

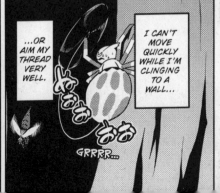

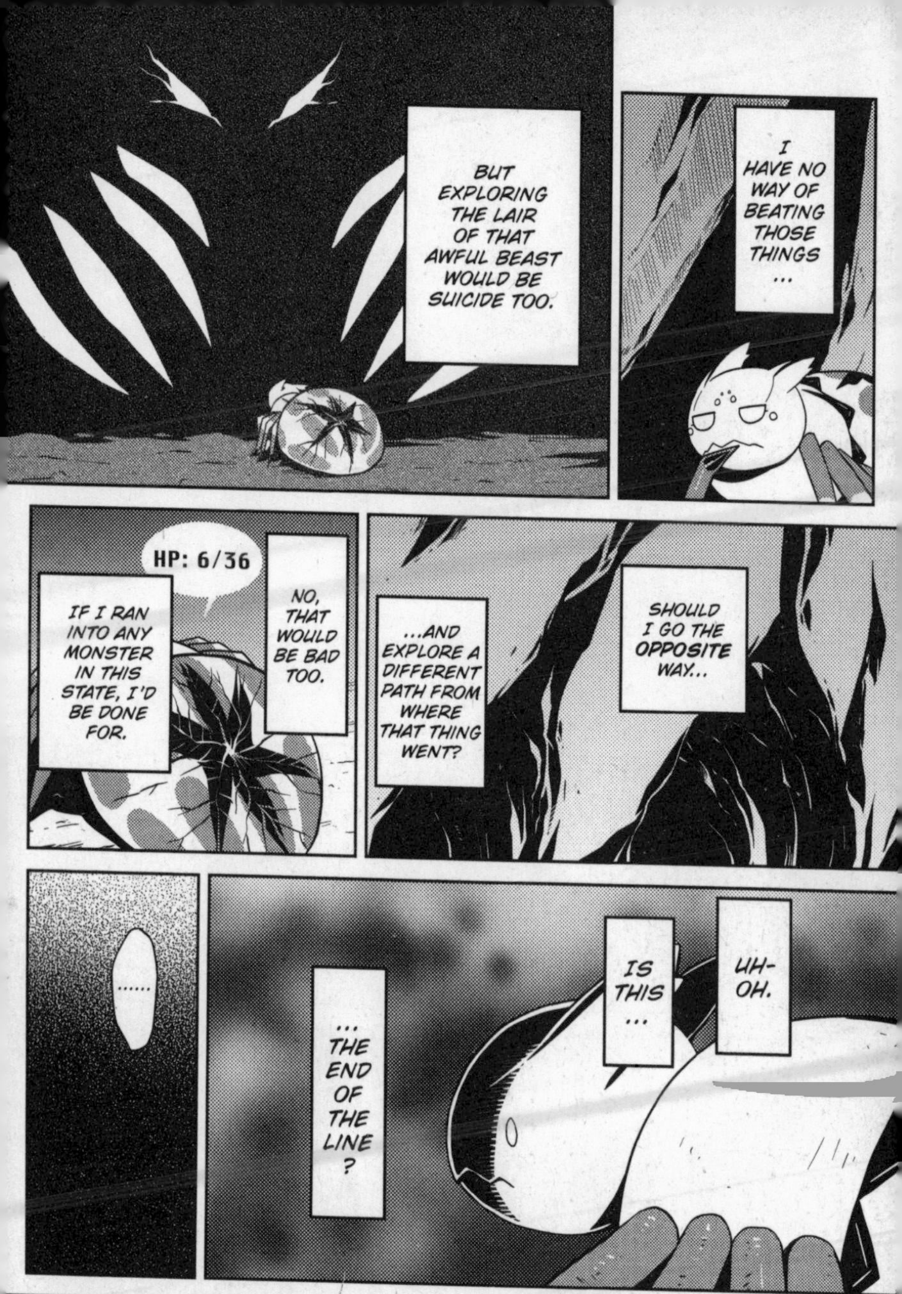
I HAVE NO WAY OF BEATING THOSE THINGS...
BUT EXPLORING THE LAIR OF THAT AWFUL BEAST WOULD BE SUICIDE TOO.
SHOULD I GO THE **OPPOSITE** WAY...
...AND EXPLORE A DIFFERENT PATH FROM WHERE THAT THING WENT?
NO, THAT WOULD BE BAD TOO.
HP: 6/36
IF I RAN INTO ANY MONSTER IN THIS STATE, I'D BE DONE FOR.
UH-OH.
IS THIS...
...THE END OF THE LINE?
......

...WHERE DID I GO WRONG?

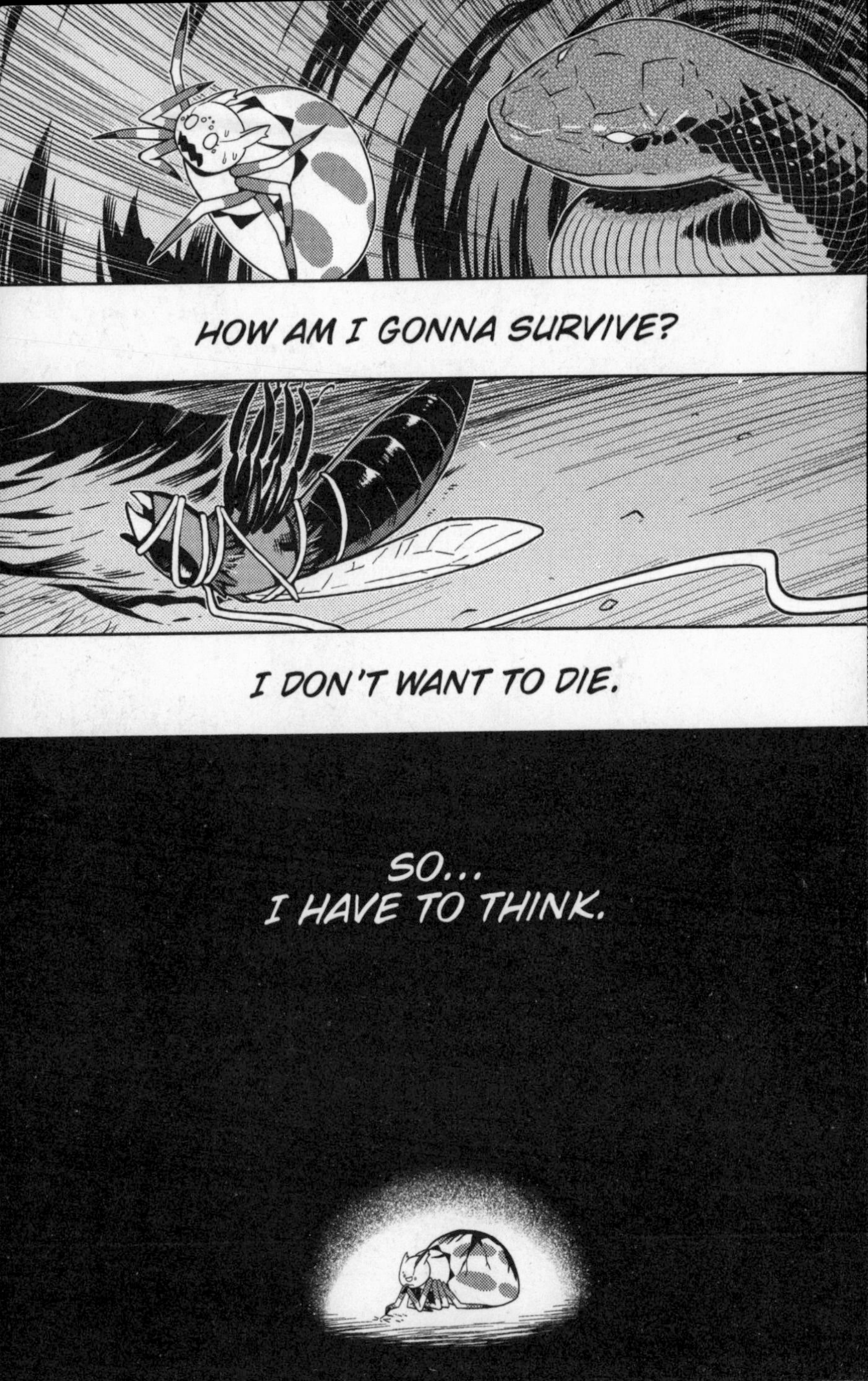
HOW AM I GONNA SURVIVE?
I DON'T WANT TO DIE.
SO...
I HAVE TO THINK.

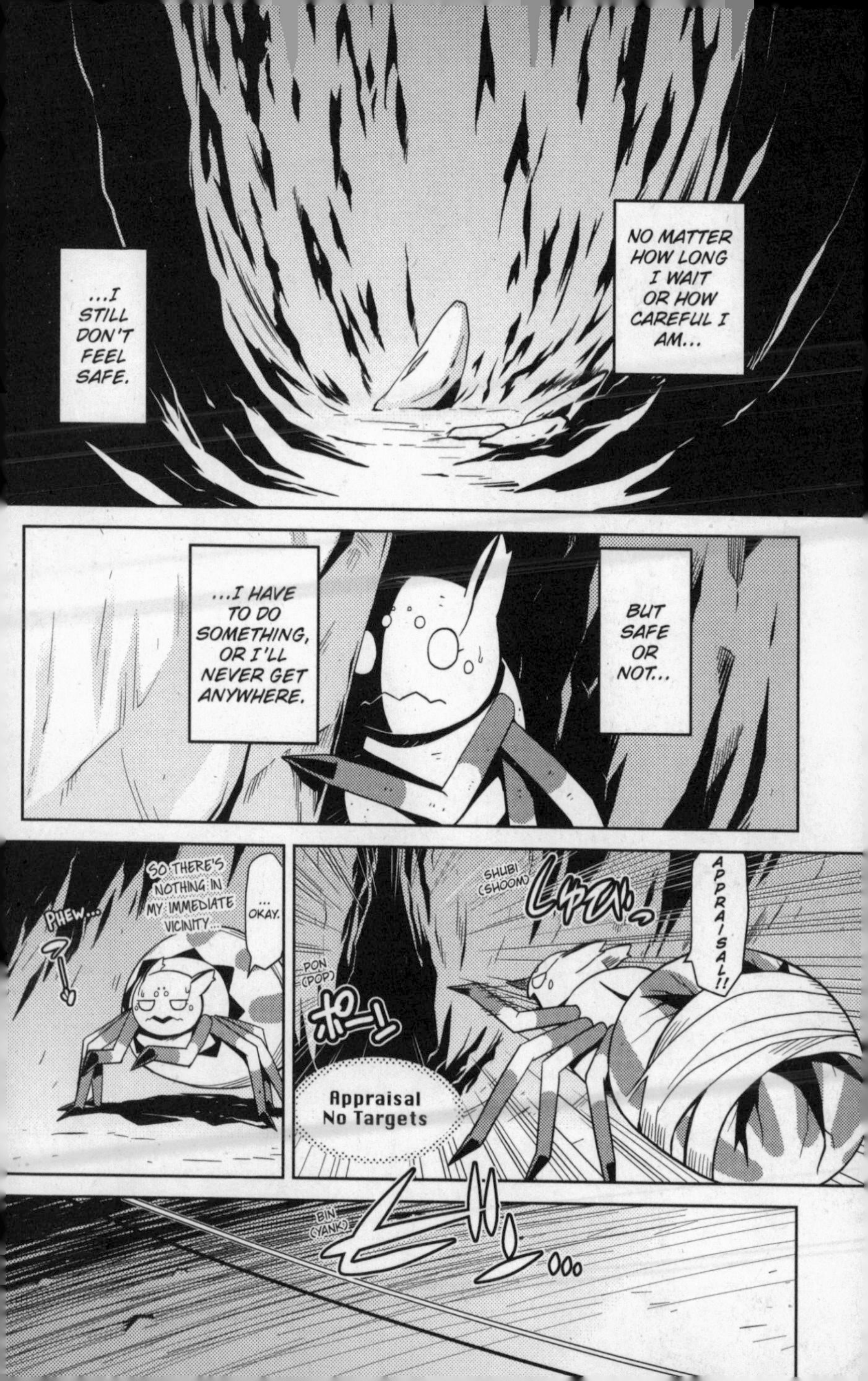
NO MATTER HOW LONG I WAIT OR HOW CAREFUL I AM...
...I STILL DON'T FEEL SAFE.
BUT SAFE OR NOT...
...I HAVE TO DO SOMETHING, OR I'LL NEVER GET ANYWHERE.
APPRAISAL!!
SHUBI (SHOOM)
PON (POP)
Appraisal
No Targets
...OKAY.
SO THERE'S NOTHING IN MY IMMEDIATE VICINITY...
PHEW...
BIN (YANK)

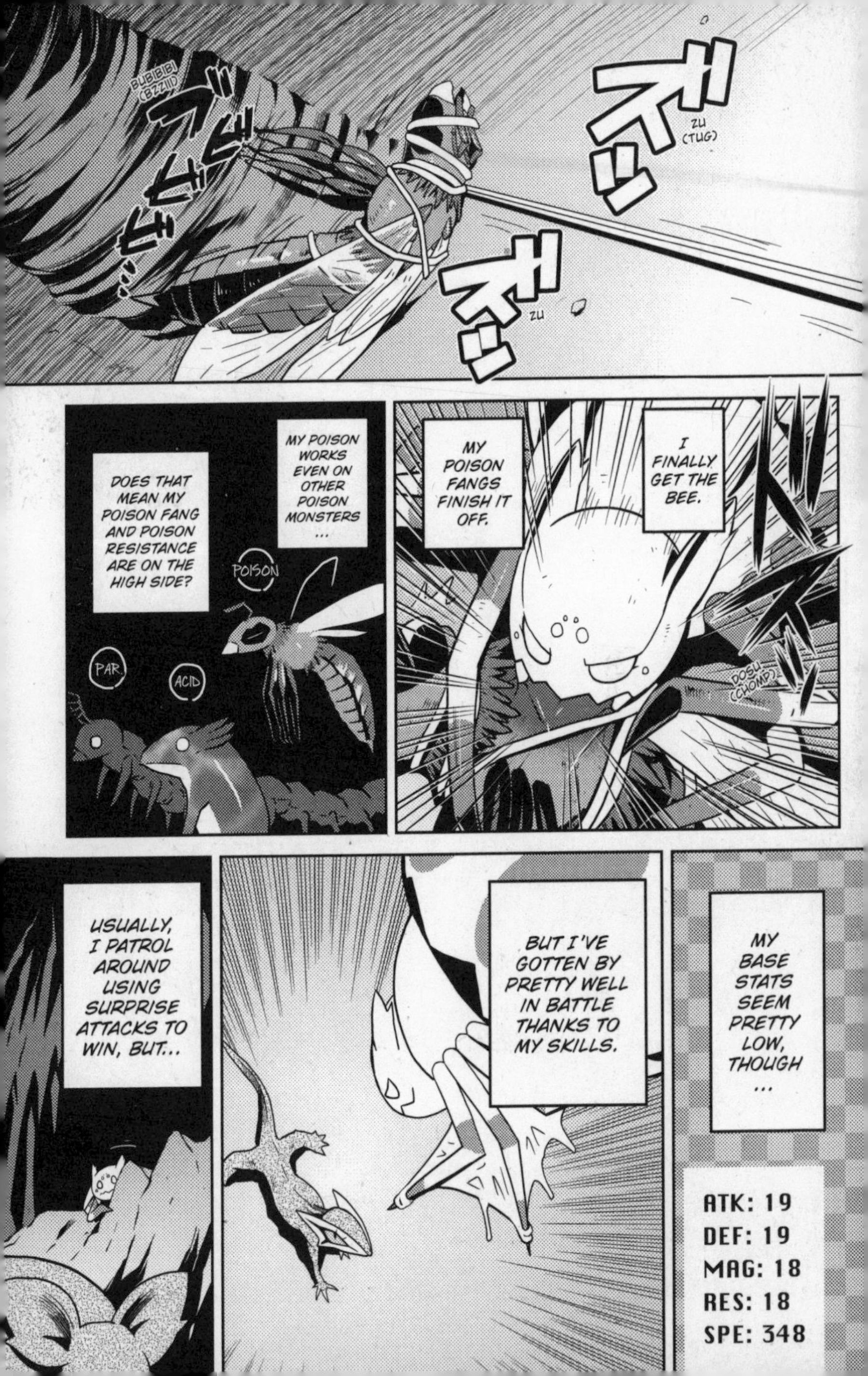
ZU
(TUG)
ZU
BUBIBIBI
(BZZIID)
I FINALLY GET THE BEE.
MY POISON FANGS FINISH IT OFF.
DOSU
(CHOMP)
MY POISON WORKS EVEN ON OTHER POISON MONSTERS...
DOES THAT MEAN MY POISON FANG AND POISON RESISTANCE ARE ON THE HIGH SIDE?
POISON
ACID
PAR.
MY BASE STATS SEEM PRETTY LOW, THOUGH...
ATK: 19
DEF: 19
MAG: 18
RES: 18
SPE: 348
BUT I'VE GOTTEN BY PRETTY WELL IN BATTLE THANKS TO MY SKILLS.
USUALLY, I PATROL AROUND USING SURPRISE ATTACKS TO WIN, BUT...

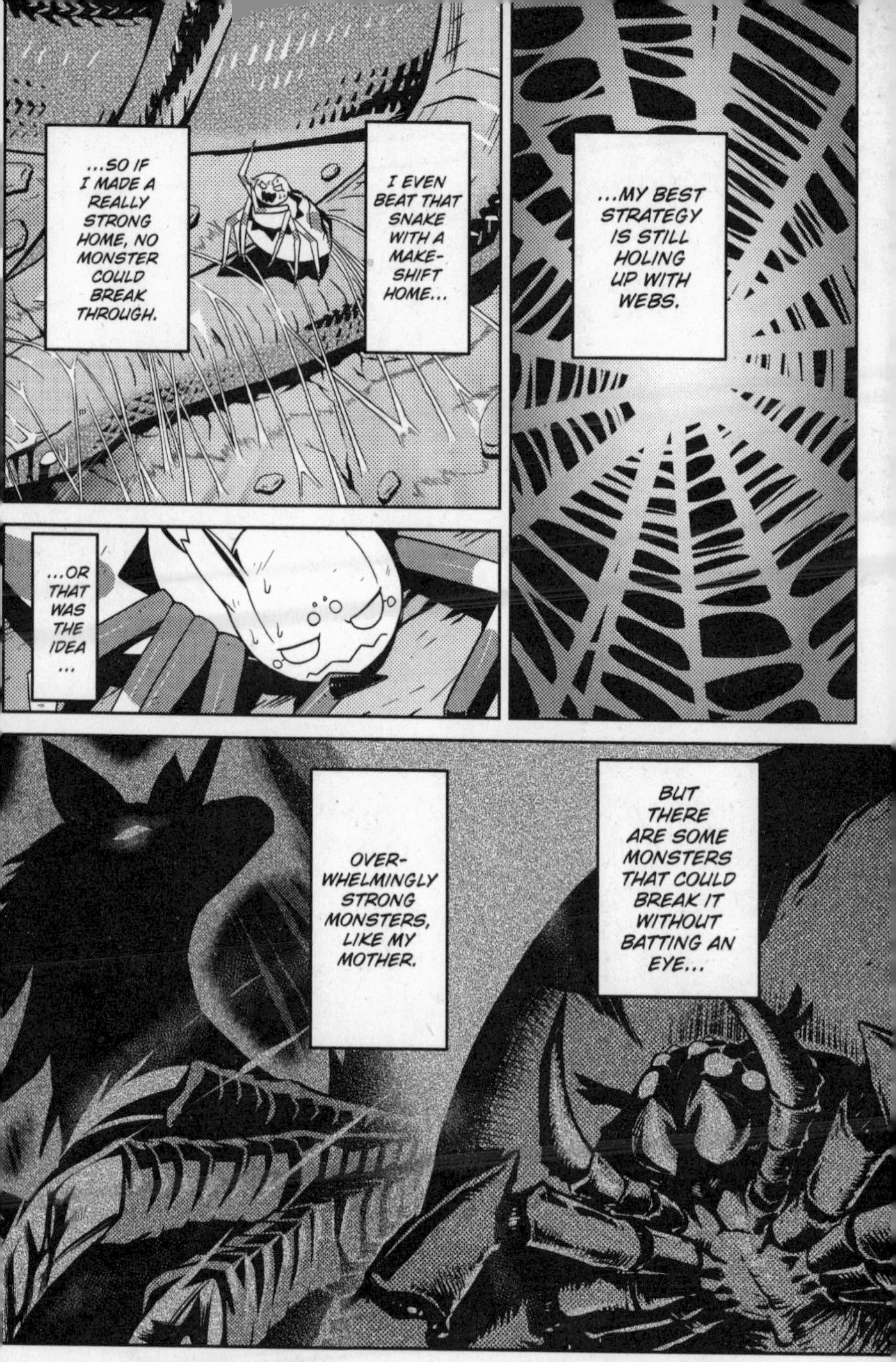
...MY BEST STRATEGY IS STILL HOLING UP WITH WEBS.
I EVEN BEAT THAT SNAKE WITH A MAKE-SHIFT HOME...
...SO IF I MADE A REALLY STRONG HOME, NO MONSTER COULD BREAK THROUGH.
...OR THAT WAS THE IDEA...
BUT THERE ARE SOME MONSTERS THAT COULD BREAK IT WITHOUT BATTING AN EYE...
OVER-WHELMINGLY STRONG MONSTERS, LIKE MY MOTHER.

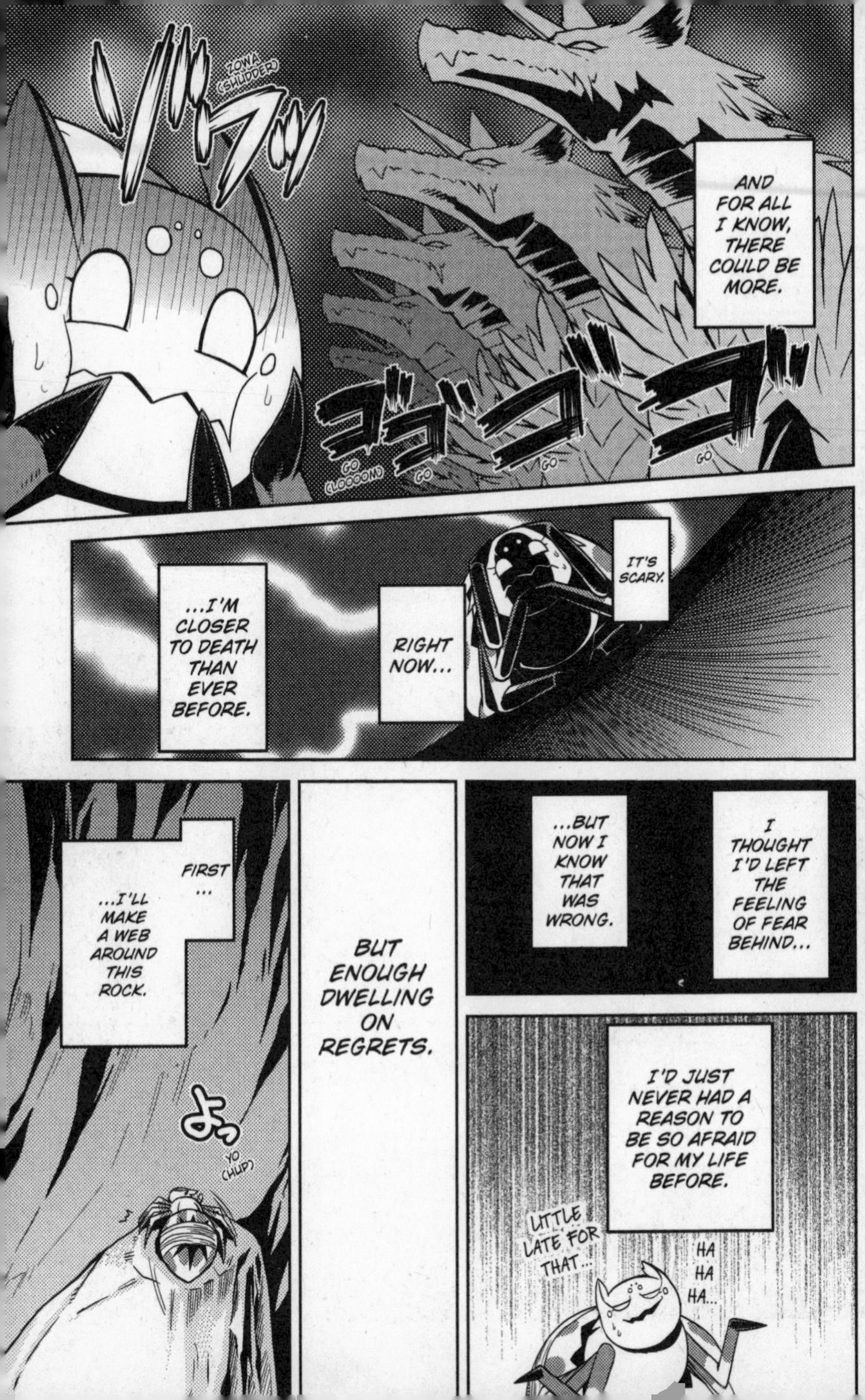
AND FOR ALL I KNOW, THERE COULD BE MORE.
ZOWA (SHUDDER)
GO (LOOOOM) GO GO GO
IT'S SCARY.
RIGHT NOW...
...I'M CLOSER TO DEATH THAN EVER BEFORE.
I THOUGHT I'D LEFT THE FEELING OF FEAR BEHIND...
...BUT NOW I KNOW THAT WAS WRONG.
I'D JUST NEVER HAD A REASON TO BE SO AFRAID FOR MY LIFE BEFORE.
HA HA HA...
LITTLE LATE FOR THAT...
BUT ENOUGH DWELLING ON REGRETS.
FIRST...
...I'LL MAKE A WEB AROUND THIS ROCK.
YO (HUP)

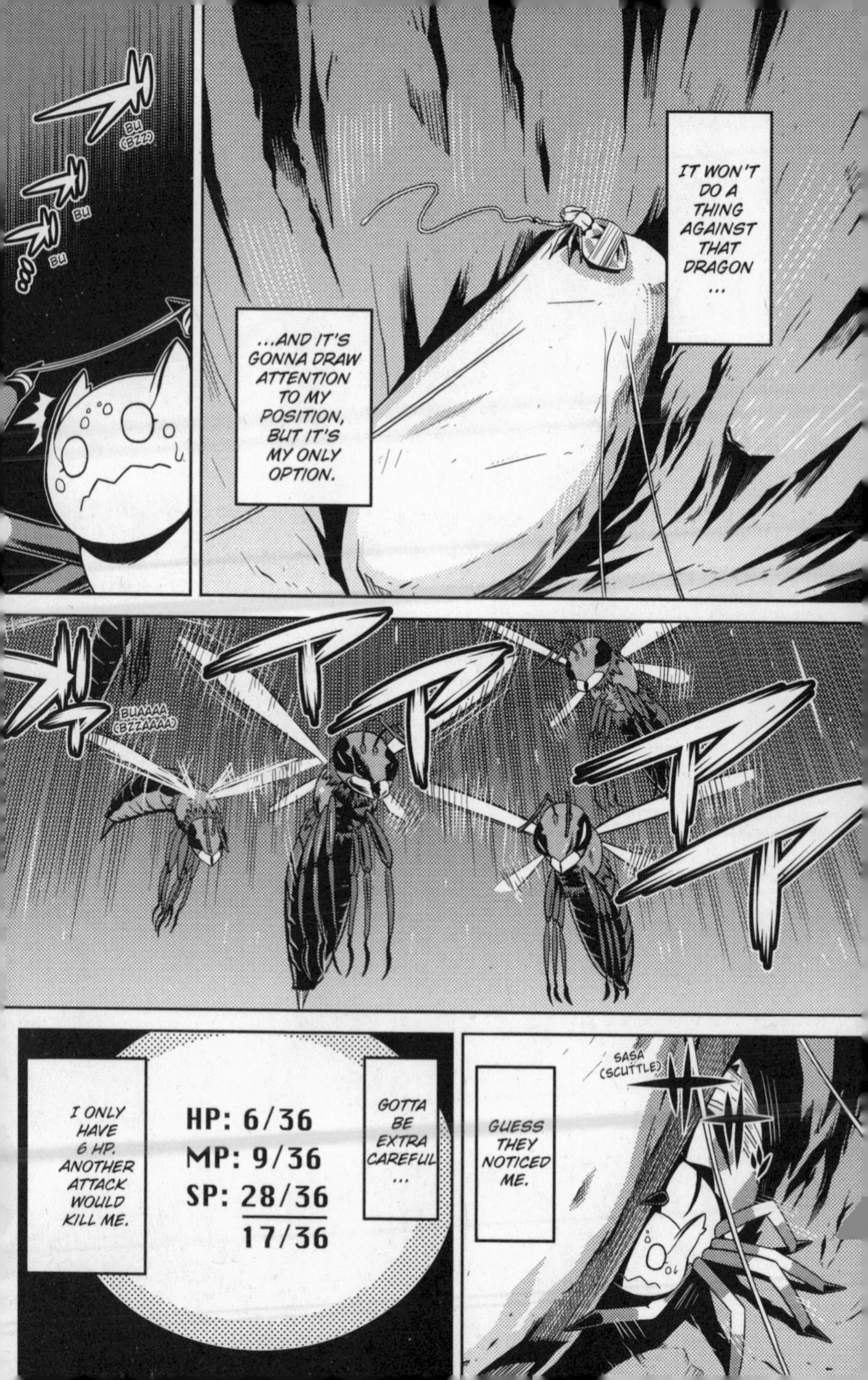
IT WON'T DO A THING AGAINST THAT DRAGON...
...AND IT'S GONNA DRAW ATTENTION TO MY POSITION, BUT IT'S MY ONLY OPTION.
BU (BZZ)
BU
BU
BUAAAA (BZZAAAA)
SASA (SCUTTLE)
GUESS THEY NOTICED ME.
GOTTA BE EXTRA CAREFUL...
HP: 6/36
MP: 9/36
SP: 28/36
17/36
I ONLY HAVE 6 HP. ANOTHER ATTACK WOULD KILL ME.

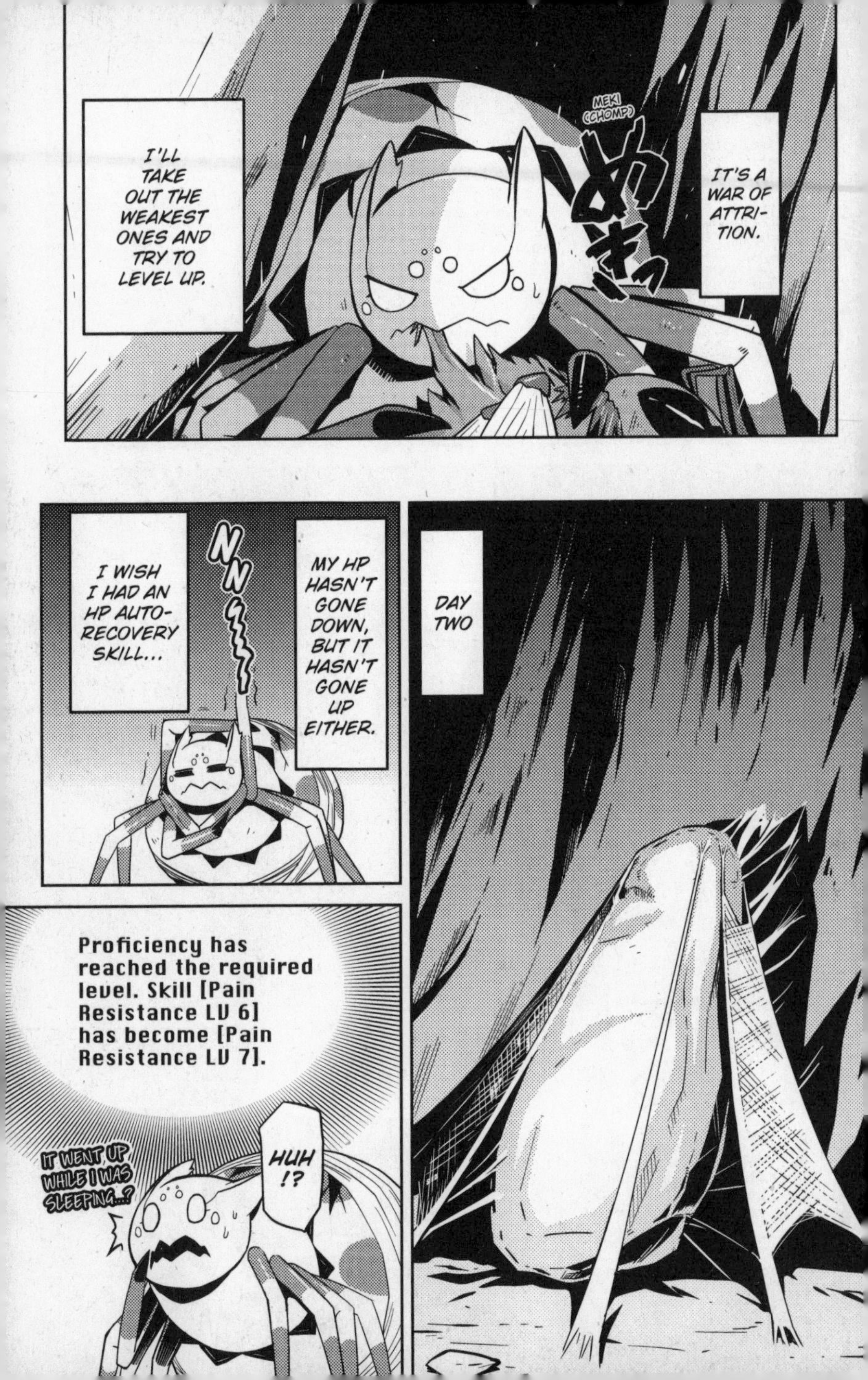
IT'S A WAR OF ATTRITION.
MEKI (CHOMP)
I'LL TAKE OUT THE WEAKEST ONES AND TRY TO LEVEL UP.
DAY TWO
MY HP HASN'T GONE DOWN, BUT IT HASN'T GONE UP EITHER.
NN
I WISH I HAD AN HP AUTO-RECOVERY SKILL...
Proficiency has reached the required level. Skill [Pain Resistance LV 6] has become [Pain Resistance LV 7].
HUH!?
IT WENT UP WHILE I WAS SLEEPING...?

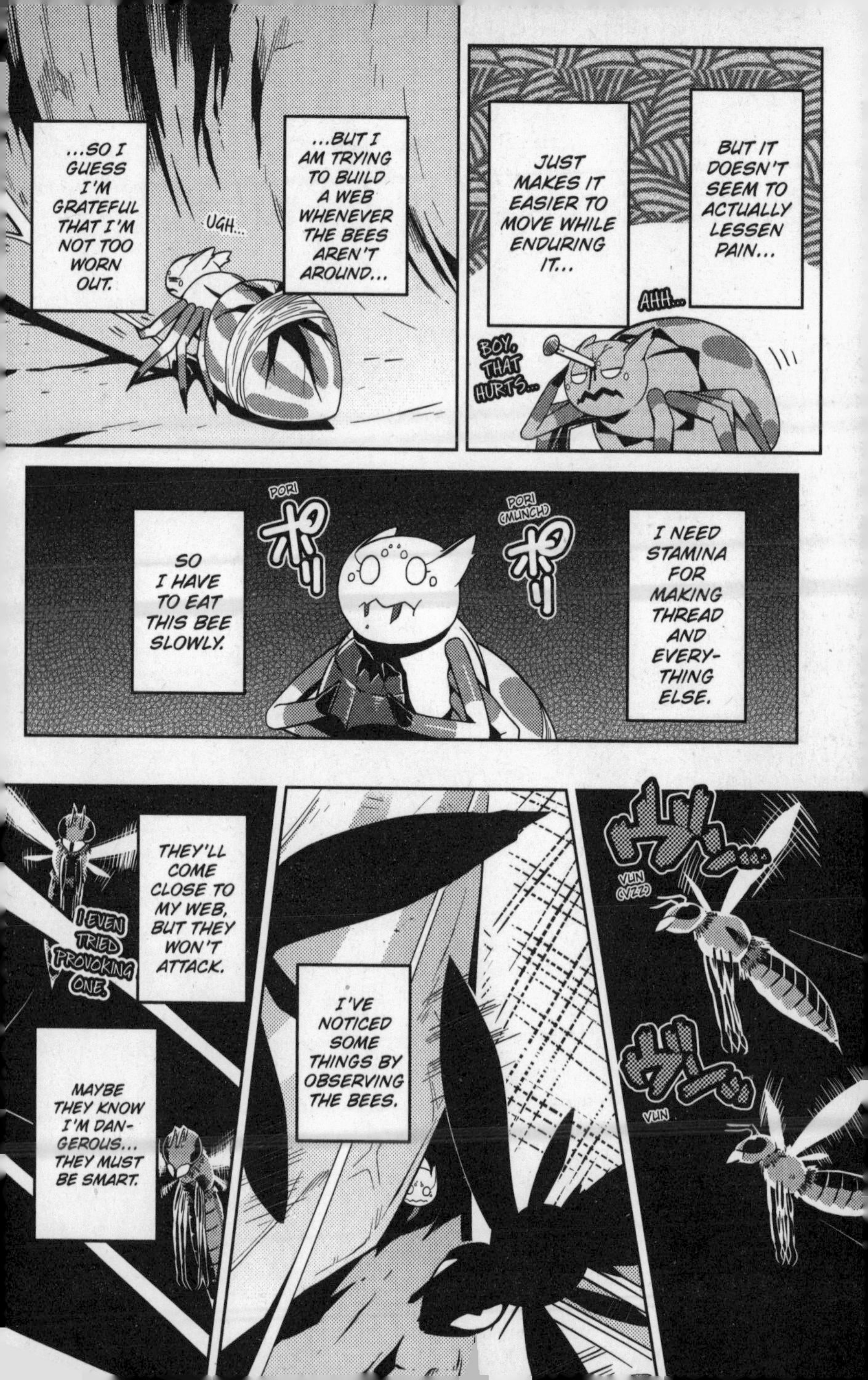
BUT IT DOESN'T SEEM TO ACTUALLY LESSEN PAIN...
JUST MAKES IT EASIER TO MOVE WHILE ENDURING IT...
AHH...
BOY. THAT HURTS...
...BUT I AM TRYING TO BUILD A WEB WHENEVER THE BEES AREN'T AROUND...
UGH...
...SO I GUESS I'M GRATEFUL THAT I'M NOT TOO WORN OUT.
I NEED STAMINA FOR MAKING THREAD AND EVERY-THING ELSE.
PORI (MUNCH)
PORI
SO I HAVE TO EAT THIS BEE SLOWLY.
VUN (VZZ)
VUN
I'VE NOTICED SOME THINGS BY OBSERVING THE BEES.
THEY'LL COME CLOSE TO MY WEB, BUT THEY WON'T ATTACK.
I EVEN TRIED PROVOKING ONE.
MAYBE THEY KNOW I'M DAN-GEROUS... THEY MUST BE SMART.

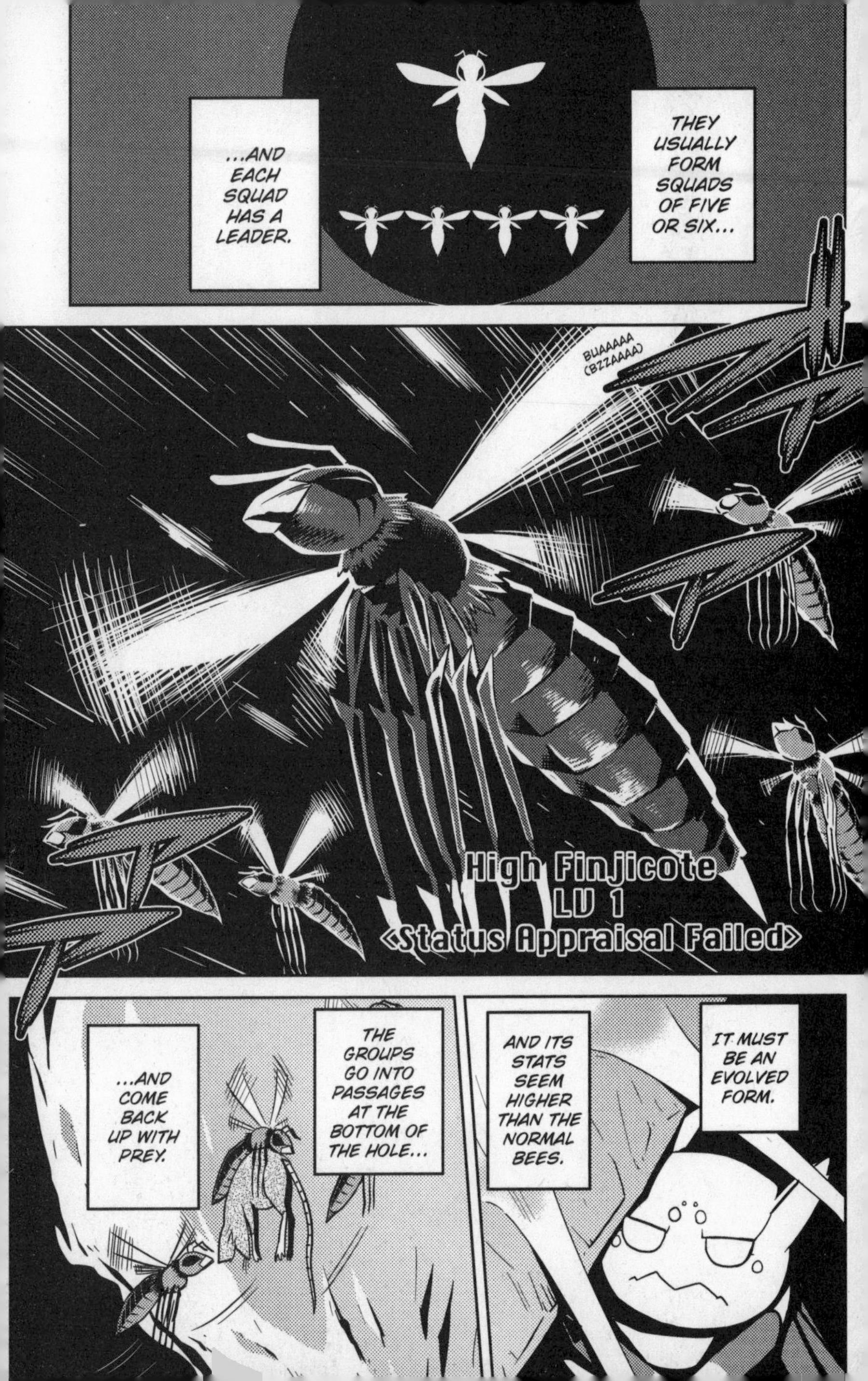
THEY USUALLY FORM SQUADS OF FIVE OR SIX...
...AND EACH SQUAD HAS A LEADER.
BUAAAAA (BZZAAAA)
High Finjicote
LV 1
«Status Appraisal Failed»
IT MUST BE AN EVOLVED FORM.
AND ITS STATS SEEM HIGHER THAN THE NORMAL BEES.
THE GROUPS GO INTO PASSAGES AT THE BOTTOM OF THE HOLE...
...AND COME BACK UP WITH PREY.

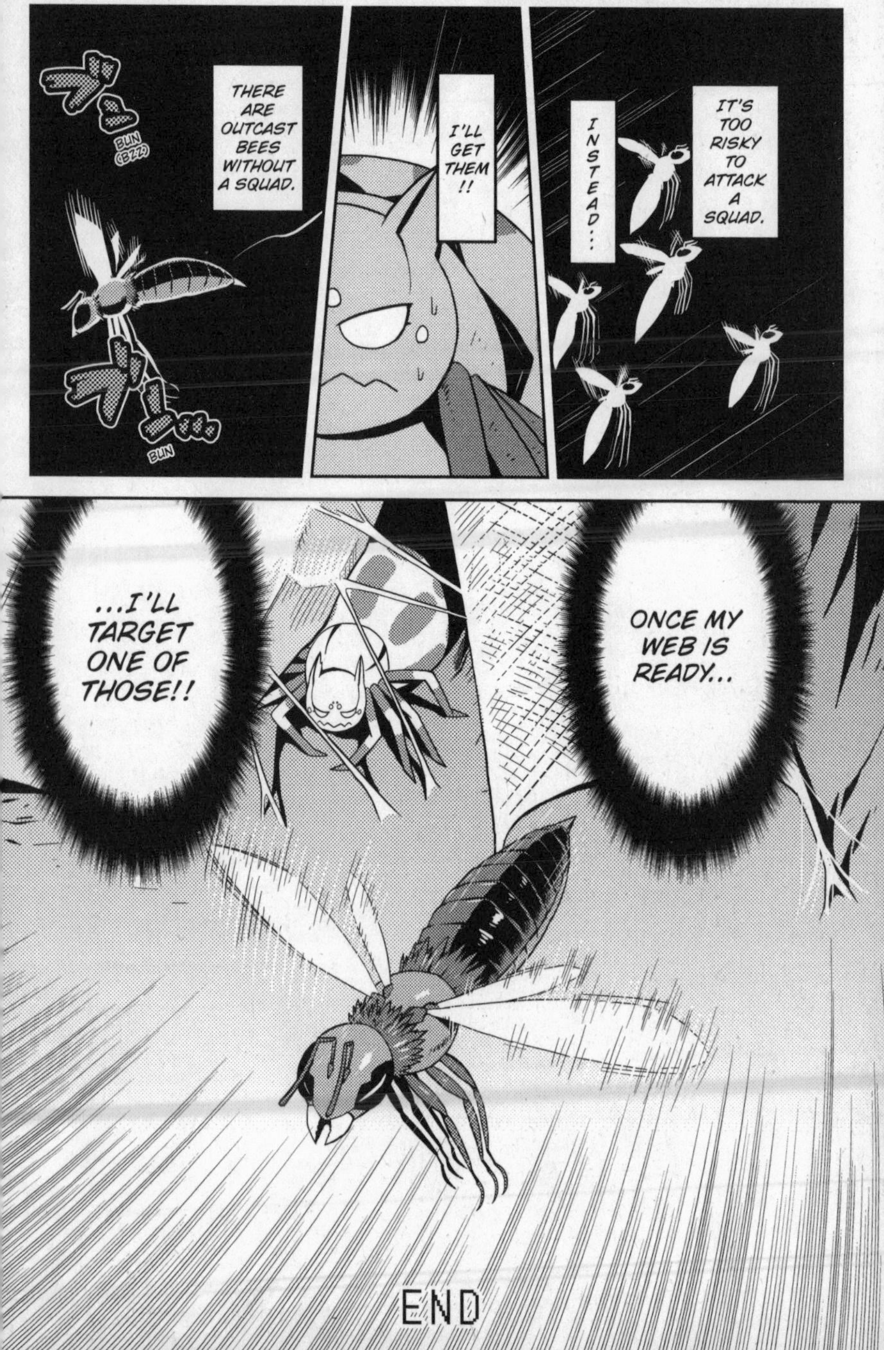
IT'S TOO RISKY TO ATTACK A SQUAD.
INSTEAD...
I'LL GET THEM!!
THERE ARE OUTCAST BEES WITHOUT A SQUAD.
BUN (BZZ)
BUN
ONCE MY WEB IS READY...
...I'LL TARGET ONE OF THOSE!!
END

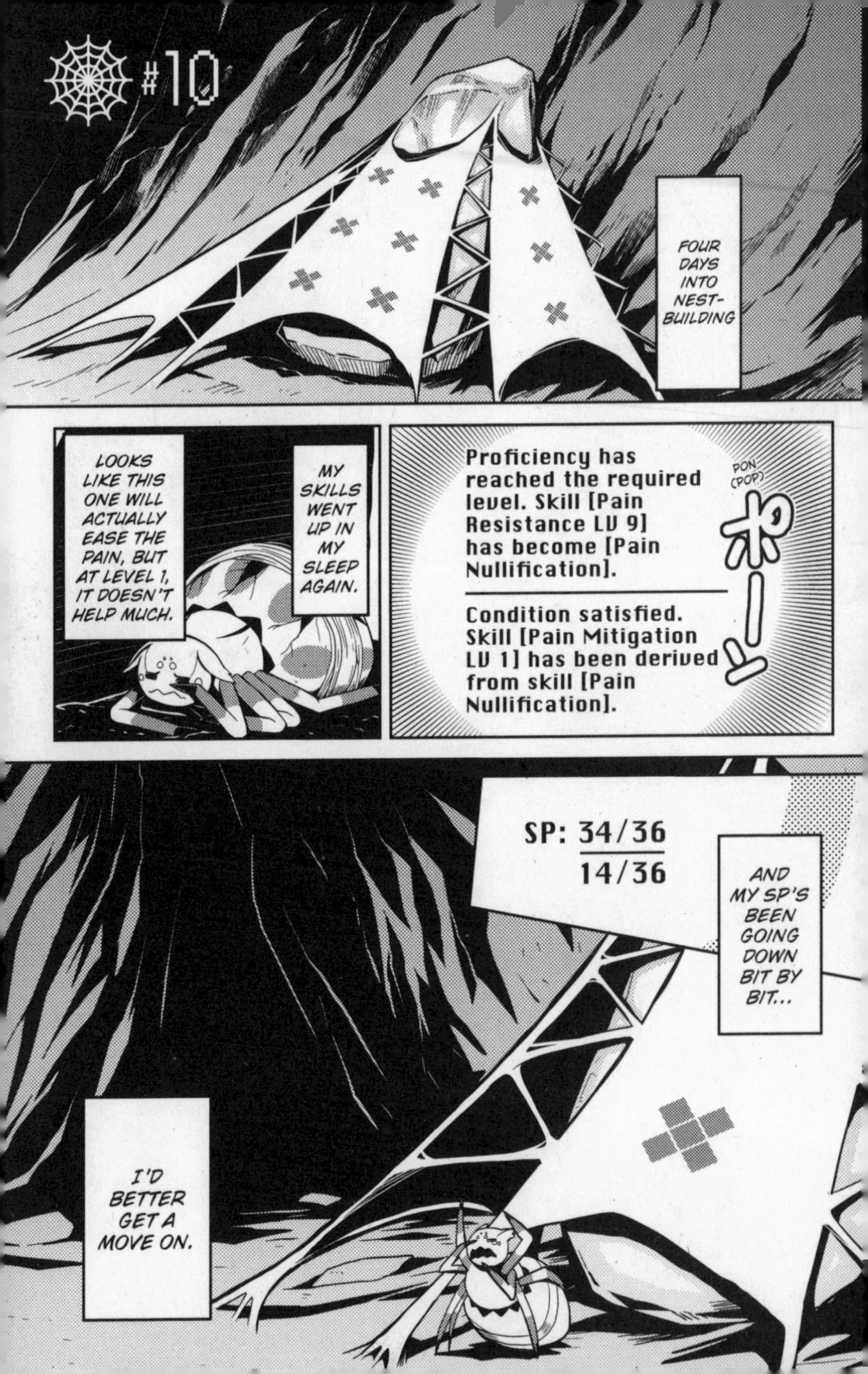
#10
FOUR DAYS INTO NEST-BUILDING
ポーン
PON (POP)
Proficiency has reached the required level. Skill [Pain Resistance LV 9] has become [Pain Nullification].
Condition satisfied. Skill [Pain Mitigation LV 1] has been derived from skill [Pain Nullification].
MY SKILLS WENT UP IN MY SLEEP AGAIN.
LOOKS LIKE THIS ONE WILL ACTUALLY EASE THE PAIN, BUT AT LEVEL 1, IT DOESN'T HELP MUCH.
SP: 34/36
14/36
AND MY SP'S BEEN GOING DOWN BIT BY BIT...
I'D BETTER GET A MOVE ON.

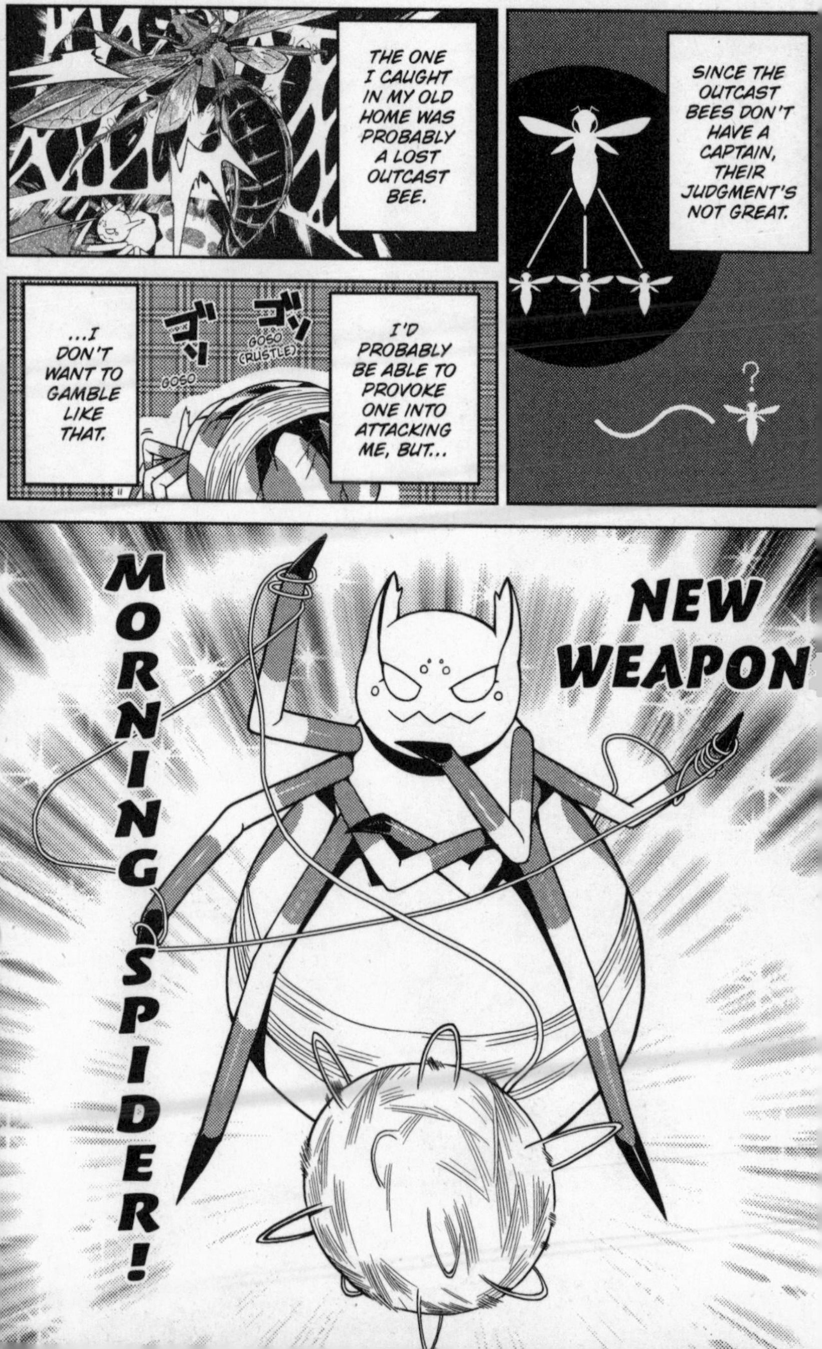
SINCE THE OUTCAST BEES DON'T HAVE A CAPTAIN, THEIR JUDGMENT'S NOT GREAT.
?
THE ONE I CAUGHT IN MY OLD HOME WAS PROBABLY A LOST OUTCAST BEE.
I'D PROBABLY BE ABLE TO PROVOKE ONE INTO ATTACKING ME, BUT...
GOSO (RUSTLE)
GOSO
...I DON'T WANT TO GAMBLE LIKE THAT.
NEW WEAPON
MORNING SPIDER!

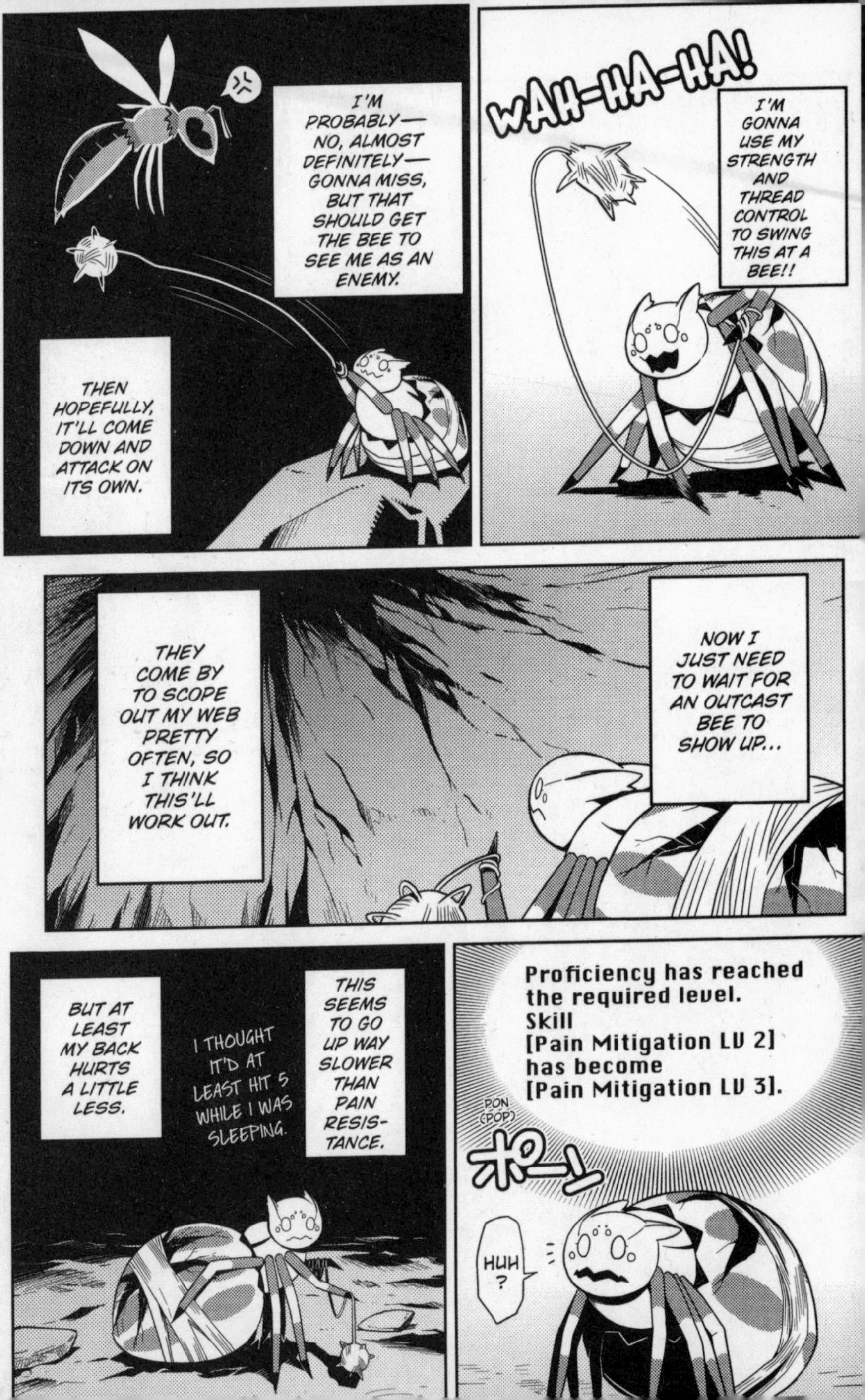
WAH-HA-HA!
I'M GONNA USE MY STRENGTH AND THREAD CONTROL TO SWING THIS AT A BEE!!
I'M PROBABLY— NO, ALMOST DEFINITELY— GONNA MISS, BUT THAT SHOULD GET THE BEE TO SEE ME AS AN ENEMY.
THEN HOPEFULLY, IT'LL COME DOWN AND ATTACK ON ITS OWN.
NOW I JUST NEED TO WAIT FOR AN OUTCAST BEE TO SHOW UP...
THEY COME BY TO SCOPE OUT MY WEB PRETTY OFTEN, SO I THINK THIS'LL WORK OUT.
Proficiency has reached the required level. Skill [Pain Mitigation LV 2] has become [Pain Mitigation LV 3].
PON (POP)
HUH?
THIS SEEMS TO GO UP WAY SLOWER THAN PAIN RESISTANCE.
I THOUGHT IT'D AT LEAST HIT 5 WHILE I WAS SLEEPING.
BUT AT LEAST MY BACK HURTS A LITTLE LESS.

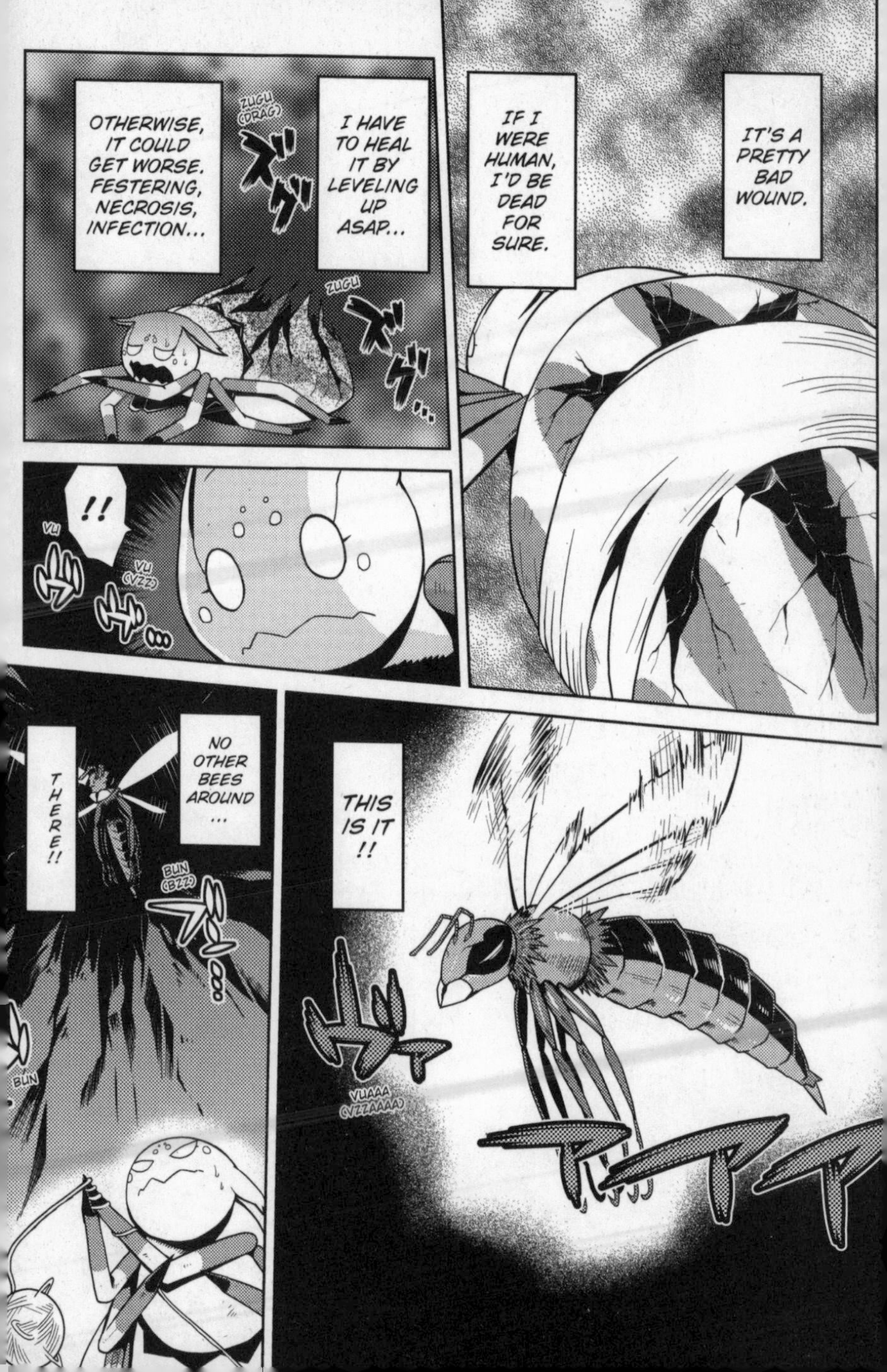
IT'S A PRETTY BAD WOUND.
IF I WERE HUMAN, I'D BE DEAD FOR SURE.
I HAVE TO HEAL IT BY LEVELING UP ASAP...
ZUGU (DRAG)
OTHERWISE, IT COULD GET WORSE. FESTERING, NECROSIS, INFECTION...
ZUGU
!!
VU (VZZ)
VU
THIS IS IT!!
VUAAA (VZZAAAA)
NO OTHER BEES AROUND...
THERE!!
BUN (BZZ)
BUN

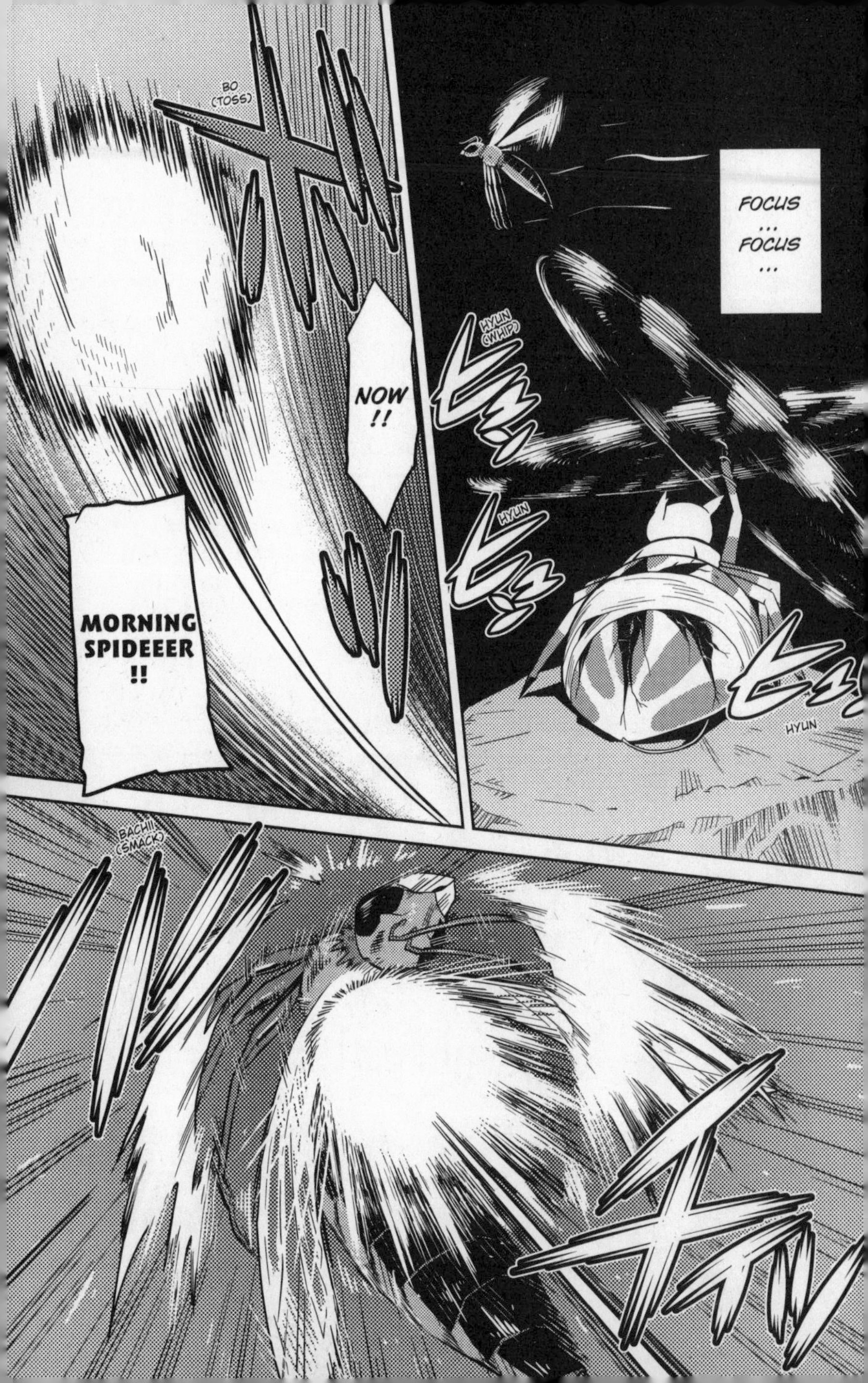
FOCUS ... FOCUS ...
HYUN (WHIP)
HYUN
HYUN
NOW !!
BO (TOSS)
MORNING SPIDEEER !!
BACHI! (SMACK)

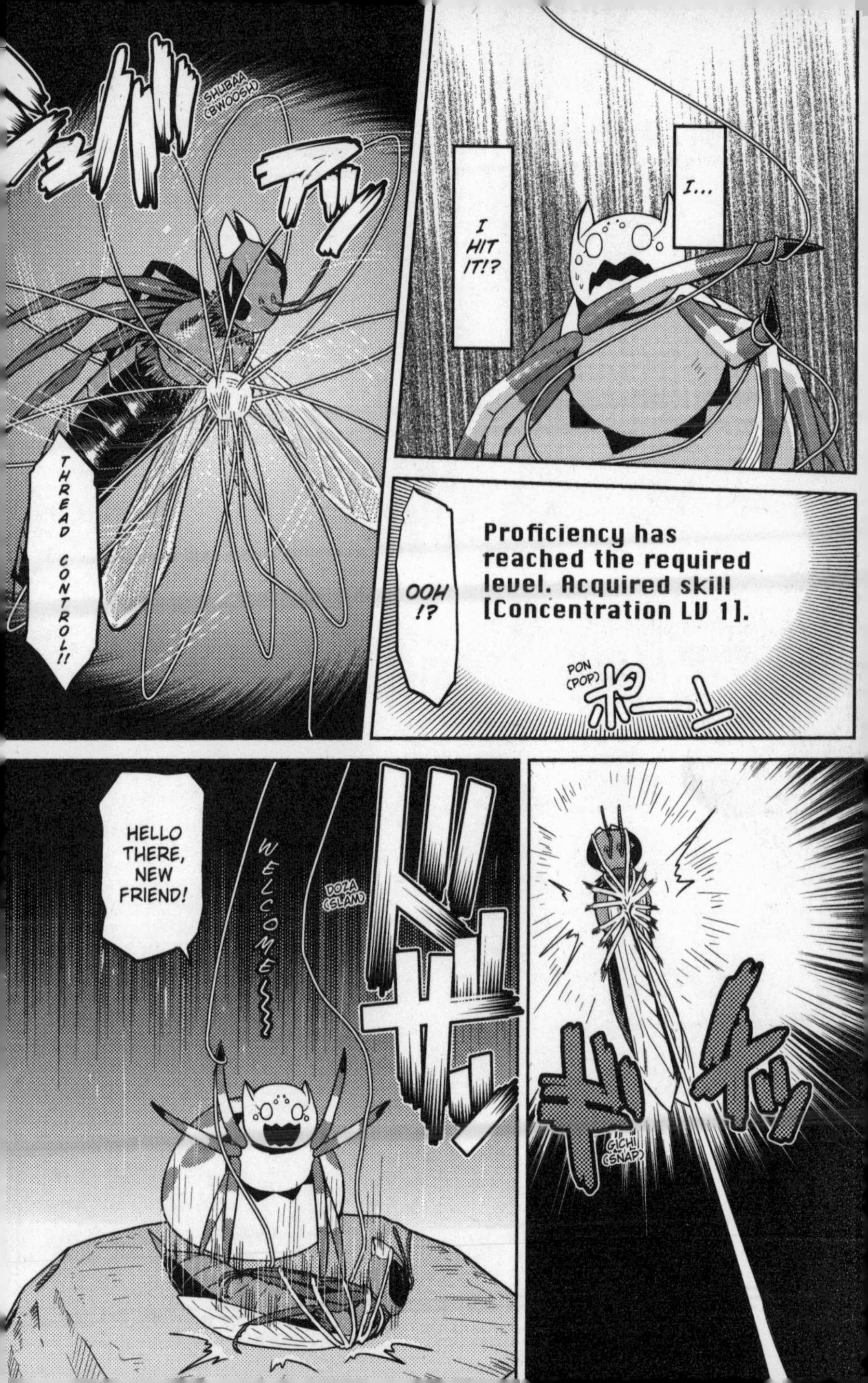
I...
I HIT IT!?
Proficiency has reached the required level. Acquired skill [Concentration LV 1].
OOH!?
PON (POP)
SHUBAA (BWOOSH)
THREAD CONTROL!!
GICHI (SNAP)
DOZA (SLAM)
WELCOME~
HELLO THERE, NEW FRIEND!

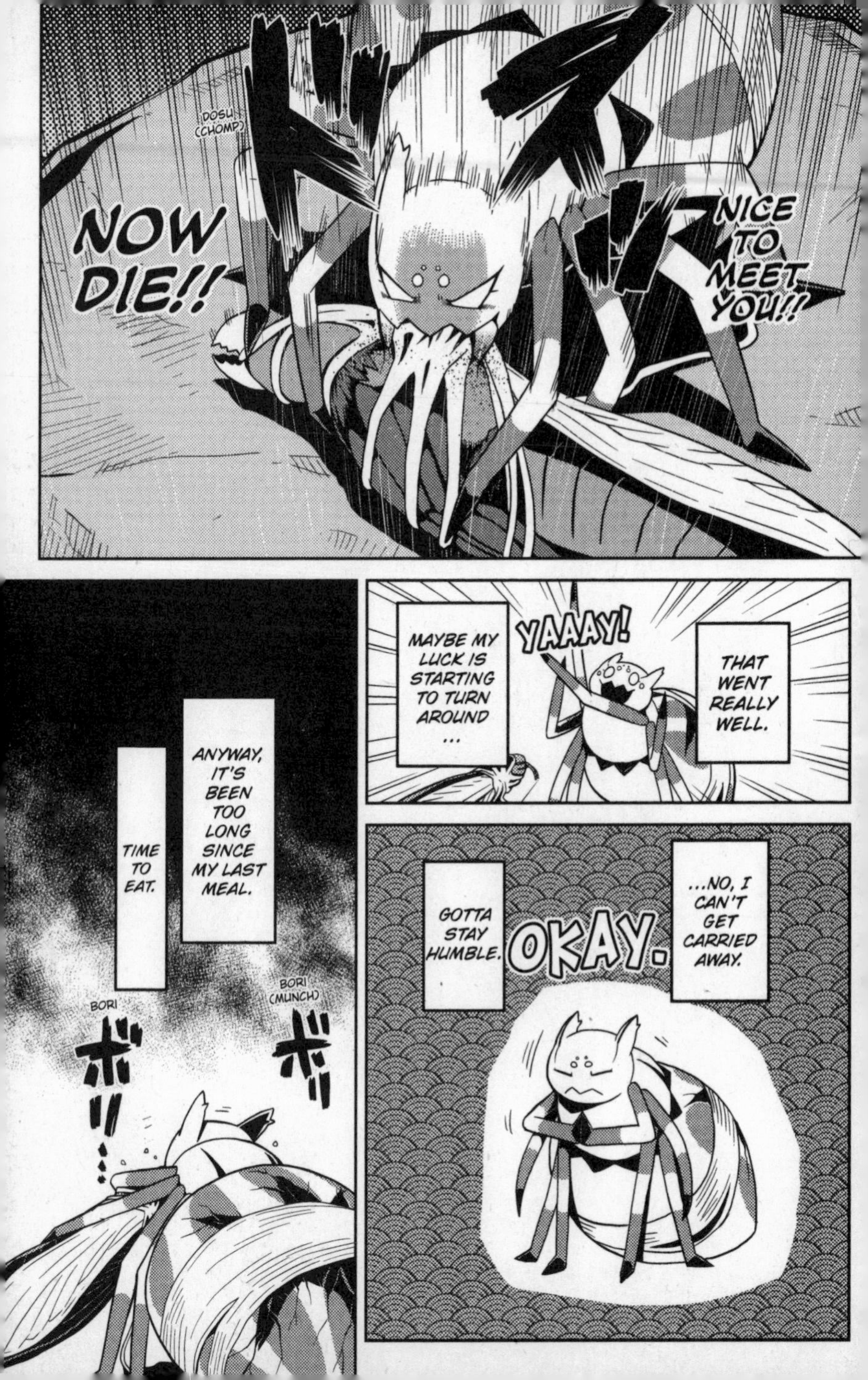
DOSU (CHOMP)
NICE TO MEET YOU!!
NOW DIE!!
THAT WENT REALLY WELL.
YAAAY!
MAYBE MY LUCK IS STARTING TO TURN AROUND...
...NO, I CAN'T GET CARRIED AWAY.
OKAY.
GOTTA STAY HUMBLE.
ANYWAY, IT'S BEEN TOO LONG SINCE MY LAST MEAL.
TIME TO EAT.
BORI (MUNCH)
BORI

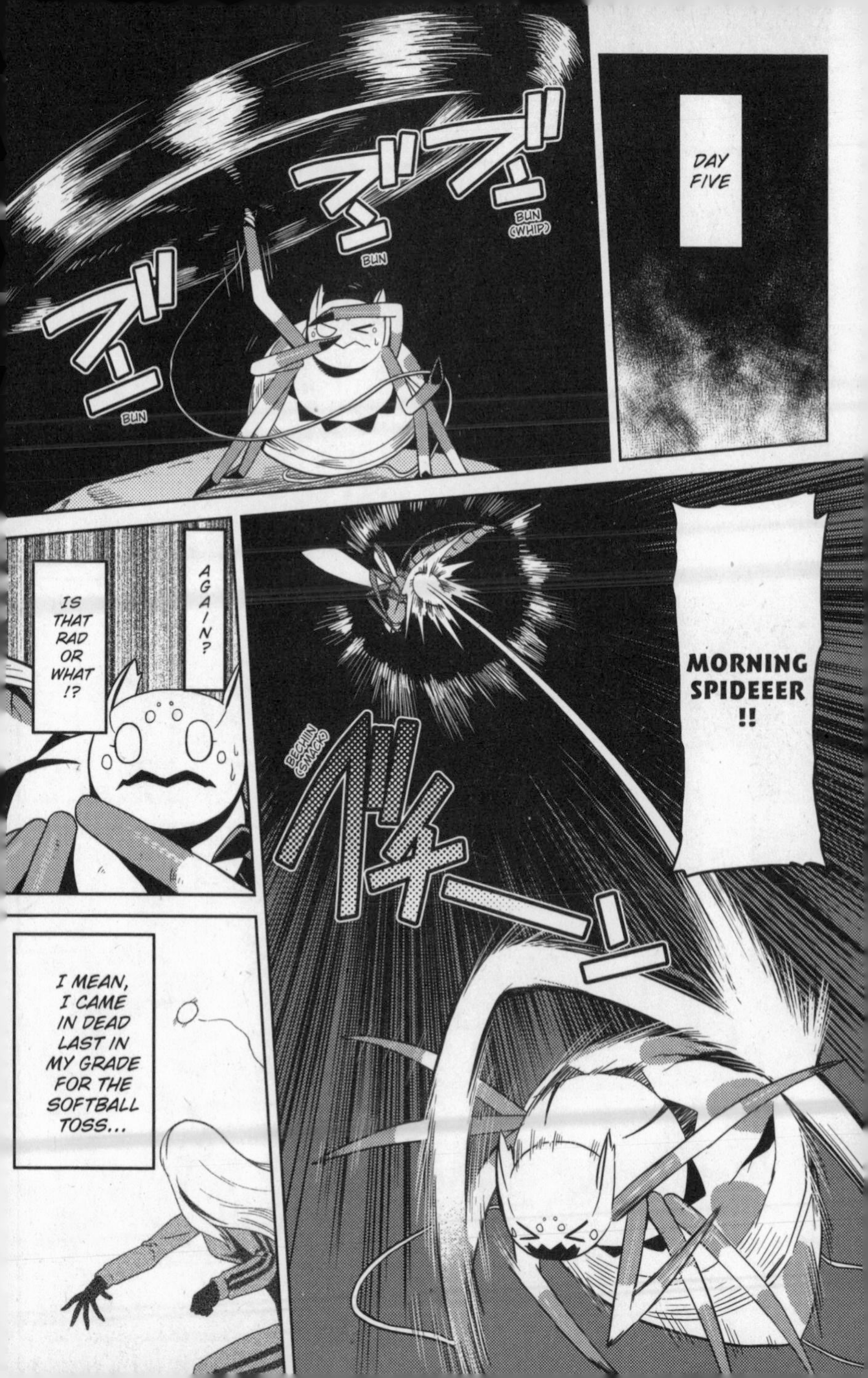
DAY FIVE
BUN (WHIP)
BUN
BUN
MORNING SPIDEEER!!
BECHIIN (SMACK)
AGAIN?
IS THAT RAD OR WHAT!?
I MEAN, I CAME IN DEAD LAST IN MY GRADE FOR THE SOFTBALL TOSS...

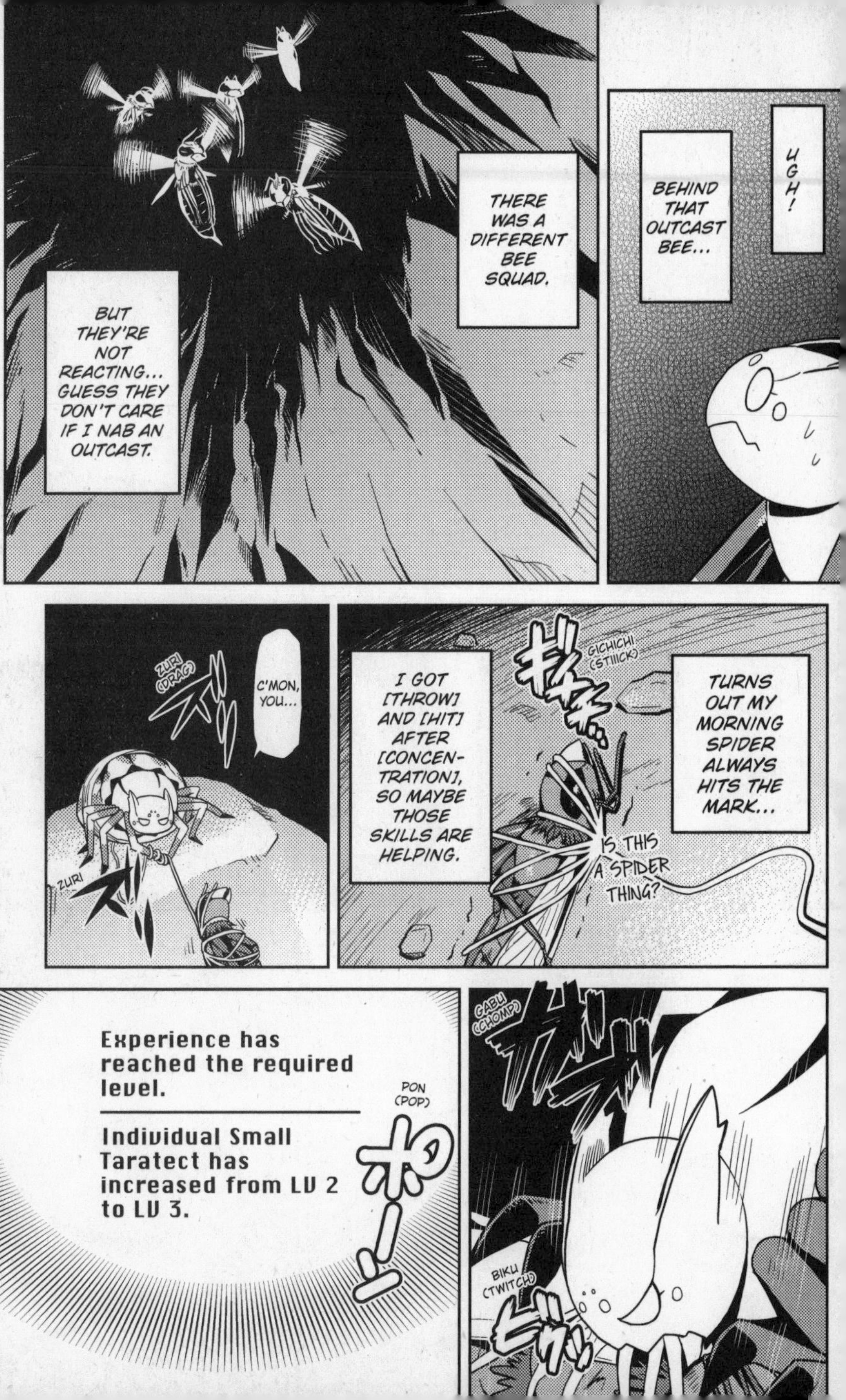
UGH!
BEHIND THAT OUTCAST BEE...
THERE WAS A DIFFERENT BEE SQUAD.
BUT THEY'RE NOT REACTING... GUESS THEY DON'T CARE IF I NAB AN OUTCAST.
TURNS OUT MY MORNING SPIDER ALWAYS HITS THE MARK...
GICHICHI (STIIICK)
I GOT [THROW] AND [HIT] AFTER [CONCEN-TRATION], SO MAYBE THOSE SKILLS ARE HELPING.
IS THIS A SPIDER THING?
C'MON, YOU...
ZURI (DRAG)
ZURI
GABU (CHOMP)
BIKU (TWITCH)
Experience has reached the required level.
Individual Small Taratect has increased from LV 2 to LV 3.
PON (POP)

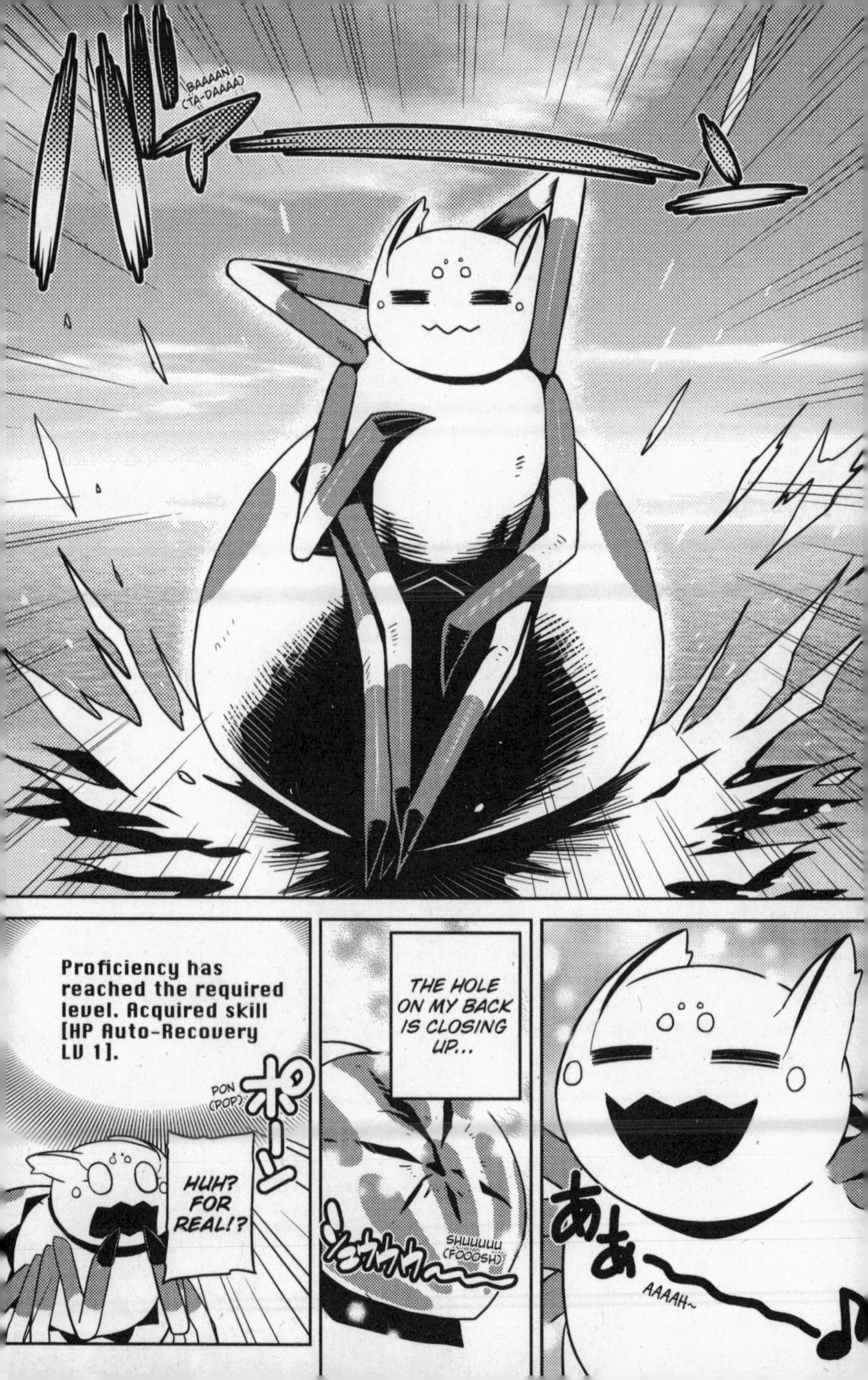
BAAAAN (TA-DAAAA)
AAAAH~
THE HOLE ON MY BACK IS CLOSING UP...
SHUUUUU (FOOOSH)
Proficiency has reached the required level. Acquired skill [HP Auto-Recovery LV 1].
PON (POP)
HUH? FOR REAL!?

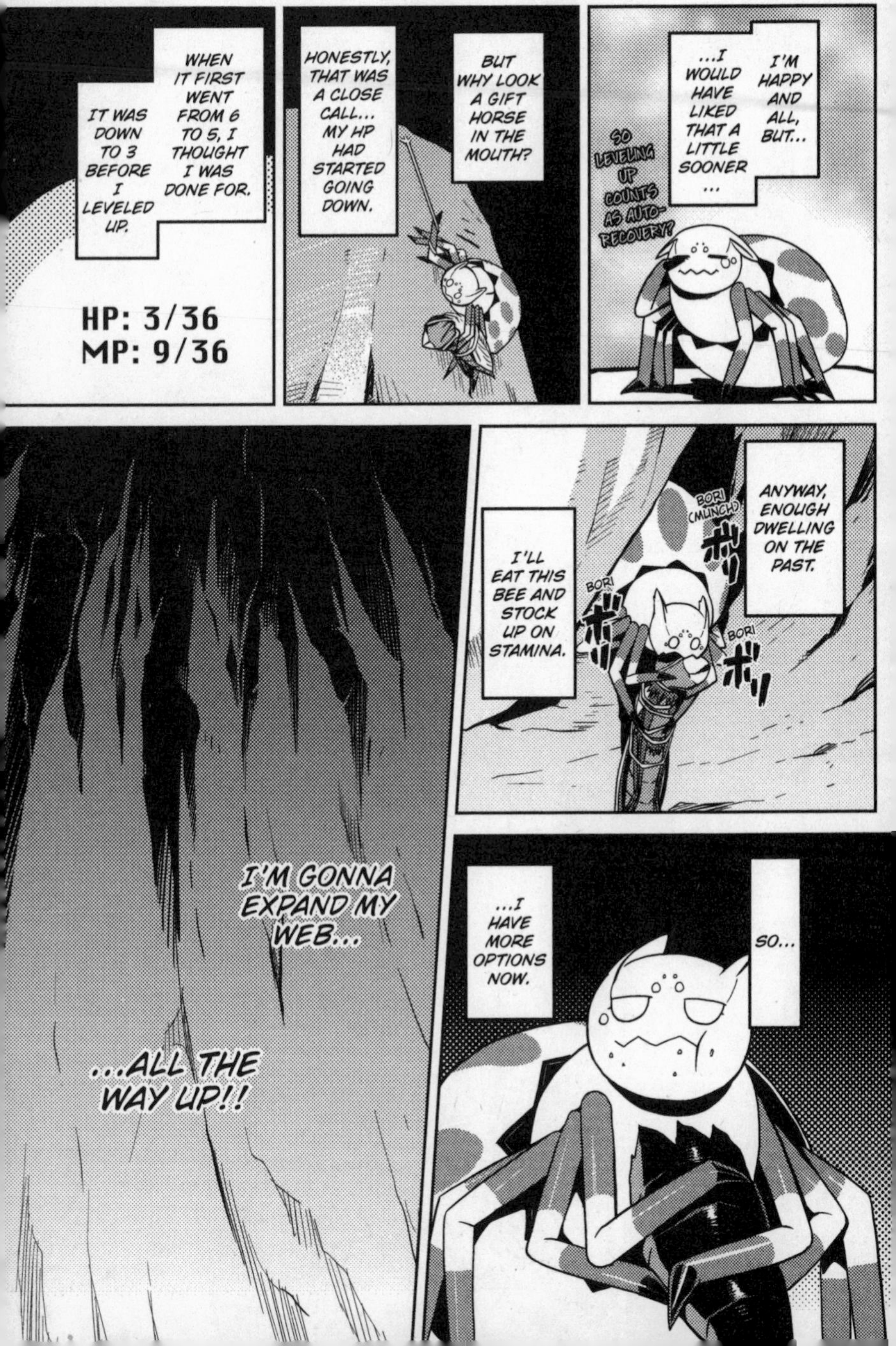
I'M HAPPY AND ALL, BUT...
...I WOULD HAVE LIKED THAT A LITTLE SOONER...
SO LEVELING UP COUNTS AS AUTO-RECOVERY?
BUT WHY LOOK A GIFT HORSE IN THE MOUTH?
HONESTLY, THAT WAS A CLOSE CALL... MY HP HAD STARTED GOING DOWN.
WHEN IT FIRST WENT FROM 6 TO 5, I THOUGHT I WAS DONE FOR.
IT WAS DOWN TO 3 BEFORE I LEVELED UP.
HP: 3/36
MP: 9/36
ANYWAY, ENOUGH DWELLING ON THE PAST.
ボリ
BORI (MUNCH)
I'LL EAT THIS BEE AND STOCK UP ON STAMINA.
ボリ
BORI
ボリ
BORI
SO...
...I HAVE MORE OPTIONS NOW.
I'M GONNA EXPAND MY WEB...
...ALL THE WAY UP!!

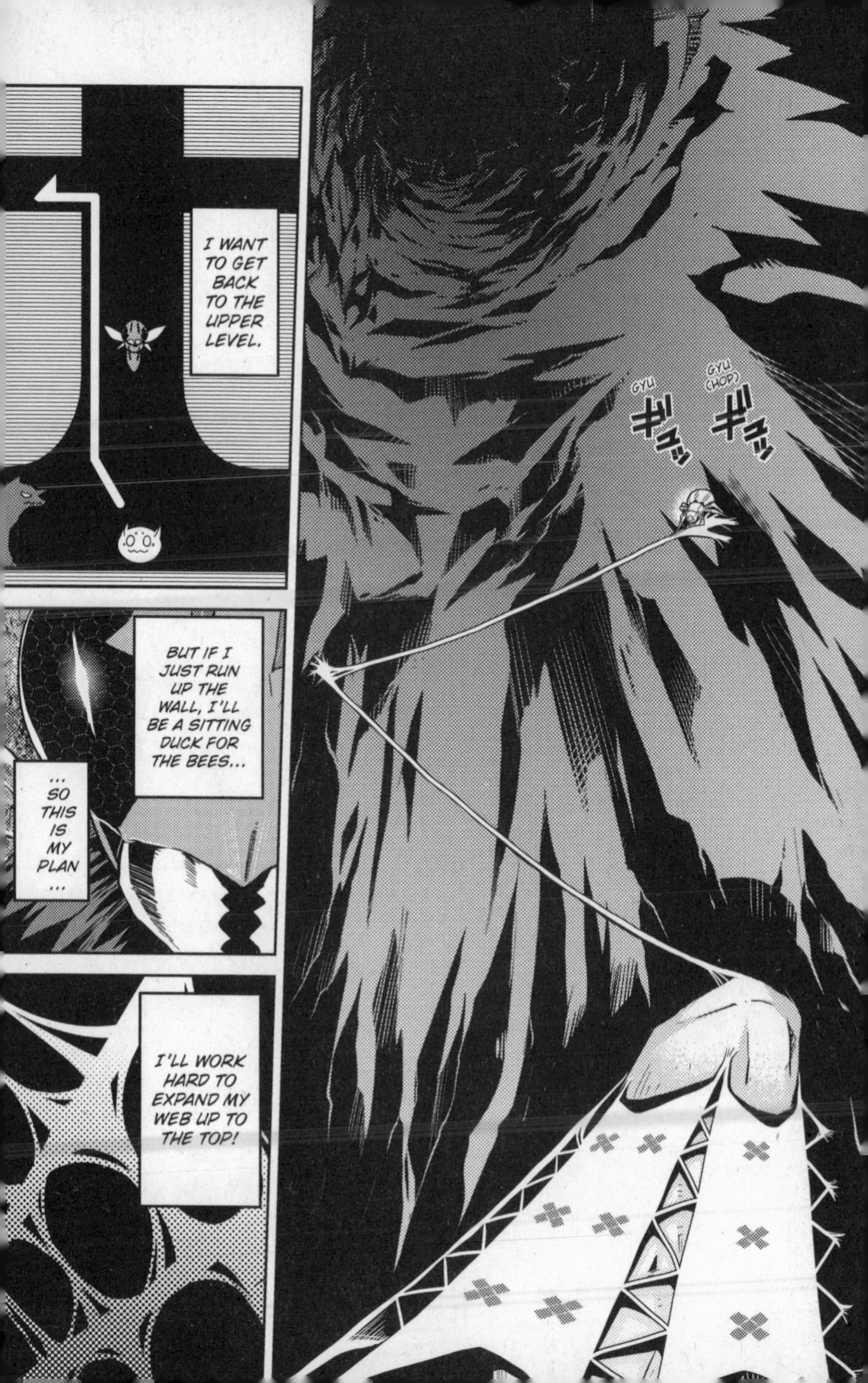
GYU (HOP)
ギュッ
GYU
ギュッ
I WANT TO GET BACK TO THE UPPER LEVEL.
BUT IF I JUST RUN UP THE WALL, I'LL BE A SITTING DUCK FOR THE BEES...
...SO THIS IS MY PLAN...
I'LL WORK HARD TO EXPAND MY WEB UP TO THE TOP!

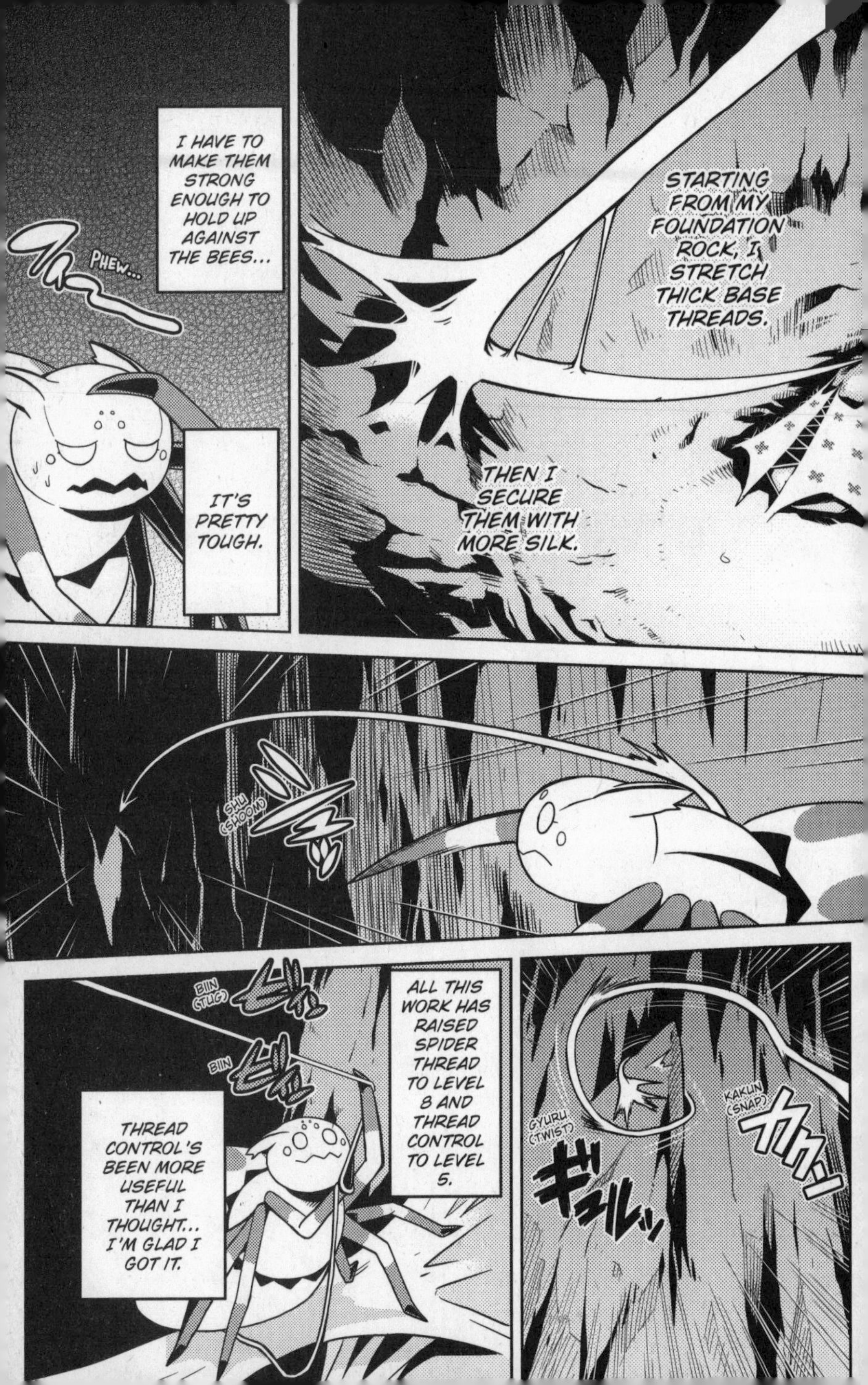
STARTING FROM MY FOUNDATION ROCK, I STRETCH THICK BASE THREADS.
THEN I SECURE THEM WITH MORE SILK.
I HAVE TO MAKE THEM STRONG ENOUGH TO HOLD UP AGAINST THE BEES...
PHEW...
IT'S PRETTY TOUGH.
SHU (SHOOM)
KAKUN (SNAP)
GYURU (TWIST)
ALL THIS WORK HAS RAISED SPIDER THREAD TO LEVEL 8 AND THREAD CONTROL TO LEVEL 5.
BIIN (TUG)
BIIN
THREAD CONTROL'S BEEN MORE USEFUL THAN I THOUGHT... I'M GLAD I GOT IT.

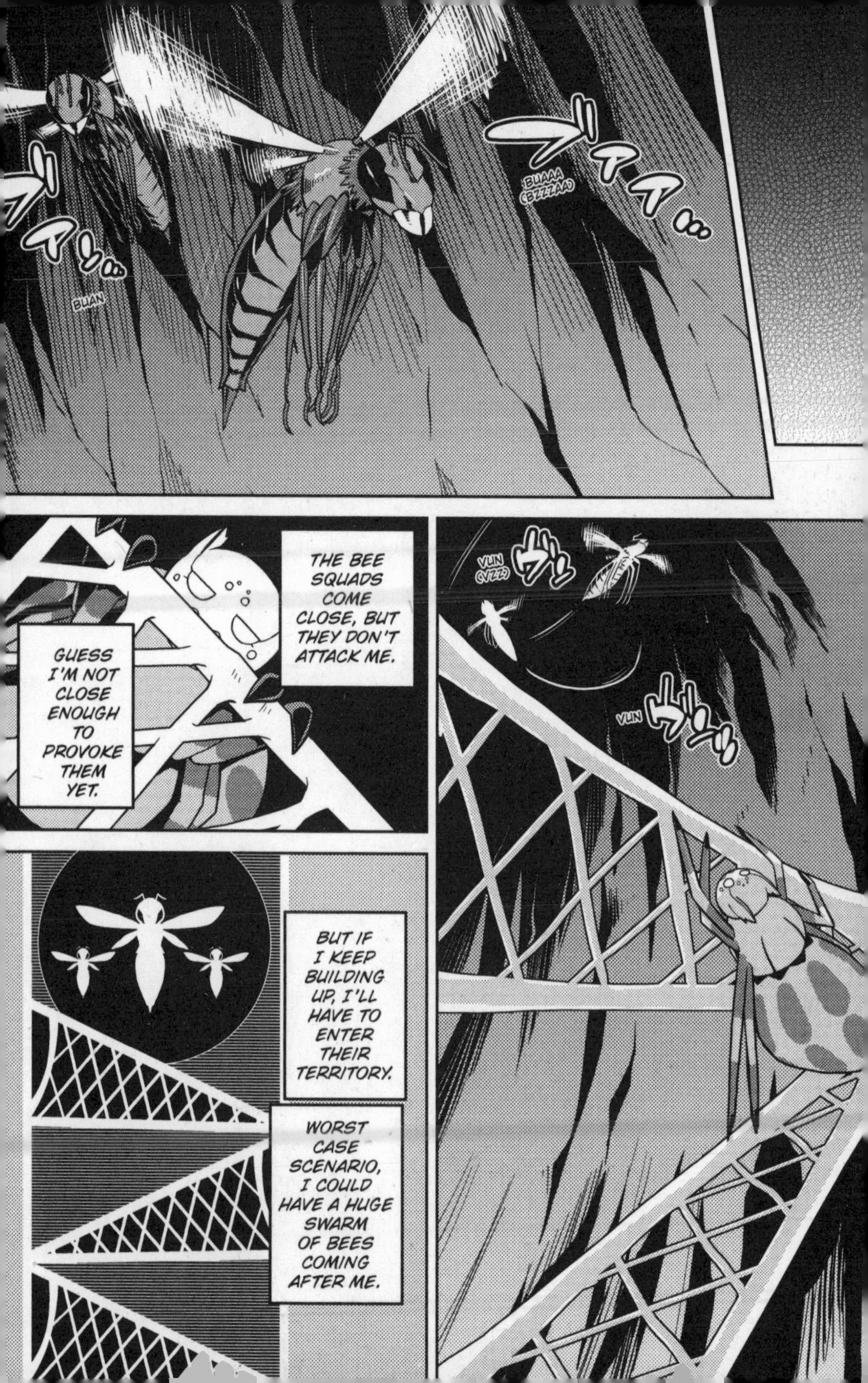
BUAAA (BZZZAA)
BUAN
VUN (VZZ)
VUN
THE BEE SQUADS COME CLOSE, BUT THEY DON'T ATTACK ME.
GUESS I'M NOT CLOSE ENOUGH TO PROVOKE THEM YET.
BUT IF I KEEP BUILDING UP, I'LL HAVE TO ENTER THEIR TERRITORY.
WORST CASE SCENARIO, I COULD HAVE A HUGE SWARM OF BEES COMING AFTER ME.

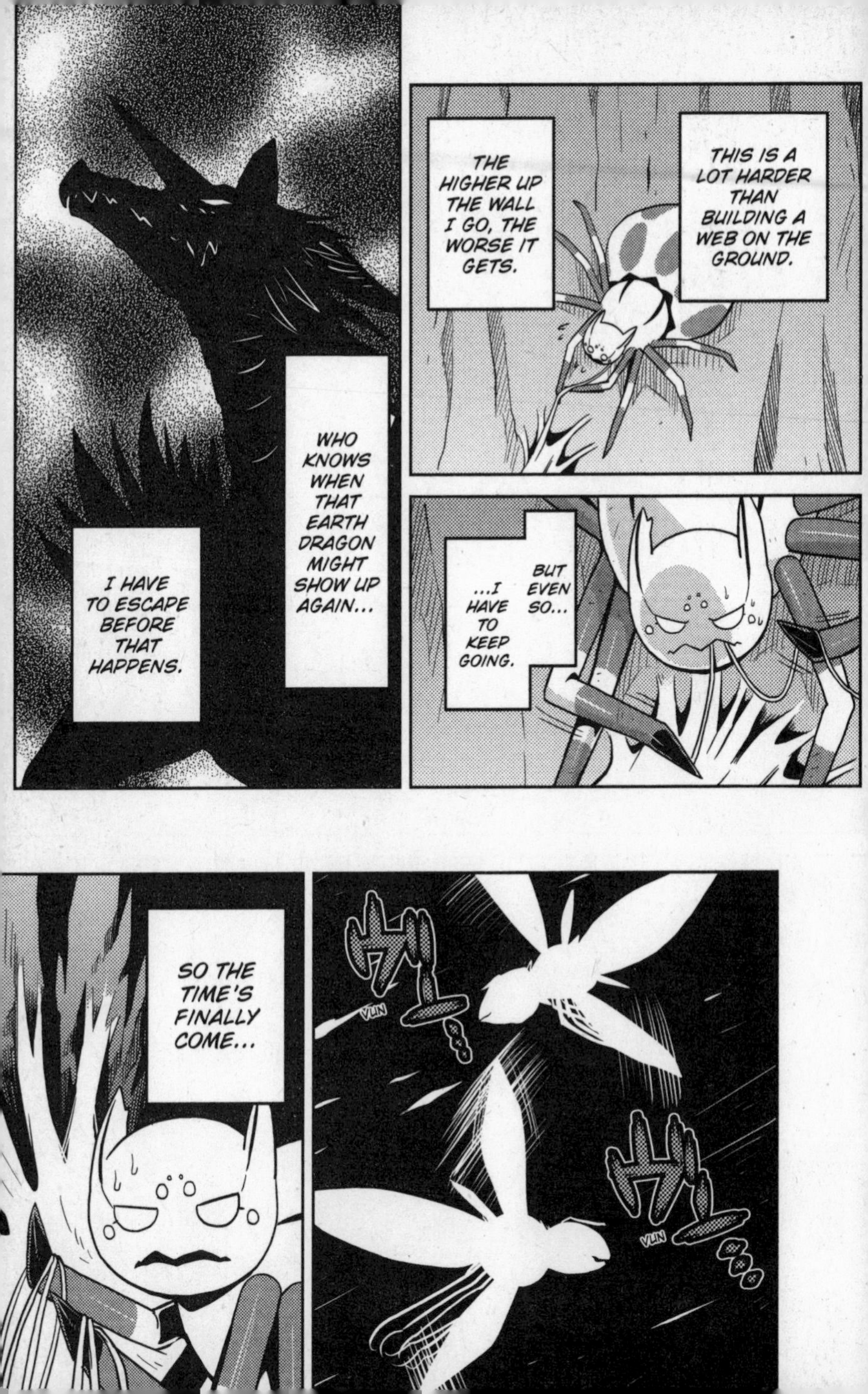
THIS IS A LOT HARDER THAN BUILDING A WEB ON THE GROUND.
THE HIGHER UP THE WALL I GO, THE WORSE IT GETS.
BUT EVEN SO...
...I HAVE TO KEEP GOING.
WHO KNOWS WHEN THAT EARTH DRAGON MIGHT SHOW UP AGAIN...
I HAVE TO ESCAPE BEFORE THAT HAPPENS.
VUN
VUN
SO THE TIME'S FINALLY COME...

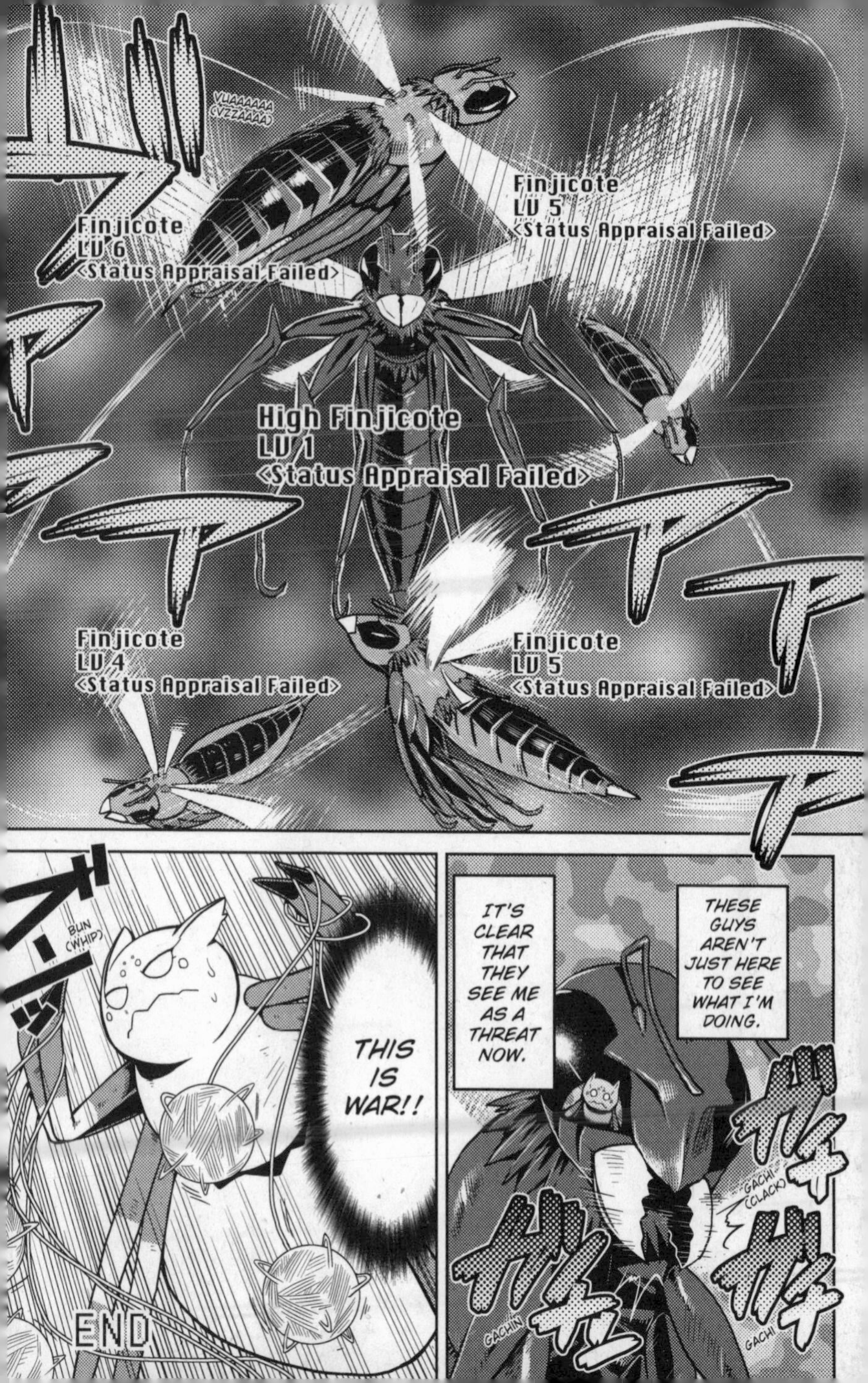
Finjicote
LV 5
<Status Appraisal Failed>
VUAAAAAA (VZZAAAAA)
Finjicote
LV 6
<Status Appraisal Failed>
High Finjicote
LV 1
<Status Appraisal Failed>
Finjicote
LV 5
<Status Appraisal Failed>
Finjicote
LV 4
<Status Appraisal Failed>
THESE GUYS AREN'T JUST HERE TO SEE WHAT I'M DOING.
IT'S CLEAR THAT THEY SEE ME AS A THREAT NOW.
GACHI (CLACK)
GACHI
GACHIN
BUN (WHIP)
THIS IS WAR!!
END

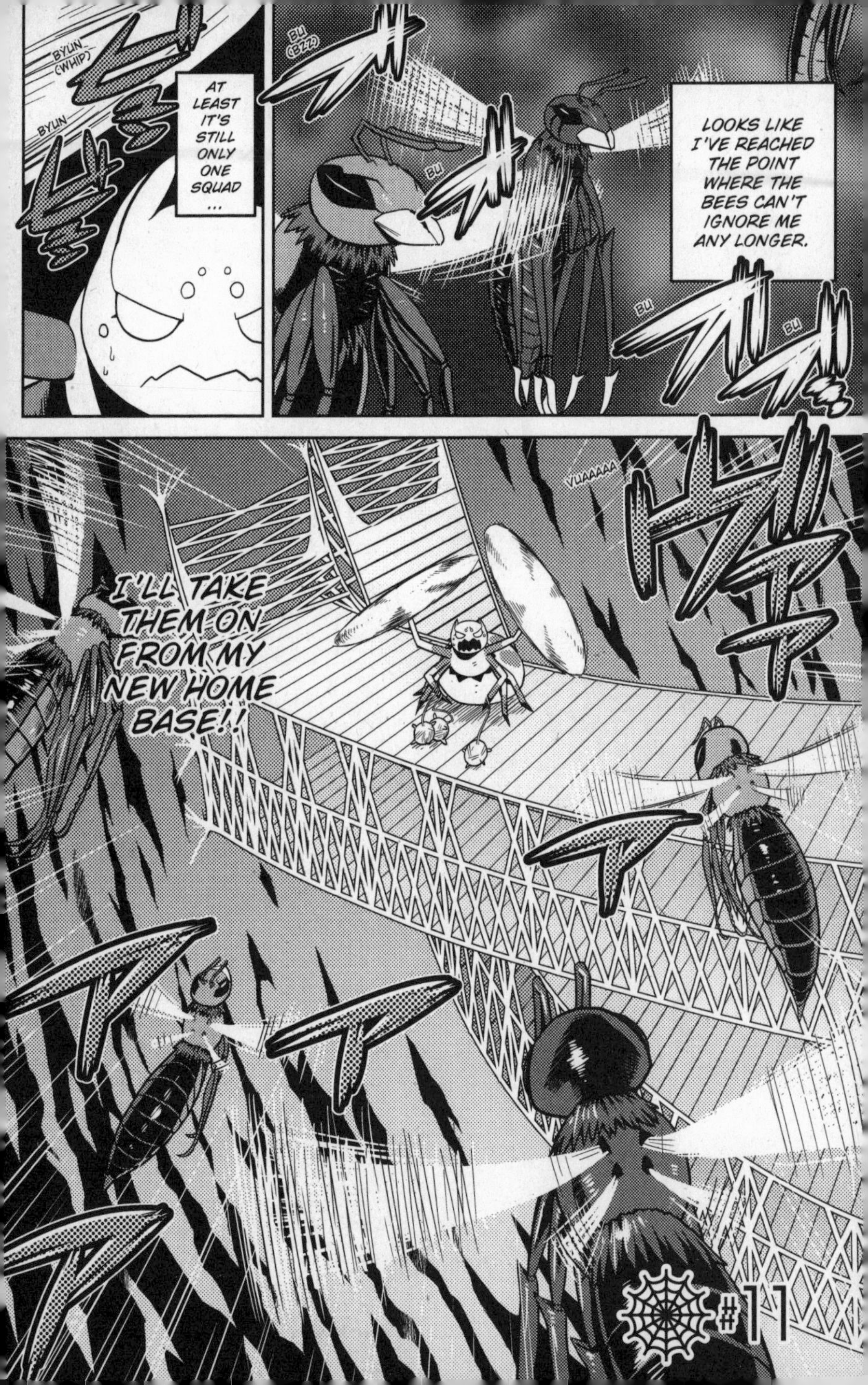
LOOKS LIKE I'VE REACHED THE POINT WHERE THE BEES CAN'T IGNORE ME ANY LONGER.
BU (BZZ)
BU
BU
BU
BYUN (WHIP)
BYUN
AT LEAST IT'S STILL ONLY ONE SQUAD...
VUAAAAA
I'LL TAKE THEM ON FROM MY NEW HOME BASE!!
#11

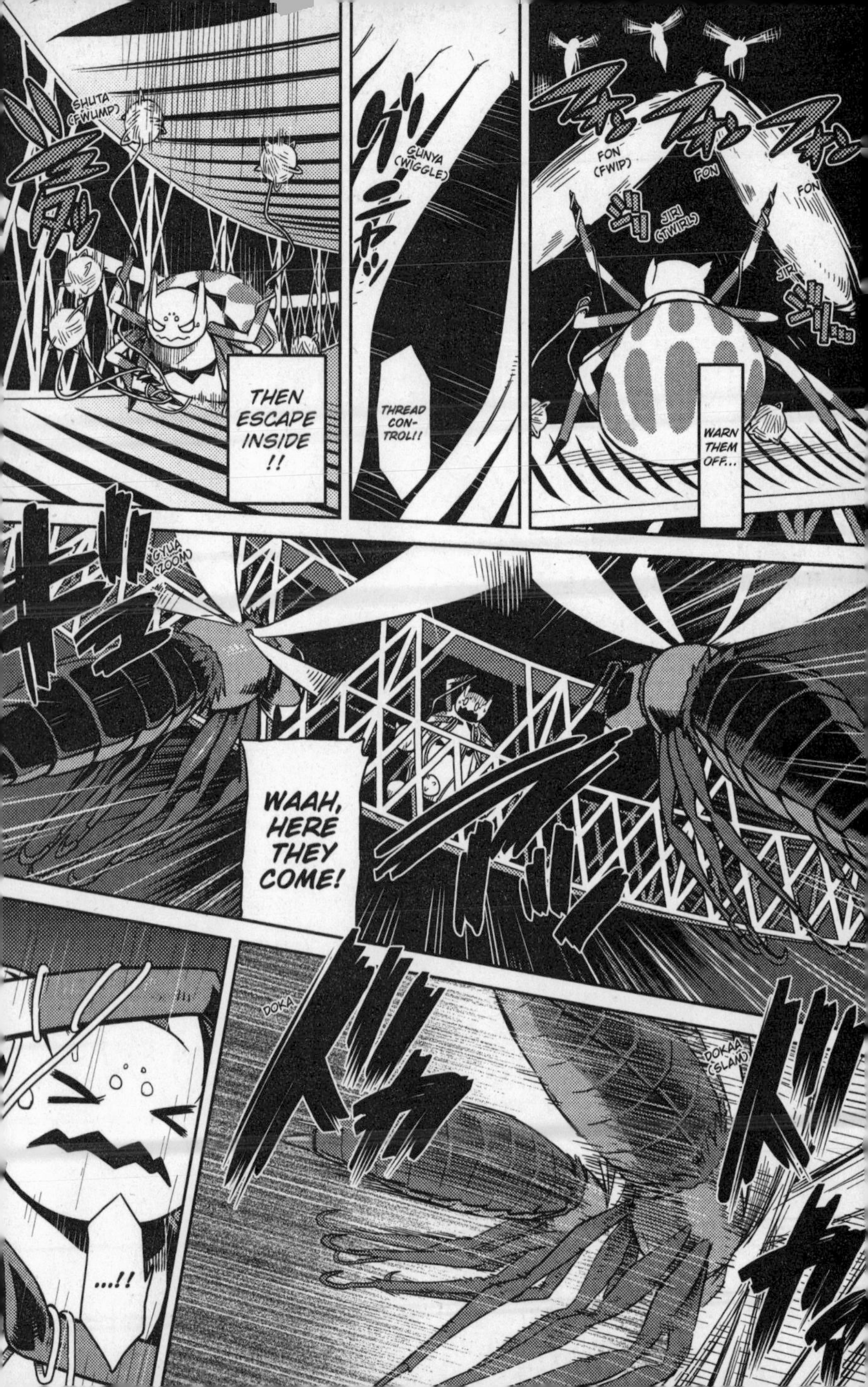
FON (FWIP)
FON
FON
JIRI (TWIRL)
JIRI
WARN THEM OFF...
GUNYA (WIGGLE)
THREAD CON-TROL!!
SHUTA (FWUMP)
THEN ESCAPE INSIDE!!
GYUA (ZOOM)
WAAH, HERE THEY COME!
DOKAA (SLAM)
DOKA
...!!

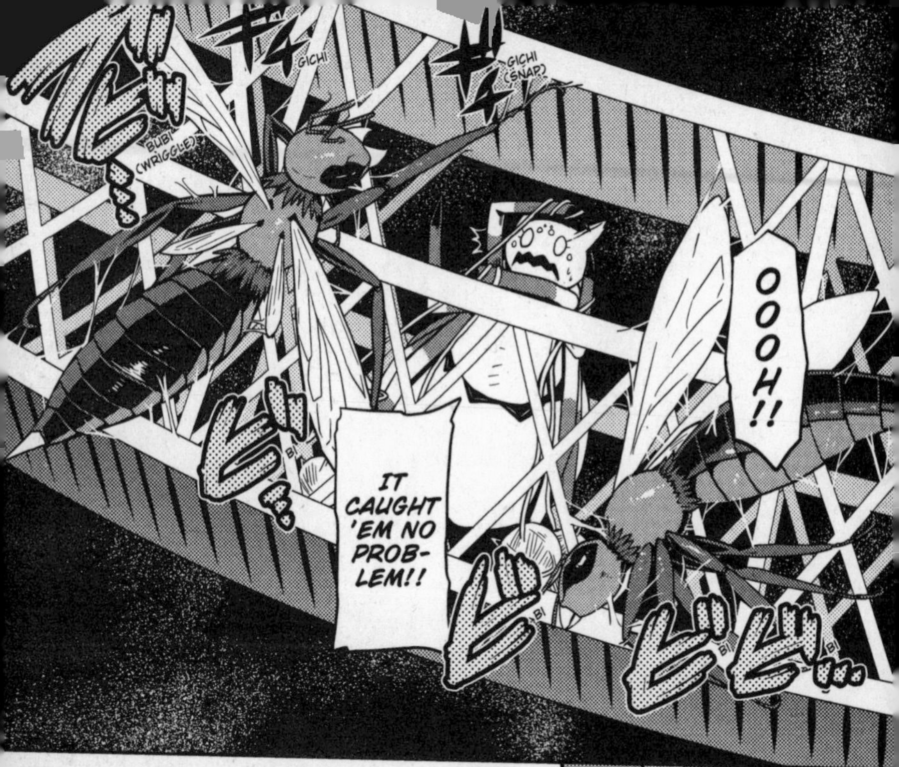
GICHI (SNAP)
GICHI
OOOOH!!
BUBI (WRIGGLE)
IT CAUGHT 'EM NO PROBLEM!!
BI
BI
BI
BI

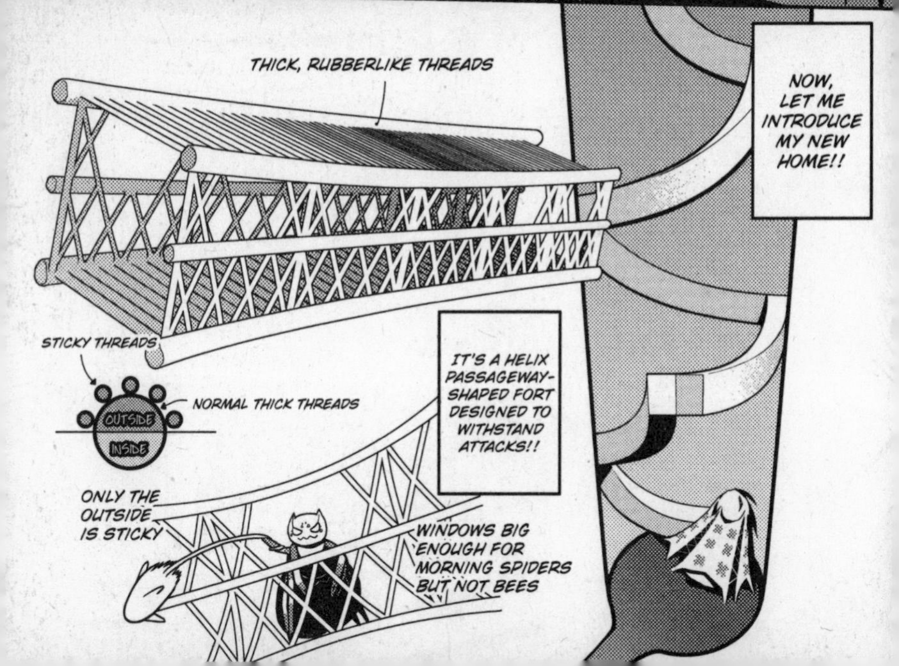
NOW, LET ME INTRODUCE MY NEW HOME!!
THICK, RUBBERLIKE THREADS
IT'S A HELIX PASSAGEWAY-SHAPED FORT DESIGNED TO WITHSTAND ATTACKS!!
STICKY THREADS
NORMAL THICK THREADS
OUTSIDE
INSIDE
ONLY THE OUTSIDE IS STICKY
WINDOWS BIG ENOUGH FOR MORNING SPIDERS BUT NOT BEES

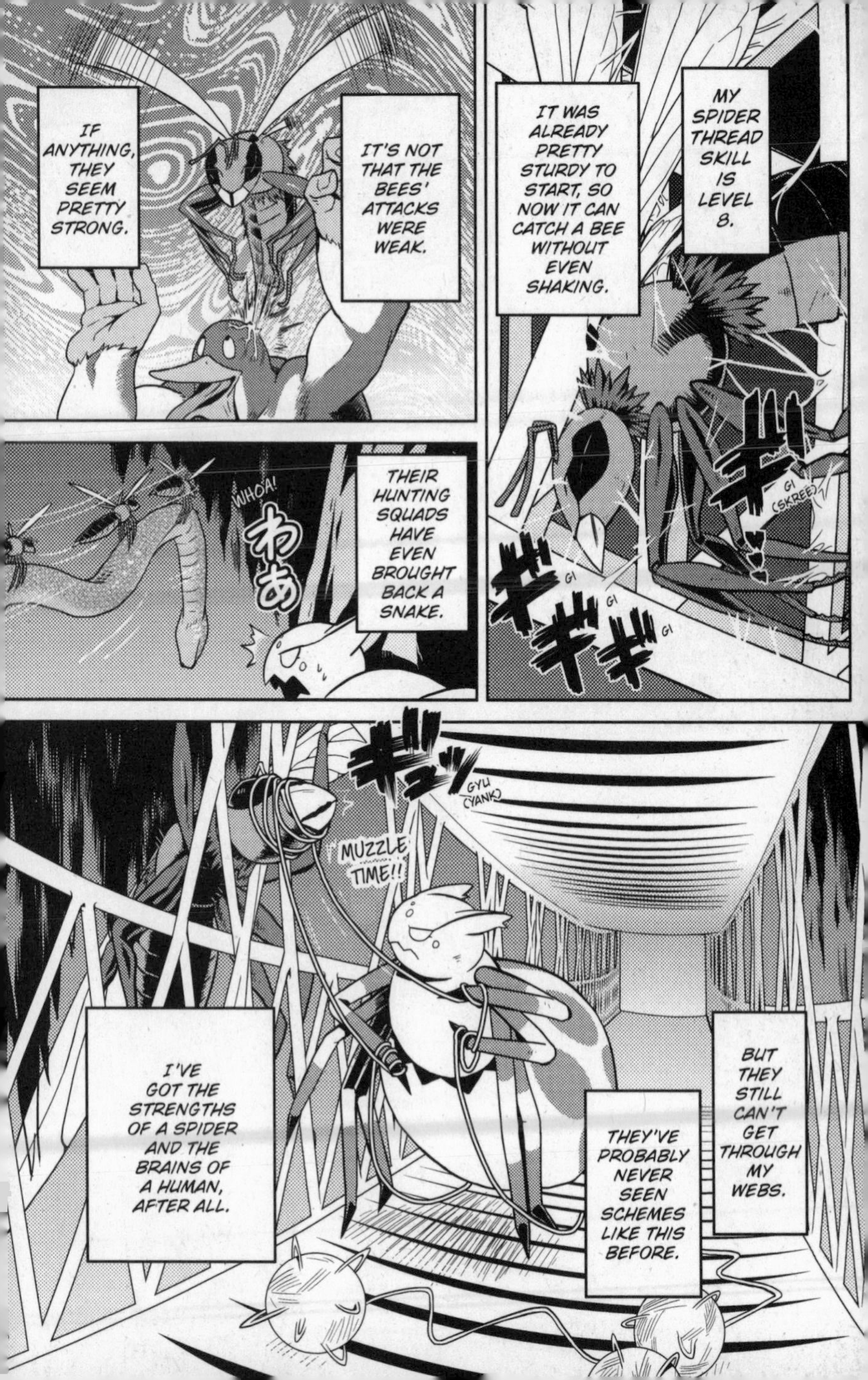
MY SPIDER THREAD SKILL IS LEVEL 8.
IT WAS ALREADY PRETTY STURDY TO START, SO NOW IT CAN CATCH A BEE WITHOUT EVEN SHAKING.
ギ
GI (SKREE)
ギ
GI
ギ
GI
ギ
GI
IT'S NOT THAT THE BEES' ATTACKS WERE WEAK.
IF ANYTHING, THEY SEEM PRETTY STRONG.
THEIR HUNTING SQUADS HAVE EVEN BROUGHT BACK A SNAKE.
わあ
WHOA!
ギュッ
GYU (YANK)
MUZZLE TIME!!
BUT THEY STILL CAN'T GET THROUGH MY WEBS.
THEY'VE PROBABLY NEVER SEEN SCHEMES LIKE THIS BEFORE.
I'VE GOT THE STRENGTHS OF A SPIDER AND THE BRAINS OF A HUMAN, AFTER ALL.

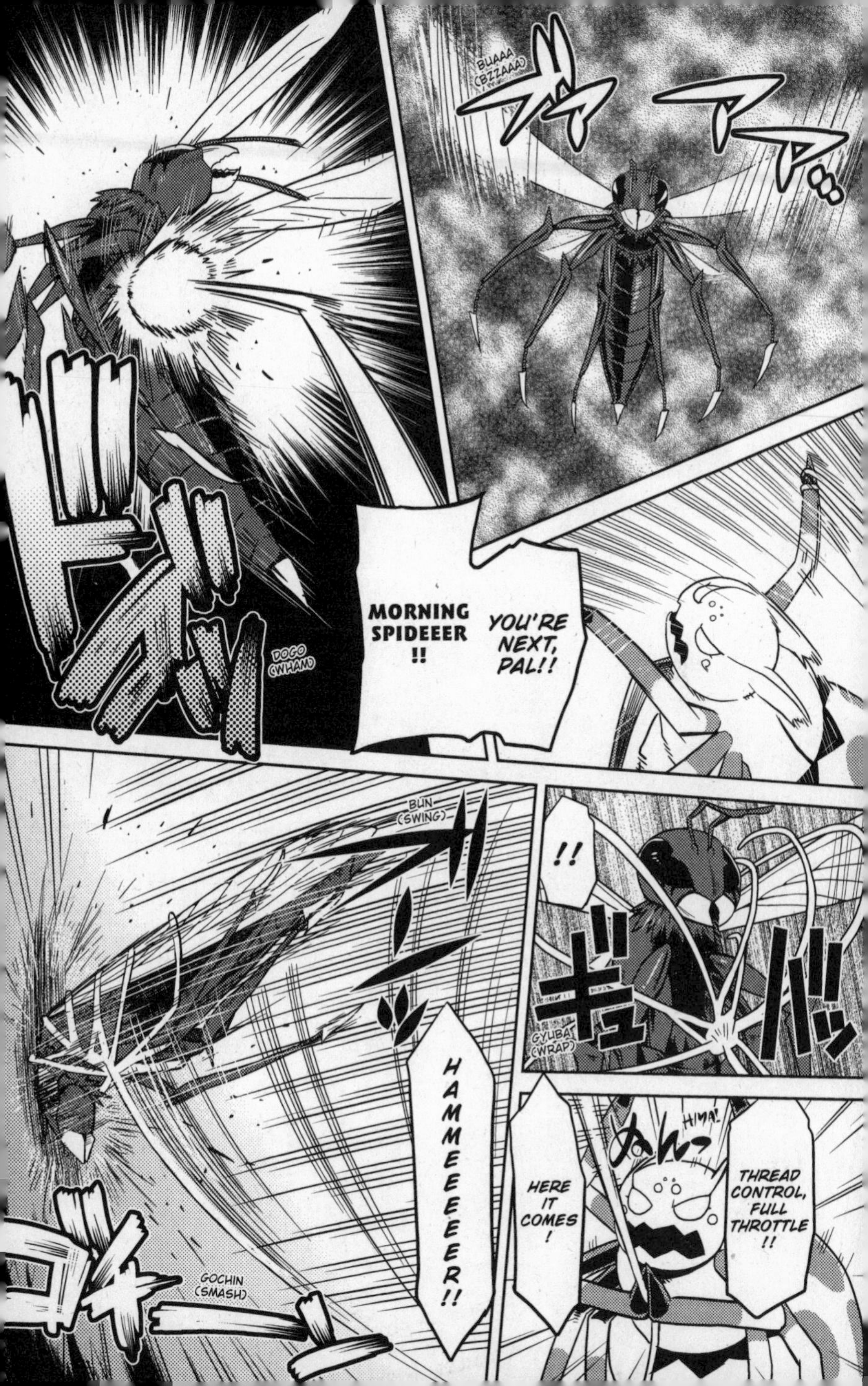
BUAAA (BZZAAA)
YOU'RE NEXT, PAL!!
MORNING SPIDEEEER!!
DOGO (WHAM)
!!
GYUBA (WRAP)
THREAD CONTROL, FULL THROTTLE!!
HIMA!
HERE IT COMES!
BUN (SWING)
HAMMEEEEEER!!
GOCHIN (SMASH)

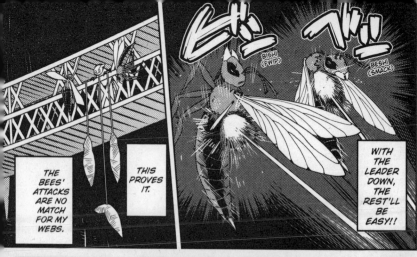

BESHI (SMACK)
BISHI (FWIP)
WITH THE LEADER DOWN, THE REST'LL BE EASY!!
THIS PROVES IT.
THE BEES' ATTACKS ARE NO MATCH FOR MY WEBS.
THERE ARE STILL HUNDREDS OF BEES FLYING AROUND ABOVE ME.
AT FIRST, I WAS AFRAID OF THAT HUGE NUMBER, BUT...
...WHETHER THERE'S 100 OR 1,000, IT DOESN'T MATTER IF THEY CAN'T BREAK THROUGH.
FINALLY, MY CHANCES OF ESCAPE ARE STARTING TO IMPROVE.
SO I'LL KEEP EXPANDING MY WEB!

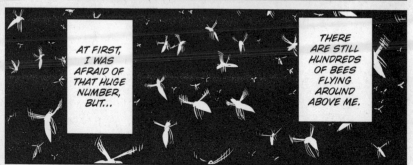

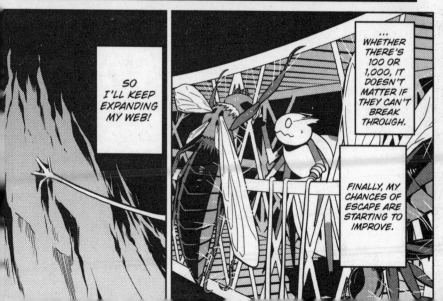

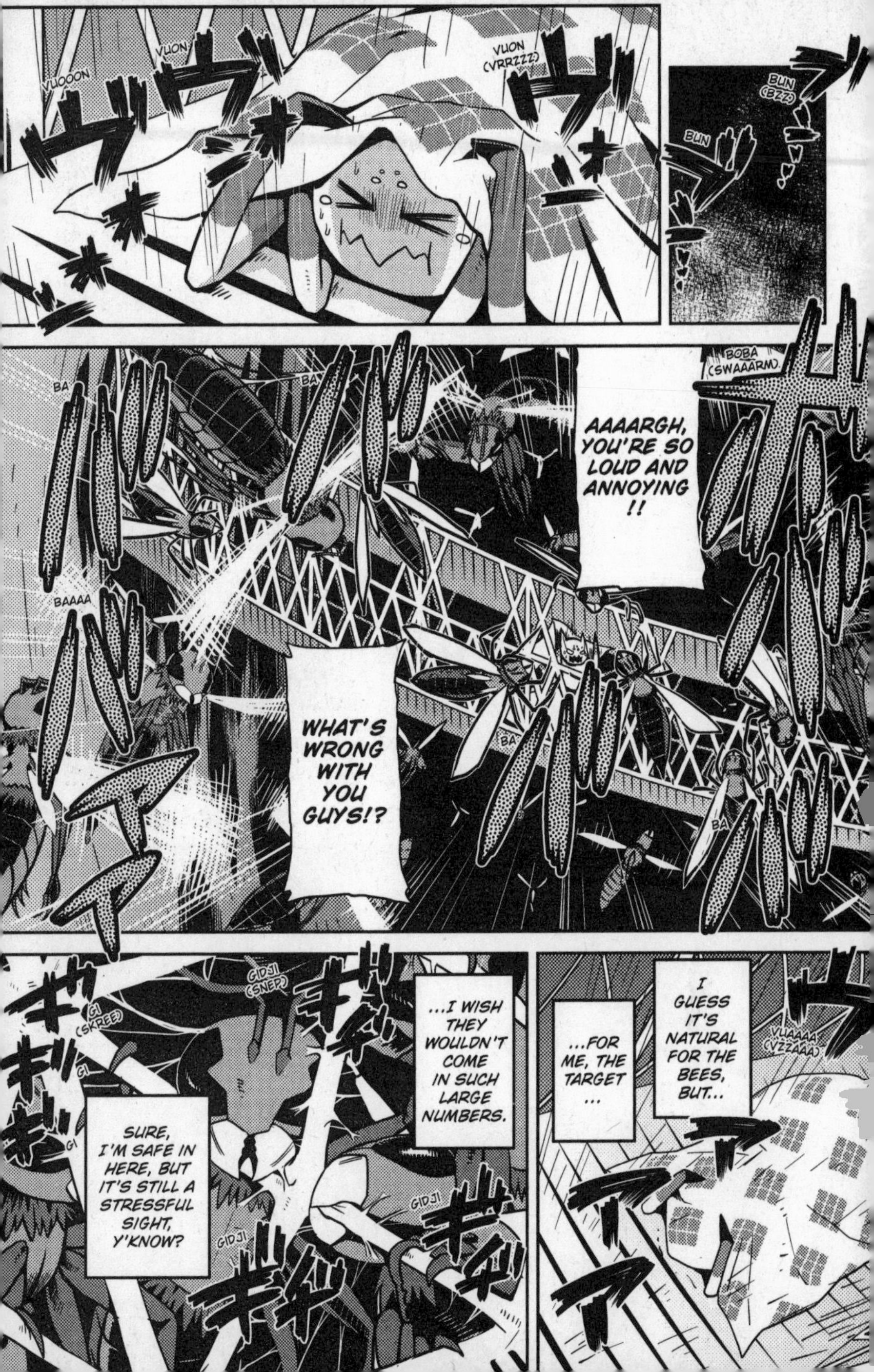
BUN (BZZ)
BUN
VUON (VRRZZZ)
VUON
VUOOOON
BOBA (SWAAARM)
AAAARGH, YOU'RE SO LOUD AND ANNOYING !!
BA
BA
WHAT'S WRONG WITH YOU GUYS!?
BAAAA
BA
BA
VUAAAA (VZZAAA)
I GUESS IT'S NATURAL FOR THE BEES, BUT...
...FOR ME, THE TARGET...
...I WISH THEY WOULDN'T COME IN SUCH LARGE NUMBERS.
GIDJI (SNEP)
GI (SKREE)
GI
GI
SURE, I'M SAFE IN HERE, BUT IT'S STILL A STRESSFUL SIGHT, Y'KNOW?
GIDJI
GIDJI

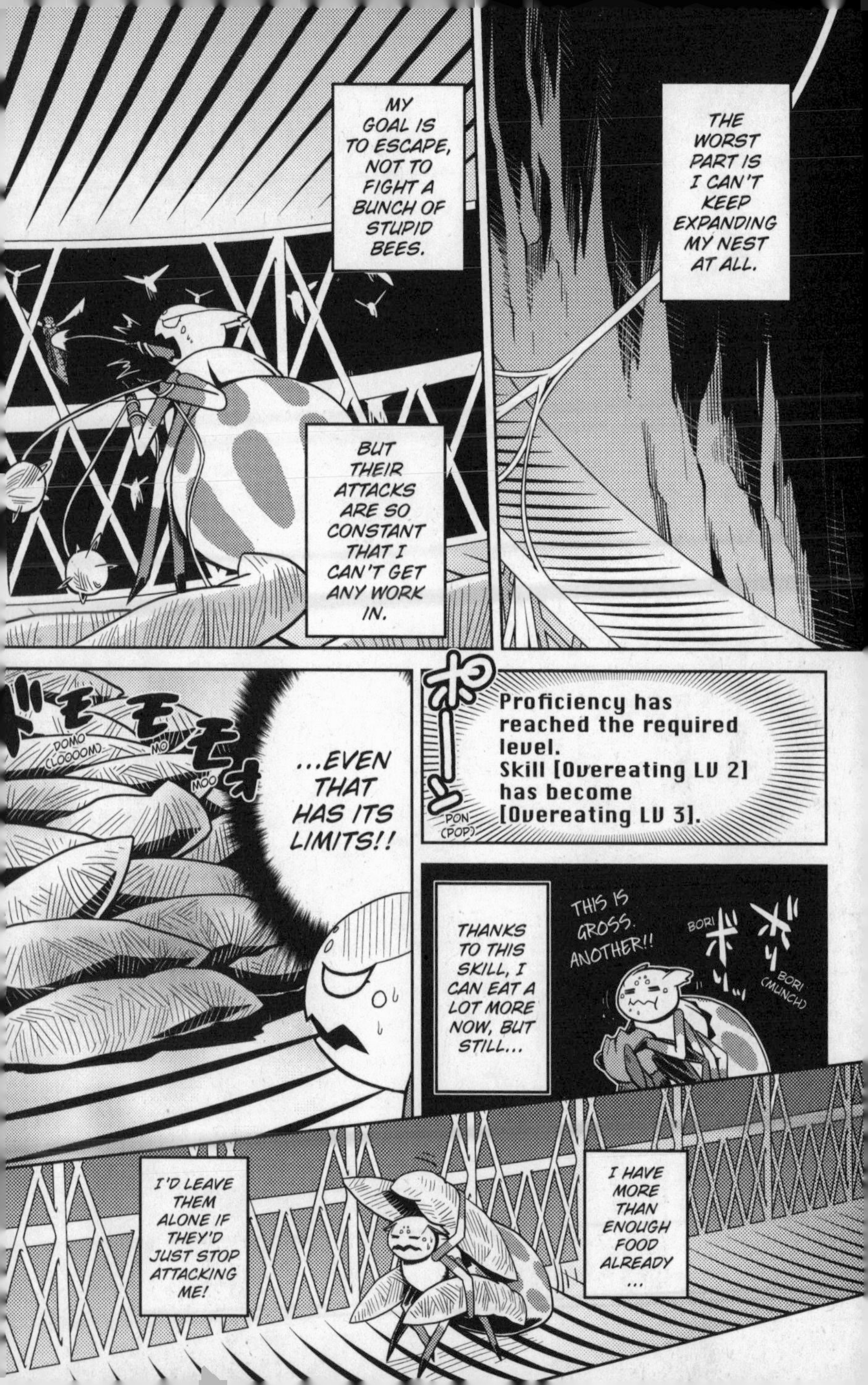
THE WORST PART IS I CAN'T KEEP EXPANDING MY NEST AT ALL.
MY GOAL IS TO ESCAPE, NOT TO FIGHT A BUNCH OF STUPID BEES.
BUT THEIR ATTACKS ARE SO CONSTANT THAT I CAN'T GET ANY WORK IN.
PON (POP)
Proficiency has reached the required level.
Skill [Overeating LV 2] has become [Overeating LV 3].
THANKS TO THIS SKILL, I CAN EAT A LOT MORE NOW, BUT STILL...
THIS IS GROSS. ANOTHER!!
BORI
BORI (MUNCH)
DOMO (LOOOOM)
MO
MOO
...EVEN THAT HAS ITS LIMITS!!
I HAVE MORE THAN ENOUGH FOOD ALREADY ...
I'D LEAVE THEM ALONE IF THEY'D JUST STOP ATTACKING ME!

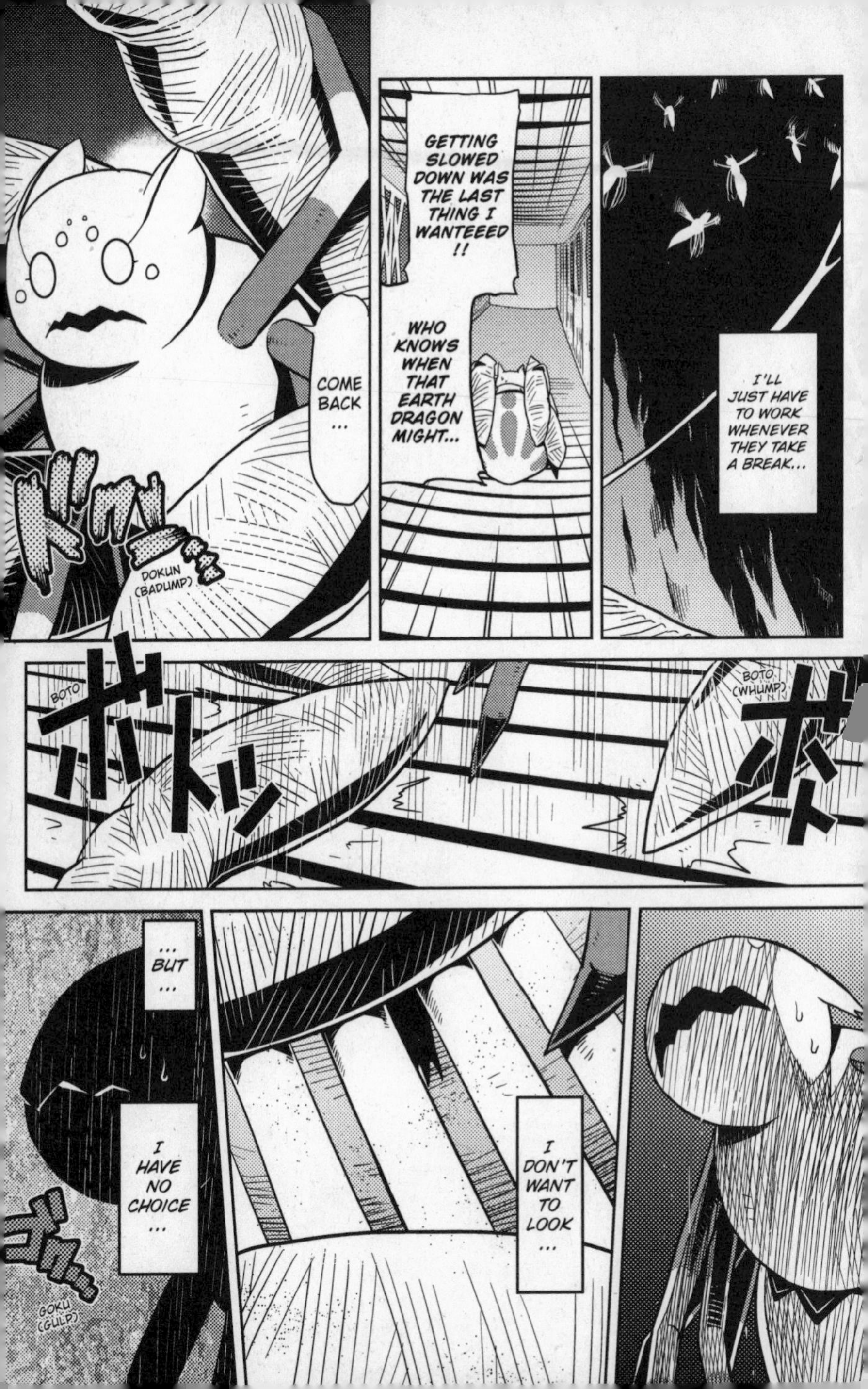
I'LL JUST HAVE TO WORK WHENEVER THEY TAKE A BREAK...
GETTING SLOWED DOWN WAS THE LAST THING I WANTEEED!!
WHO KNOWS WHEN THAT EARTH DRAGON MIGHT...
COME BACK...
DOKUN (BADUMP)
BOTO (WHUMP)
BOTO
I DON'T WANT TO LOOK...
...BUT...
I HAVE NO CHOICE...
GOKU (GULP)

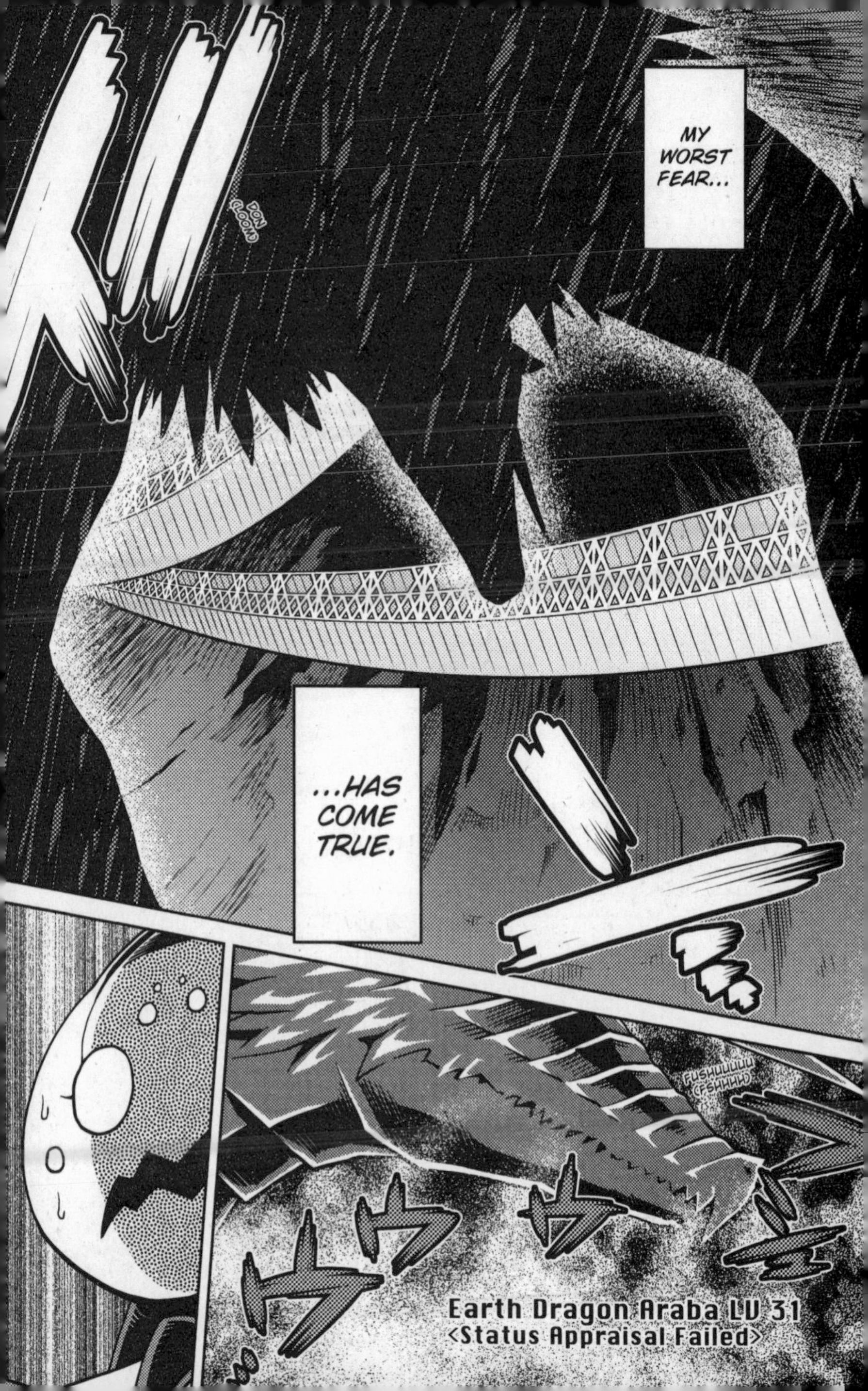
MY WORST FEAR...
DON (GLOOM)
...HAS COME TRUE.
FUSHUUUUUU (FSHHHH)
Earth Dragon Araba LV 31
<Status Appraisal Failed>

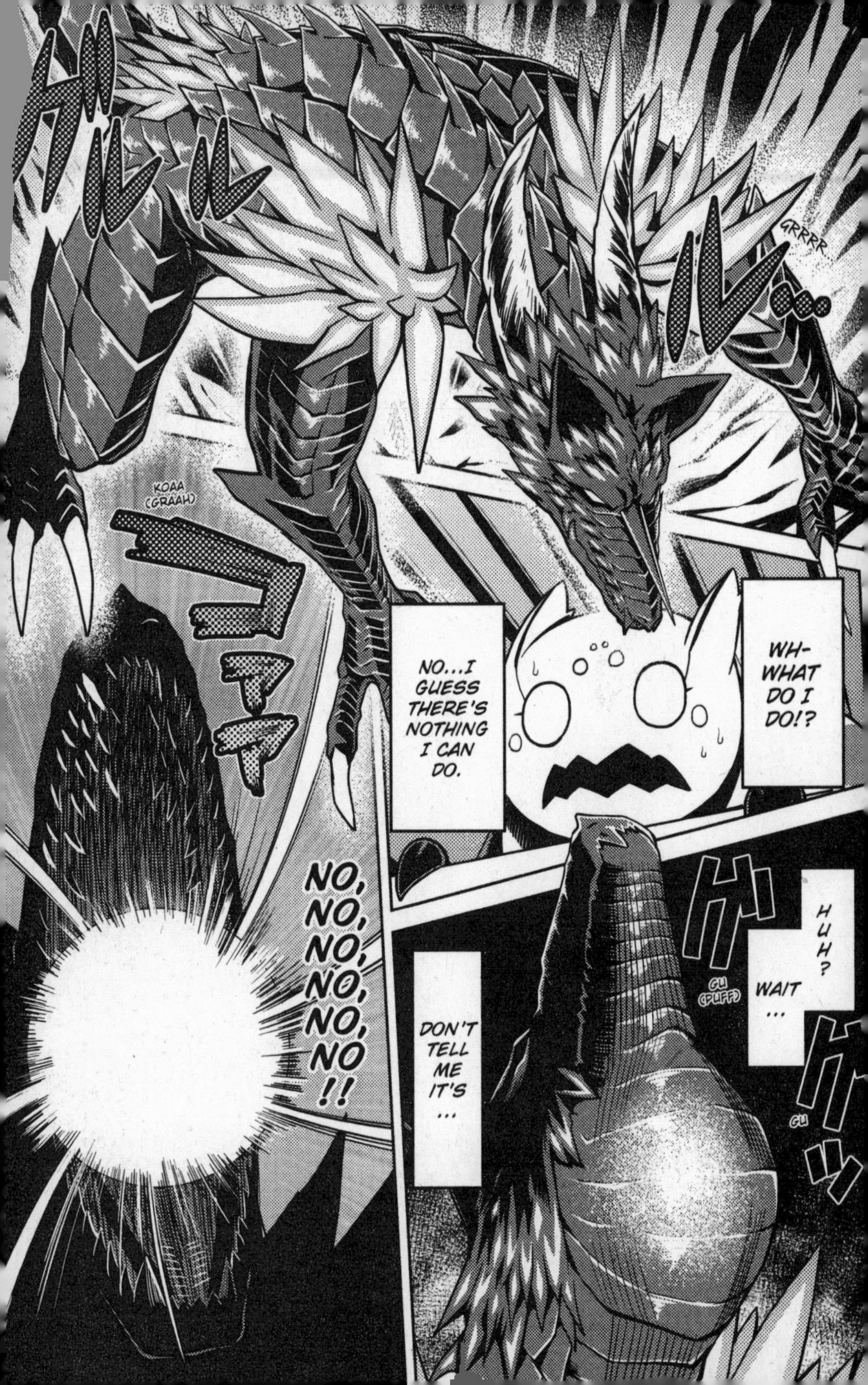
GRRRR
KOAA (GRAAH)
WH- WHAT DO I DO!?
NO...I GUESS THERE'S NOTHING I CAN DO.
HUH? WAIT ...
GU (PUFF)
GU
DON'T TELL ME IT'S ...
NO, NO, NO, NO, NO, NO!!

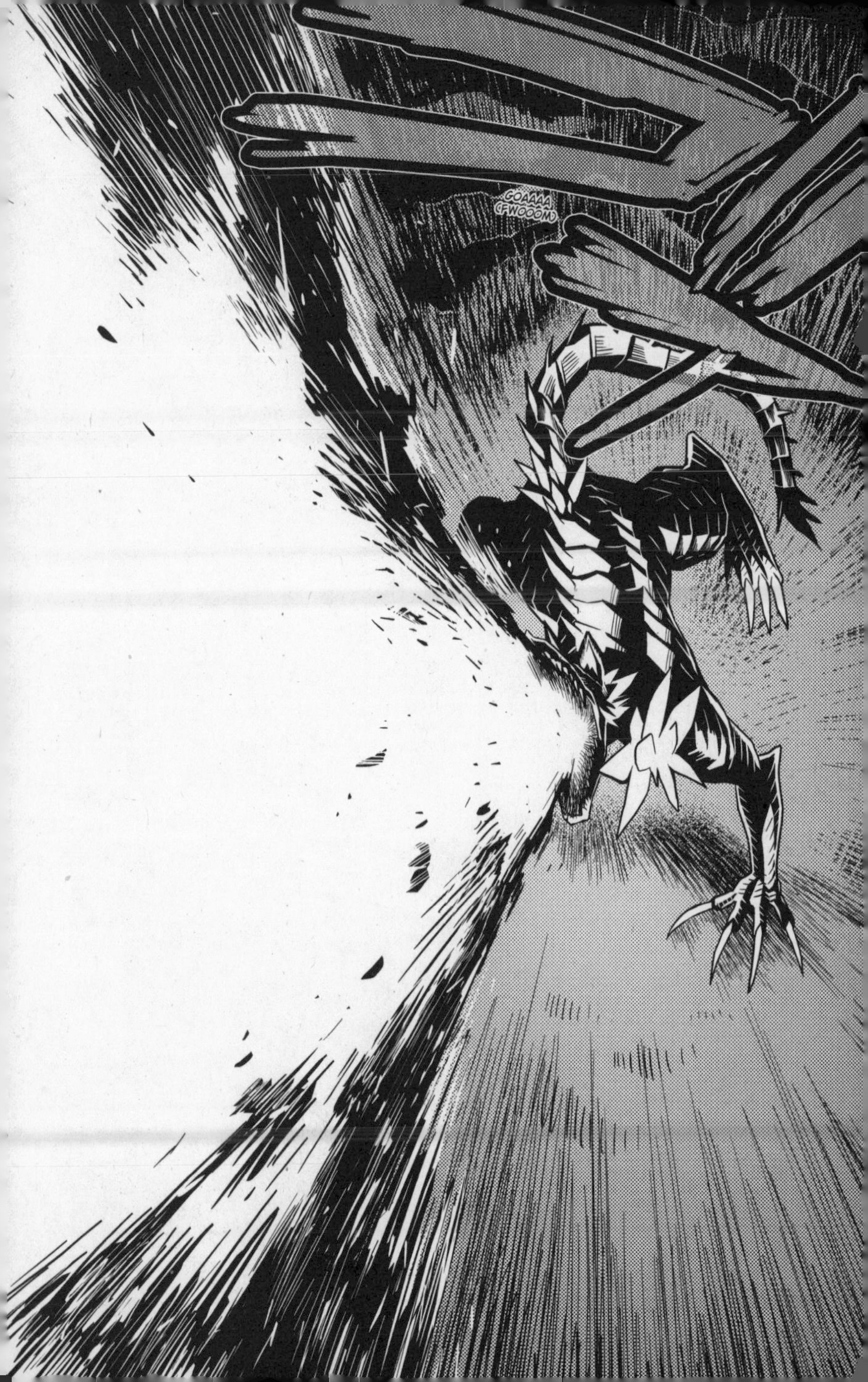
GOAAAA
(FWOOOM)

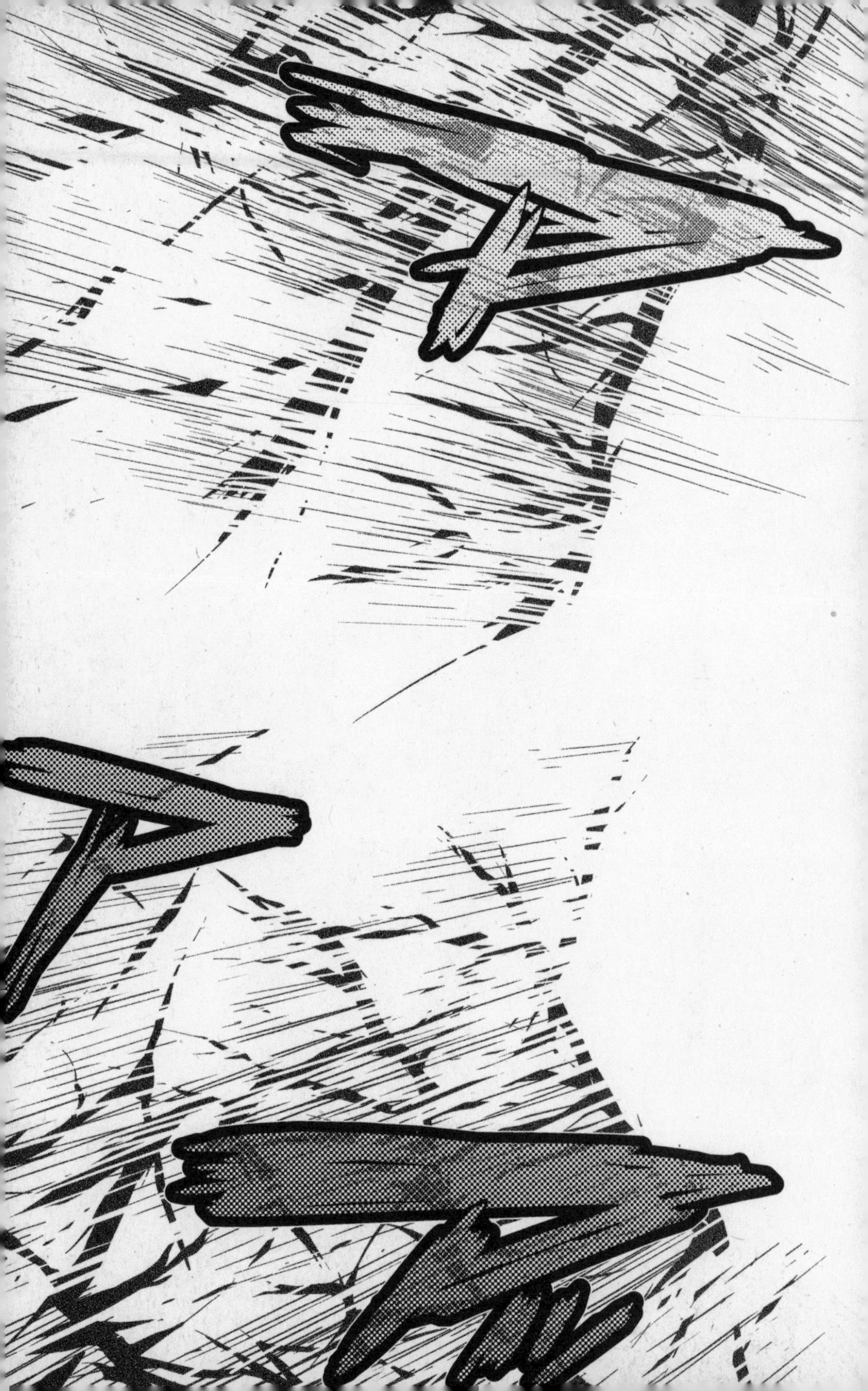

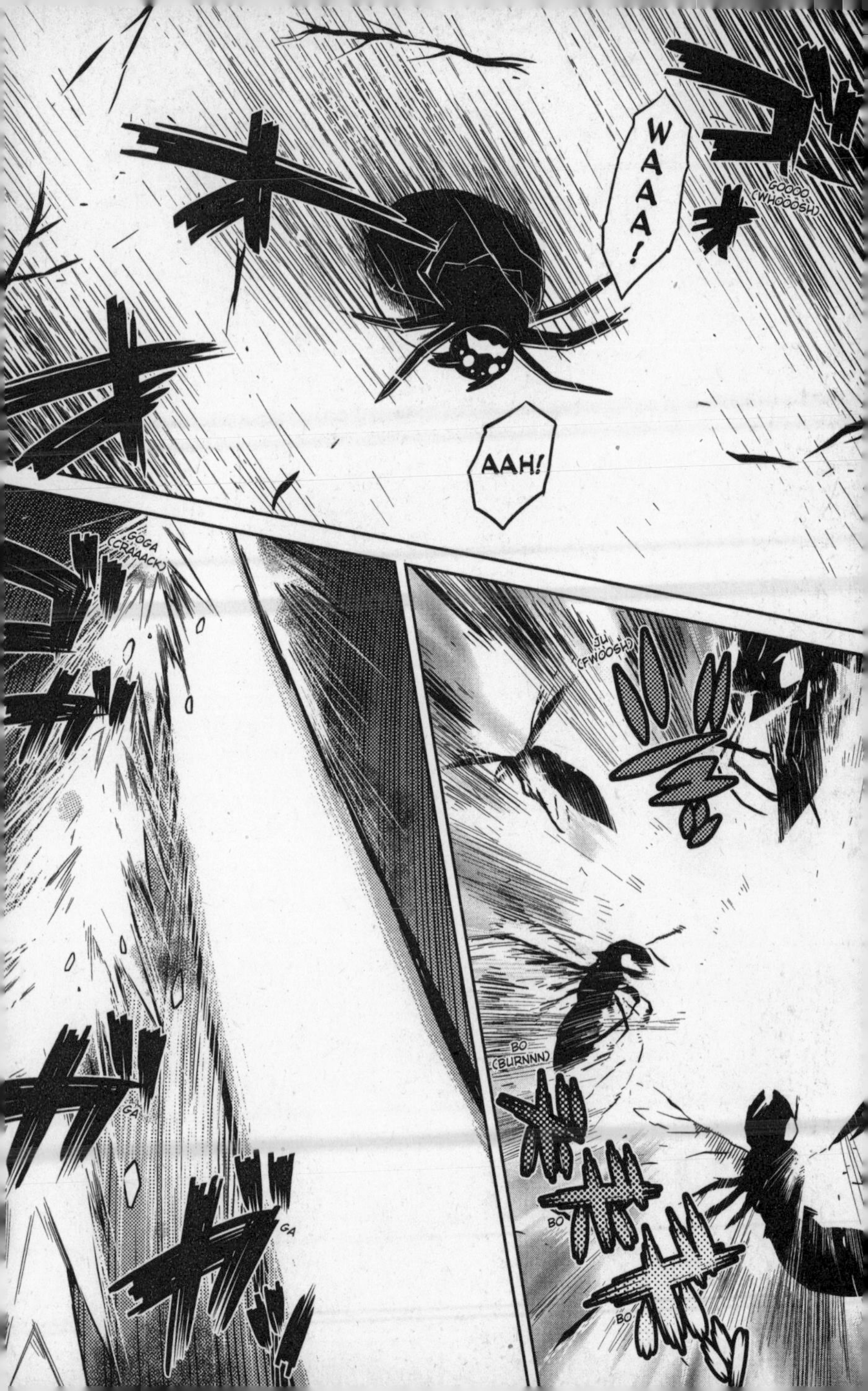
GOOOO (WHOOOSH)
WAAA!
AAH!
JU (FWOOSH)
BO (BURNNN)
BO
BO
GOGA (CRAAACK)
GA
GA

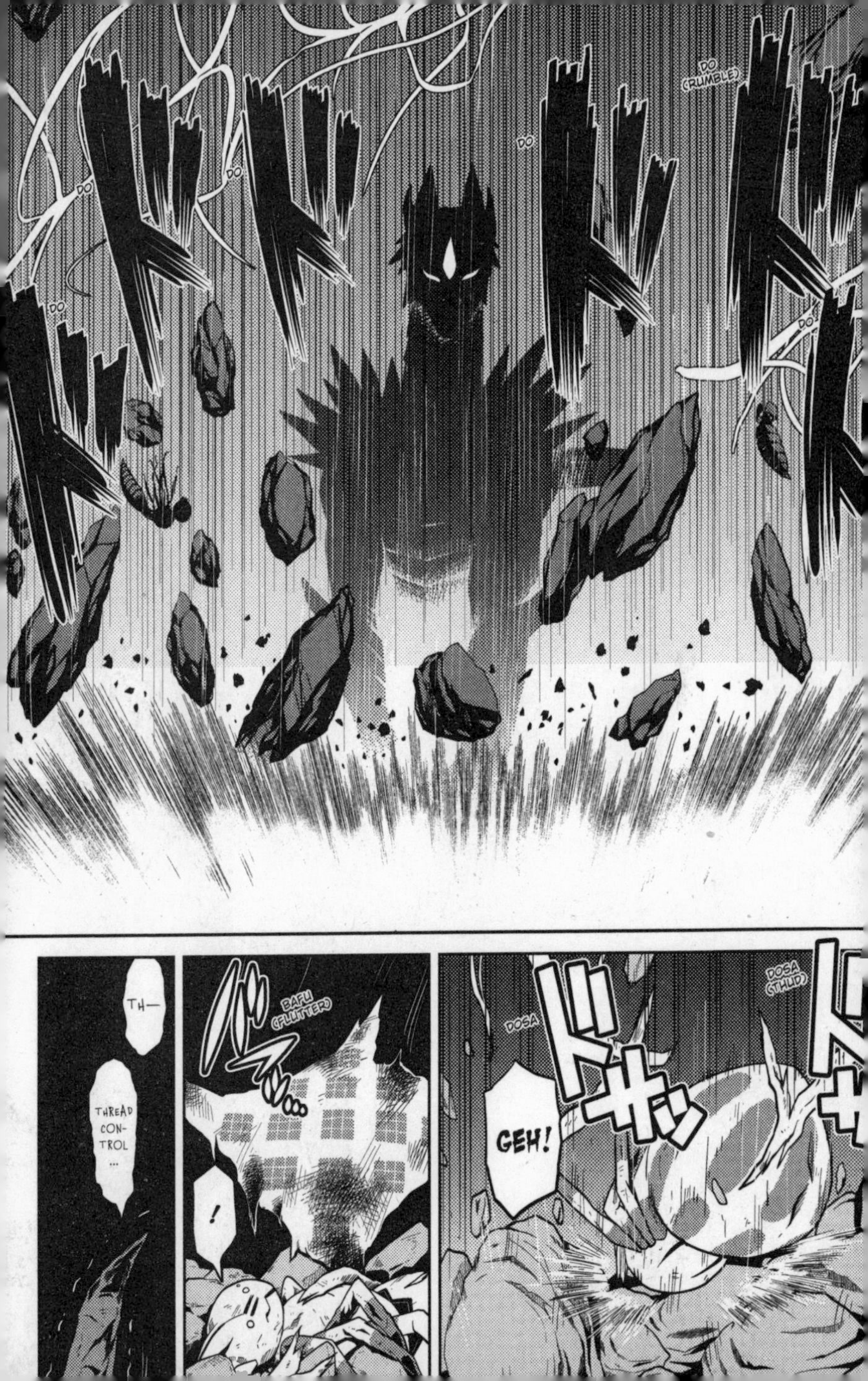
DO
(RUMBLE)
DO
DO
DO
DO
DO
DOSA
(THUD)
DOSA
GEH!
BAFU
(FLUTTER)
!
TH—
THREAD CON-TROL...

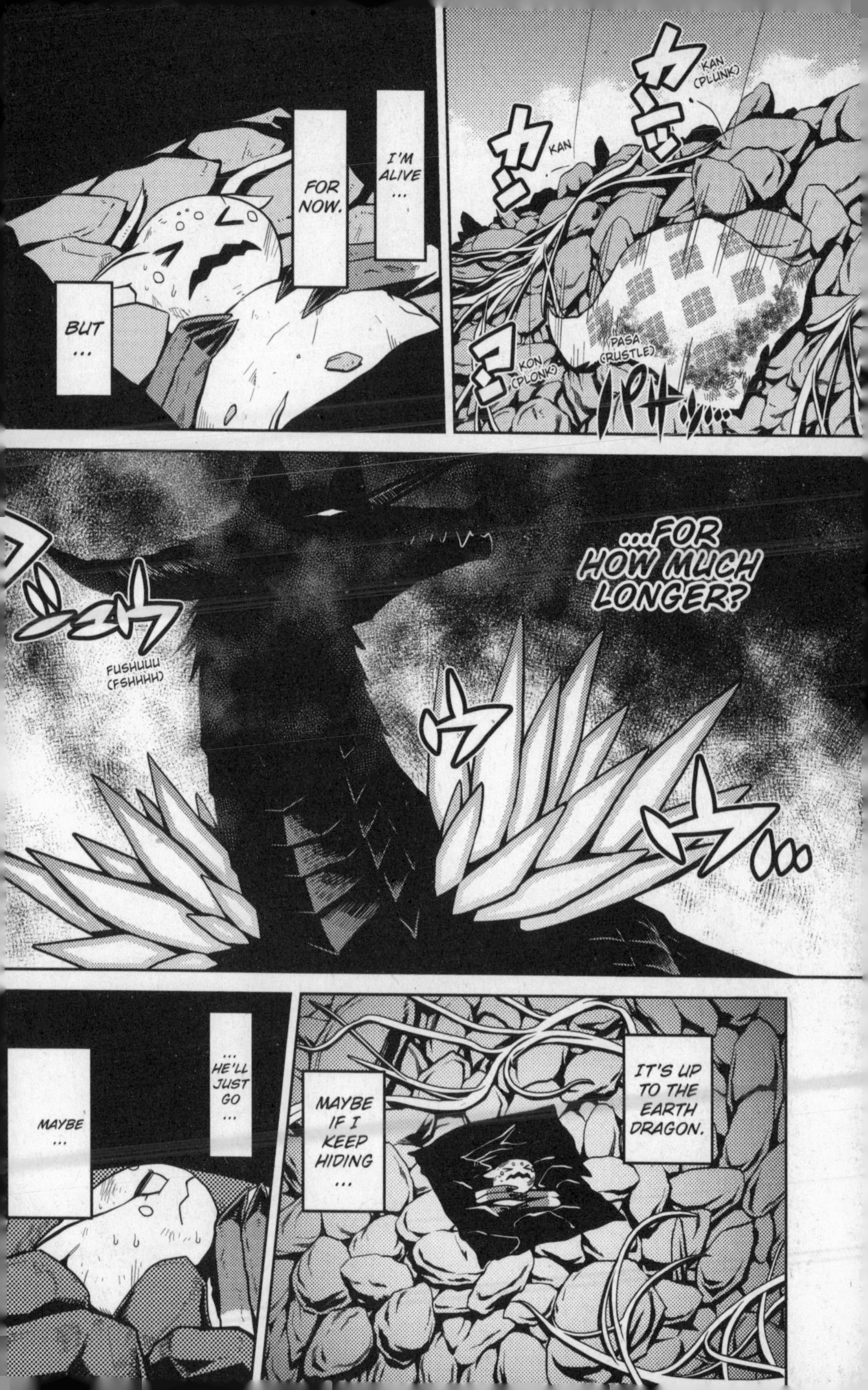
KAN (PLUNK)
KAN
PASA (RUSTLE)
KON (PLONK)
I'M ALIVE ...
FOR NOW.
BUT ...
...FOR HOW MUCH LONGER?
FUSHUUU (FSHHHH)
IT'S UP TO THE EARTH DRAGON.
MAYBE IF I KEEP HIDING ...
... HE'LL JUST GO ...
MAYBE ...

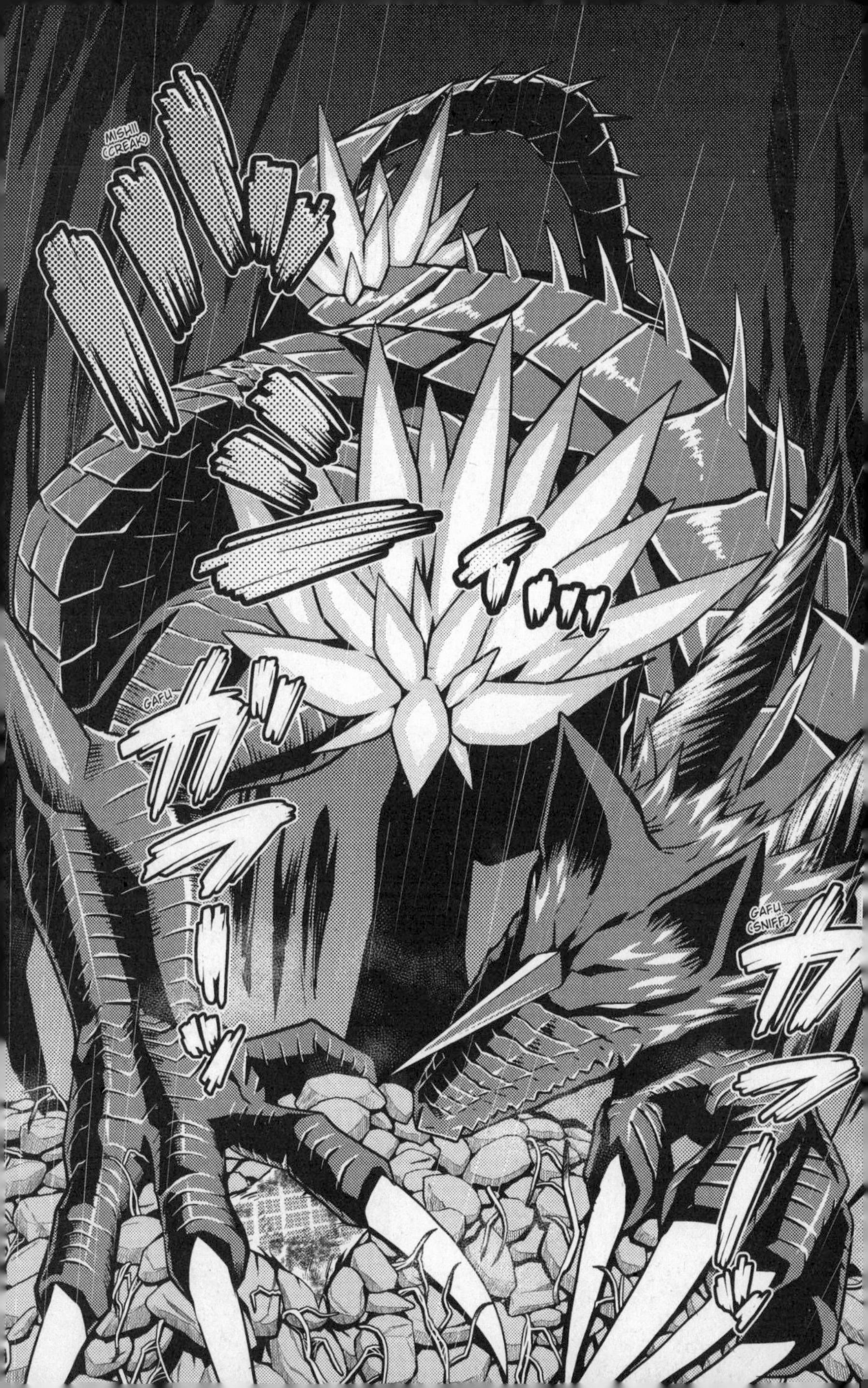
GAFU
(SNIFF)
MISHII
(CREAK)
GAFU

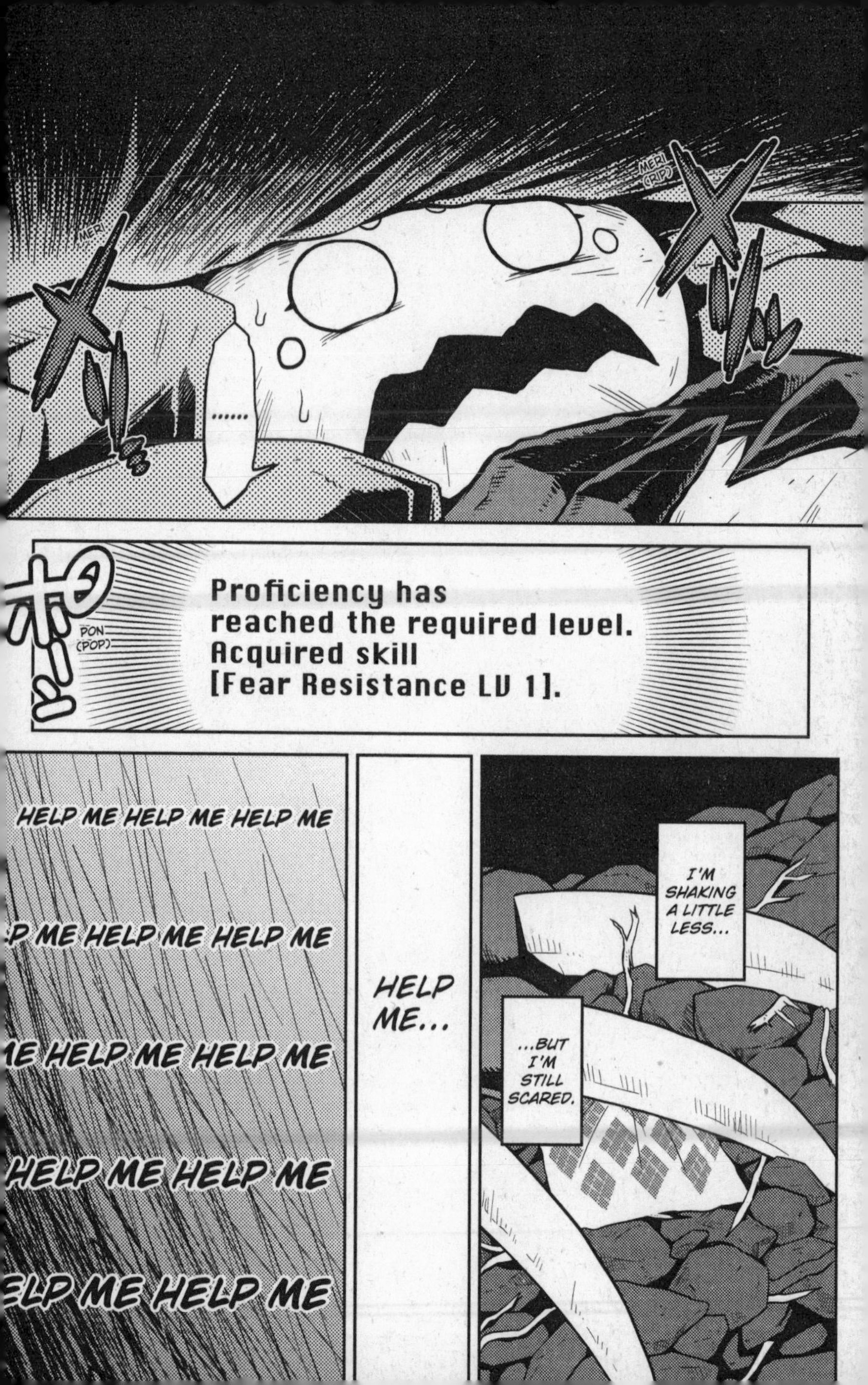
MERI (RIP)
MERI
......
PON (POP)
Proficiency has reached the required level.
Acquired skill [Fear Resistance LV 1].
I'M SHAKING A LITTLE LESS...
...BUT I'M STILL SCARED.
HELP ME...
HELP ME HELP ME HELP ME
P ME HELP ME HELP ME
E HELP ME HELP ME
HELP ME HELP ME
ELP ME HELP ME

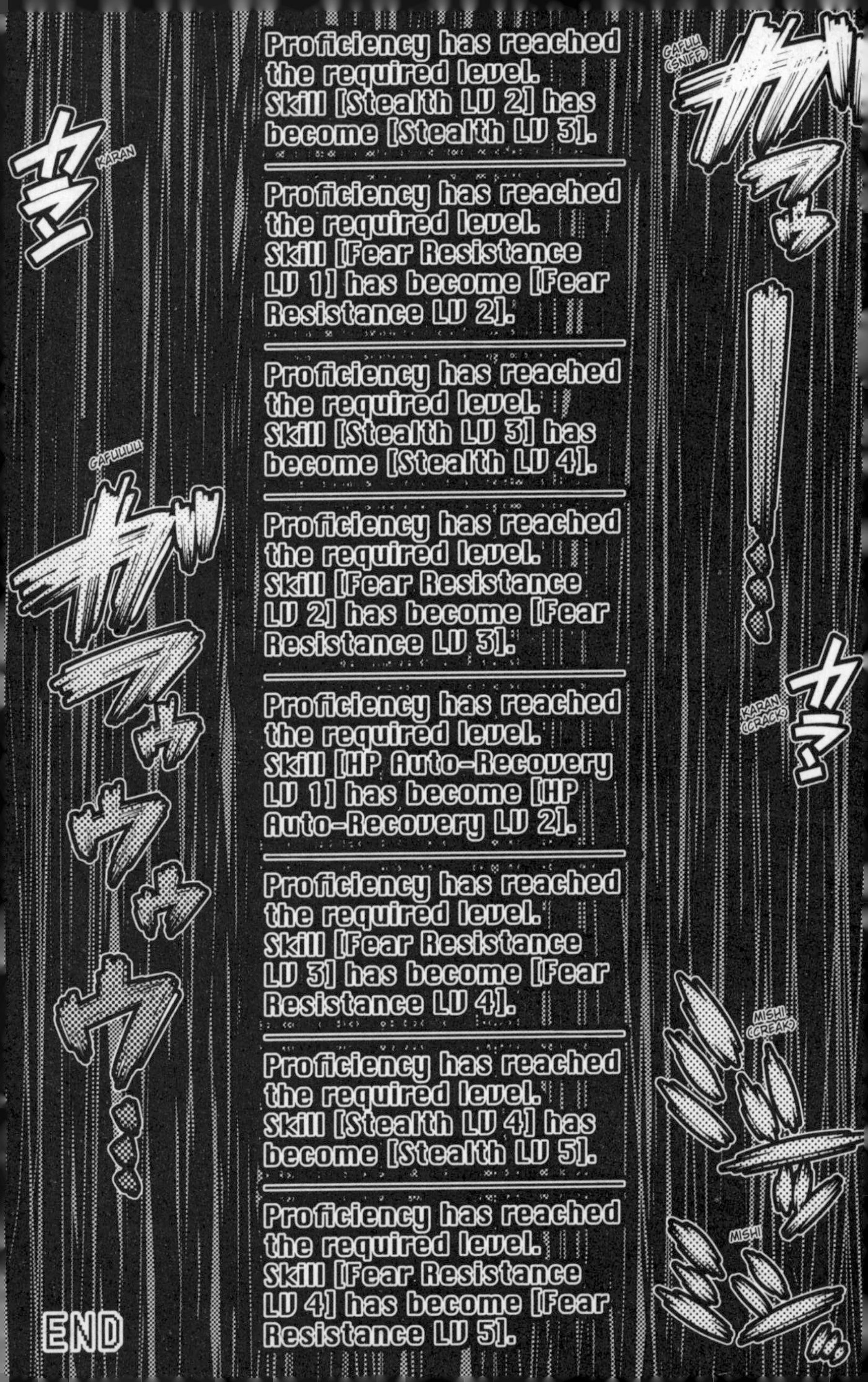
GAFUU (SNIFF)
KARAN (CRACK)
MISHI (CREAK)
MISHI
Proficiency has reached the required level. Skill [Stealth LV 2] has become [Stealth LV 3].
Proficiency has reached the required level. Skill [Fear Resistance LV 1] has become [Fear Resistance LV 2].
Proficiency has reached the required level. Skill [Stealth LV 3] has become [Stealth LV 4].
Proficiency has reached the required level. Skill [Fear Resistance LV 2] has become [Fear Resistance LV 3].
Proficiency has reached the required level. Skill [HP Auto-Recovery LV 1] has become [HP Auto-Recovery LV 2].
Proficiency has reached the required level. Skill [Fear Resistance LV 3] has become [Fear Resistance LV 4].
Proficiency has reached the required level. Skill [Stealth LV 4] has become [Stealth LV 5].
Proficiency has reached the required level. Skill [Fear Resistance LV 4] has become [Fear Resistance LV 5].
KARAN
GAFULULU
END

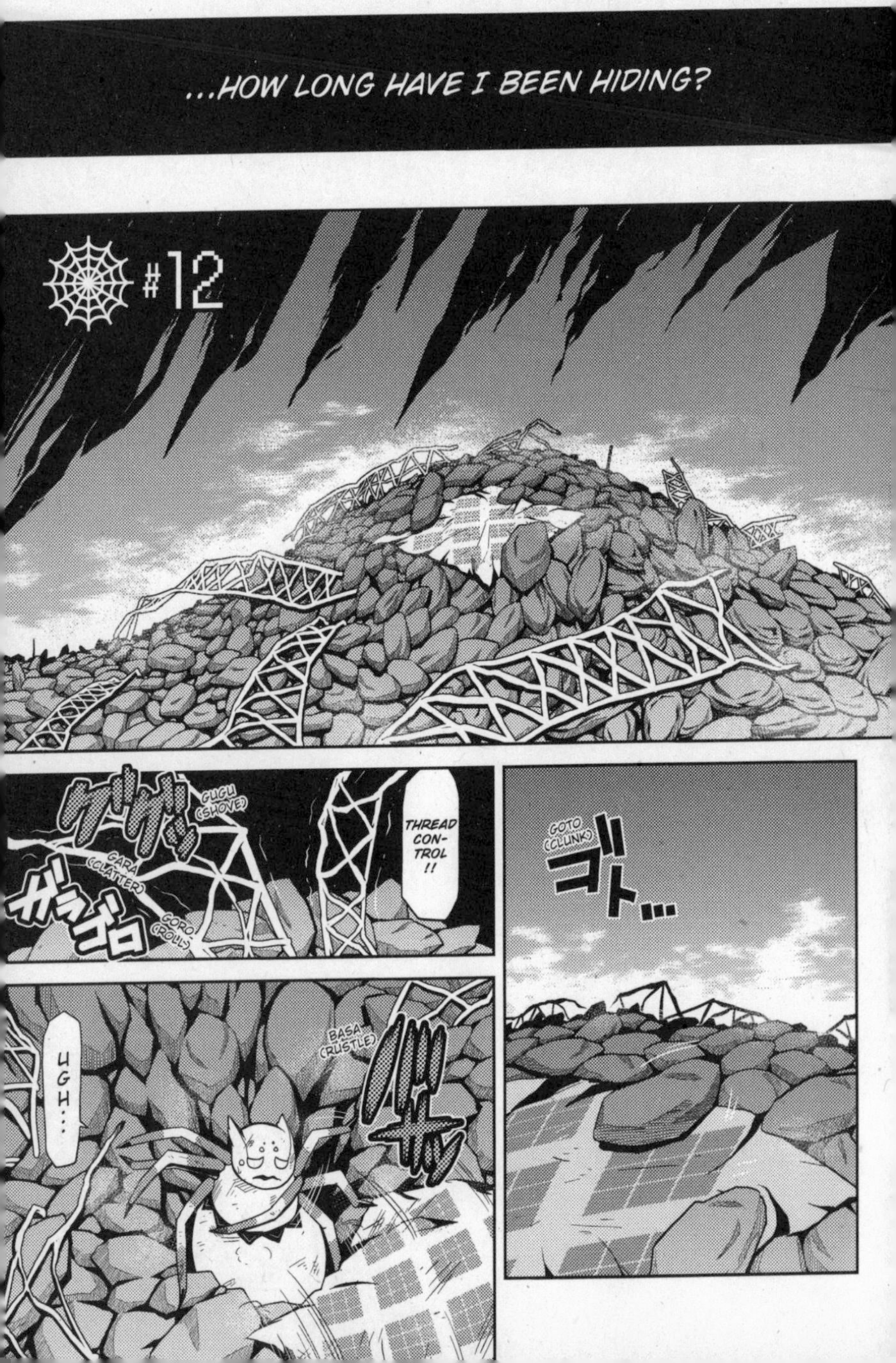
...HOW LONG HAVE I BEEN HIDING?
#12
GOTO (CLUNK)
THREAD CONTROL!!
GUGU (SHOVE)
GARA (CLATTER)
GORO (ROLL)
BASA (RUSTLE)
UGH...

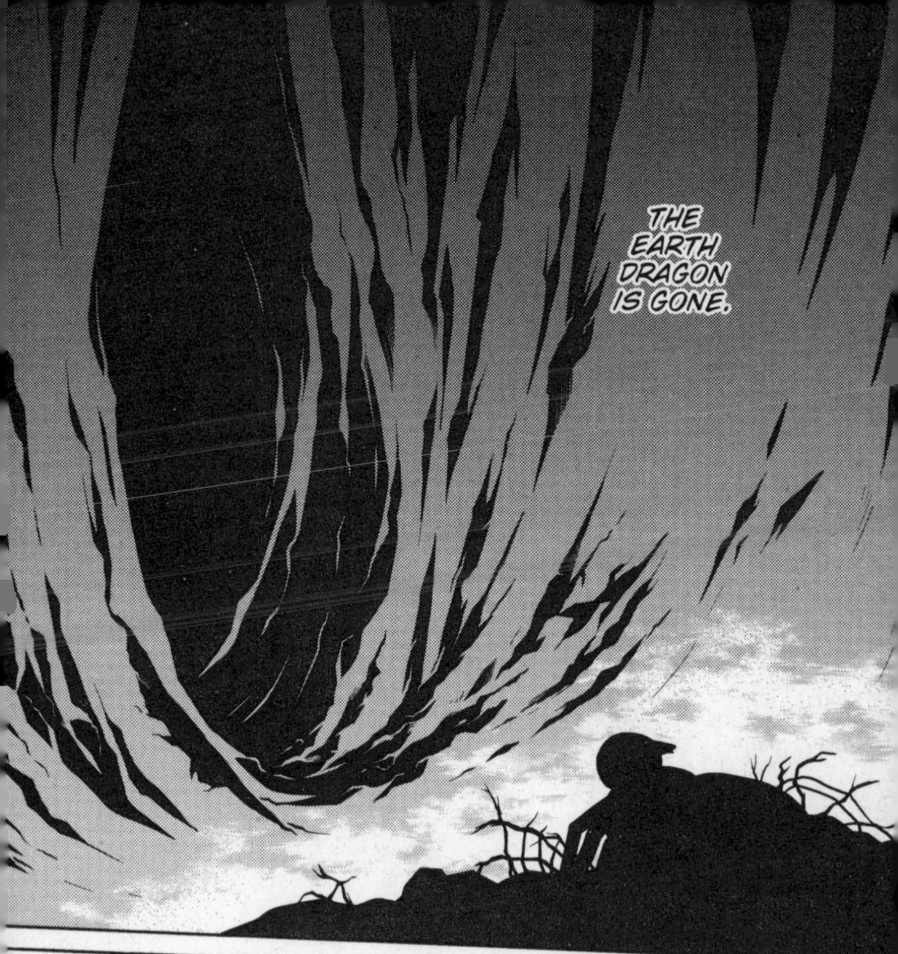
THE EARTH DRAGON IS GONE.
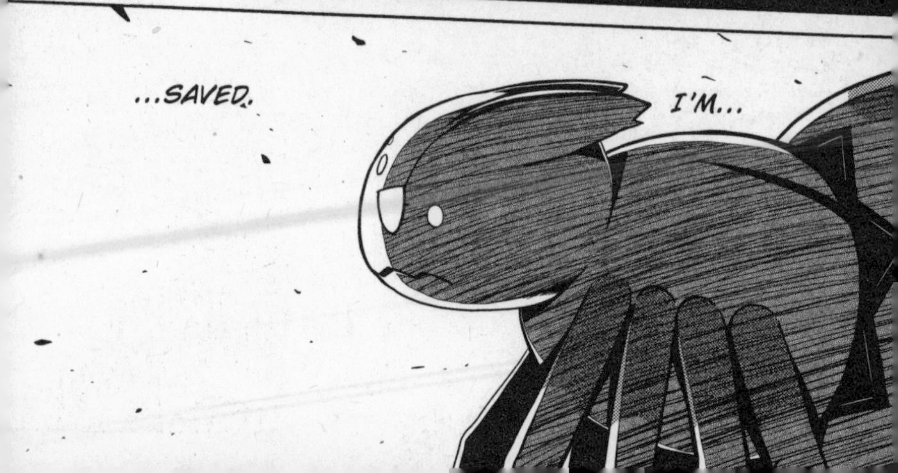
I'M...
...SAVED.

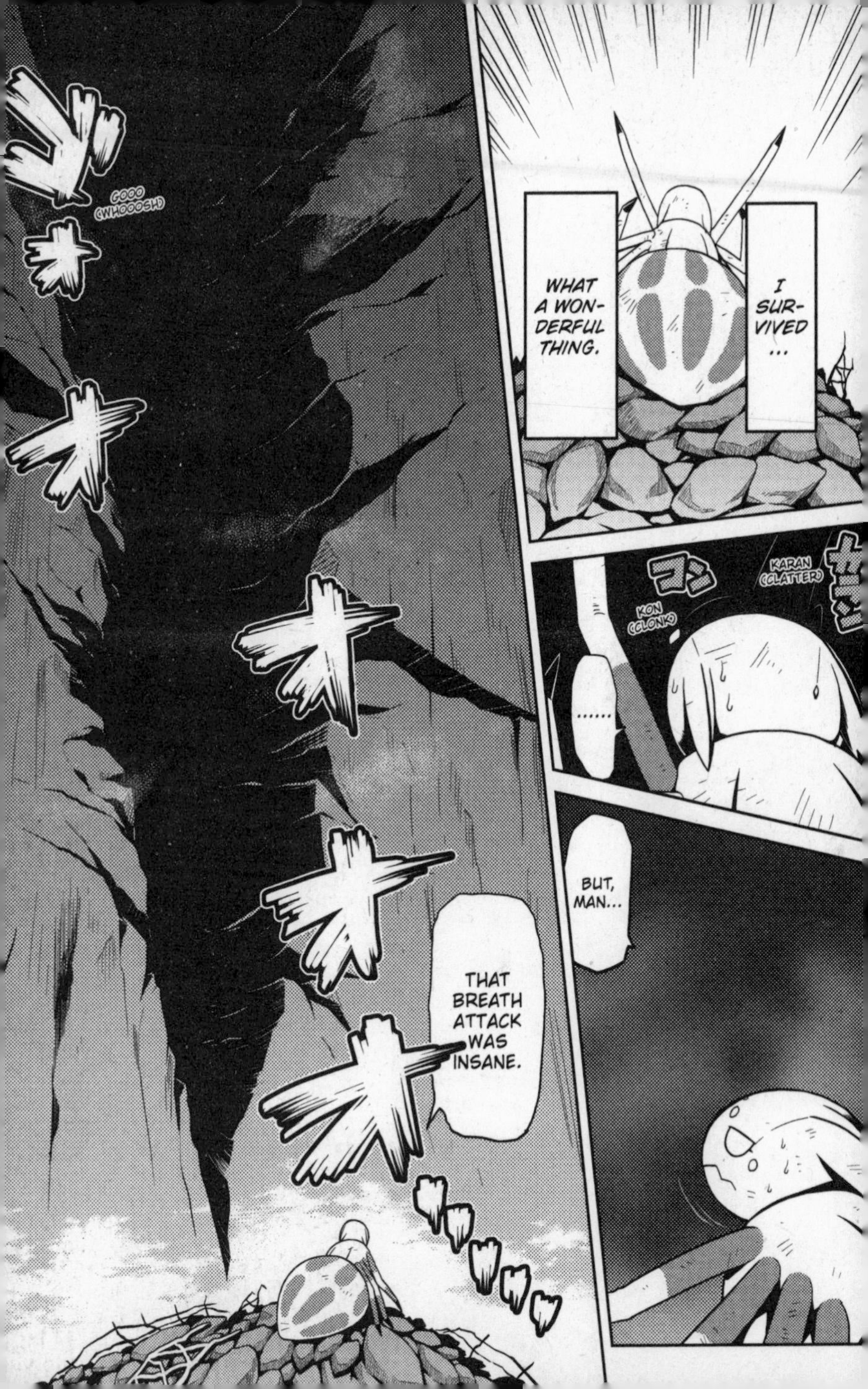
I SURVIVED...
WHAT A WONDERFUL THING.
KARAN (CLATTER)
KON (CLONK)
......
BUT, MAN...
GOOO (WHOOOSH)
THAT BREATH ATTACK WAS INSANE.

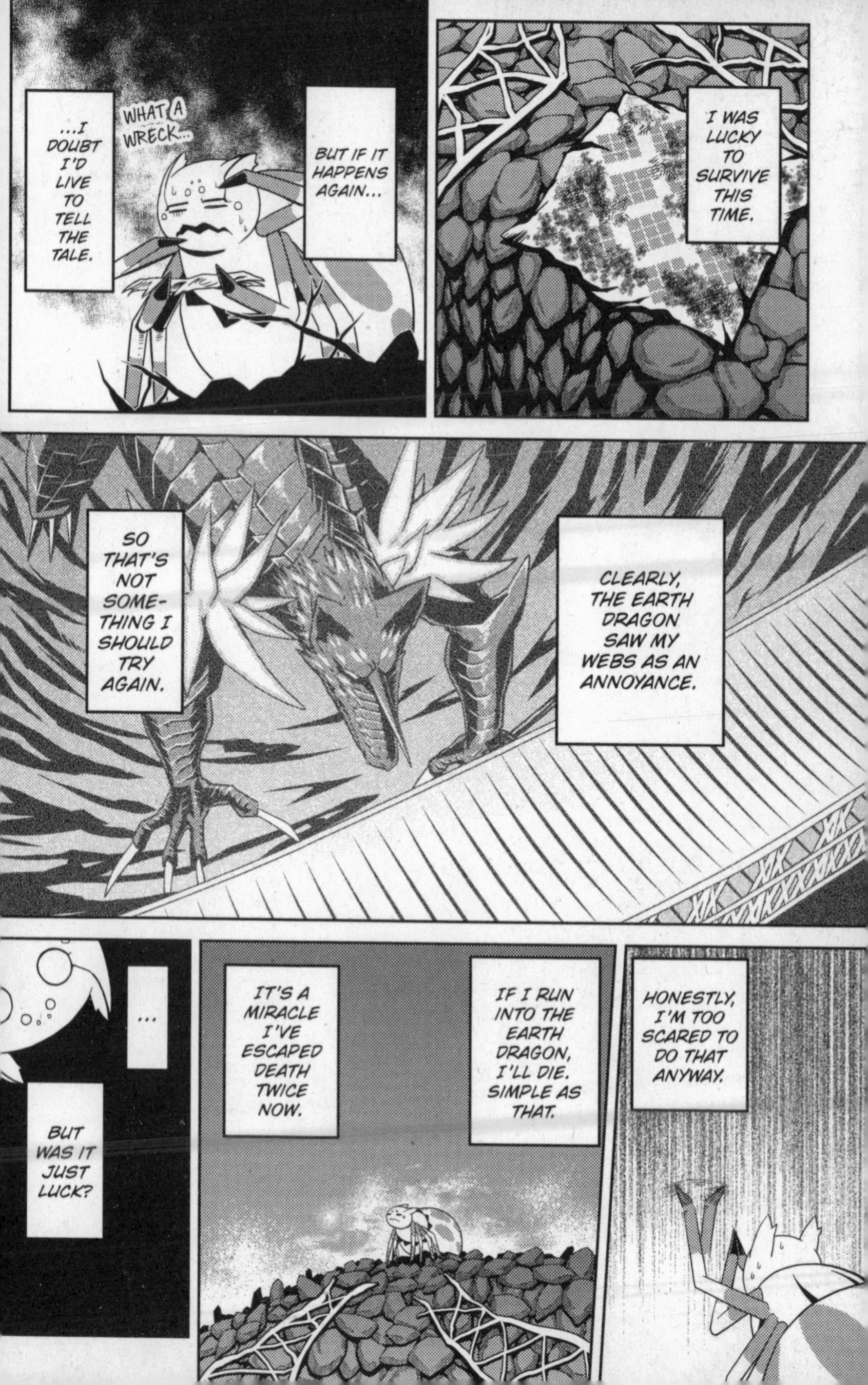
I WAS LUCKY TO SURVIVE THIS TIME.
BUT IF IT HAPPENS AGAIN...
WHAT A WRECK...
...I DOUBT I'D LIVE TO TELL THE TALE.
CLEARLY, THE EARTH DRAGON SAW MY WEBS AS AN ANNOYANCE.
SO THAT'S NOT SOME-THING I SHOULD TRY AGAIN.
HONESTLY, I'M TOO SCARED TO DO THAT ANYWAY.
IF I RUN INTO THE EARTH DRAGON, I'LL DIE. SIMPLE AS THAT.
IT'S A MIRACLE I'VE ESCAPED DEATH TWICE NOW.
...
BUT WAS IT JUST LUCK?

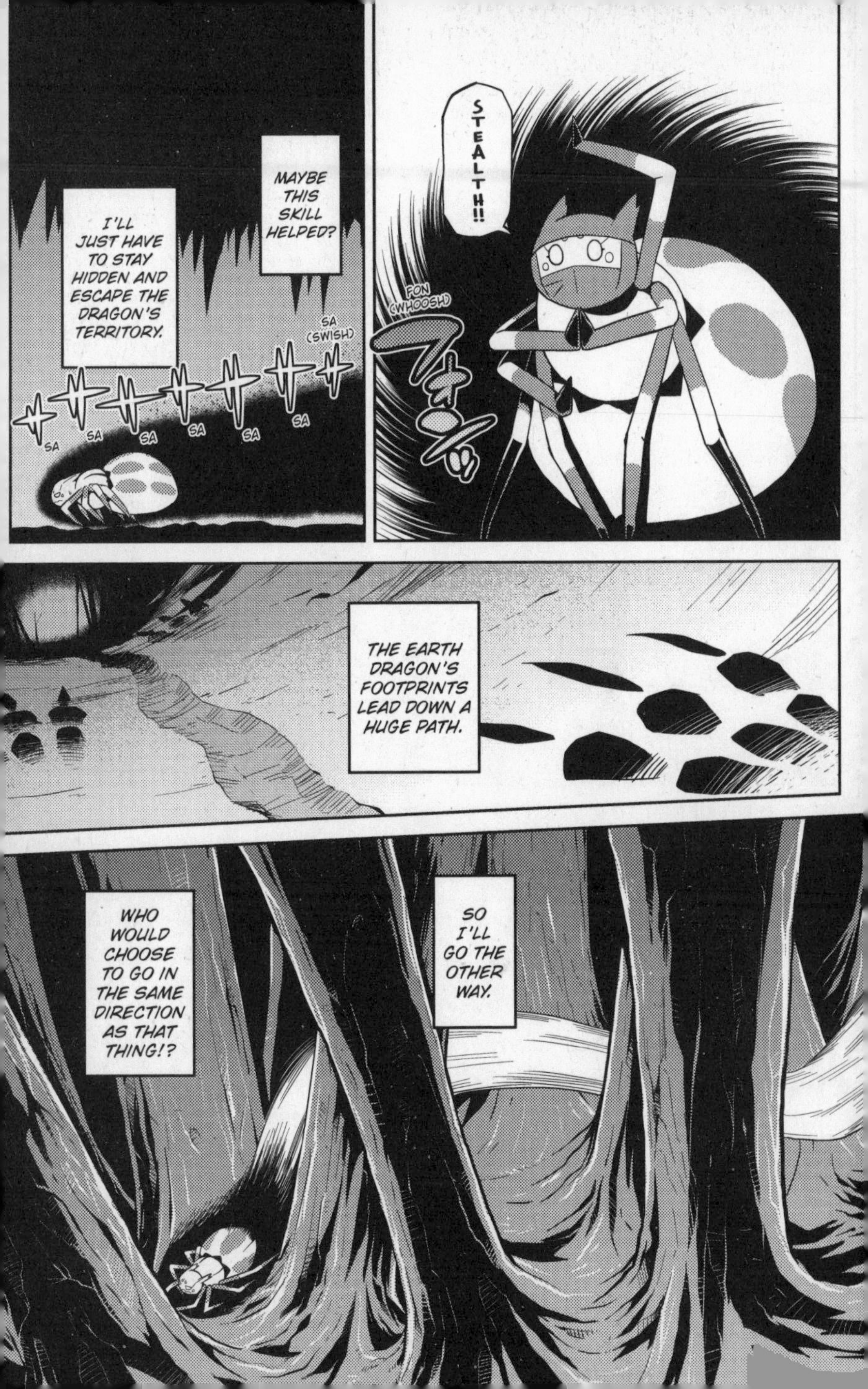
STEALTH!!
FON (WHOOSH)
MAYBE THIS SKILL HELPED?
I'LL JUST HAVE TO STAY HIDDEN AND ESCAPE THE DRAGON'S TERRITORY.
SA (SWISH)
SA
SA
SA
SA
SA
SA
THE EARTH DRAGON'S FOOTPRINTS LEAD DOWN A HUGE PATH.
SO I'LL GO THE OTHER WAY.
WHO WOULD CHOOSE TO GO IN THE SAME DIRECTION AS THAT THING!?

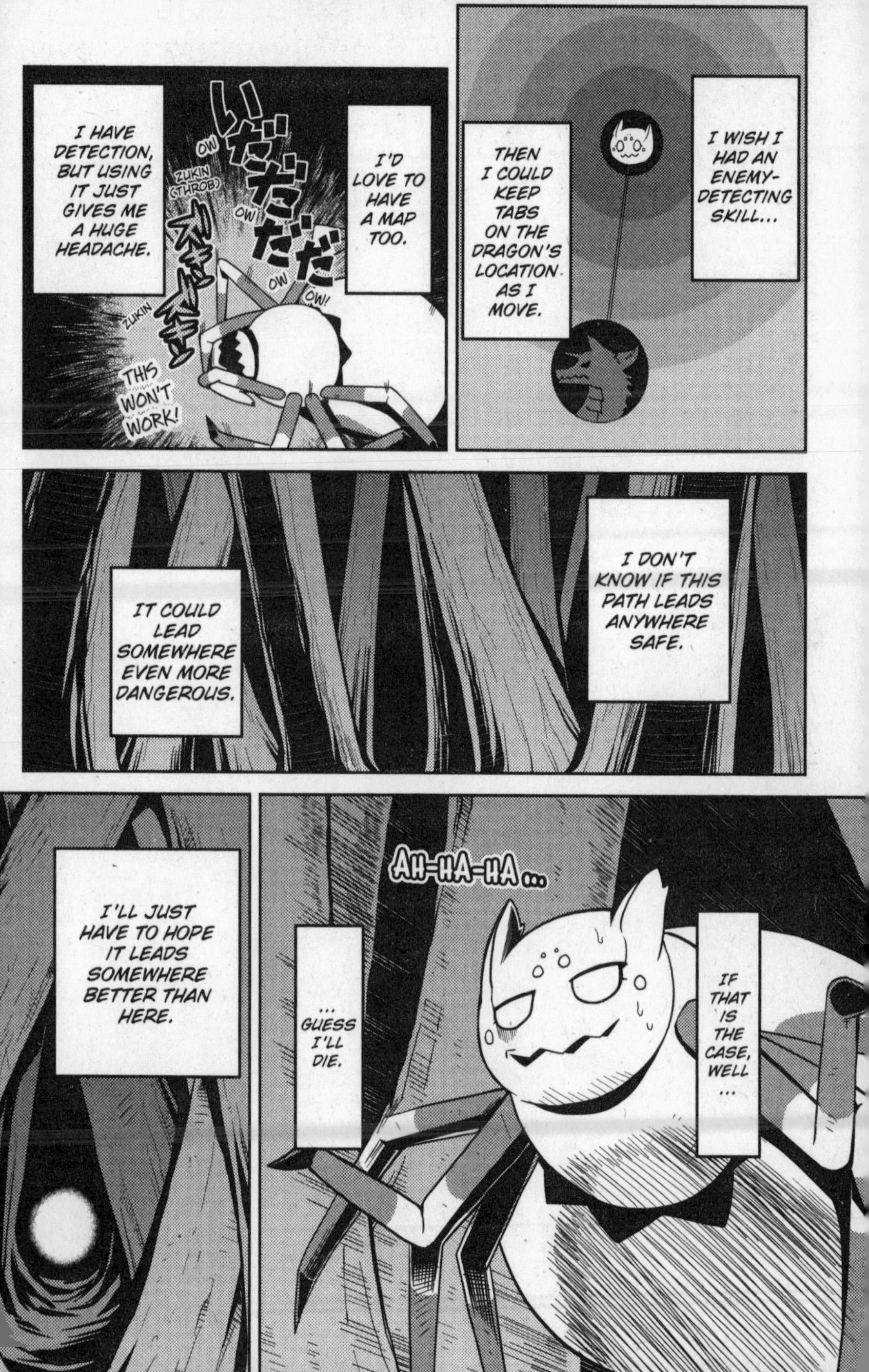
I WISH I HAD AN ENEMY-DETECTING SKILL...
THEN I COULD KEEP TABS ON THE DRAGON'S LOCATION AS I MOVE.
I'D LOVE TO HAVE A MAP TOO.
OW
OW
OW
OW!
ZUKIN (THROB)
ZUKIN
I HAVE DETECTION, BUT USING IT JUST GIVES ME A HUGE HEADACHE.
THIS WON'T WORK!
I DON'T KNOW IF THIS PATH LEADS ANYWHERE SAFE.
IT COULD LEAD SOMEWHERE EVEN MORE DANGEROUS.
AH-HA-HA...
IF THAT IS THE CASE, WELL...
...GUESS I'LL DIE.
I'LL JUST HAVE TO HOPE IT LEADS SOMEWHERE BETTER THAN HERE.

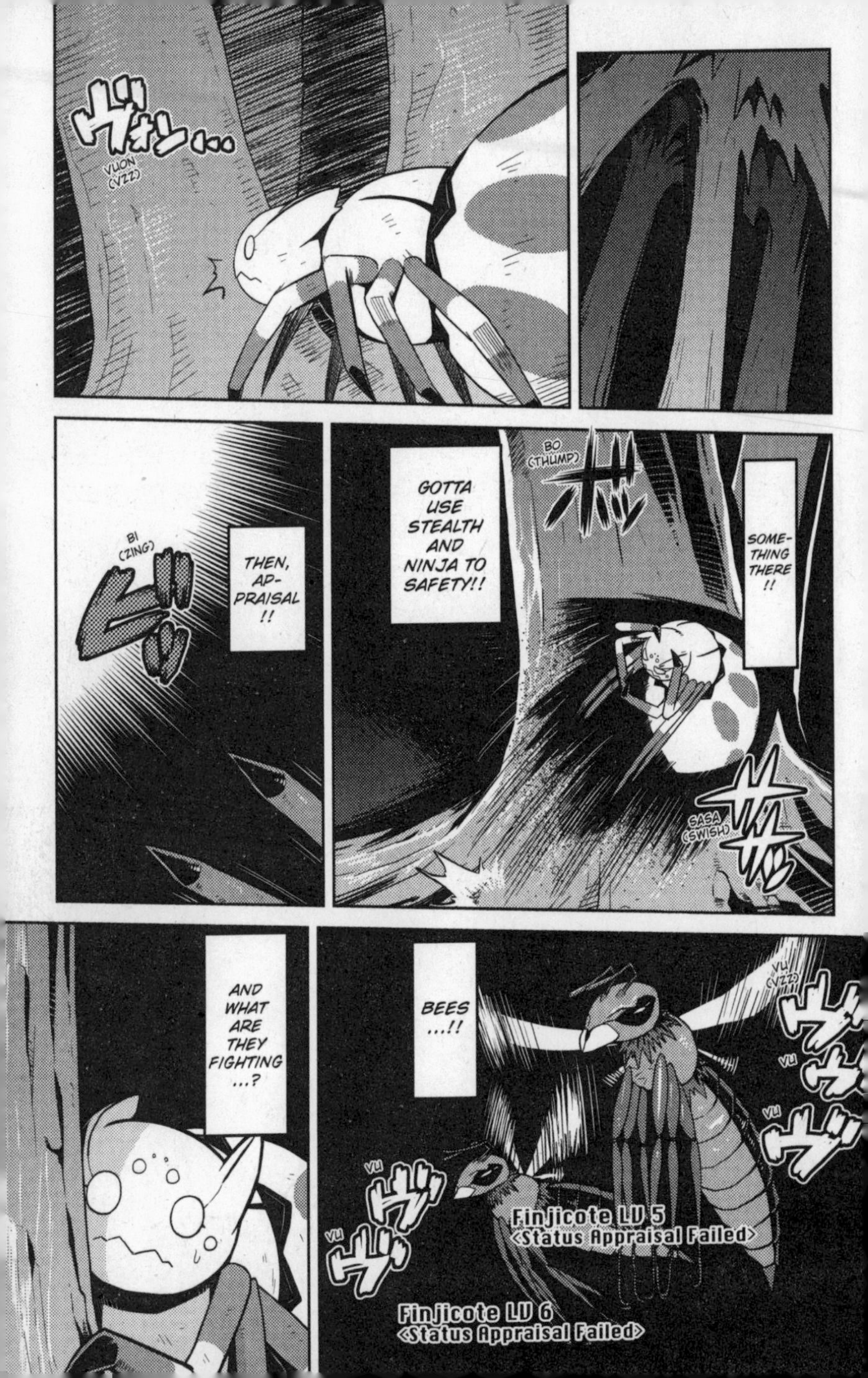

VUON (VZZ)
SOME-THING THERE!!
BO (THUMP)
GOTTA USE STEALTH AND NINJA TO SAFETY!!
SASA (SWISH)
THEN, AP-PRAISAL!!
BI (ZING)
VU (VZZ)
BEES...!!
VU
VU
Finjicote LV 5
<Status Appraisal Failed>
VU
VU
Finjicote LV 6
<Status Appraisal Failed>
AND WHAT ARE THEY FIGHTING...?

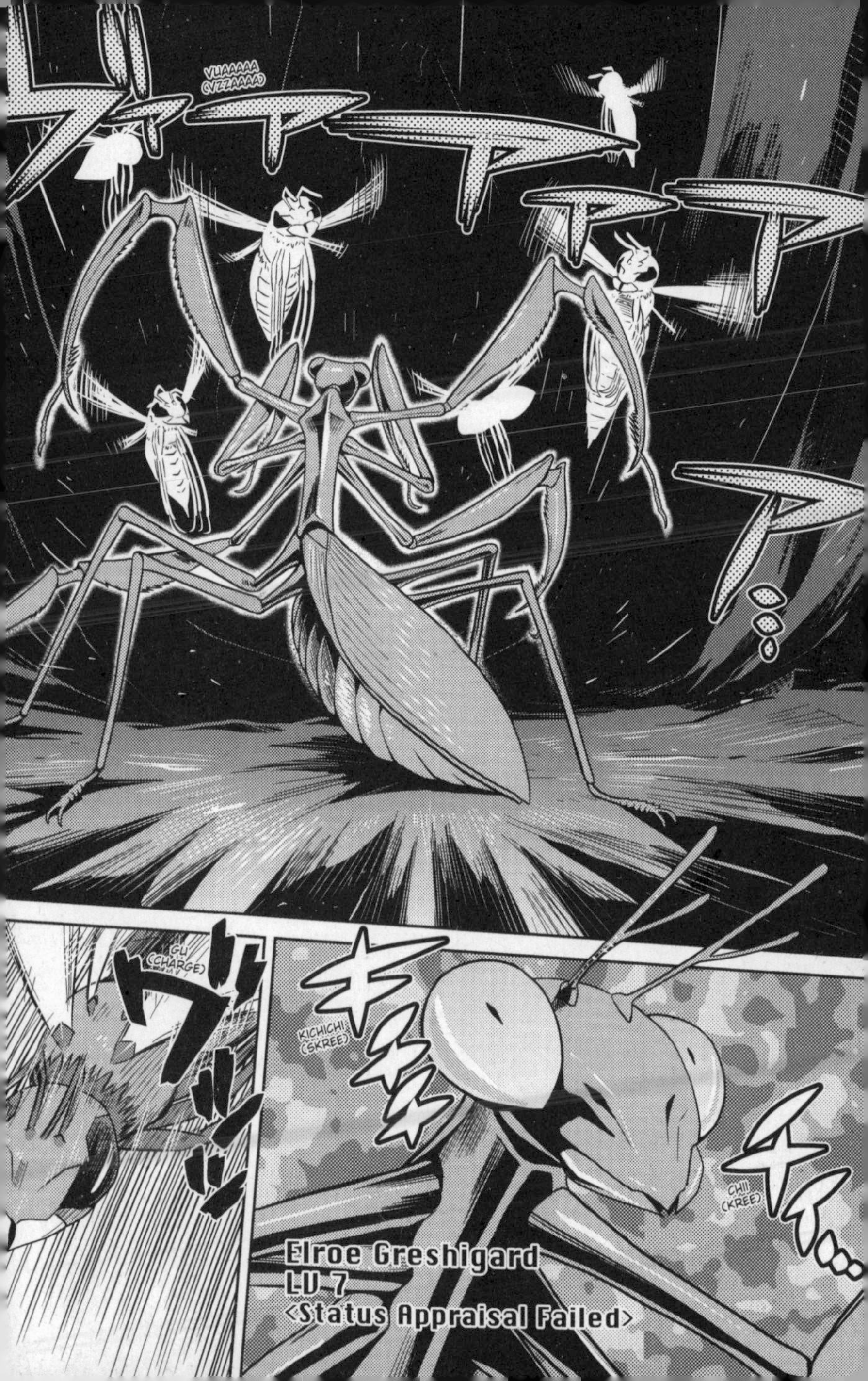
VUAAAAA
(VZZAAAA)
KICHICHI
(SKREE)
CHII
(KREE)
Elroe Greshigard
LV 7
<Status Appraisal Failed>
GU
(CHARGE)

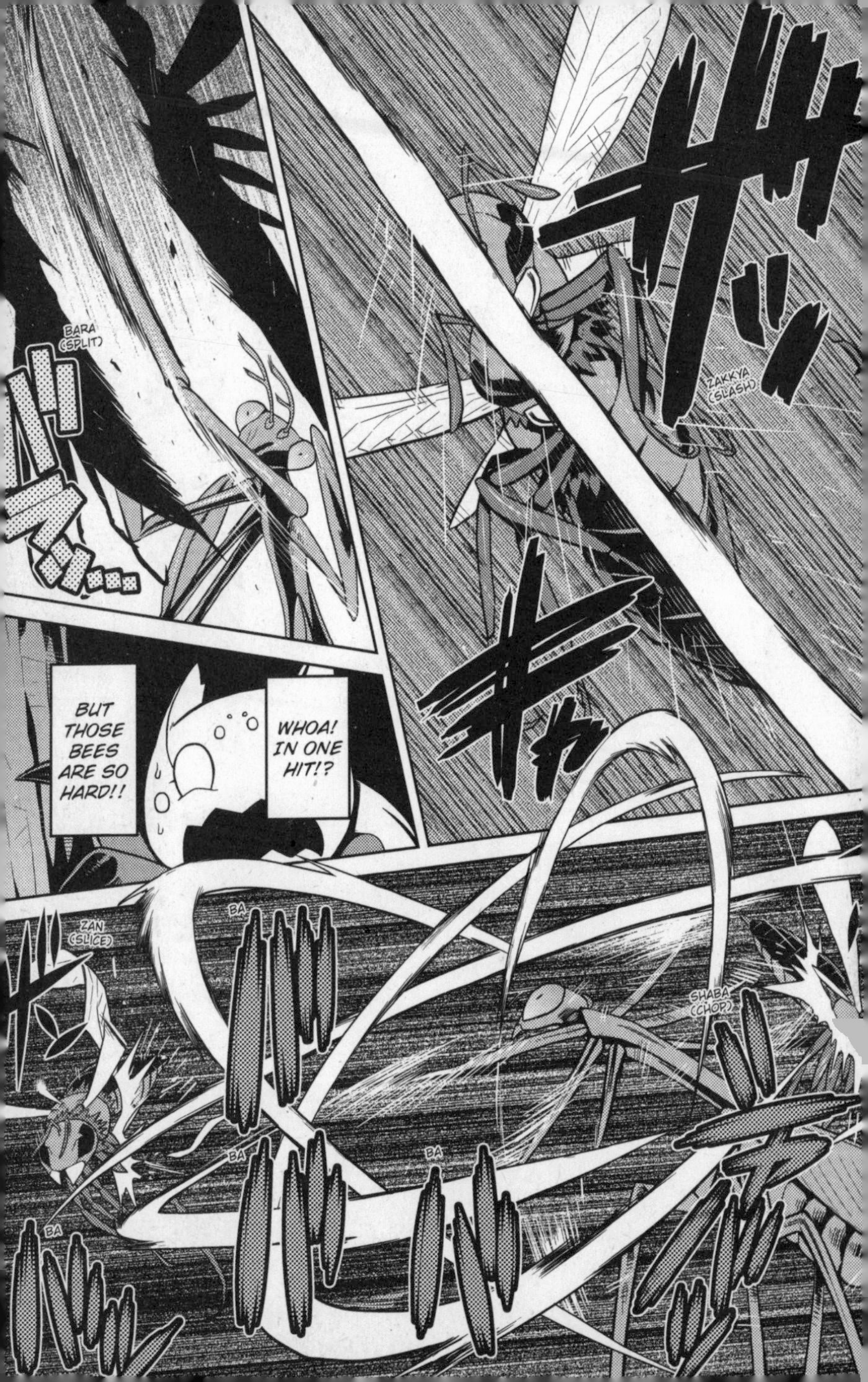
ZAKKYA (SLASH)
BARA (SPLIT)
WHOA! IN ONE HIT!?
BUT THOSE BEES ARE SO HARD!!
SHABA (CHOP)
BA
BA
BA
ZAN (SLICE)
BA

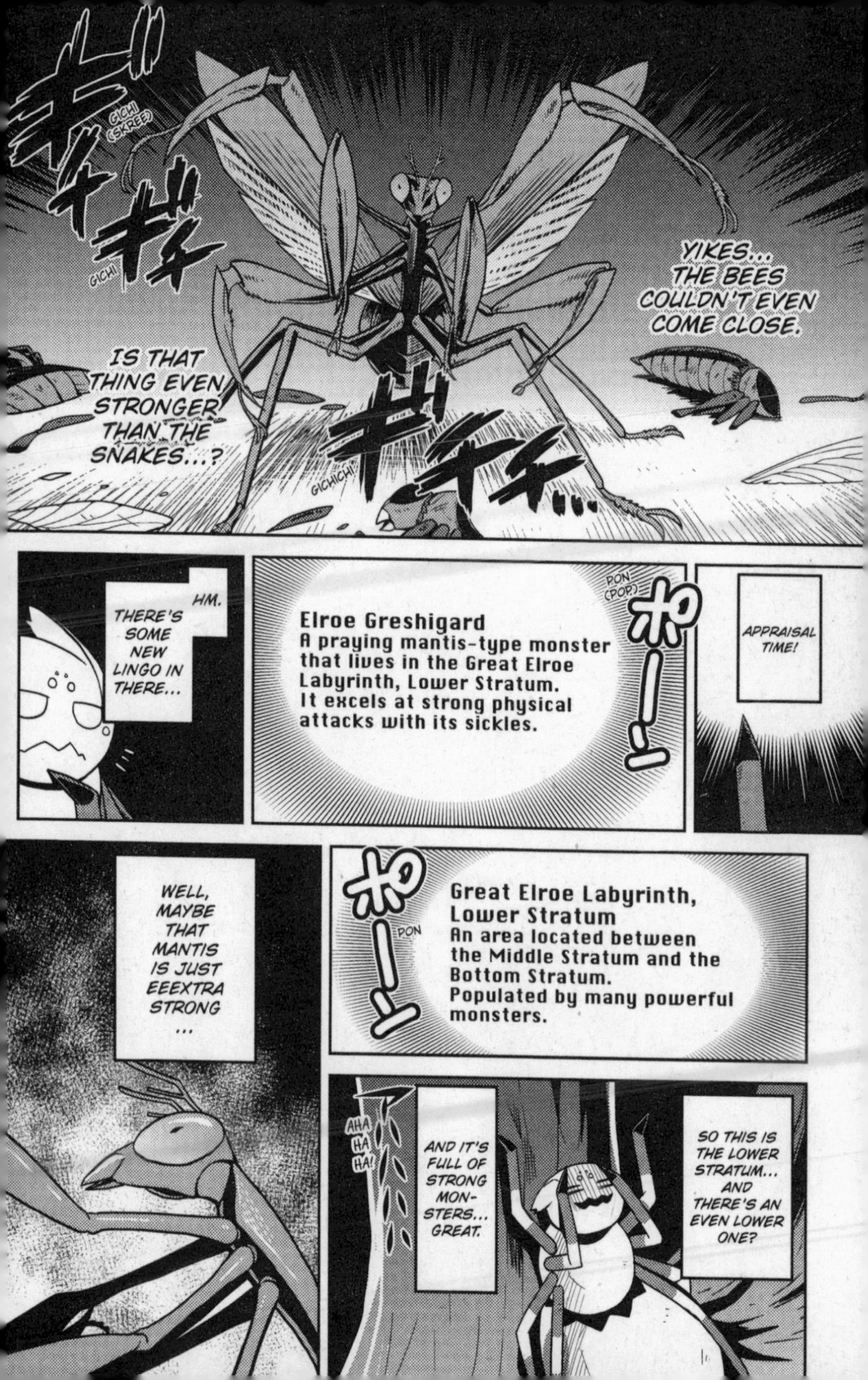
GICHI (SKREE)
GICHI
YIKES... THE BEES COULDN'T EVEN COME CLOSE.
IS THAT THING EVEN STRONGER THAN THE SNAKES...?
GICHICHI
APPRAISAL TIME!
PON (POP)
Elroe Greshigard
A praying mantis-type monster that lives in the Great Elroe Labyrinth, Lower Stratum.
It excels at strong physical attacks with its sickles.
HM.
THERE'S SOME NEW LINGO IN THERE...
PON
Great Elroe Labyrinth, Lower Stratum
An area located between the Middle Stratum and the Bottom Stratum.
Populated by many powerful monsters.
SO THIS IS THE LOWER STRATUM... AND THERE'S AN EVEN LOWER ONE?
AND IT'S FULL OF STRONG MON-STERS... GREAT.
AHA HA HA!
WELL, MAYBE THAT MANTIS IS JUST EEEXTRA STRONG...

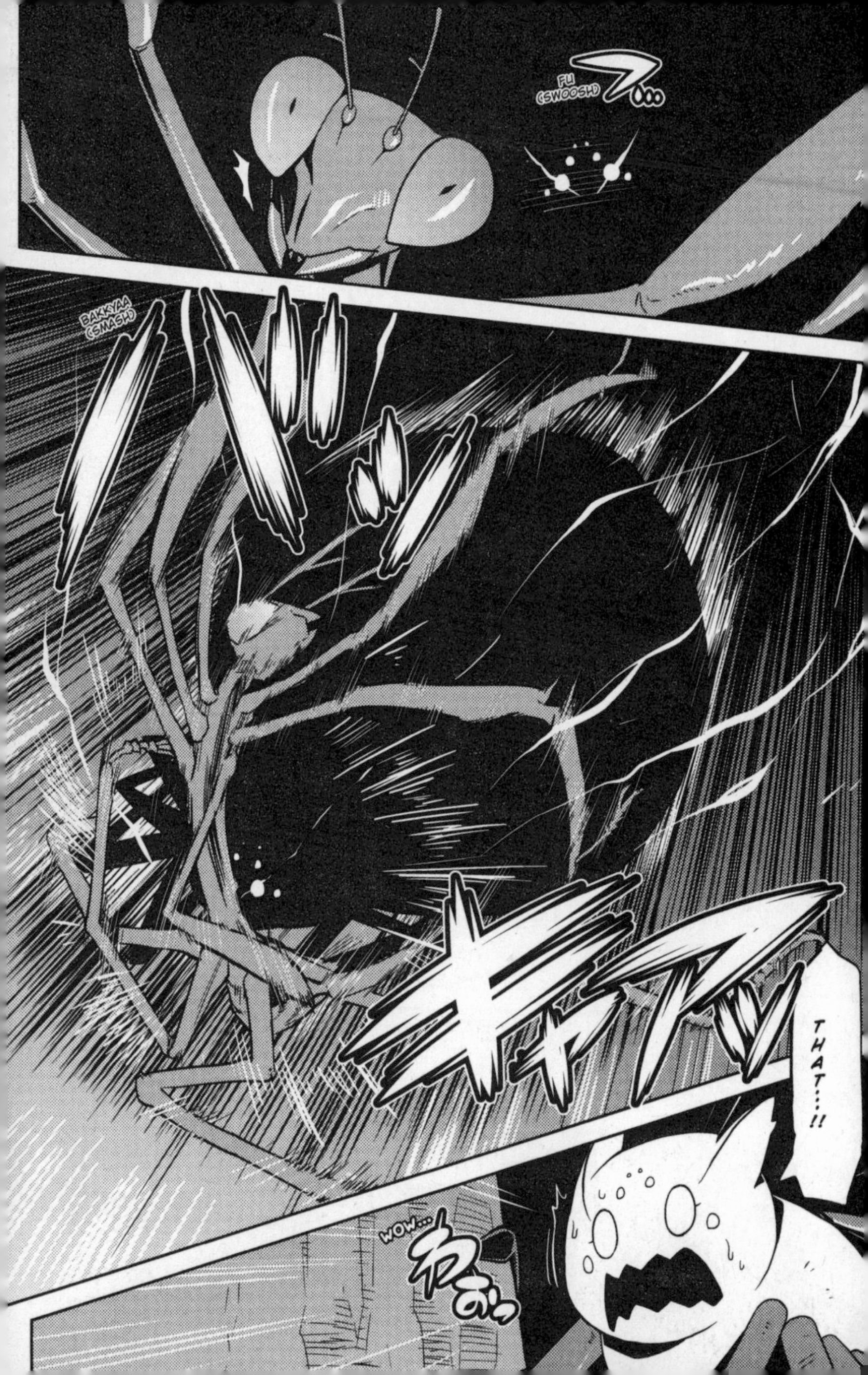
FU (SWOOSH)
BAKKYAA (SMASH)
THAT...!!
WOW...

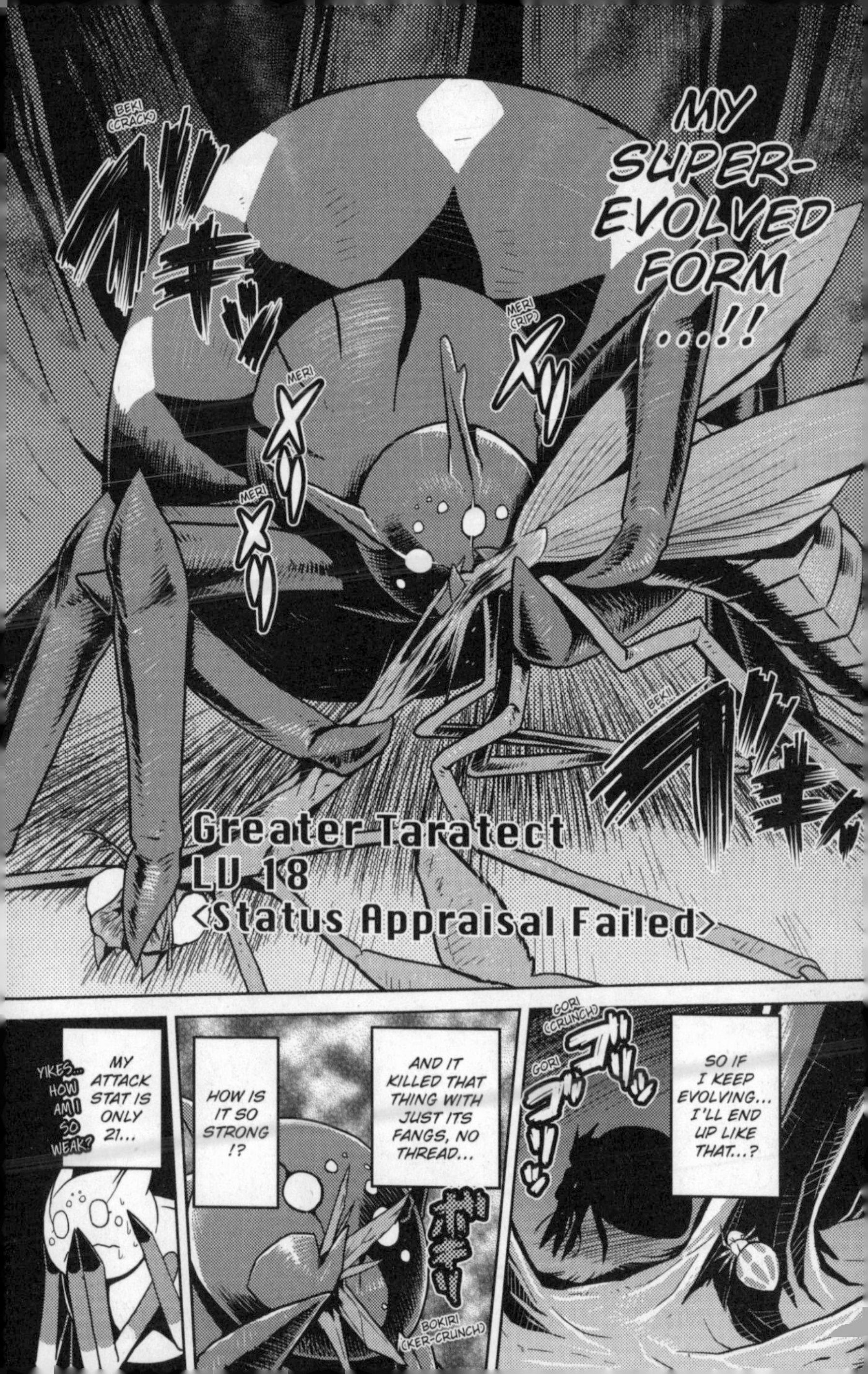
MY SUPER-EVOLVED FORM ...!!
MERI (RIP)
BEKI (CRACK)
MERI
MERI
BEKI
Greater Taratect
LV 18
<Status Appraisal Failed>
SO IF I KEEP EVOLVING... I'LL END UP LIKE THAT...?
GORI (CRUNCH)
GORI
AND IT KILLED THAT THING WITH JUST ITS FANGS, NO THREAD...
BOKIRI (KER-CRUNCH)
HOW IS IT SO STRONG !?
MY ATTACK STAT IS ONLY 21...
YIKES... HOW AM I SO WEAK?

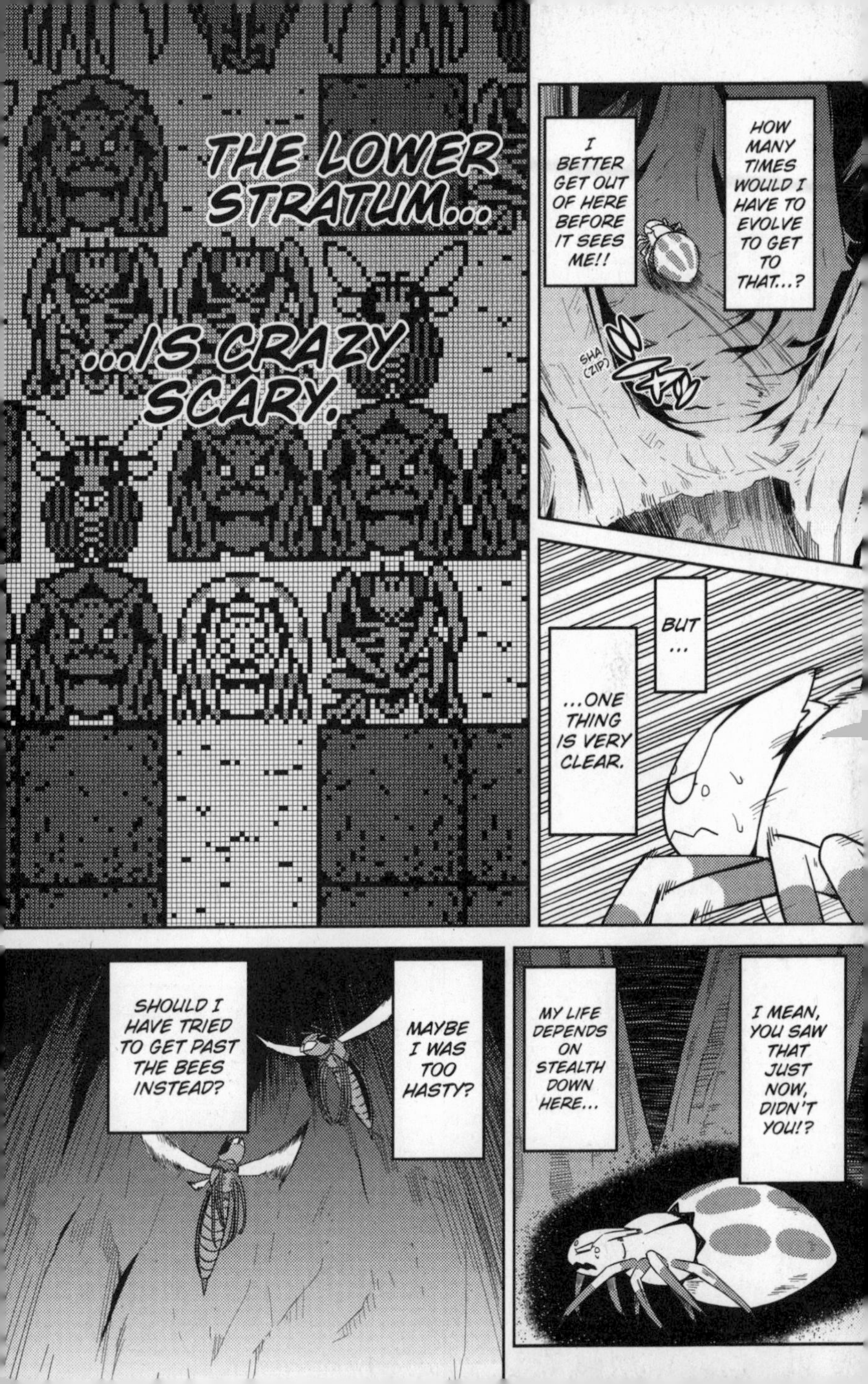
HOW MANY TIMES WOULD I HAVE TO EVOLVE TO GET TO THAT...?
I BETTER GET OUT OF HERE BEFORE IT SEES ME!!
SHA (ZIP)
BUT...
...ONE THING IS VERY CLEAR.
THE LOWER STRATUM...
...IS CRAZY SCARY.
I MEAN, YOU SAW THAT JUST NOW, DIDN'T YOU!?
MY LIFE DEPENDS ON STEALTH DOWN HERE...
MAYBE I WAS TOO HASTY?
SHOULD I HAVE TRIED TO GET PAST THE BEES INSTEAD?

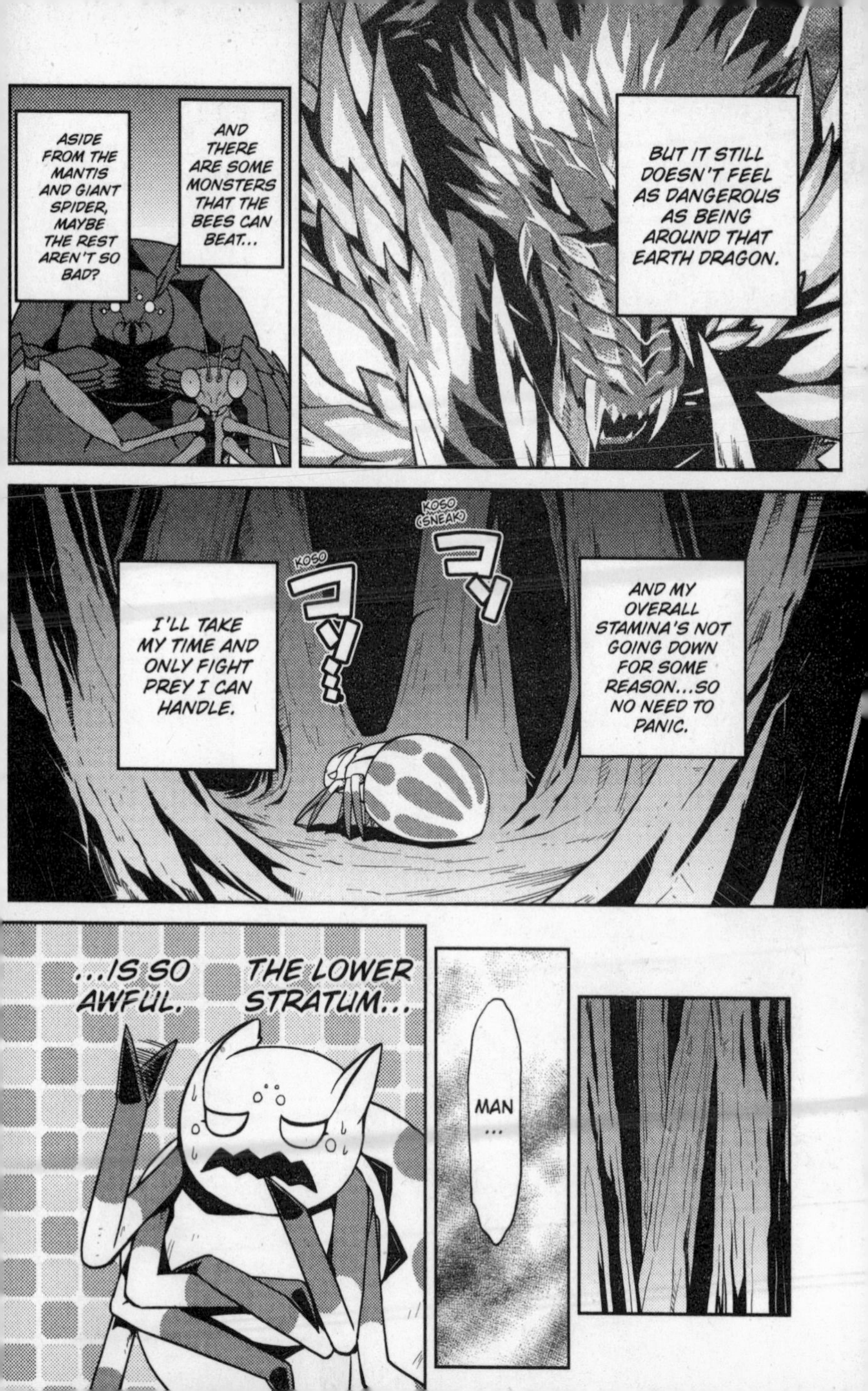
BUT IT STILL DOESN'T FEEL AS DANGEROUS AS BEING AROUND THAT EARTH DRAGON.
AND THERE ARE SOME MONSTERS THAT THE BEES CAN BEAT...
ASIDE FROM THE MANTIS AND GIANT SPIDER, MAYBE THE REST AREN'T SO BAD?
AND MY OVERALL STAMINA'S NOT GOING DOWN FOR SOME REASON...SO NO NEED TO PANIC.
KOSO (SNEAK)
KOSO
I'LL TAKE MY TIME AND ONLY FIGHT PREY I CAN HANDLE.
MAN...
THE LOWER STRATUM...
...IS SO AWFUL.

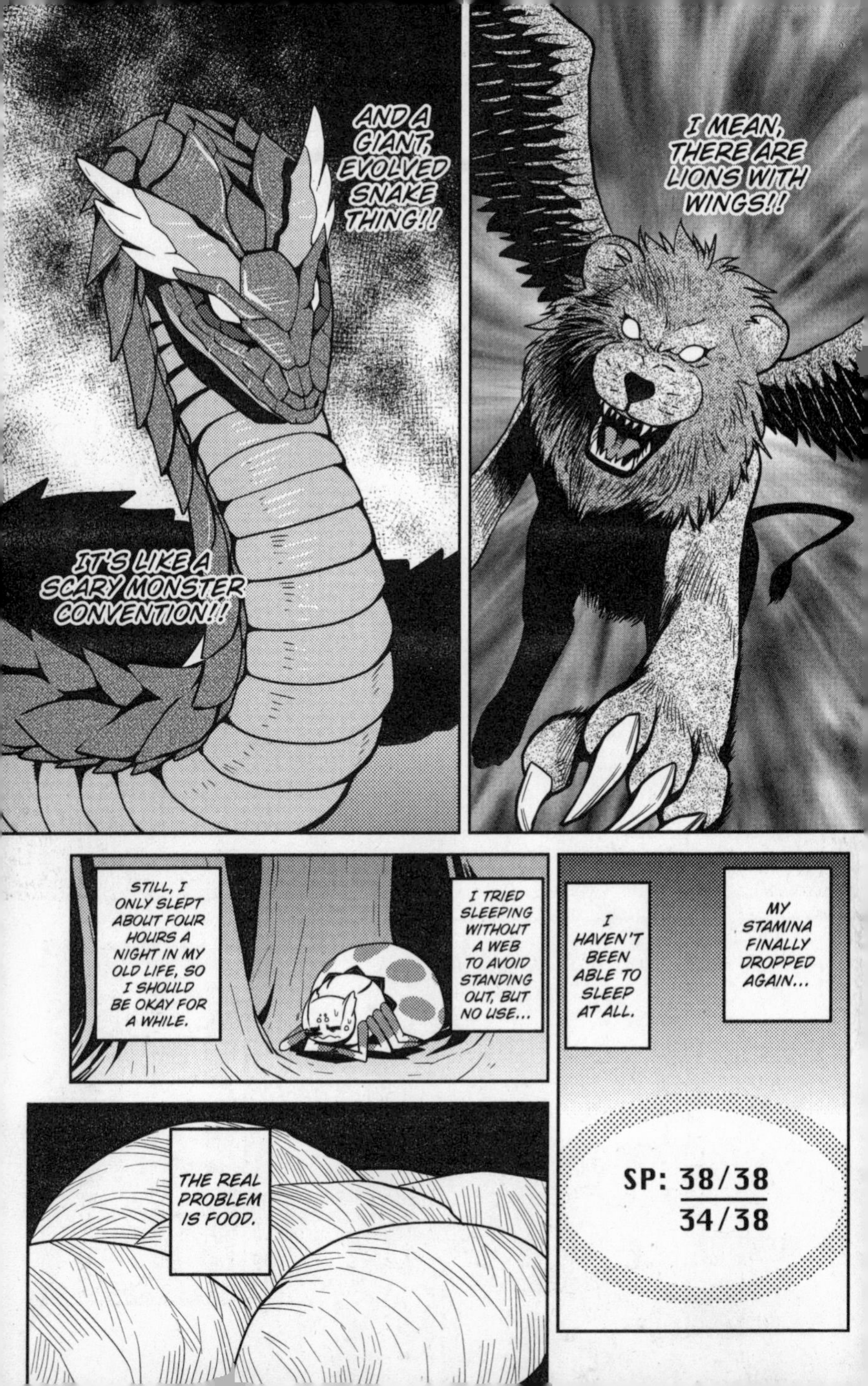
I MEAN, THERE ARE LIONS WITH WINGS!!
AND A GIANT, EVOLVED SNAKE THING!!
IT'S LIKE A SCARY MONSTER CONVENTION!!
MY STAMINA FINALLY DROPPED AGAIN...
I HAVEN'T BEEN ABLE TO SLEEP AT ALL.
SP: 38/38 34/38
I TRIED SLEEPING WITHOUT A WEB TO AVOID STANDING OUT, BUT NO USE...
STILL, I ONLY SLEPT ABOUT FOUR HOURS A NIGHT IN MY OLD LIFE, SO I SHOULD BE OKAY FOR A WHILE.
THE REAL PROBLEM IS FOOD.

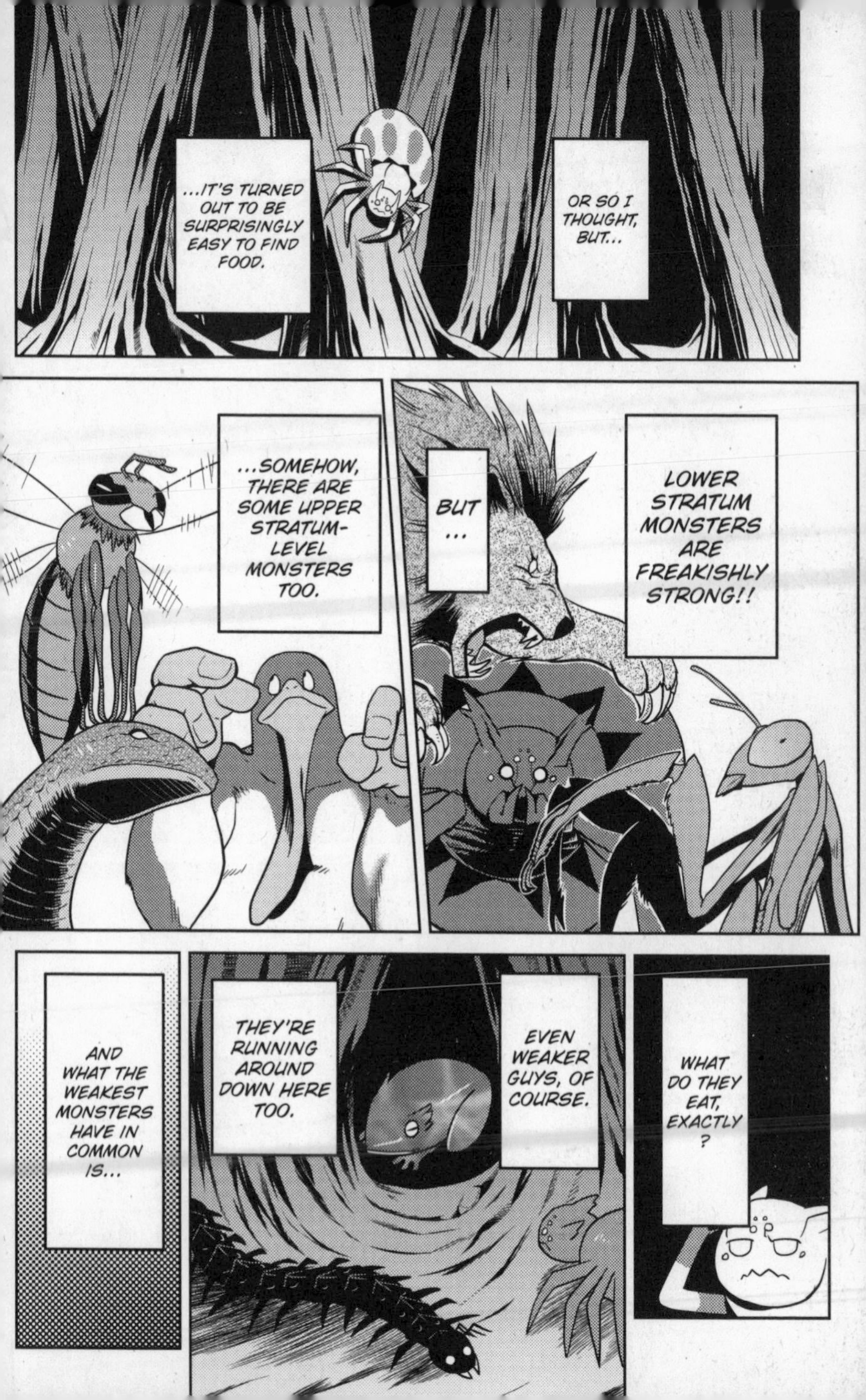
...IT'S TURNED OUT TO BE SURPRISINGLY EASY TO FIND FOOD.
OR SO I THOUGHT, BUT...
BUT ...
LOWER STRATUM MONSTERS ARE FREAKISHLY STRONG!!
...SOMEHOW, THERE ARE SOME UPPER STRATUM-LEVEL MONSTERS TOO.
WHAT DO THEY EAT, EXACTLY?
EVEN WEAKER GUYS, OF COURSE.
THEY'RE RUNNING AROUND DOWN HERE TOO.
AND WHAT THE WEAKEST MONSTERS HAVE IN COMMON IS...

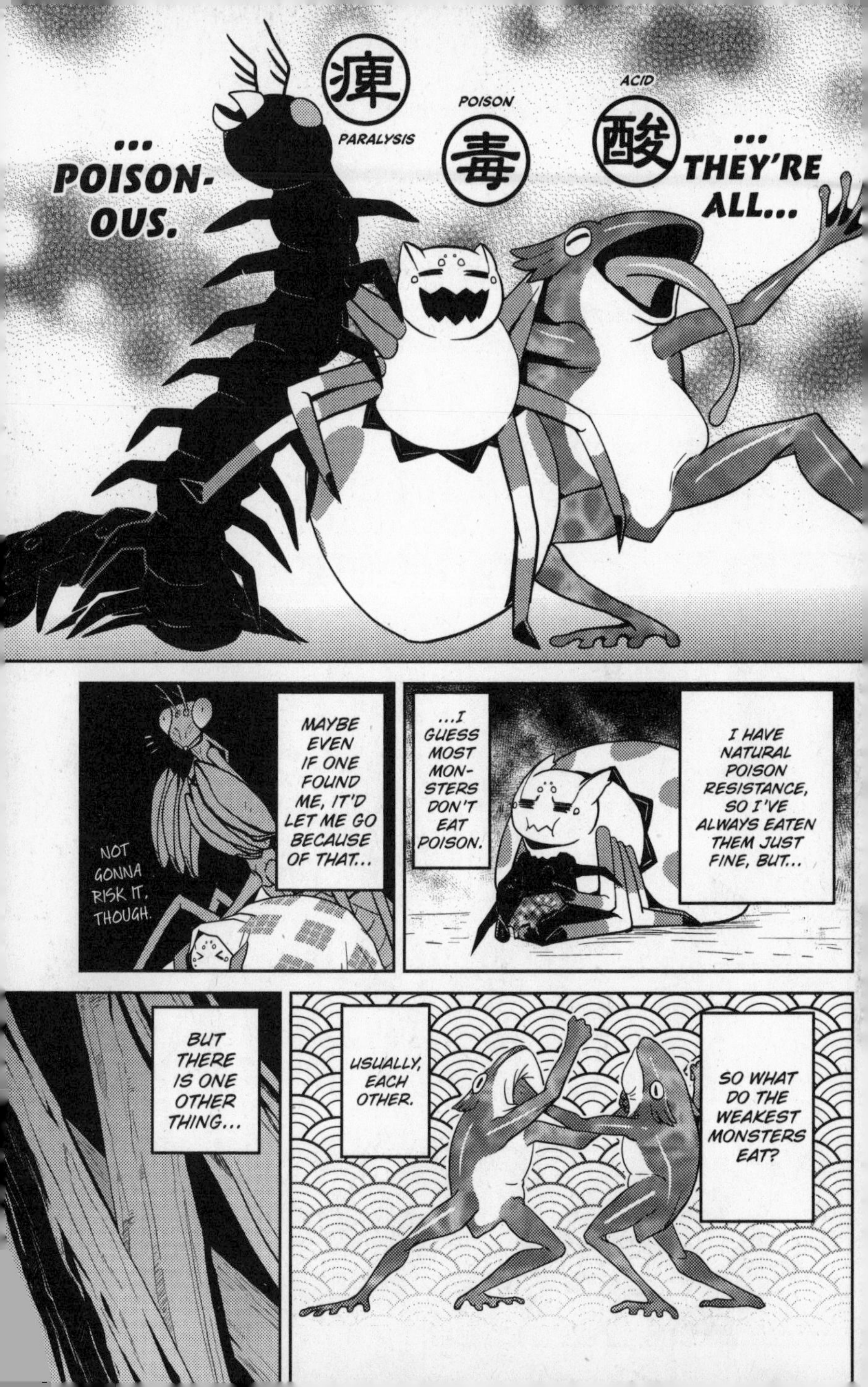
...THEY'RE ALL...
ACID
酸
POISON
毒
痺
PARALYSIS
...POISON-OUS.
I HAVE NATURAL POISON RESISTANCE, SO I'VE ALWAYS EATEN THEM JUST FINE, BUT...
...I GUESS MOST MONSTERS DON'T EAT POISON.
MAYBE EVEN IF ONE FOUND ME, IT'D LET ME GO BECAUSE OF THAT...
NOT GONNA RISK IT, THOUGH.
SO WHAT DO THE WEAKEST MONSTERS EAT?
USUALLY, EACH OTHER.
BUT THERE IS ONE OTHER THING...

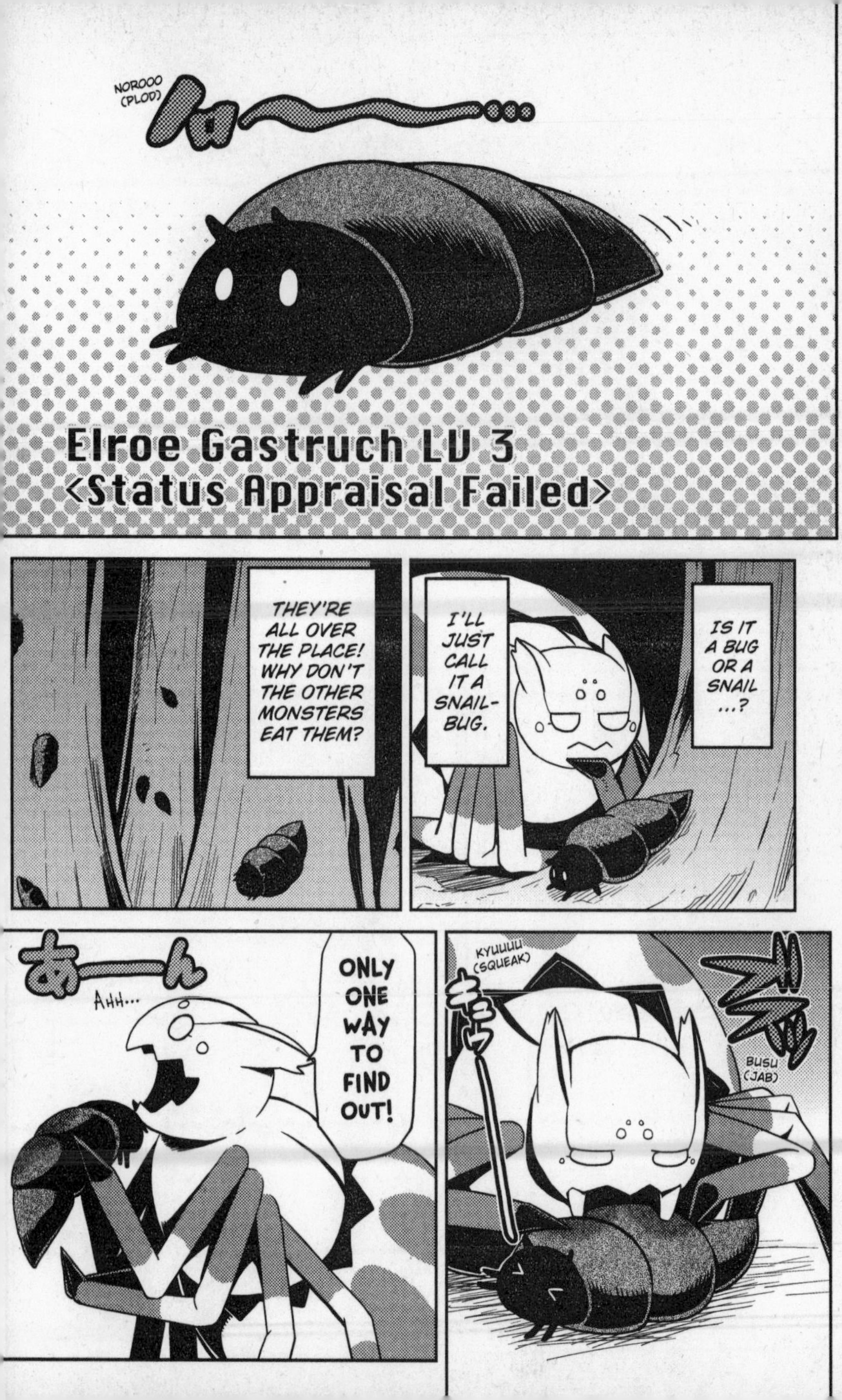
NOROOO (PLOD)
Elroe Gastruch LV 3
<Status Appraisal Failed>
IS IT A BUG OR A SNAIL ...?
I'LL JUST CALL IT A SNAIL-BUG.
THEY'RE ALL OVER THE PLACE! WHY DON'T THE OTHER MONSTERS EAT THEM?
KYUUUU (SQUEAK)
BUSU (JAB)
AHH...
ONLY ONE WAY TO FIND OUT!

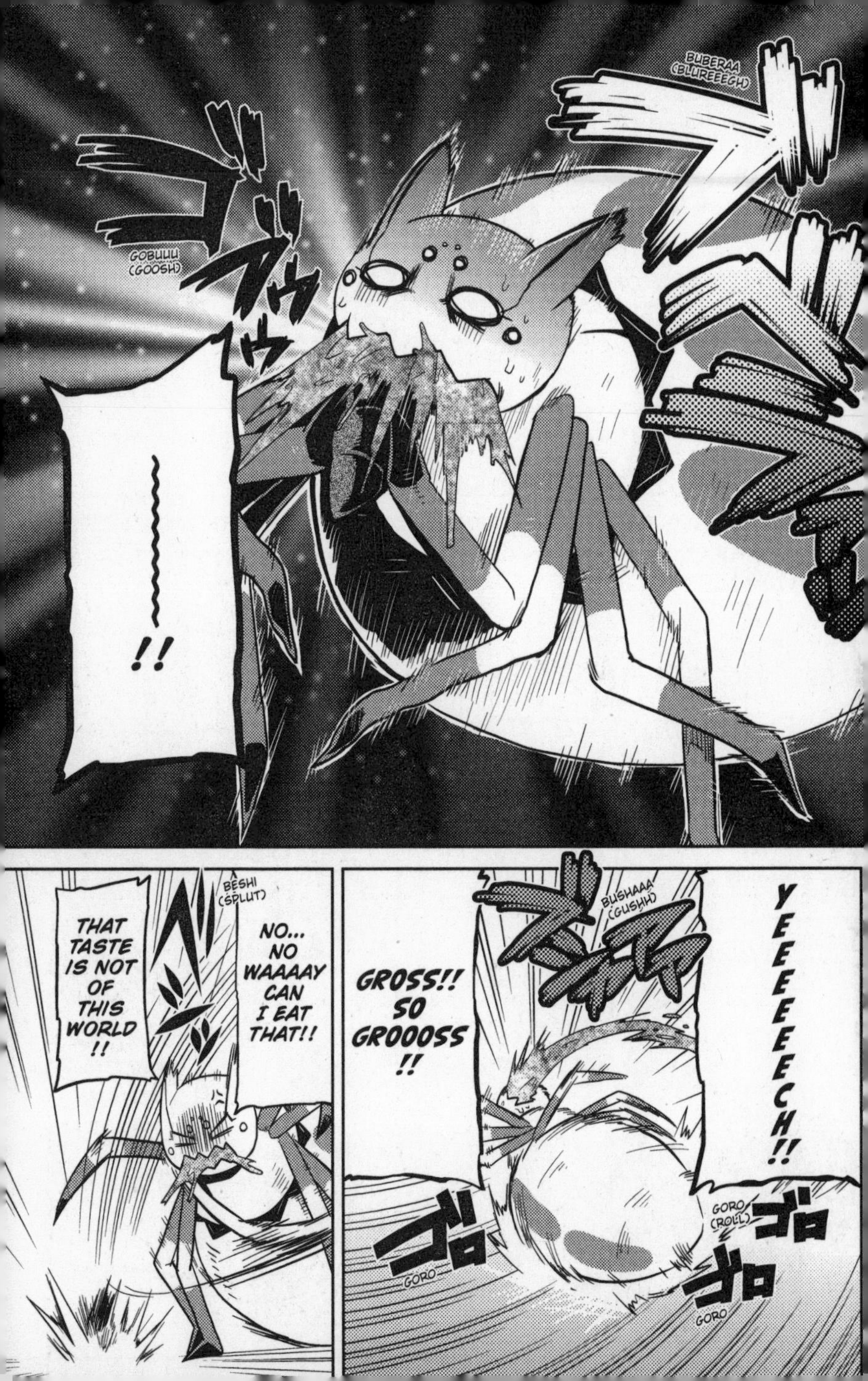
BUBERAA (BLUREEEGH)
GOBUUU (GOOSH)
——!!
YEEEEEECH!!
BUSHAAA (GUSHH)
GROSS!! SO GROOOSS!!
GORO (ROLL)
GORO
GORO
NO... NO WAAAAY CAN I EAT THAT!!
BESHI (SPLUT)
THAT TASTE IS NOT OF THIS WORLD!!

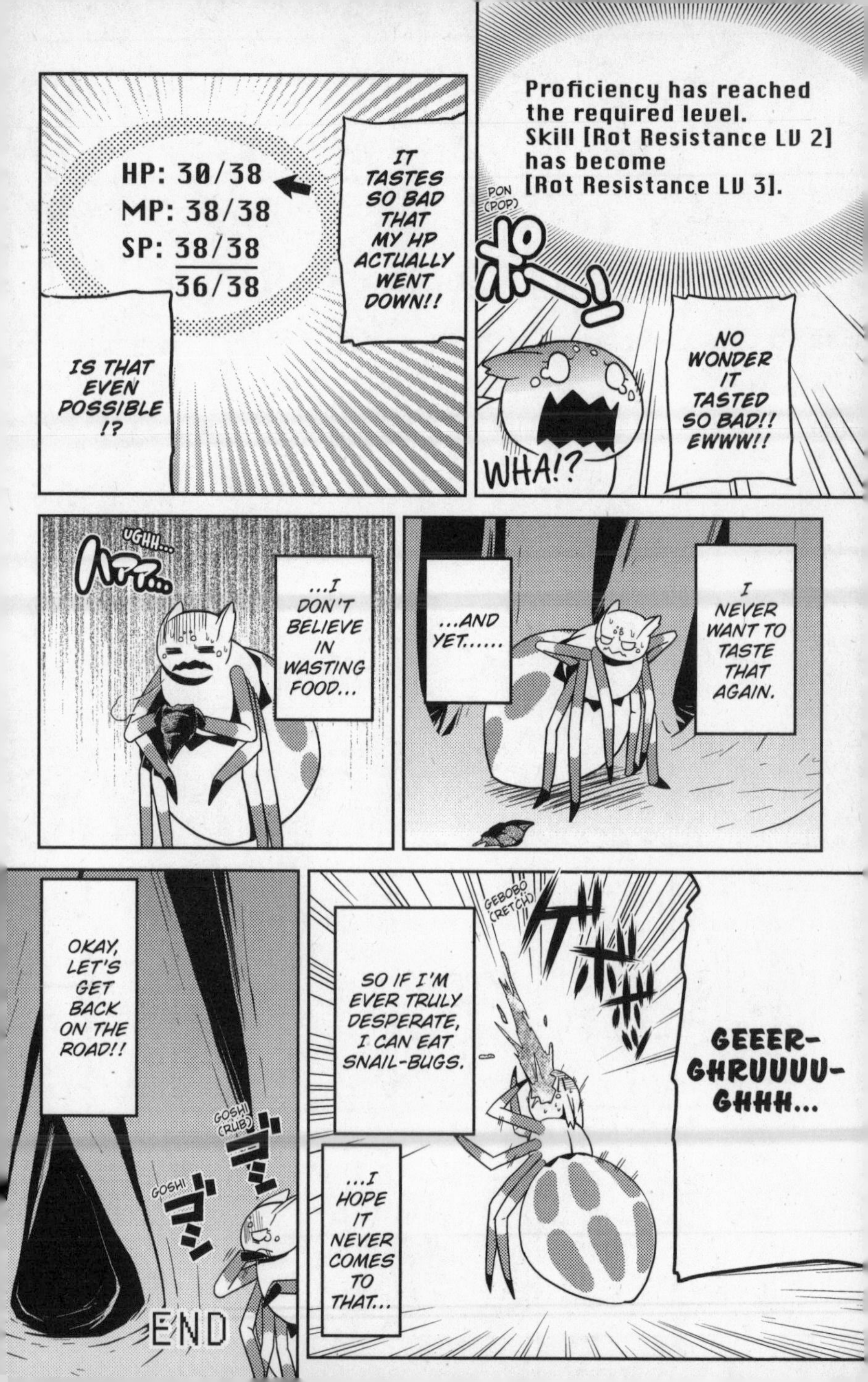

Proficiency has reached the required level. Skill [Rot Resistance LV 2] has become [Rot Resistance LV 3].
PON (POP)
NO WONDER IT TASTED SO BAD!! EWWW!!
WHA!?
IT TASTES SO BAD THAT MY HP ACTUALLY WENT DOWN!!
HP: 30/38
MP: 38/38
SP: 38/38
36/38
IS THAT EVEN POSSIBLE!?
I NEVER WANT TO TASTE THAT AGAIN.
...AND YET......
UGHH...
...I DON'T BELIEVE IN WASTING FOOD...
GEBOBO (RETCH)
GEEER-GHRUUUU-GHHH...
SO IF I'M EVER TRULY DESPERATE, I CAN EAT SNAIL-BUGS.
...I HOPE IT NEVER COMES TO THAT...
OKAY, LET'S GET BACK ON THE ROAD!!
GOSHI (RUB)
GOSHI
END

So I'm a Spider, So What?

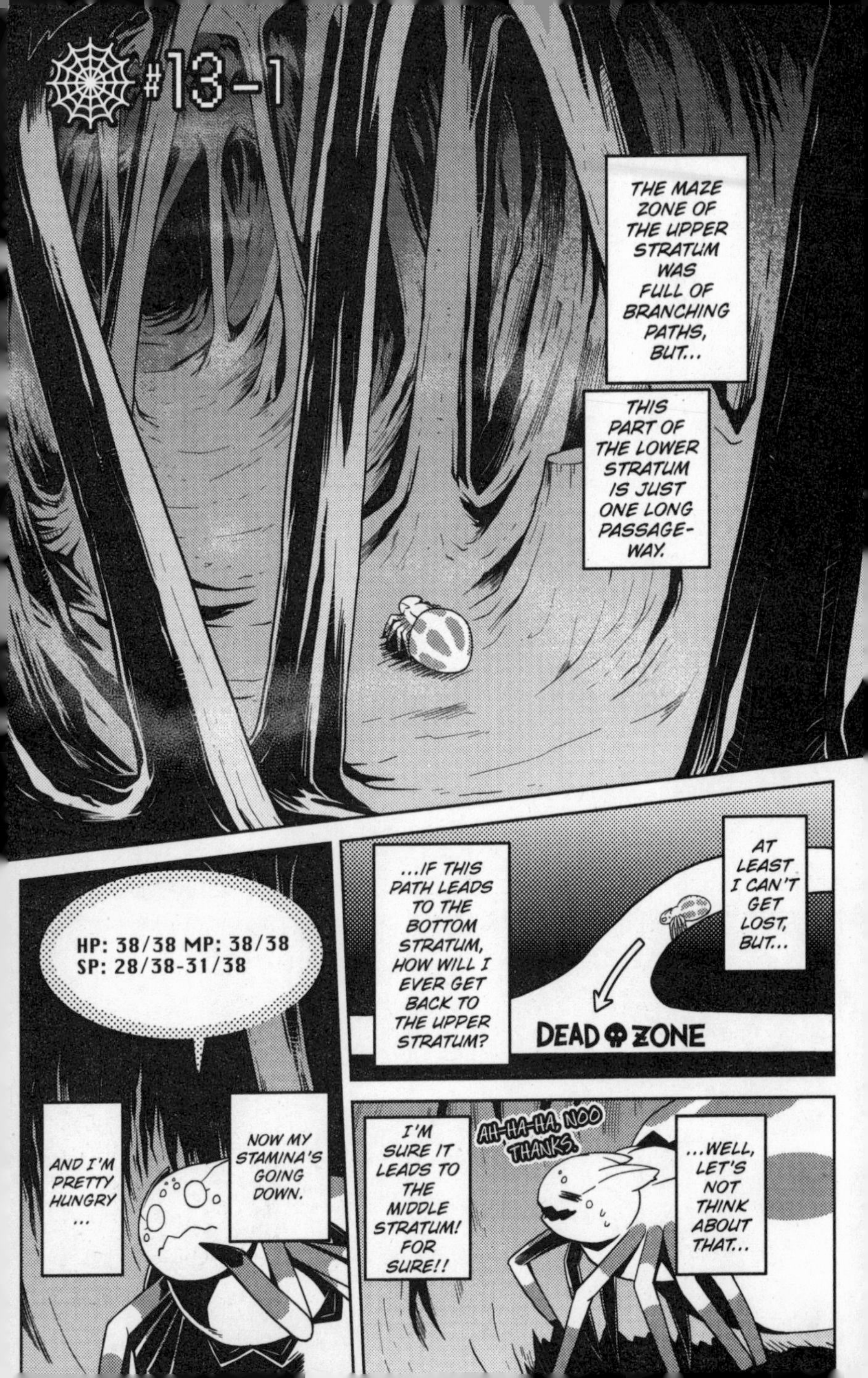
#13-1
THE MAZE ZONE OF THE UPPER STRATUM WAS FULL OF BRANCHING PATHS, BUT...
THIS PART OF THE LOWER STRATUM IS JUST ONE LONG PASSAGE-WAY.
AT LEAST I CAN'T GET LOST, BUT...
...IF THIS PATH LEADS TO THE BOTTOM STRATUM, HOW WILL I EVER GET BACK TO THE UPPER STRATUM?
DEAD ZONE
...WELL, LET'S NOT THINK ABOUT THAT...
AH-HA-HA, NOO THANKS.
I'M SURE IT LEADS TO THE MIDDLE STRATUM! FOR SURE!!
HP: 38/38 MP: 38/38
SP: 28/38-31/38
NOW MY STAMINA'S GOING DOWN.
AND I'M PRETTY HUNGRY...

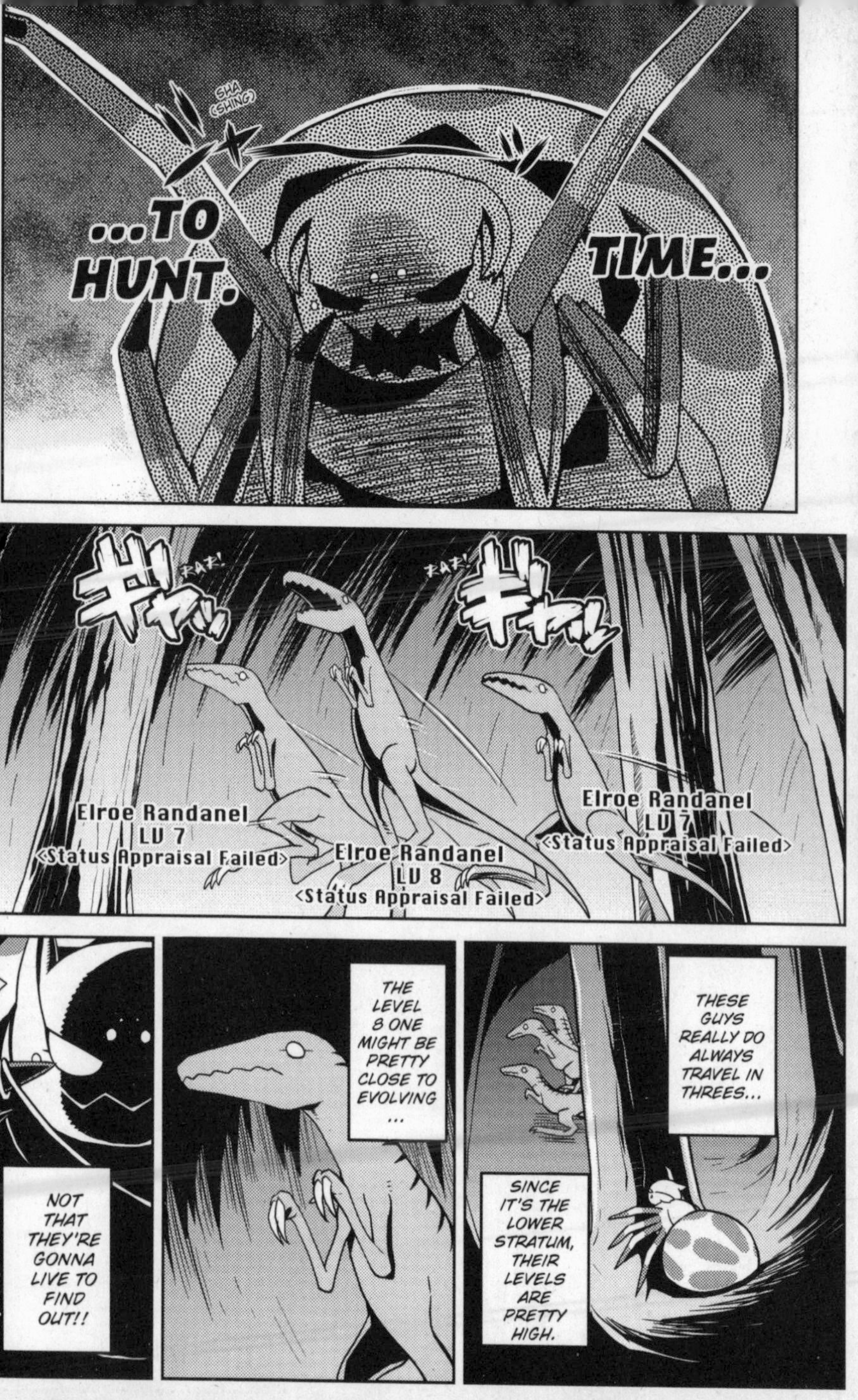
SHA (SHING)
TIME...
...TO HUNT.
RAR!
RAR!
Elroe Randanel LV 7 <Status Appraisal Failed>
Elroe Randanel LV 8 <Status Appraisal Failed>
Elroe Randanel LV 7 <Status Appraisal Failed>
THESE GUYS REALLY DO ALWAYS TRAVEL IN THREES...
SINCE IT'S THE LOWER STRATUM, THEIR LEVELS ARE PRETTY HIGH.
THE LEVEL 8 ONE MIGHT BE PRETTY CLOSE TO EVOLVING...
NOT THAT THEY'RE GONNA LIVE TO FIND OUT!!

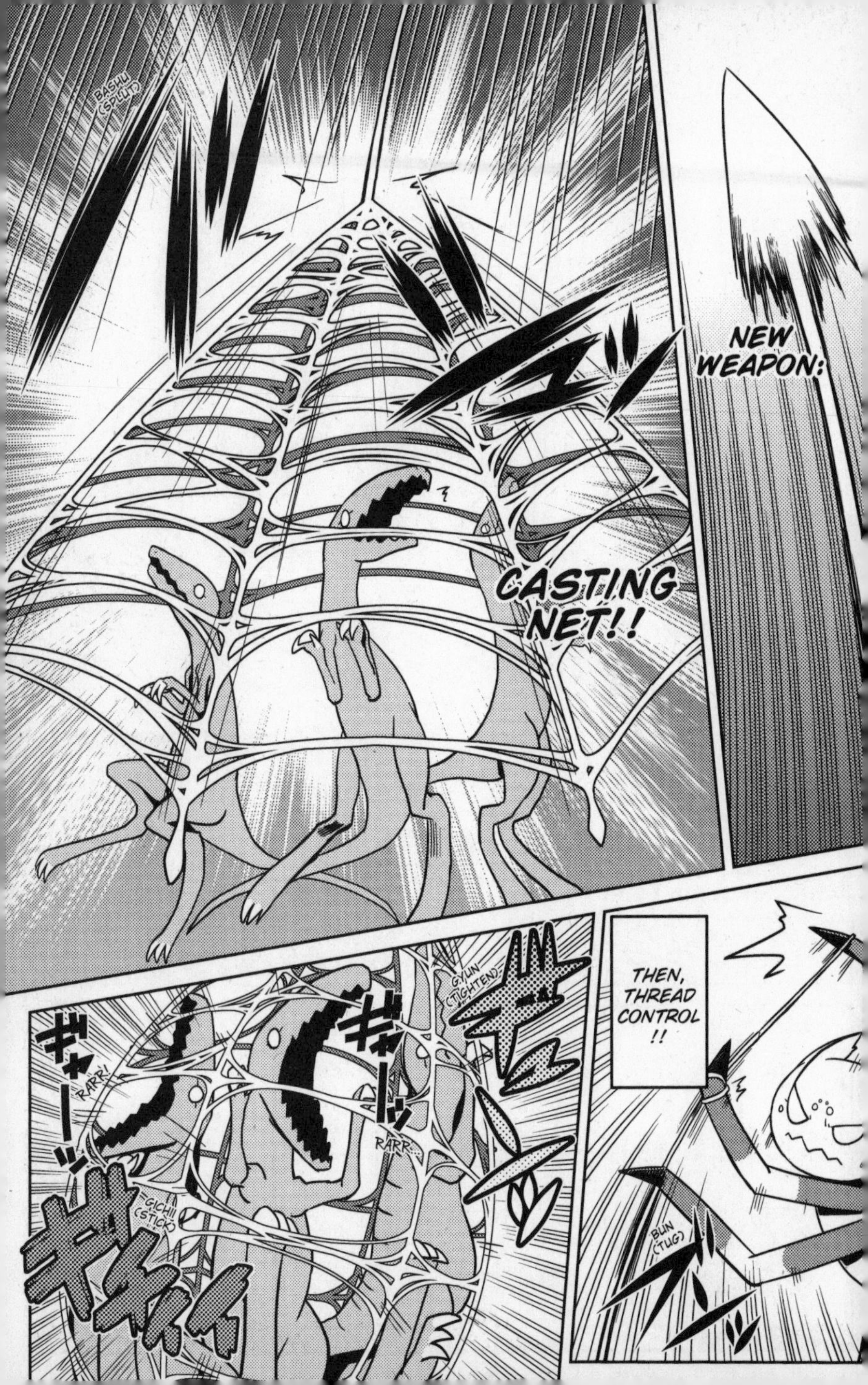
NEW WEAPON:
BASHU (SPLUT)
CASTING NET!!
THEN, THREAD CONTROL !!
BUN (TUG)
GYUN (TIGHTEN)
RARR
RARR!
GICHI! (STICK)

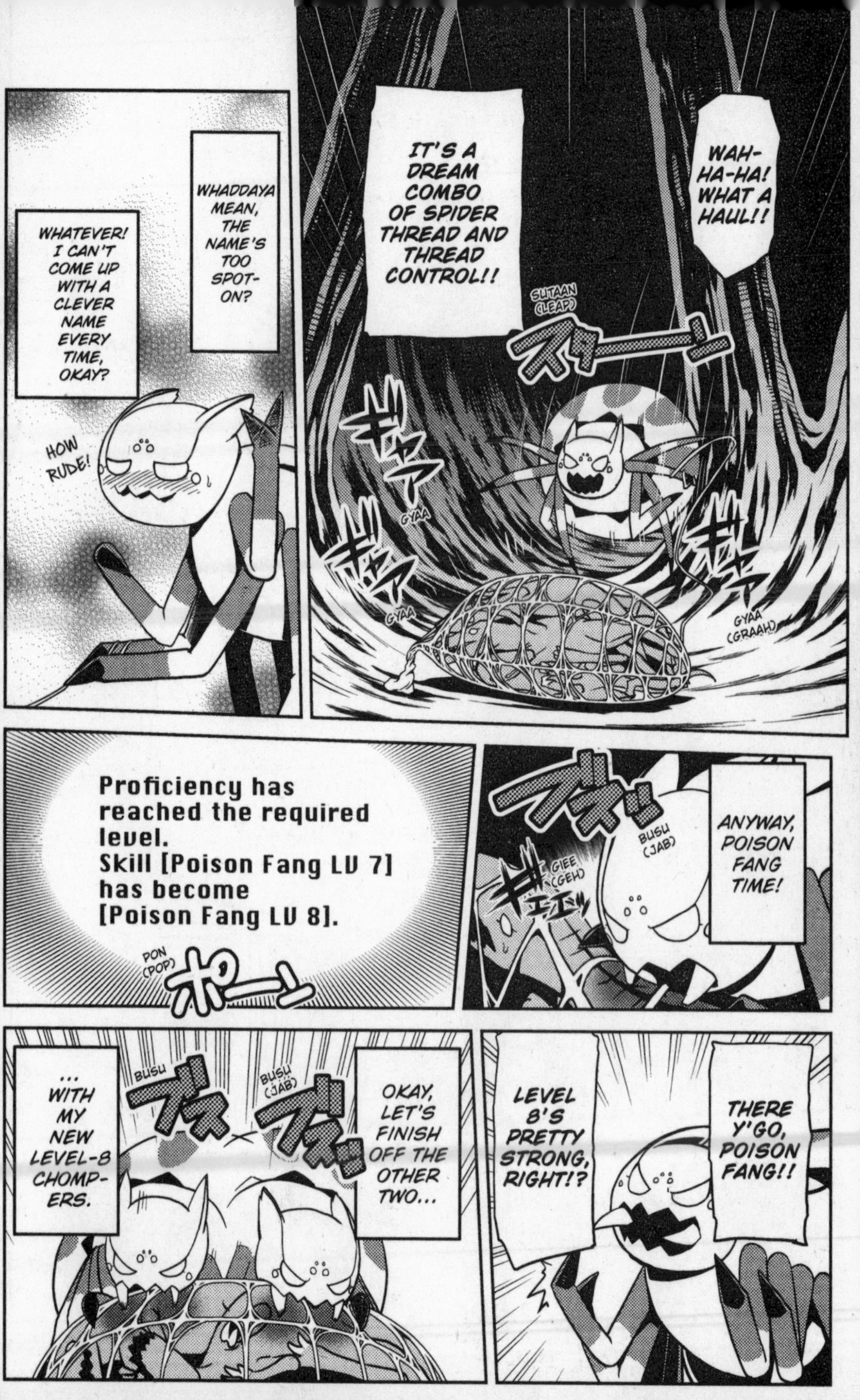
WAH-HA-HA! WHAT A HAUL!!
IT'S A DREAM COMBO OF SPIDER THREAD AND THREAD CONTROL!!
SUTAAN (LEAP)
GYAA
GYAA
GYAA (GRAAH)
WHADDAYA MEAN, THE NAME'S TOO SPOT-ON?
WHATEVER! I CAN'T COME UP WITH A CLEVER NAME EVERY TIME, OKAY?
HOW RUDE!
ANYWAY, POISON FANG TIME!
BUSU (JAB)
GIEE (GEH)
Proficiency has reached the required level. Skill [Poison Fang LV 7] has become [Poison Fang LV 8].
PON (POP)
THERE Y'GO, POISON FANG!!
LEVEL 8'S PRETTY STRONG, RIGHT!?
OKAY, LET'S FINISH OFF THE OTHER TWO...
BUSU (JAB)
BUSU
... WITH MY NEW LEVEL-8 CHOMPERS.

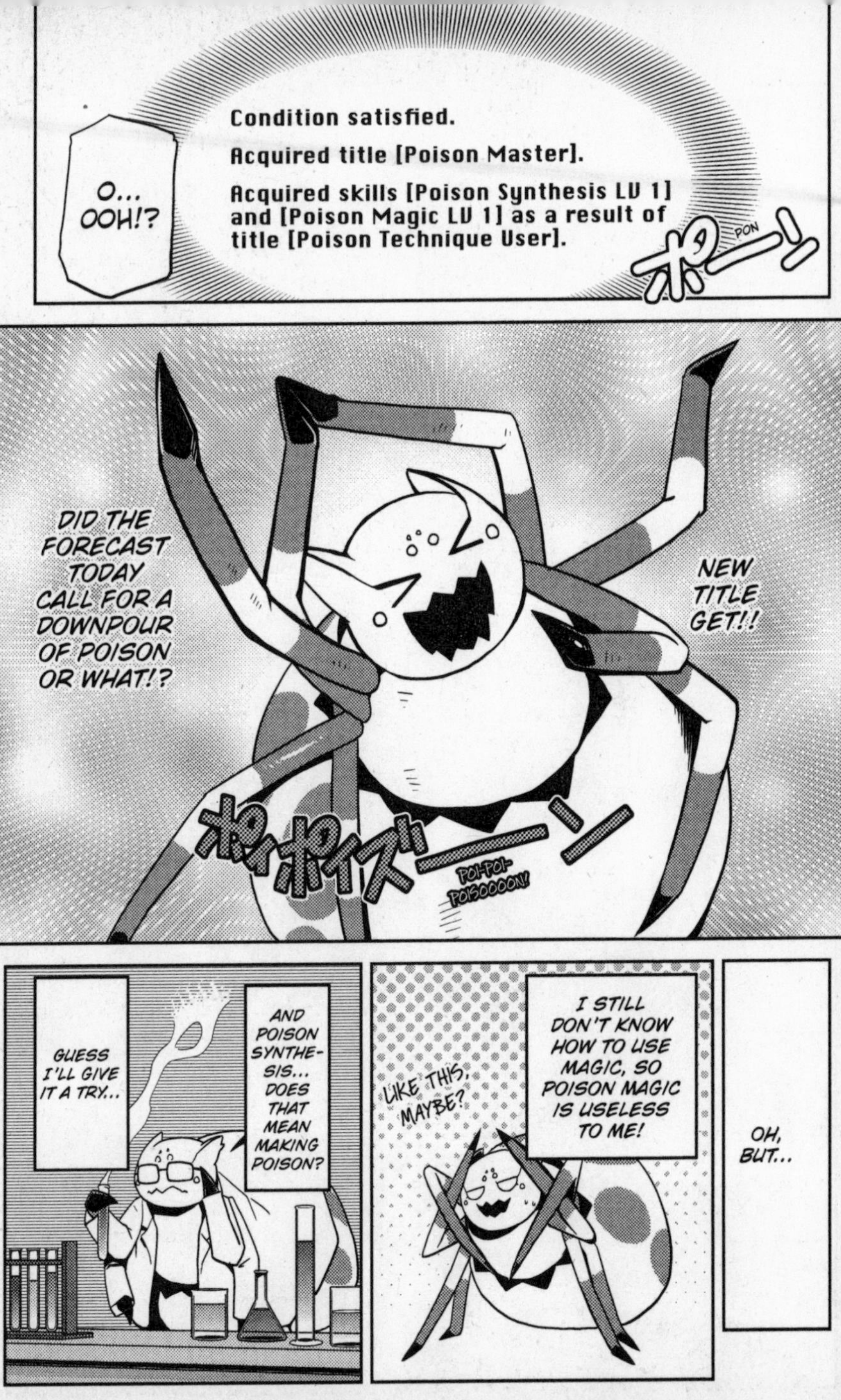
ポーン
PON
Condition satisfied.
Acquired title [Poison Master].
Acquired skills [Poison Synthesis LV 1] and [Poison Magic LV 1] as a result of title [Poison Technique User].
O... OOH!?
NEW TITLE GET!!
DID THE FORECAST TODAY CALL FOR A DOWNPOUR OF POISON OR WHAT!?
ポイポイズーン
POI-POI-POISOOOON!
OH, BUT...
I STILL DON'T KNOW HOW TO USE MAGIC, SO POISON MAGIC IS USELESS TO ME!
LIKE THIS, MAYBE?
AND POISON SYNTHESIS... DOES THAT MEAN MAKING POISON?
GUESS I'LL GIVE IT A TRY...

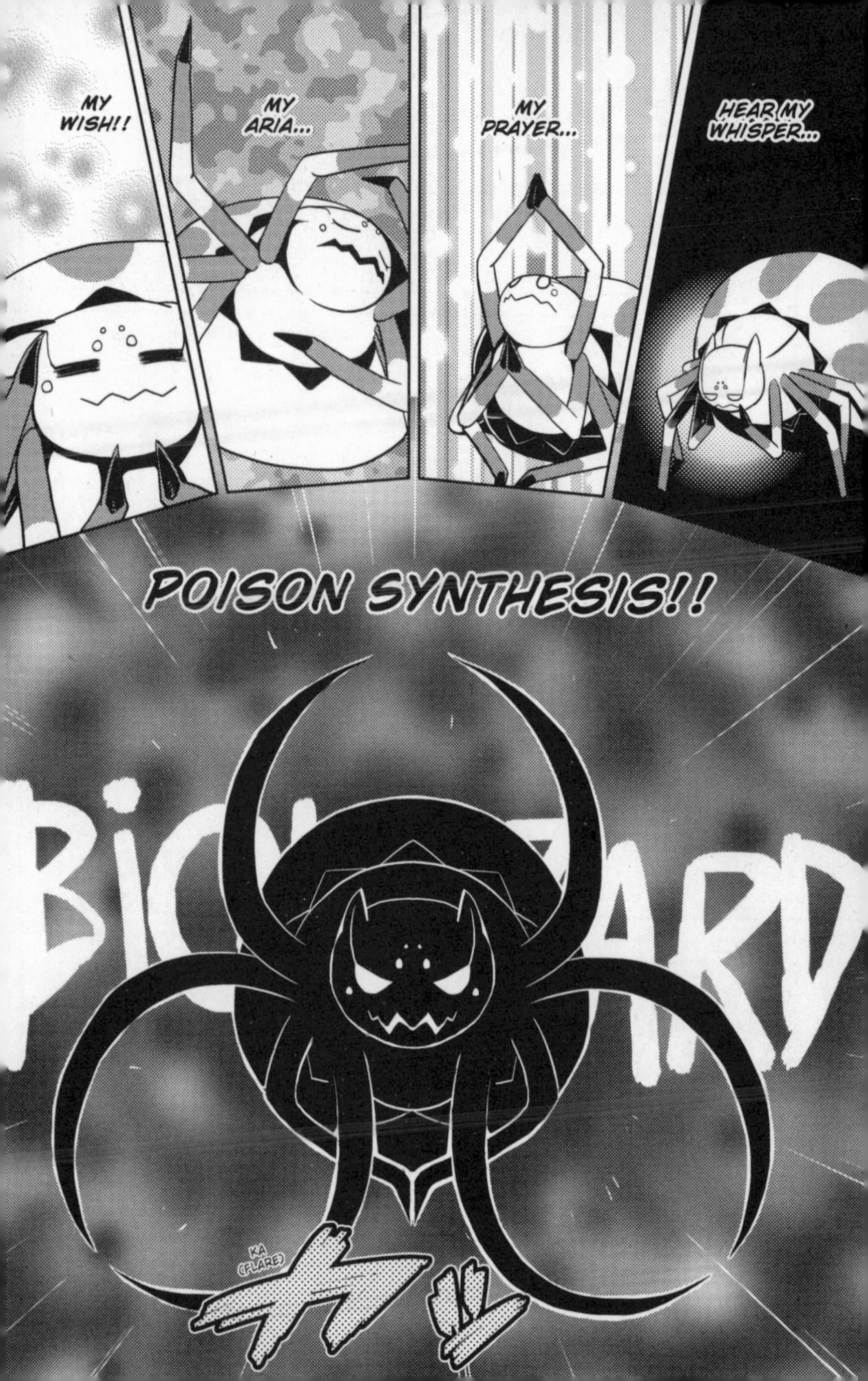
HEAR MY WHISPER...
MY PRAYER...
MY ARIA...
MY WISH!!
POISON SYNTHESIS!!
KA (FLARE)

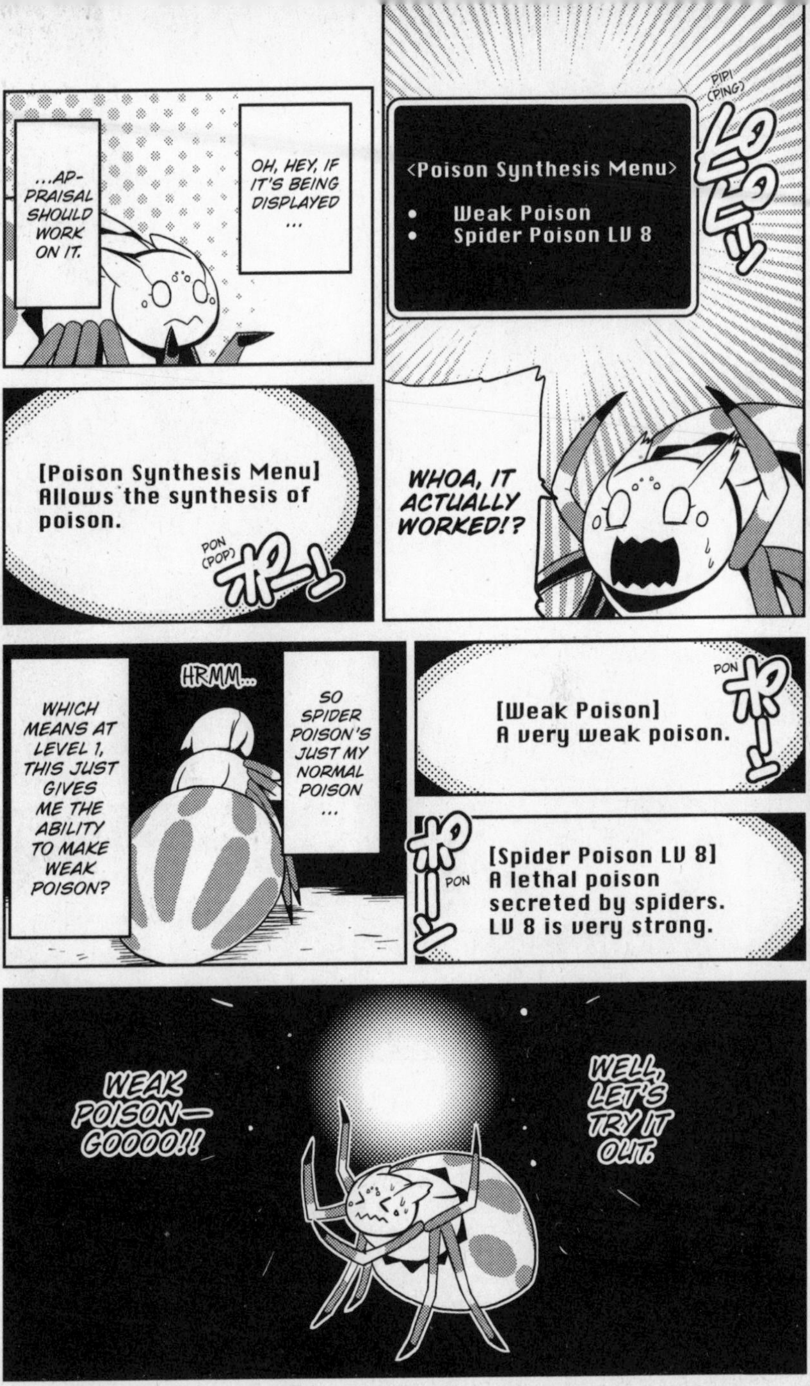
PIPI (PING)
<Poison Synthesis Menu>
• Weak Poison
• Spider Poison LV 8
WHOA, IT ACTUALLY WORKED!?
OH, HEY, IF IT'S BEING DISPLAYED ...
...AP-PRAISAL SHOULD WORK ON IT.
[Poison Synthesis Menu] Allows the synthesis of poison.
PON (POP)
PON
[Weak Poison] A very weak poison.
PON
[Spider Poison LV 8] A lethal poison secreted by spiders. LV 8 is very strong.
HRMM...
SO SPIDER POISON'S JUST MY NORMAL POISON ...
WHICH MEANS AT LEVEL 1, THIS JUST GIVES ME THE ABILITY TO MAKE WEAK POISON?
WELL, LET'S TRY IT OUT.
WEAK POISON—GOOOO!!

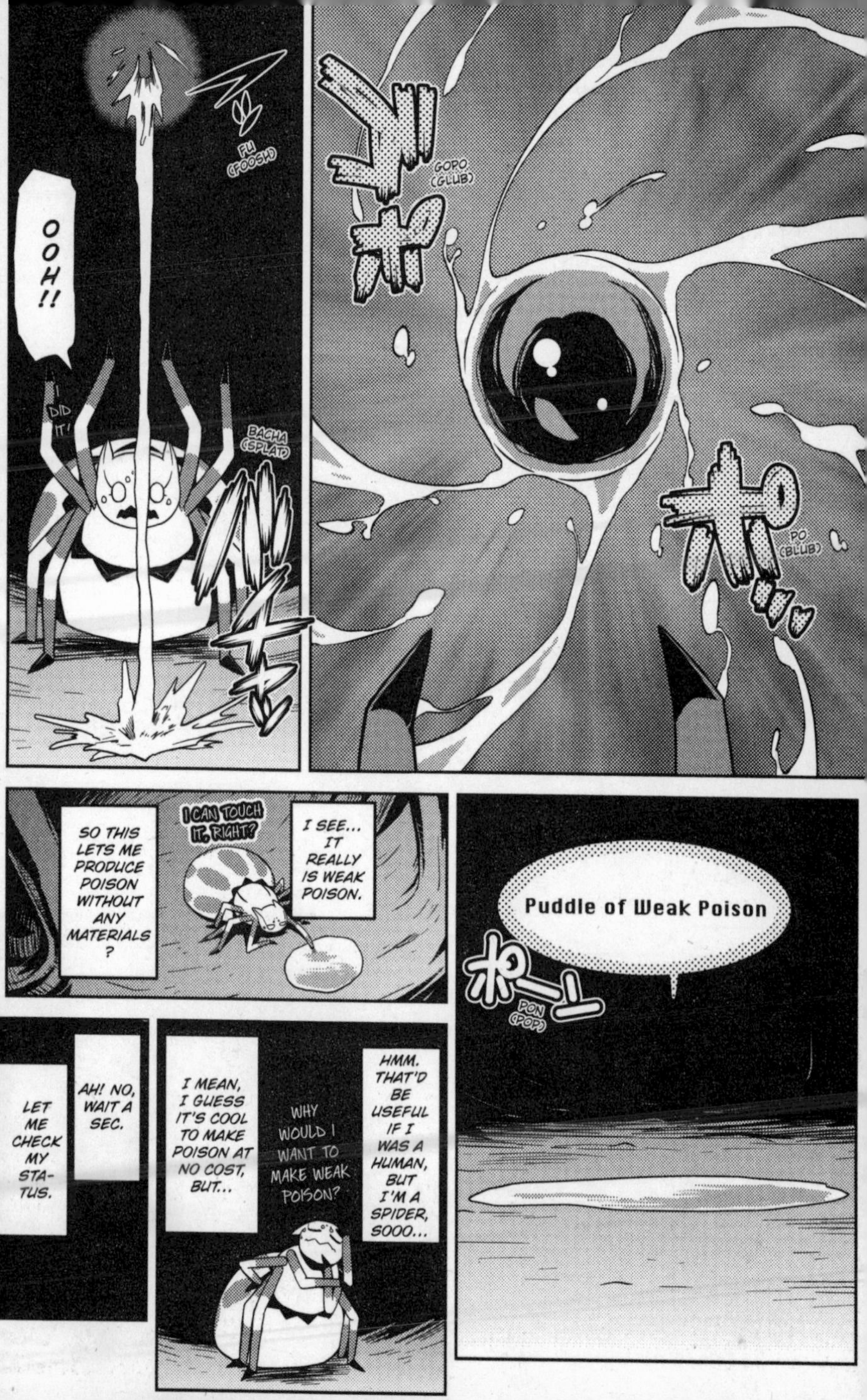
GOPO (GLUB)
PO (BLUB)
FU (FOOSH)
OOH!!
I DID IT!
BACHA (SPLAT)
Puddle of Weak Poison
PON (POP)
I SEE... IT REALLY IS WEAK POISON.
I CAN TOUCH IT, RIGHT?
SO THIS LETS ME PRODUCE POISON WITHOUT ANY MATERIALS?
HMM. THAT'D BE USEFUL IF I WAS A HUMAN, BUT I'M A SPIDER, SOOO...
WHY WOULD I WANT TO MAKE WEAK POISON?
I MEAN, I GUESS IT'S COOL TO MAKE POISON AT NO COST, BUT...
AH! NO, WAIT A SEC.
LET ME CHECK MY STATUS.

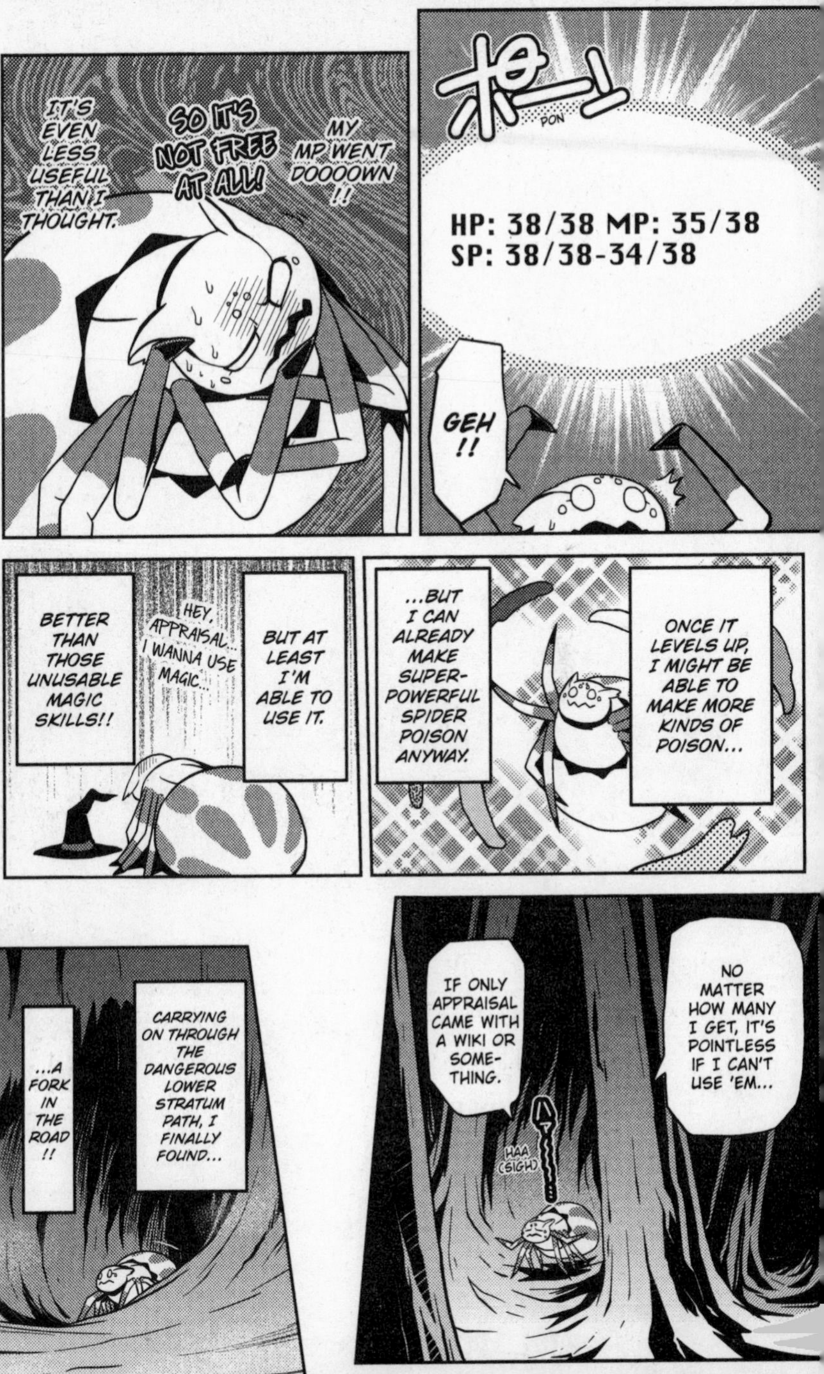
PON
HP: 38/38 MP: 35/38
SP: 38/38-34/38
GEH!!
MY MP WENT DOOOOWN!!
SO IT'S NOT FREE AT ALL!
IT'S EVEN LESS USEFUL THAN I THOUGHT.
ONCE IT LEVELS UP, I MIGHT BE ABLE TO MAKE MORE KINDS OF POISON...
...BUT I CAN ALREADY MAKE SUPER-POWERFUL SPIDER POISON ANYWAY.
BUT AT LEAST I'M ABLE TO USE IT.
HEY, APPRAISAL. I WANNA USE MAGIC...
BETTER THAN THOSE UNUSABLE MAGIC SKILLS!!
NO MATTER HOW MANY I GET, IT'S POINTLESS IF I CAN'T USE 'EM...
IF ONLY APPRAISAL CAME WITH A WIKI OR SOME-THING.
HAA (SIGH)
CARRYING ON THROUGH THE DANGEROUS LOWER STRATUM PATH, I FINALLY FOUND...
...A FORK IN THE ROAD!!

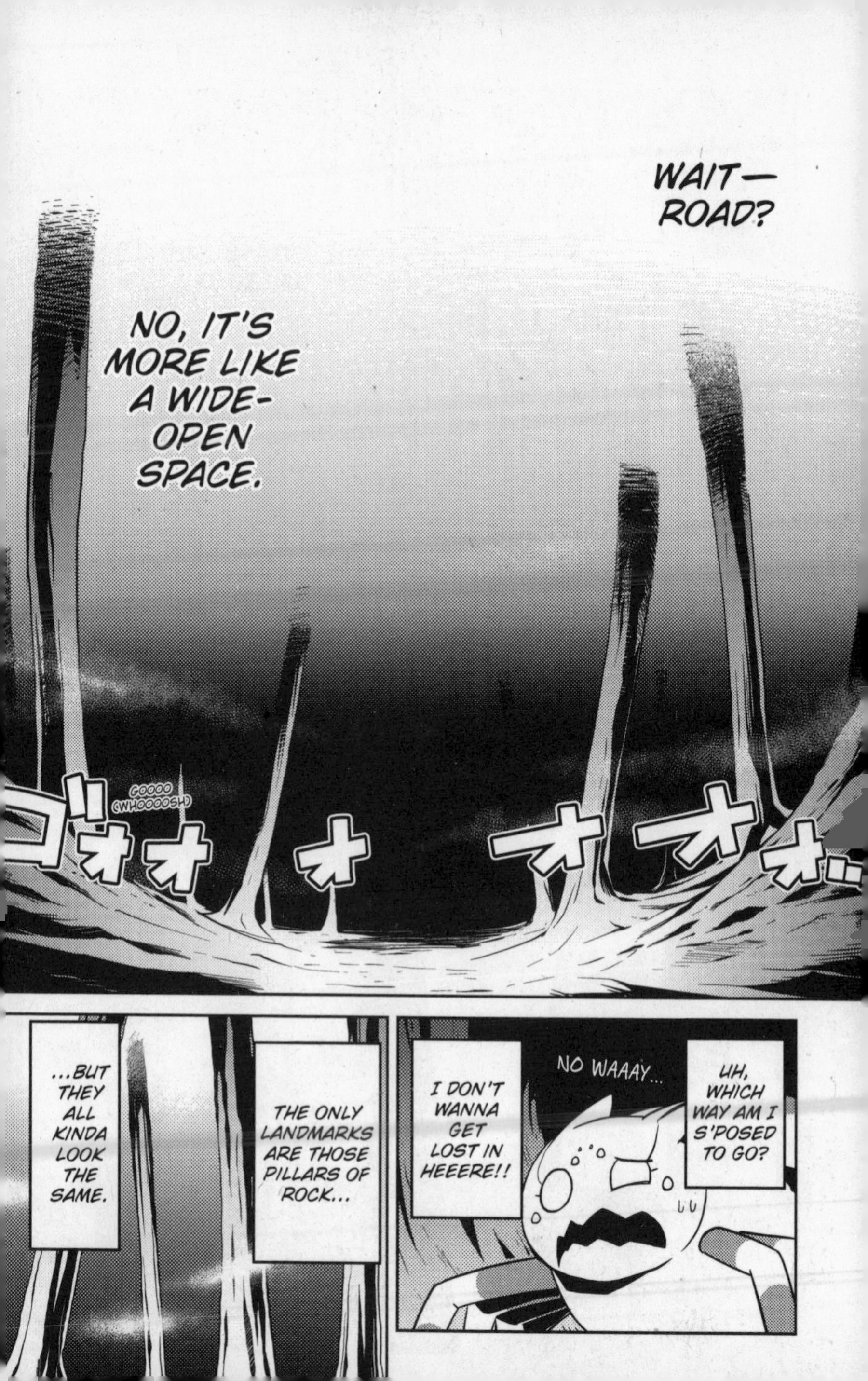
WAIT—
ROAD?
NO, IT'S MORE LIKE A WIDE-OPEN SPACE.
GOOOO (WHOOOOSH)
UH, WHICH WAY AM I S'POSED TO GO?
NO WAAAY...
I DON'T WANNA GET LOST IN HEEERE!!
THE ONLY LANDMARKS ARE THOSE PILLARS OF ROCK...
...BUT THEY ALL KINDA LOOK THE SAME.

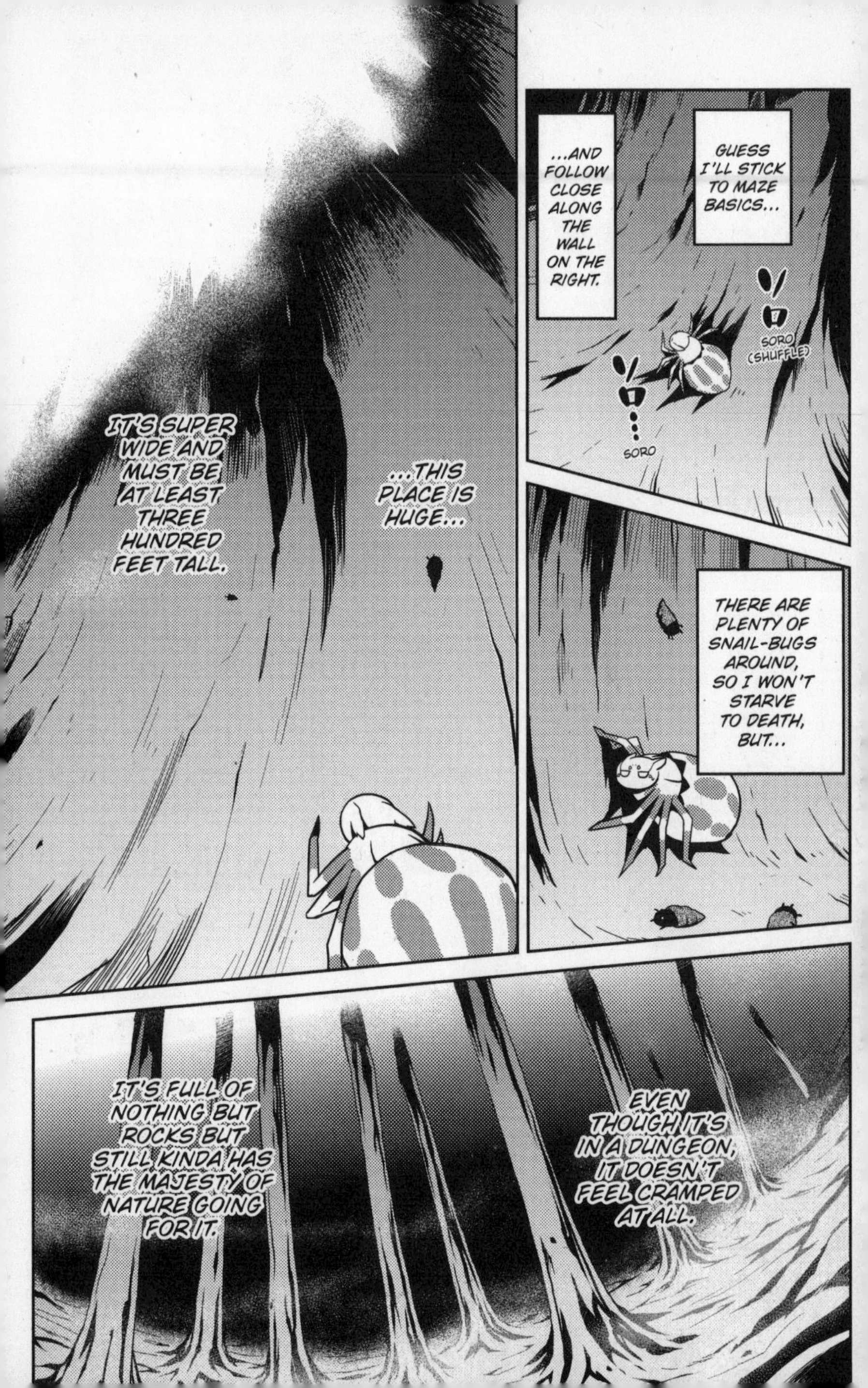
GUESS I'LL STICK TO MAZE BASICS...
...AND FOLLOW CLOSE ALONG THE WALL ON THE RIGHT.
SORO (SHUFFLE)
SORO
THERE ARE PLENTY OF SNAIL-BUGS AROUND, SO I WON'T STARVE TO DEATH, BUT...
...THIS PLACE IS HUGE...
IT'S SUPER WIDE AND MUST BE AT LEAST THREE HUNDRED FEET TALL.
EVEN THOUGH IT'S IN A DUNGEON, IT DOESN'T FEEL CRAMPED AT ALL.
IT'S FULL OF NOTHING BUT ROCKS BUT STILL KINDA HAS THE MAJESTY OF NATURE GOING FOR IT.

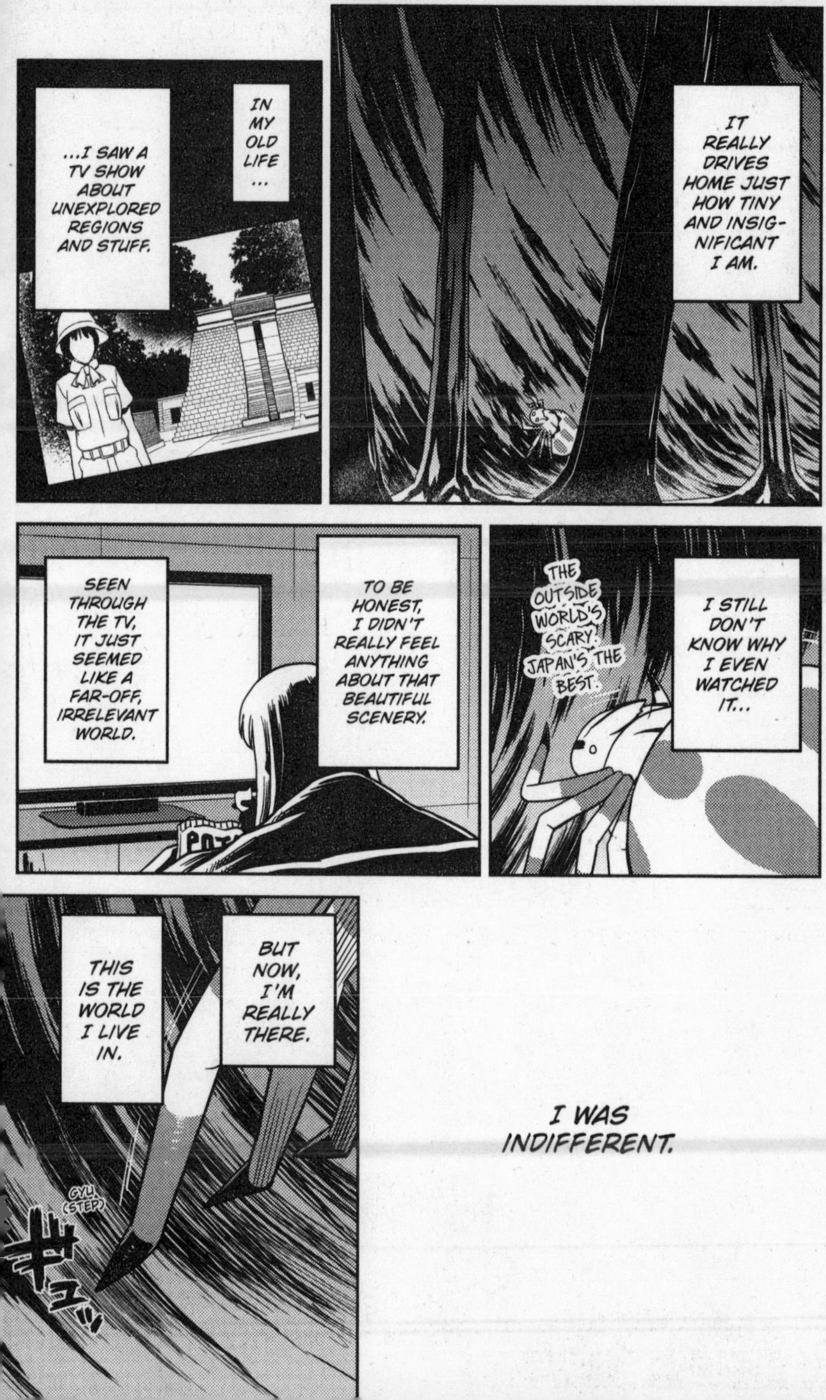
IT REALLY DRIVES HOME JUST HOW TINY AND INSIGNIFICANT I AM.
IN MY OLD LIFE...
...I SAW A TV SHOW ABOUT UNEXPLORED REGIONS AND STUFF.
I STILL DON'T KNOW WHY I EVEN WATCHED IT...
THE OUTSIDE WORLD'S SCARY. JAPAN'S THE BEST.
TO BE HONEST, I DIDN'T REALLY FEEL ANYTHING ABOUT THAT BEAUTIFUL SCENERY.
SEEN THROUGH THE TV, IT JUST SEEMED LIKE A FAR-OFF, IRRELEVANT WORLD.
I WAS INDIFFERENT.
BUT NOW, I'M REALLY THERE.
THIS IS THE WORLD I LIVE IN.
GYU (STEP)
ギュッ

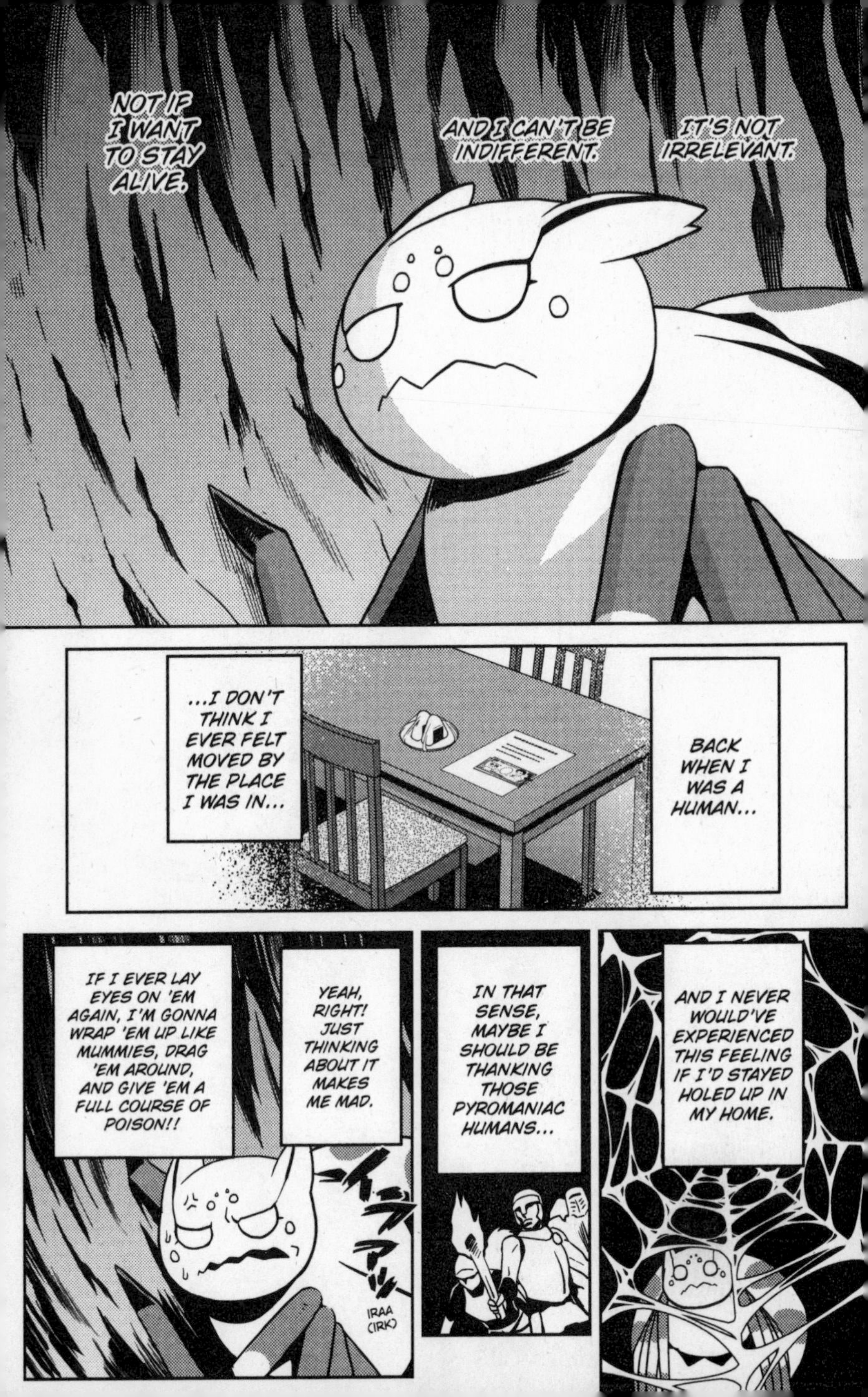
IT'S NOT IRRELEVANT.
AND I CAN'T BE INDIFFERENT.
NOT IF I WANT TO STAY ALIVE.
BACK WHEN I WAS A HUMAN...
...I DON'T THINK I EVER FELT MOVED BY THE PLACE I WAS IN...
AND I NEVER WOULD'VE EXPERIENCED THIS FEELING IF I'D STAYED HOLED UP IN MY HOME.
IN THAT SENSE, MAYBE I SHOULD BE THANKING THOSE PYROMANIAC HUMANS...
YEAH, RIGHT! JUST THINKING ABOUT IT MAKES ME MAD.
IF I EVER LAY EYES ON 'EM AGAIN, I'M GONNA WRAP 'EM UP LIKE MUMMIES, DRAG 'EM AROUND, AND GIVE 'EM A FULL COURSE OF POISON!!
IRAA (IRK)

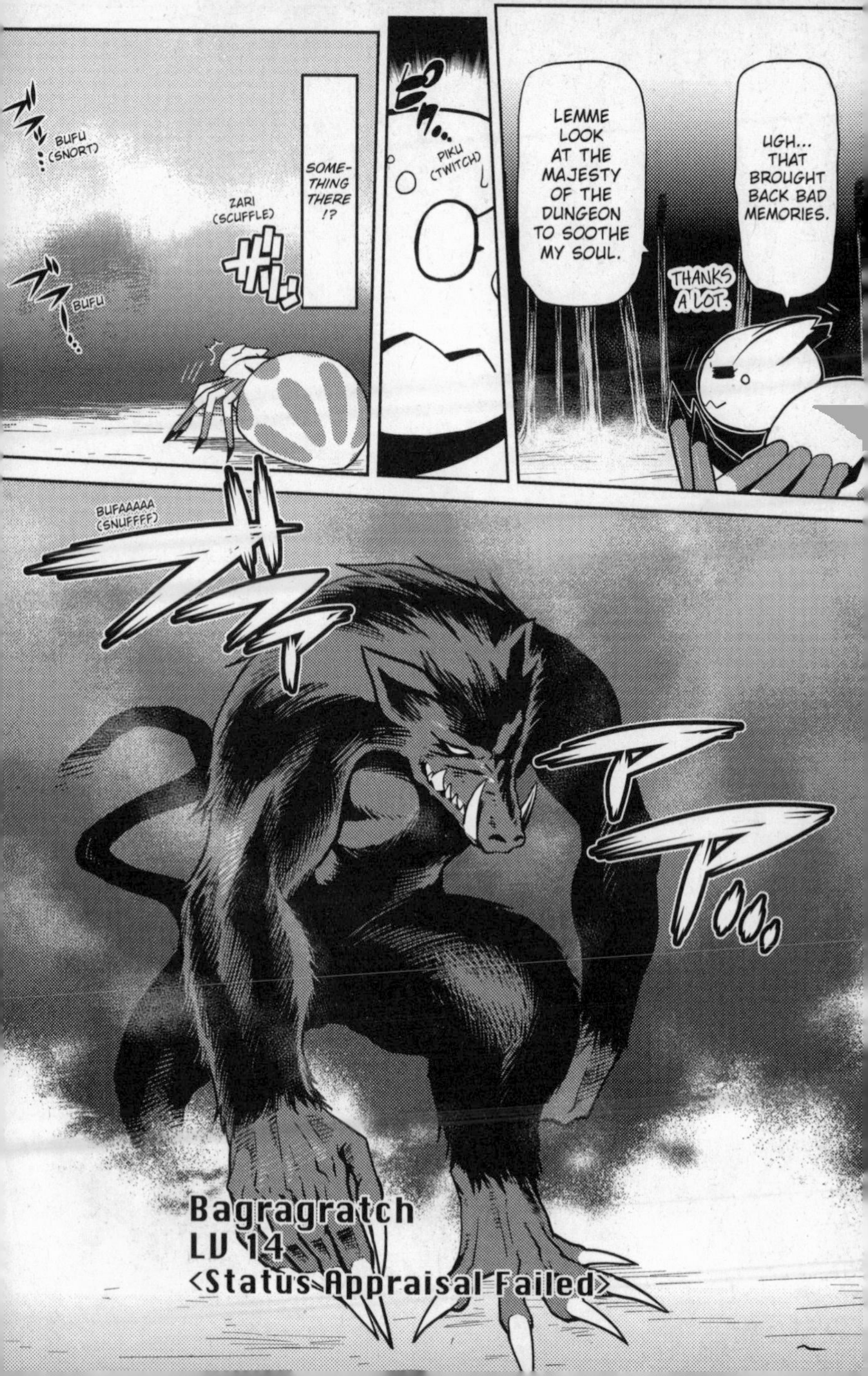
UGH... THAT BROUGHT BACK BAD MEMORIES.
THANKS A LOT.
LEMME LOOK AT THE MAJESTY OF THE DUNGEON TO SOOTHE MY SOUL.
PIKU (TWITCH)
SOME-THING THERE !?
ZARI (SCUFFLE)
BUFU (SNORT)
BUFU
BUFAAAAA (SNUFFFF)
Bagragratch
LV 14
<Status Appraisal Failed>

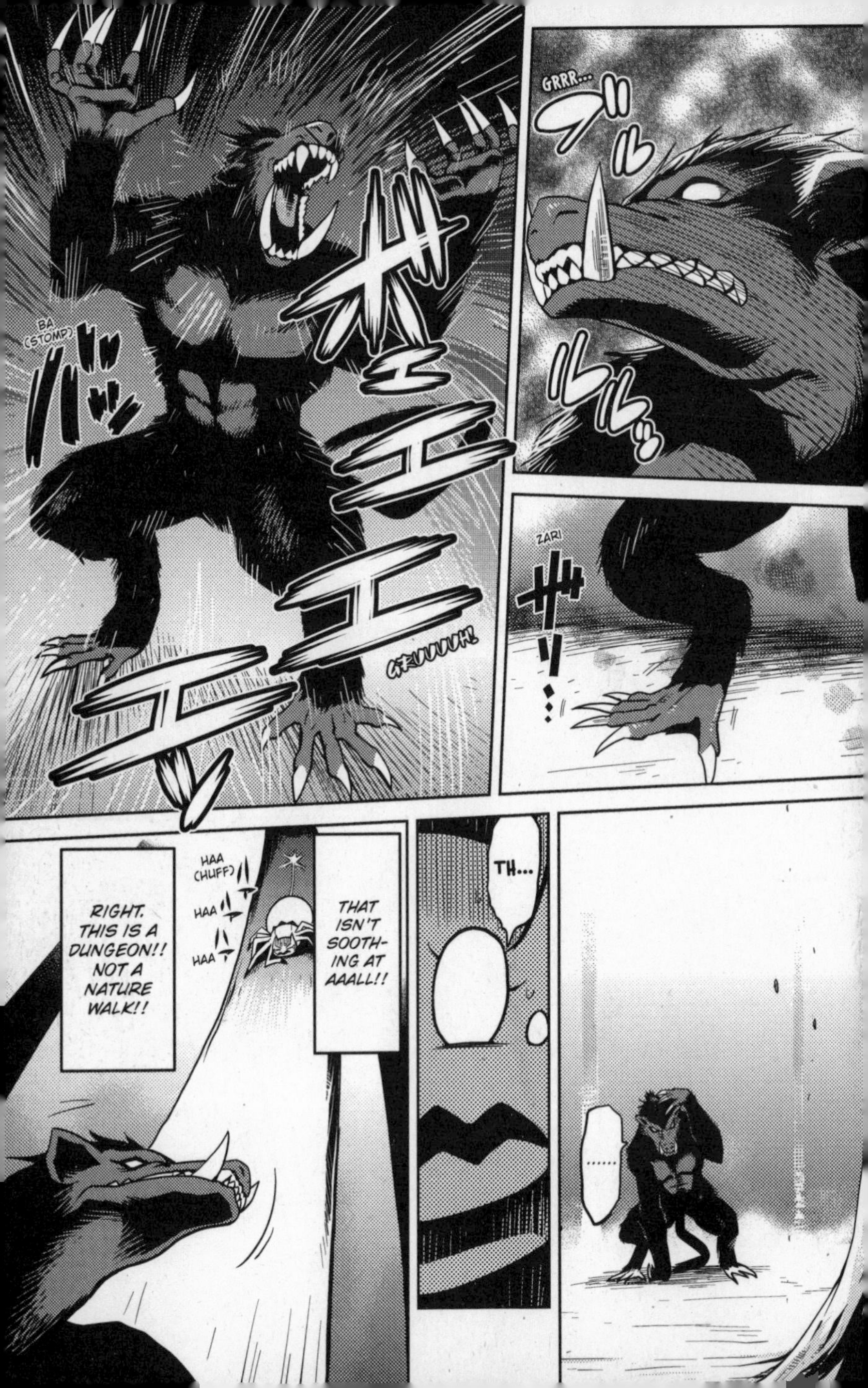
GRRR...
ZARI
BA (STOMP)
GRUUUUH!
......
TH...
THAT ISN'T SOOTHING AT AAALL!!
HAA (HUFF)
HAA
HAA
RIGHT. THIS IS A DUNGEON!! NOT A NATURE WALK!!

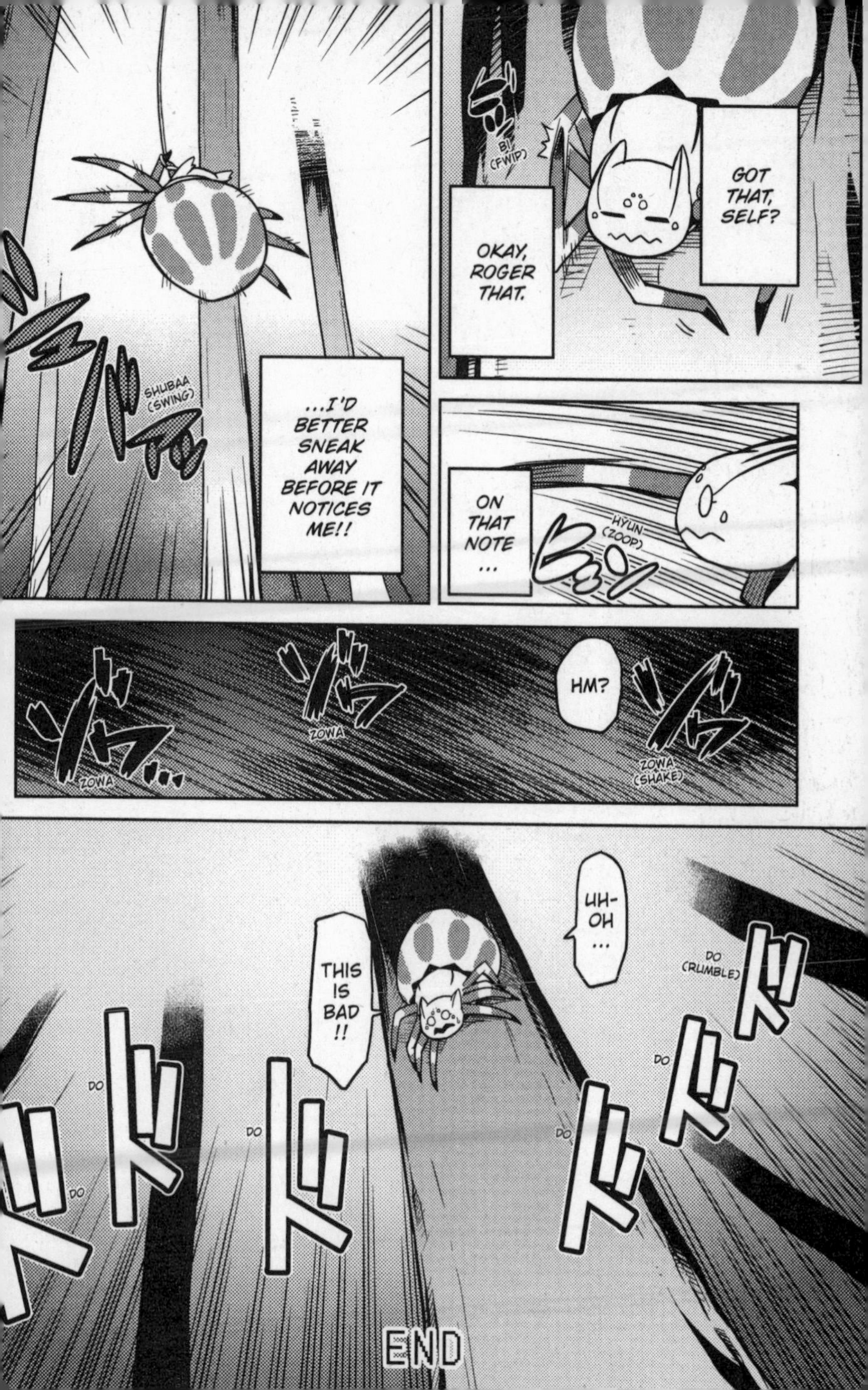

GOT THAT, SELF?
BI (FWIP)
OKAY, ROGER THAT.
HYUN (ZOOP)
ON THAT NOTE...
...I'D BETTER SNEAK AWAY BEFORE IT NOTICES ME!!
SHUBAA (SWING)
ZOWA (SHAKE)
HM?
ZOWA
ZOWA
DO (RUMBLE)
UH-OH...
DO
DO
THIS IS BAD!!
DO
DO
DO
END

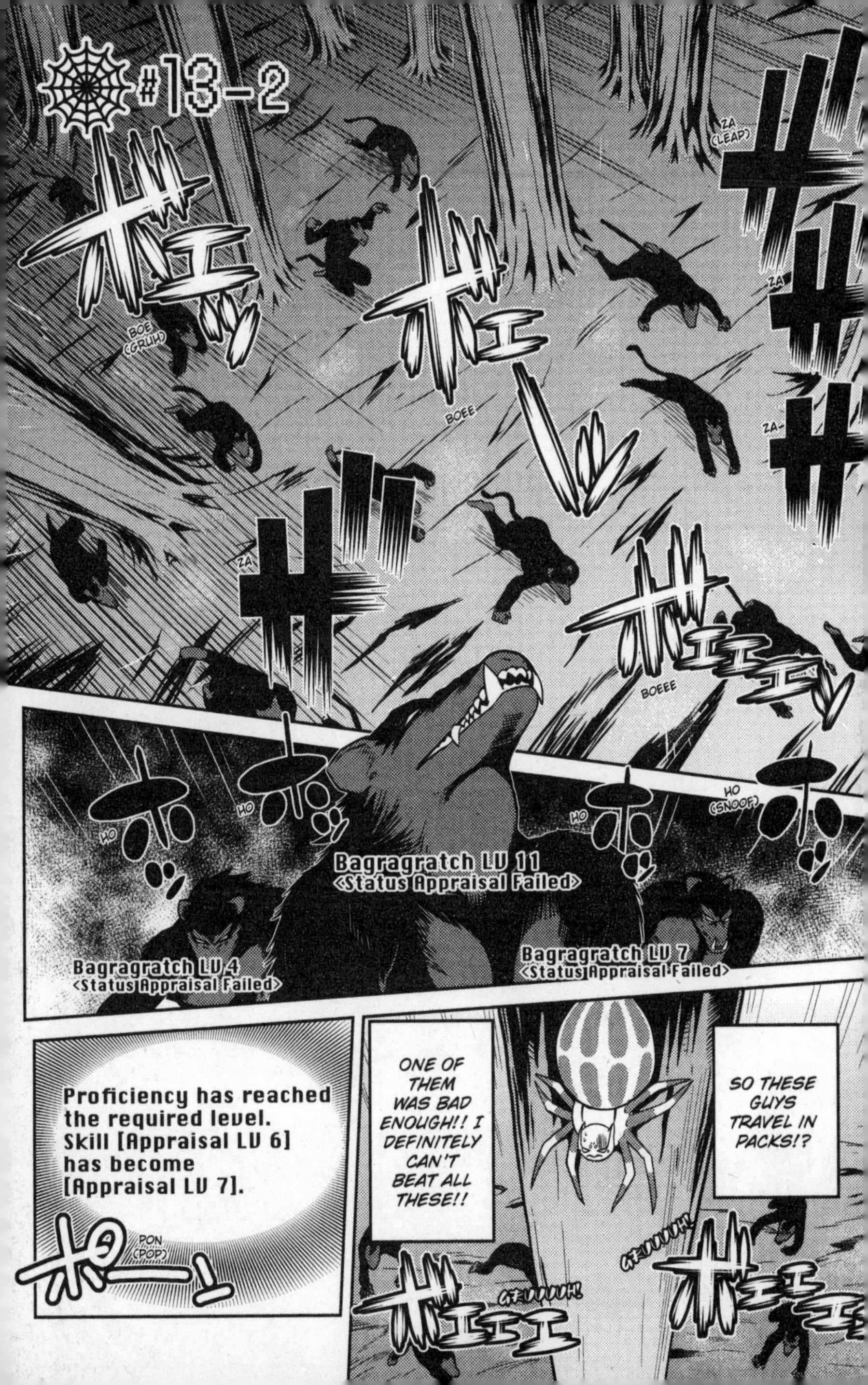

#13-2
ZA (LEAP)
ZA
ZA
BOEE
BOE (GRUH)
ZA
BOEEE
HO (SNOOF)
HO
HO
HO
Bagragratch LV 11
<Status Appraisal Failed>
Bagragratch LV 7
<Status Appraisal Failed>
Bagragratch LV 4
<Status Appraisal Failed>
SO THESE GUYS TRAVEL IN PACKS!?
ONE OF THEM WAS BAD ENOUGH!! I DEFINITELY CAN'T BEAT ALL THESE!!
GRUUUUH!
GRUUUUH!
Proficiency has reached the required level. Skill [Appraisal LV 6] has become [Appraisal LV 7].
PON (POP)

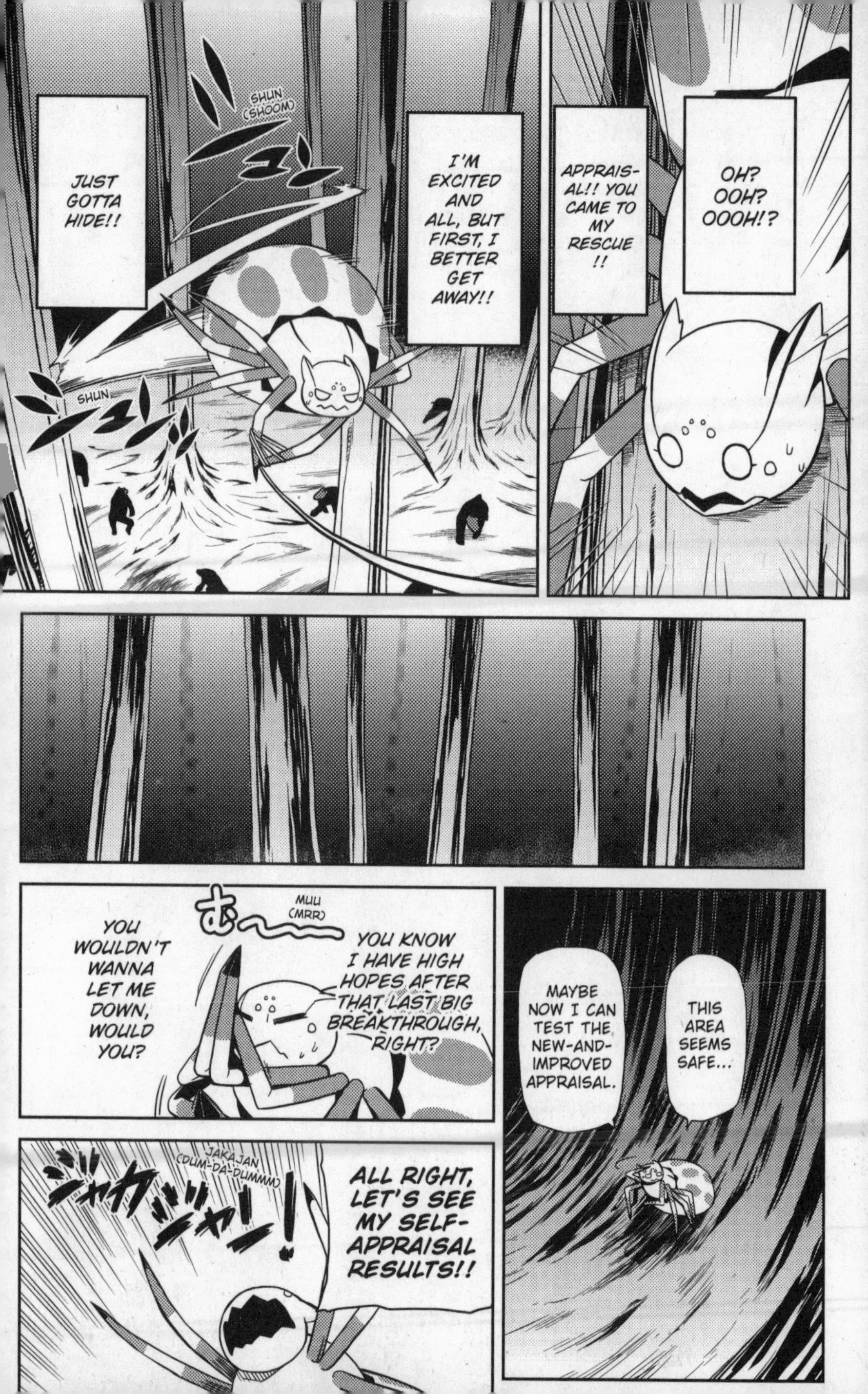

OH? OOH? OOOH!?
APPRAISAL!! YOU CAME TO MY RESCUE!!
I'M EXCITED AND ALL, BUT FIRST, I BETTER GET AWAY!!
SHUN (SHOOM)
JUST GOTTA HIDE!!
SHUN
THIS AREA SEEMS SAFE...
MAYBE NOW I CAN TEST THE NEW-AND-IMPROVED APPRAISAL.
MUU (MRR)
YOU KNOW I HAVE HIGH HOPES AFTER THAT LAST BIG BREAKTHROUGH, RIGHT?
YOU WOULDN'T WANNA LET ME DOWN, WOULD YOU?
ALL RIGHT, LET'S SEE MY SELF-APPRAISAL RESULTS!!
JAKAJAN (DUM-DA-DUMMM)

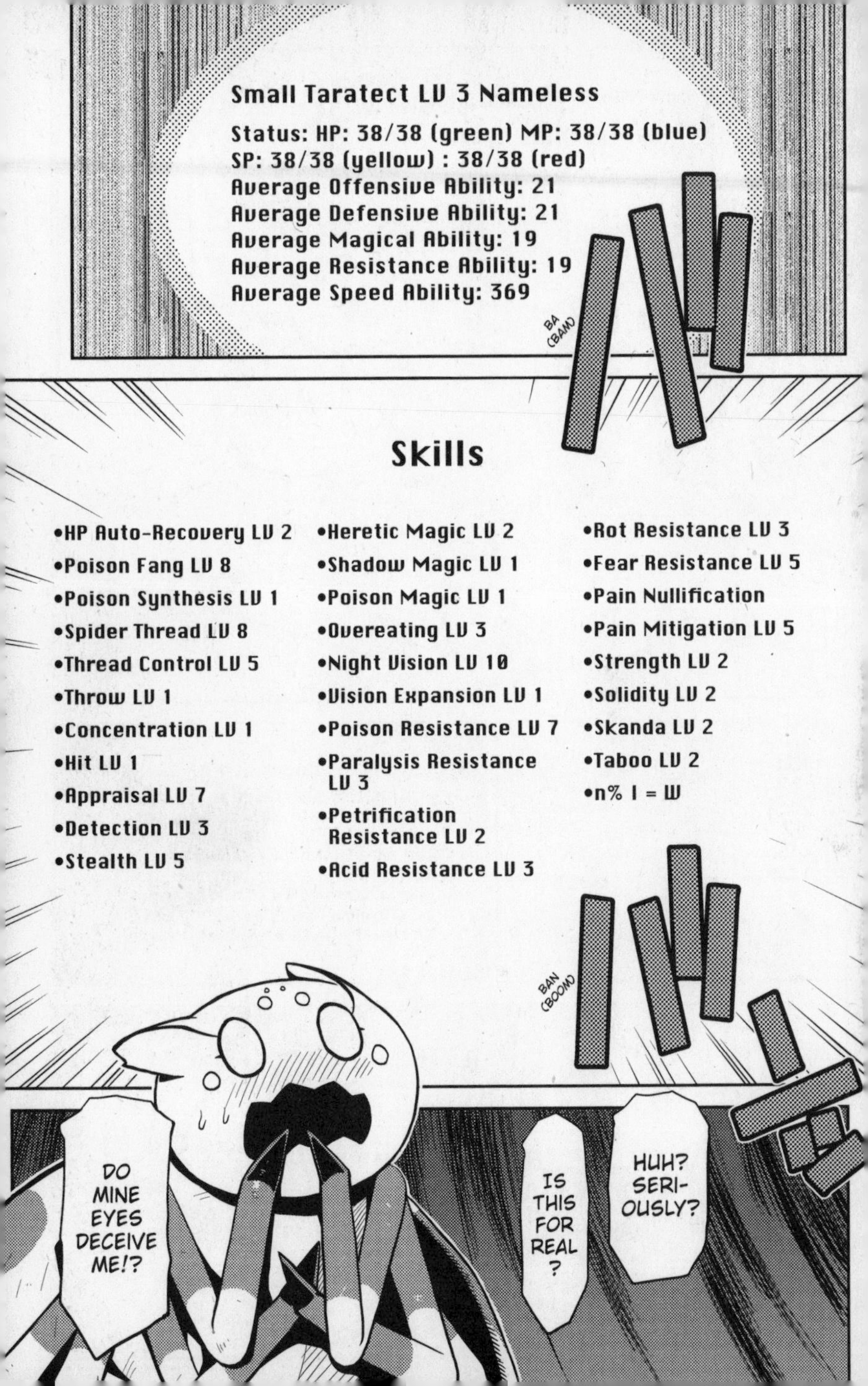
Small Taratect LV 3 Nameless
Status: HP: 38/38 (green) MP: 38/38 (blue)
SP: 38/38 (yellow) : 38/38 (red)
Average Offensive Ability: 21
Average Defensive Ability: 21
Average Magical Ability: 19
Average Resistance Ability: 19
Average Speed Ability: 369
BA (BAM)
Skills
•HP Auto-Recovery LV 2
•Poison Fang LV 8
•Poison Synthesis LV 1
•Spider Thread LV 8
•Thread Control LV 5
•Throw LV 1
•Concentration LV 1
•Hit LV 1
•Appraisal LV 7
•Detection LV 3
•Stealth LV 5
•Heretic Magic LV 2
•Shadow Magic LV 1
•Poison Magic LV 1
•Overeating LV 3
•Night Vision LV 10
•Vision Expansion LV 1
•Poison Resistance LV 7
•Paralysis Resistance LV 3
•Petrification Resistance LV 2
•Acid Resistance LV 3
•Rot Resistance LV 3
•Fear Resistance LV 5
•Pain Nullification
•Pain Mitigation LV 5
•Strength LV 2
•Solidity LV 2
•Skanda LV 2
•Taboo LV 2
•n% I = W
BAN (BOOM)
HUH? SERIOUSLY?
IS THIS FOR REAL?
DO MINE EYES DECEIVE ME!?

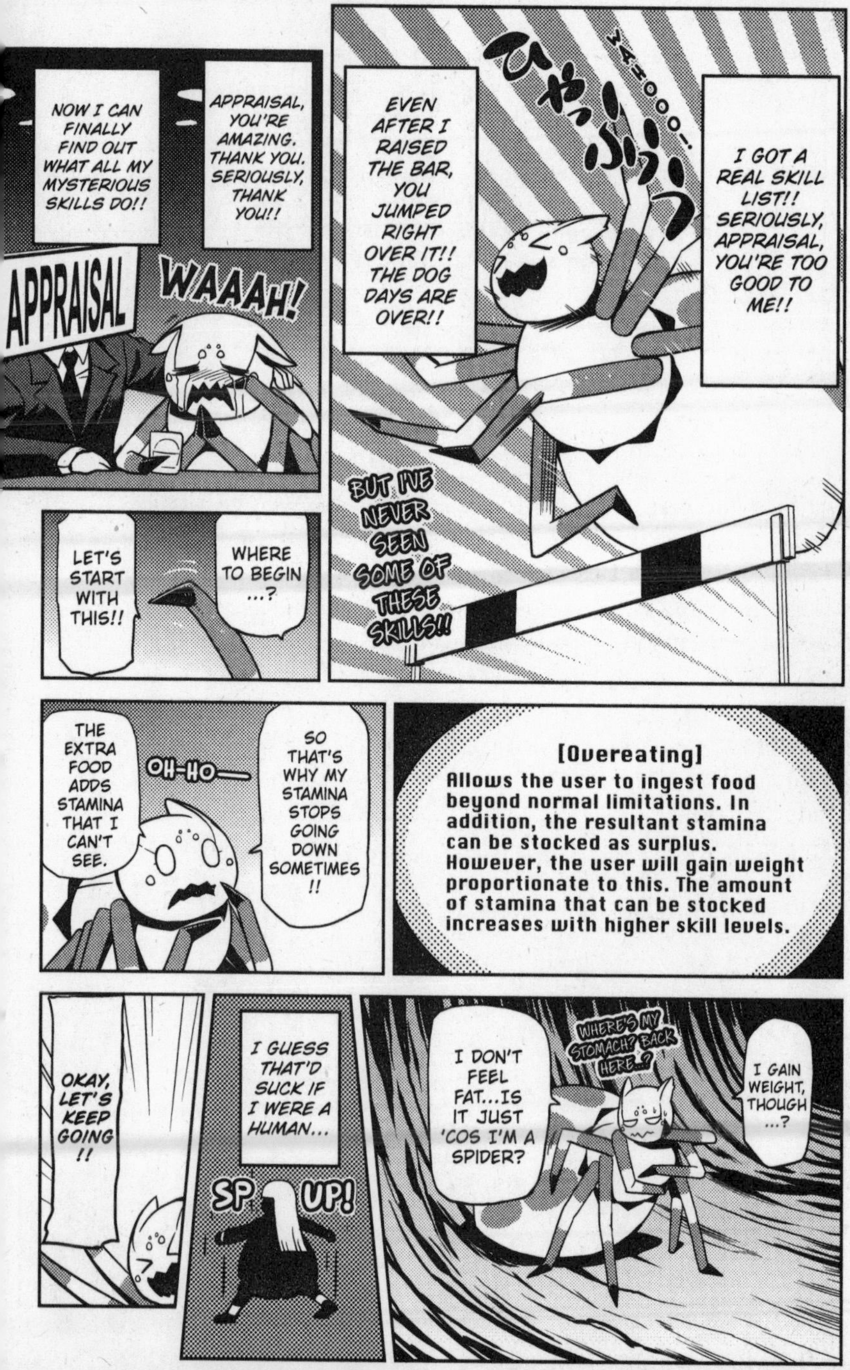
I GOT A REAL SKILL LIST!! SERIOUSLY, APPRAISAL, YOU'RE TOO GOOD TO ME!!
ひゃっふぅぅ
WAHOOOO!
EVEN AFTER I RAISED THE BAR, YOU JUMPED RIGHT OVER IT!! THE DOG DAYS ARE OVER!!
BUT I'VE NEVER SEEN SOME OF THESE SKILLS!!
APPRAISAL, YOU'RE AMAZING. THANK YOU. SERIOUSLY, THANK YOU!!
NOW I CAN FINALLY FIND OUT WHAT ALL MY MYSTERIOUS SKILLS DO!!
WAAAH!
APPRAISAL
WHERE TO BEGIN ...?
LET'S START WITH THIS!!
[Overeating]
Allows the user to ingest food beyond normal limitations. In addition, the resultant stamina can be stocked as surplus. However, the user will gain weight proportionate to this. The amount of stamina that can be stocked increases with higher skill levels.
SO THAT'S WHY MY STAMINA STOPS GOING DOWN SOMETIMES!!
OH-HO—
THE EXTRA FOOD ADDS STAMINA THAT I CAN'T SEE.
I GAIN WEIGHT, THOUGH...?
WHERE'S MY STOMACH? BACK HERE...?
I DON'T FEEL FAT...IS IT JUST 'COS I'M A SPIDER?
I GUESS THAT'D SUCK IF I WERE A HUMAN...
SP UP!
OKAY, LET'S KEEP GOING!!

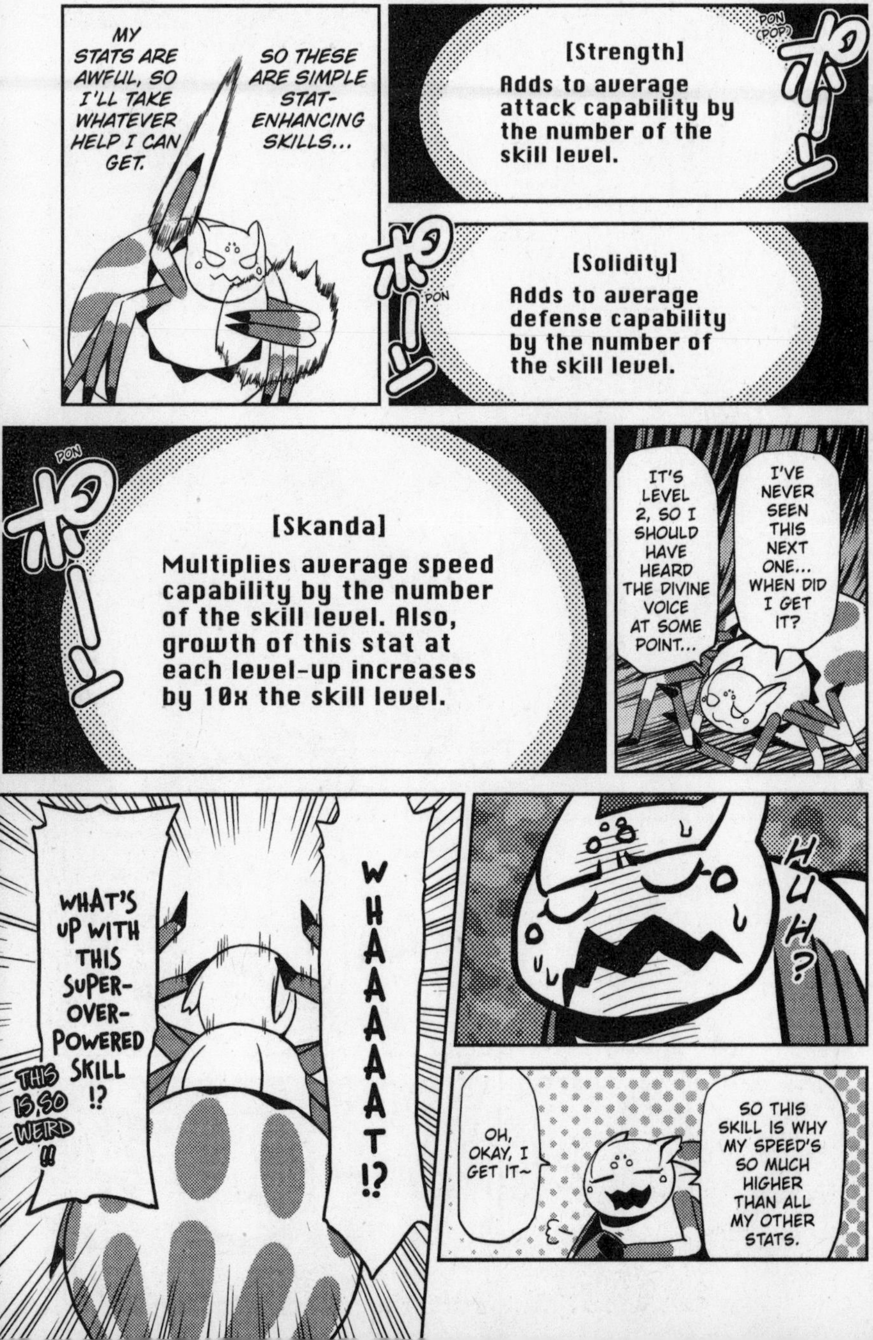
PON (POP)
[Strength]
Adds to average attack capability by the number of the skill level.
PON
[Solidity]
Adds to average defense capability by the number of the skill level.
SO THESE ARE SIMPLE STAT-ENHANCING SKILLS...
MY STATS ARE AWFUL, SO I'LL TAKE WHATEVER HELP I CAN GET.
I'VE NEVER SEEN THIS NEXT ONE... WHEN DID I GET IT?
IT'S LEVEL 2, SO I SHOULD HAVE HEARD THE DIVINE VOICE AT SOME POINT...
PON
[Skanda]
Multiplies average speed capability by the number of the skill level. Also, growth of this stat at each level-up increases by 10x the skill level.
HUH?
SO THIS SKILL IS WHY MY SPEED'S SO MUCH HIGHER THAN ALL MY OTHER STATS.
OH, OKAY, I GET IT~
WHAAAAAAT!?
WHAT'S UP WITH THIS SUPER-OVER-POWERED SKILL!?
THIS IS SO WEIRD!!

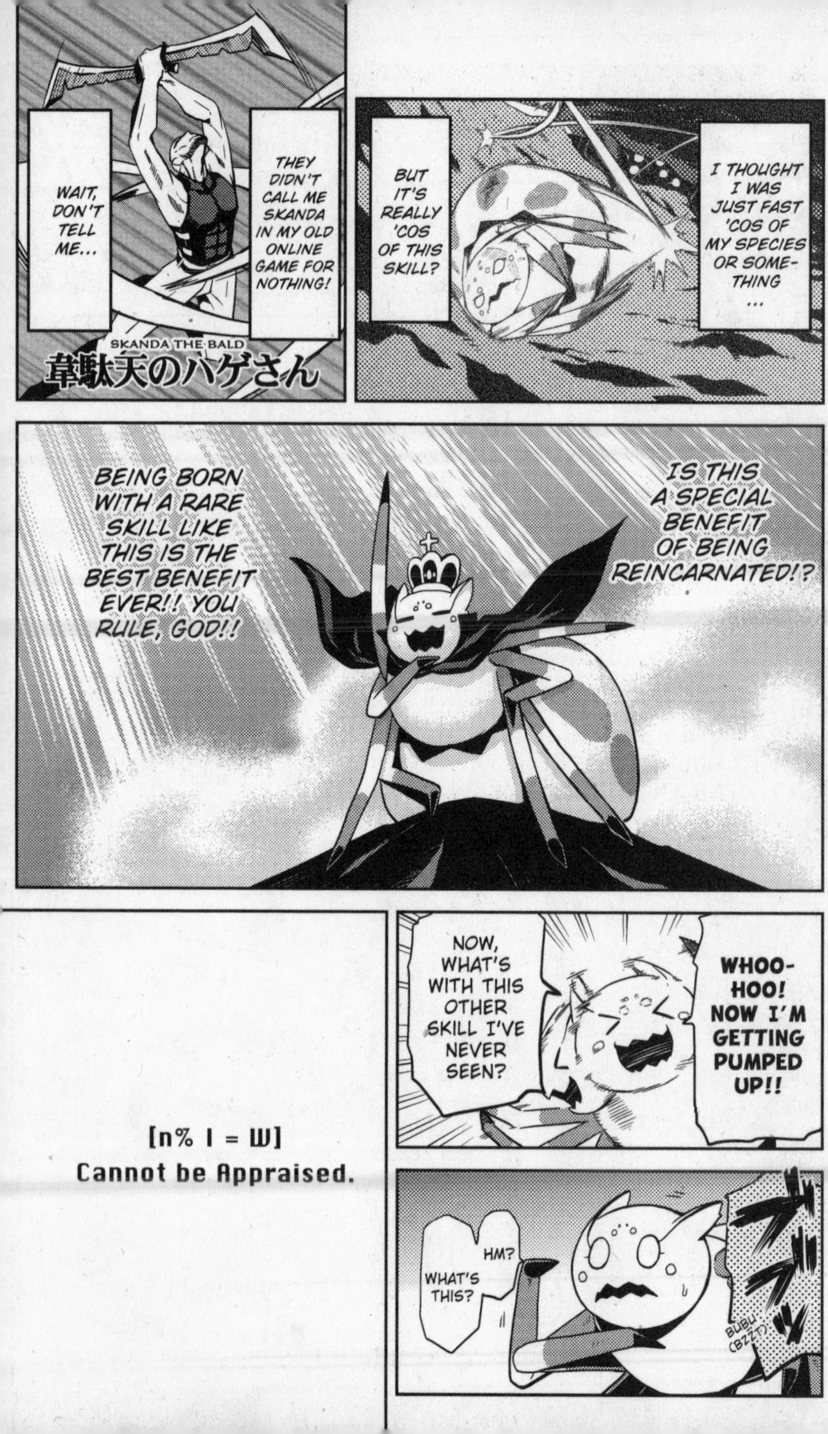
I THOUGHT I WAS JUST FAST 'COS OF MY SPECIES OR SOME-THING...
BUT IT'S REALLY 'COS OF THIS SKILL?
THEY DIDN'T CALL ME SKANDA IN MY OLD ONLINE GAME FOR NOTHING!
WAIT, DON'T TELL ME...
SKANDA THE BALD
韋駄天のハゲさん
IS THIS A SPECIAL BENEFIT OF BEING REINCARNATED!?
BEING BORN WITH A RARE SKILL LIKE THIS IS THE BEST BENEFIT EVER!! YOU RULE, GOD!!
WHOO-HOO! NOW I'M GETTING PUMPED UP!!
NOW, WHAT'S WITH THIS OTHER SKILL I'VE NEVER SEEN?
BUBU (BZZT)
HM?
WHAT'S THIS?
[n% I = W]
Cannot be Appraised.

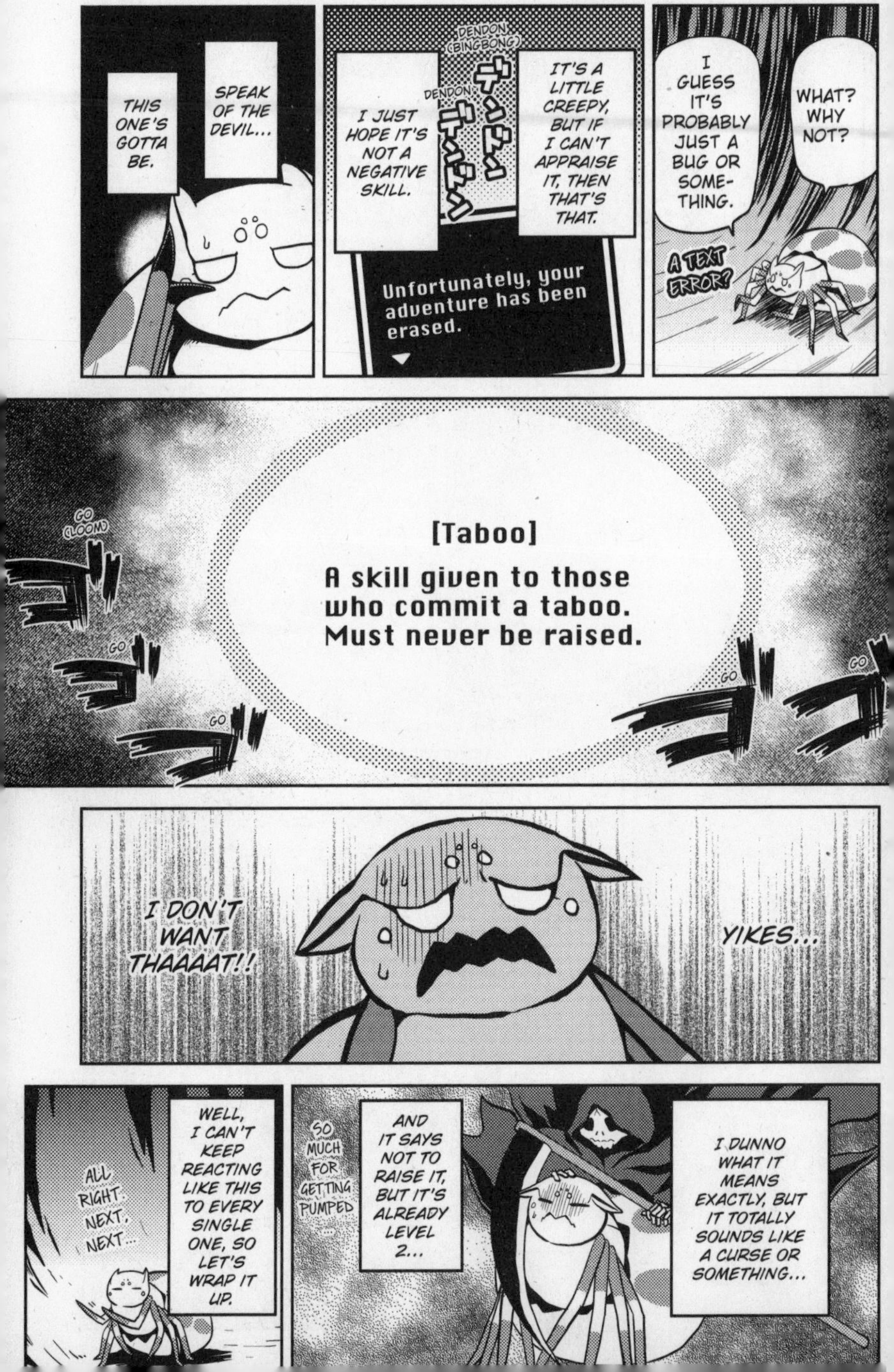
WHAT? WHY NOT?
I GUESS IT'S PROBABLY JUST A BUG OR SOME-THING.
A TEXT ERROR?
IT'S A LITTLE CREEPY, BUT IF I CAN'T APPRAISE IT, THEN THAT'S THAT.
DENDON (BINGBONG)
DENDON
I JUST HOPE IT'S NOT A NEGATIVE SKILL.
Unfortunately, your adventure has been erased.
SPEAK OF THE DEVIL...
THIS ONE'S GOTTA BE.
GO
GO
[Taboo]
A skill given to those who commit a taboo. Must never be raised.
GO (LOOM)
GO
GO
YIKES...
I DON'T WANT THAAAAT!!
I DUNNO WHAT IT MEANS EXACTLY, BUT IT TOTALLY SOUNDS LIKE A CURSE OR SOMETHING...
AND IT SAYS NOT TO RAISE IT, BUT IT'S ALREADY LEVEL 2...
SO MUCH FOR GETTING PUMPED...
WELL, I CAN'T KEEP REACTING LIKE THIS TO EVERY SINGLE ONE, SO LET'S WRAP IT UP.
ALL RIGHT. NEXT, NEXT...

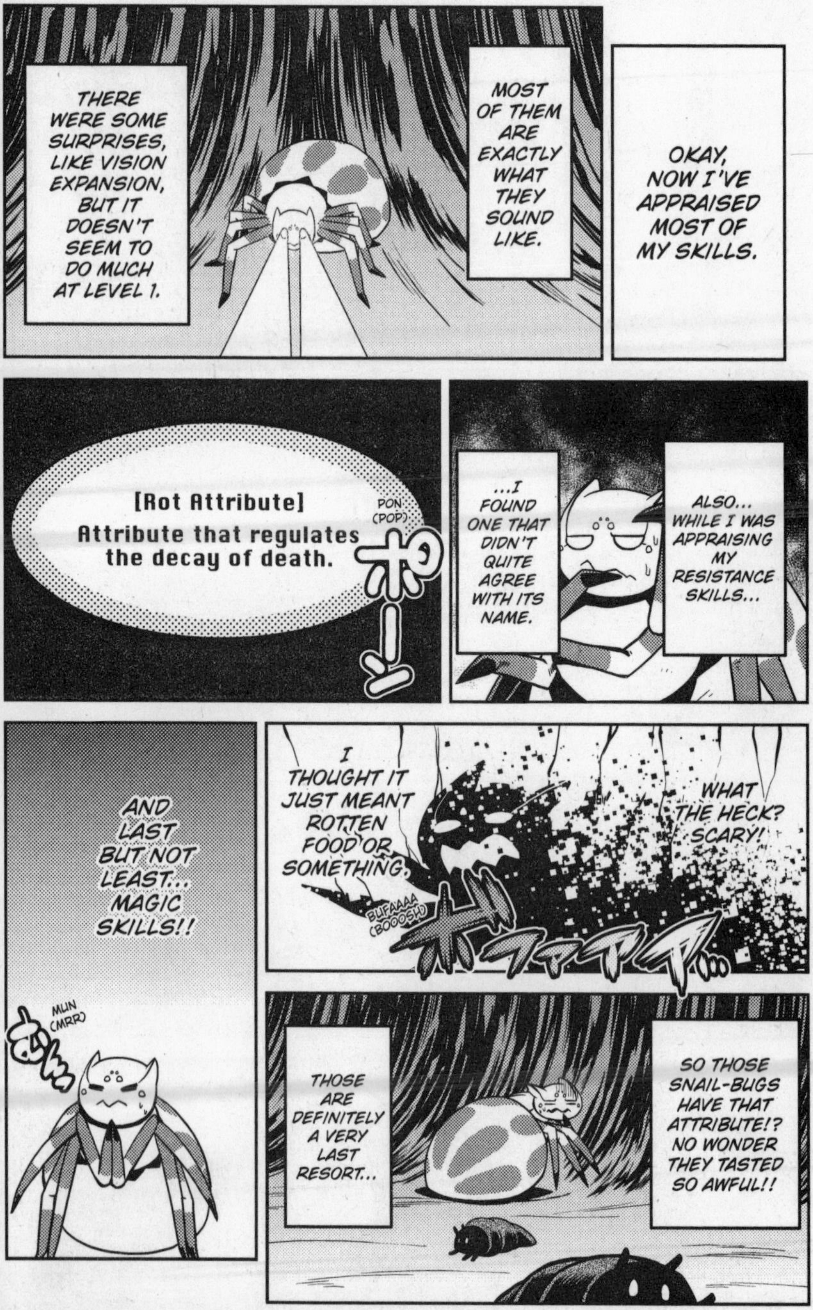
OKAY, NOW I'VE APPRAISED MOST OF MY SKILLS.
MOST OF THEM ARE EXACTLY WHAT THEY SOUND LIKE.
THERE WERE SOME SURPRISES, LIKE VISION EXPANSION, BUT IT DOESN'T SEEM TO DO MUCH AT LEVEL 1.
ALSO... WHILE I WAS APPRAISING MY RESISTANCE SKILLS...
...I FOUND ONE THAT DIDN'T QUITE AGREE WITH ITS NAME.
PON (POP)
[Rot Attribute]
Attribute that regulates the decay of death.
WHAT THE HECK? SCARY!
I THOUGHT IT JUST MEANT ROTTEN FOOD OR SOMETHING.
BUFAAAA (BOOOSH)
SO THOSE SNAIL-BUGS HAVE THAT ATTRIBUTE!? NO WONDER THEY TASTED SO AWFUL!!
THOSE ARE DEFINITELY A VERY LAST RESORT...
AND LAST BUT NOT LEAST... MAGIC SKILLS!!
MUN (MRR)

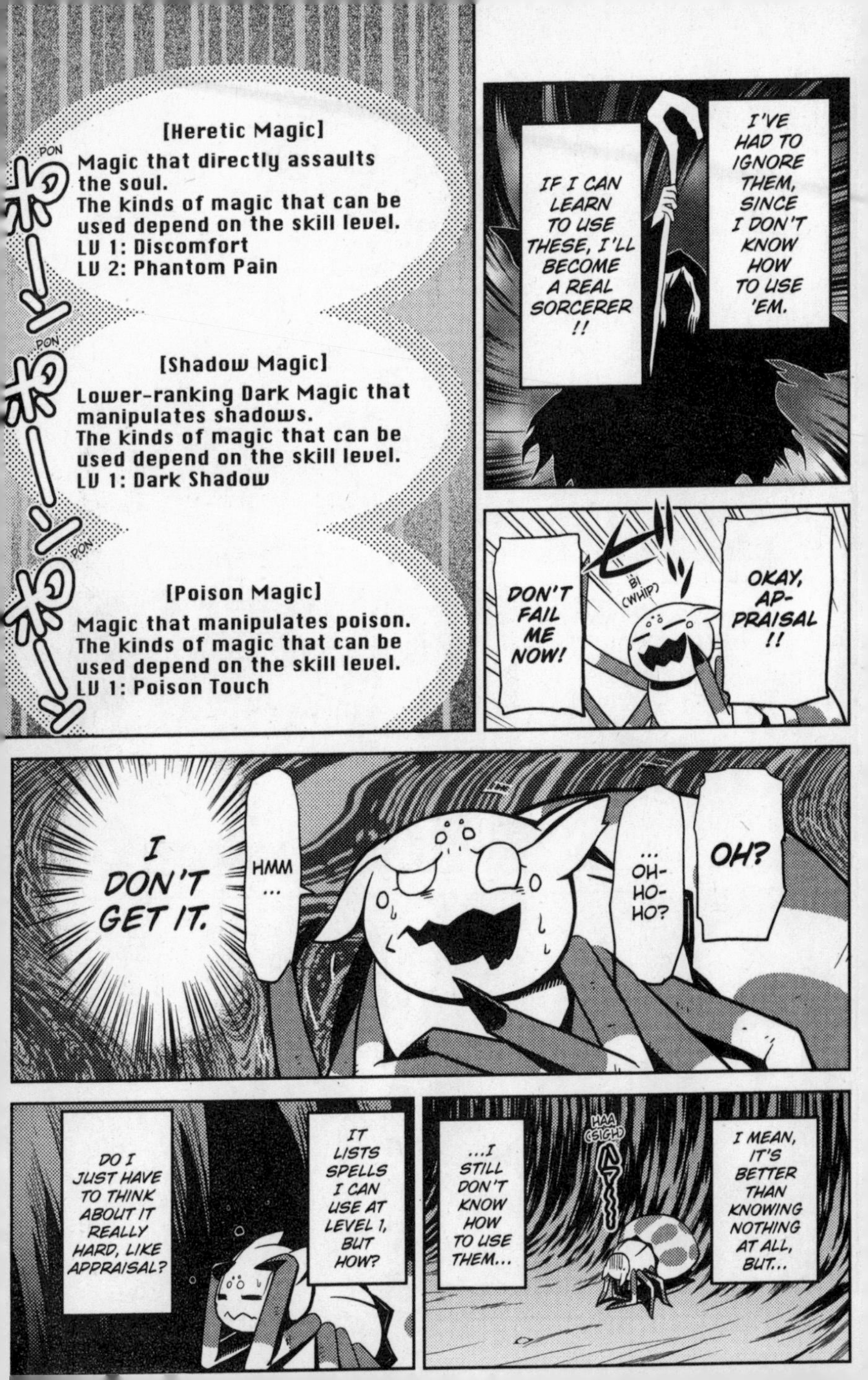
I'VE HAD TO IGNORE THEM, SINCE I DON'T KNOW HOW TO USE 'EM.
IF I CAN LEARN TO USE THESE, I'LL BECOME A REAL SORCERER!!
OKAY, AP-PRAISAL!!
BI (WHIP)
DON'T FAIL ME NOW!
[Heretic Magic]
Magic that directly assaults the soul.
The kinds of magic that can be used depend on the skill level.
LV 1: Discomfort
LV 2: Phantom Pain
PON
[Shadow Magic]
Lower-ranking Dark Magic that manipulates shadows.
The kinds of magic that can be used depend on the skill level.
LV 1: Dark Shadow
PON
[Poison Magic]
Magic that manipulates poison.
The kinds of magic that can be used depend on the skill level.
LV 1: Poison Touch
PON
OH?
...OH-HO-HO?
HMM...
I DON'T GET IT.
I MEAN, IT'S BETTER THAN KNOWING NOTHING AT ALL, BUT...
HAA (SIGH)
...I STILL DON'T KNOW HOW TO USE THEM...
IT LISTS SPELLS I CAN USE AT LEVEL 1, BUT HOW?
DO I JUST HAVE TO THINK ABOUT IT REALLY HARD, LIKE APPRAISAL?

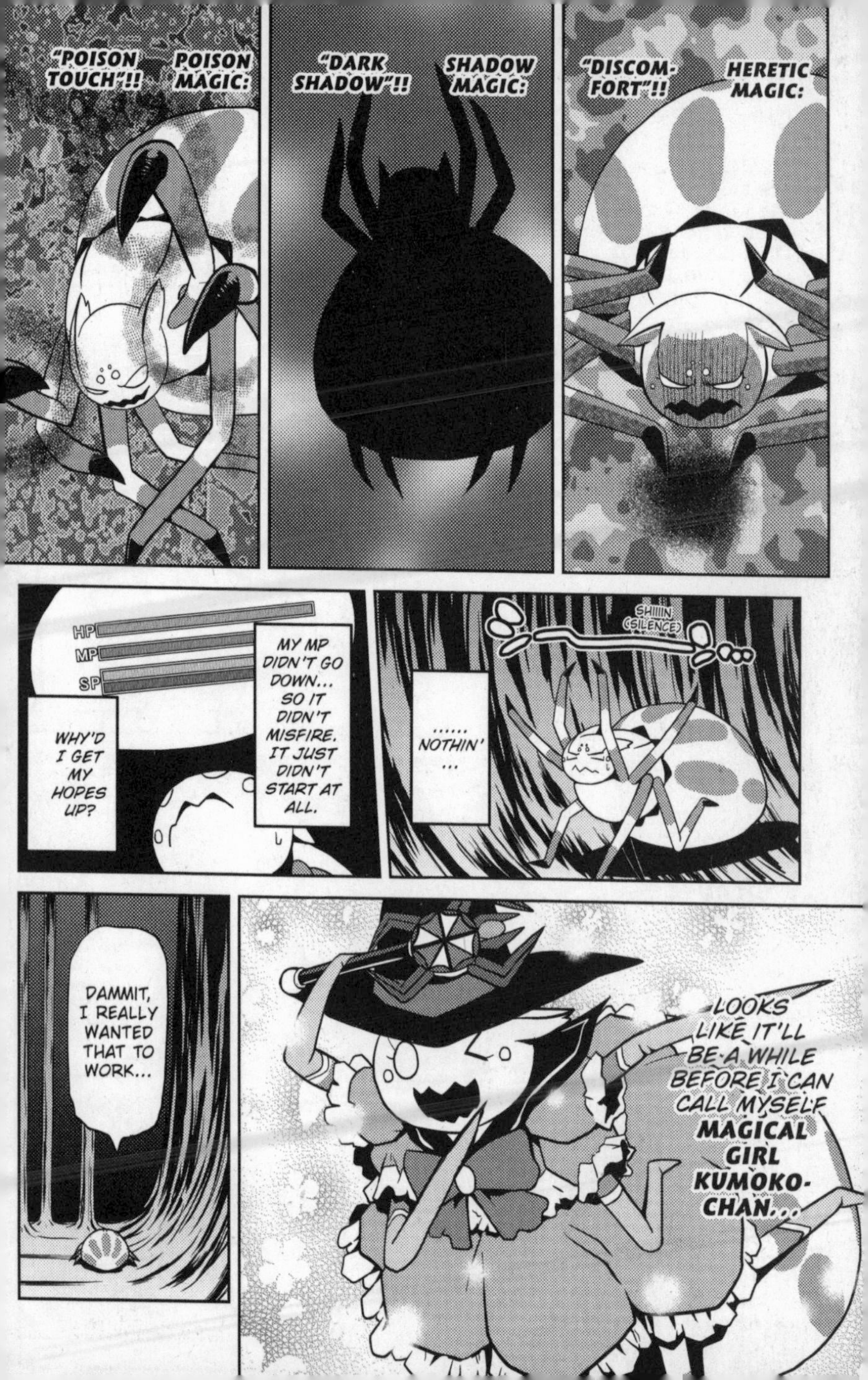
HERETIC MAGIC:
"DISCOM-FORT"!!
SHADOW MAGIC:
"DARK SHADOW"!!
POISON MAGIC:
"POISON TOUCH"!!
SHIIIN (SILENCE)
...... NOTHIN' ...
HP
MP
SP
MY MP DIDN'T GO DOWN... SO IT DIDN'T MISFIRE. IT JUST DIDN'T START AT ALL.
WHY'D I GET MY HOPES UP?
LOOKS LIKE IT'LL BE A WHILE BEFORE I CAN CALL MYSELF MAGICAL GIRL KUMOKO-CHAN...
DAMMIT, I REALLY WANTED THAT TO WORK...

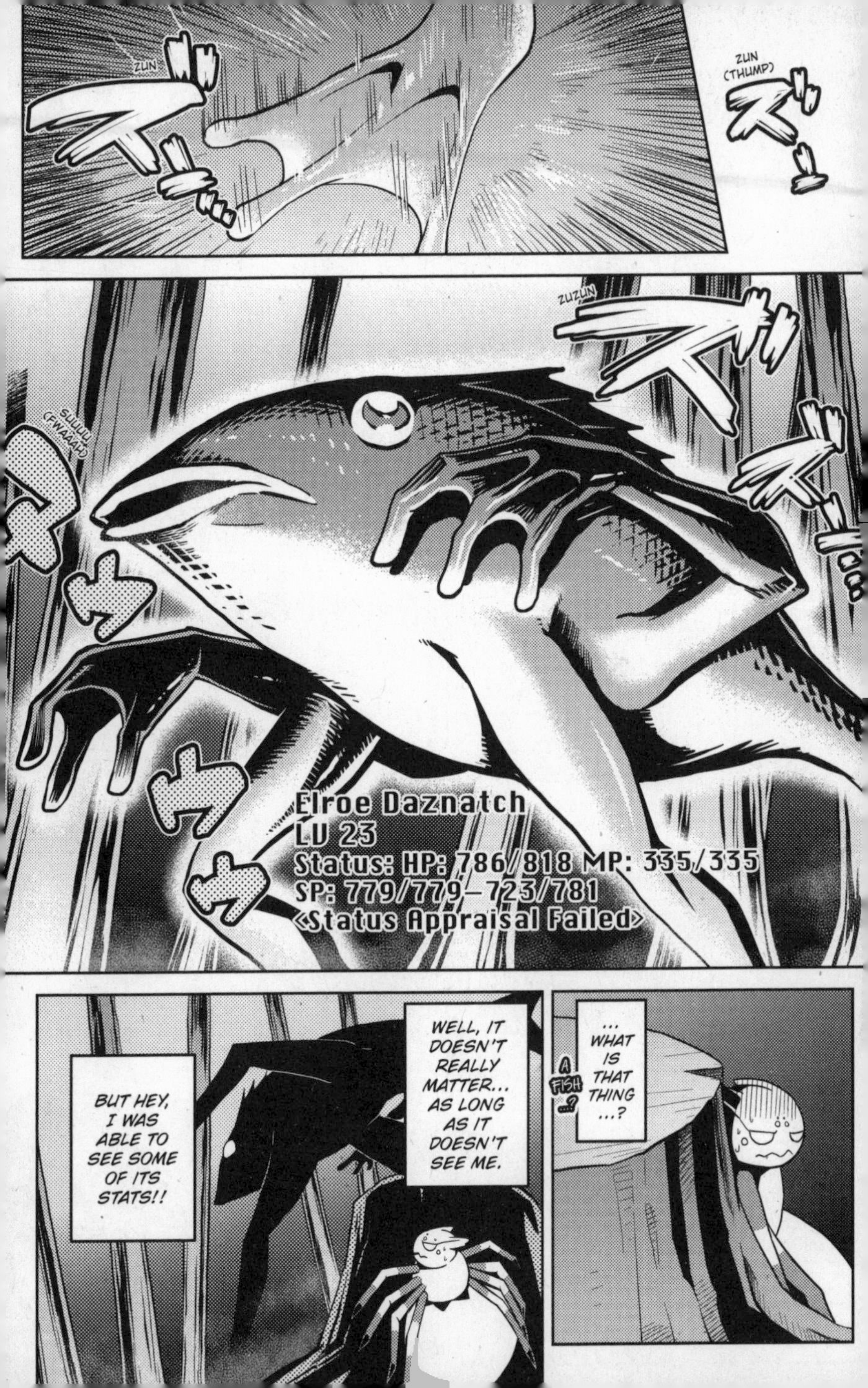
ZUN (THUMP)
ZUN
ZUZUN
SUUUU (FWAAAH)
Elroe Daznatch
LV 23
Status: HP: 786/818 MP: 335/335
SP: 779/779 723/781
«Status Appraisal Failed»
... WHAT IS THAT THING ...?
A FISH ...?
WELL, IT DOESN'T REALLY MATTER... AS LONG AS IT DOESN'T SEE ME.
BUT HEY, I WAS ABLE TO SEE SOME OF ITS STATS!!

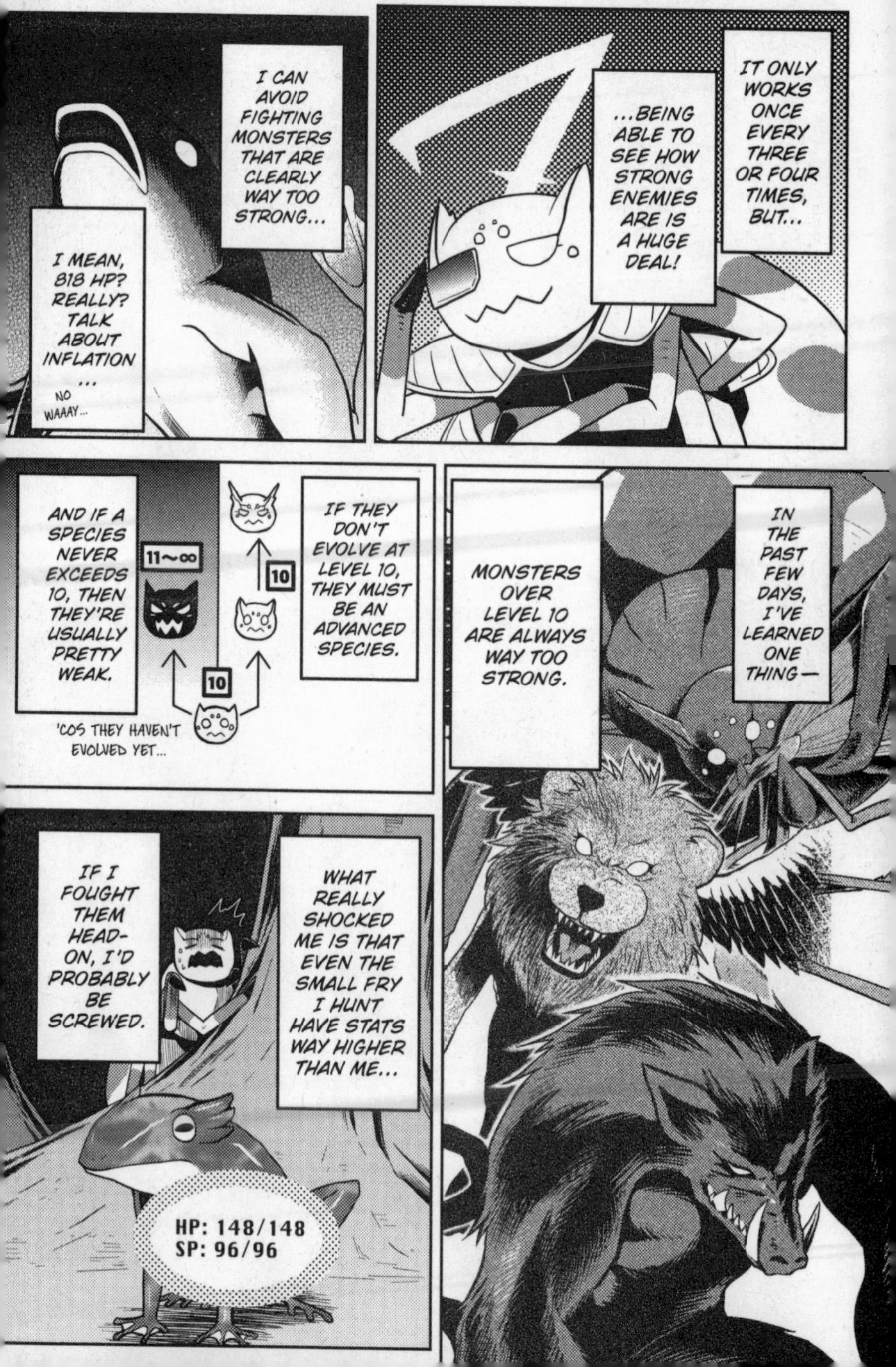
IT ONLY WORKS ONCE EVERY THREE OR FOUR TIMES, BUT...
...BEING ABLE TO SEE HOW STRONG ENEMIES ARE IS A HUGE DEAL!
I CAN AVOID FIGHTING MONSTERS THAT ARE CLEARLY WAY TOO STRONG...
I MEAN, 818 HP? REALLY? TALK ABOUT INFLATION...
NO WAAAY...
IN THE PAST FEW DAYS, I'VE LEARNED ONE THING—
MONSTERS OVER LEVEL 10 ARE ALWAYS WAY TOO STRONG.
IF THEY DON'T EVOLVE AT LEVEL 10, THEY MUST BE AN ADVANCED SPECIES.
10
10
11~∞
AND IF A SPECIES NEVER EXCEEDS 10, THEN THEY'RE USUALLY PRETTY WEAK.
'COS THEY HAVEN'T EVOLVED YET...
WHAT REALLY SHOCKED ME IS THAT EVEN THE SMALL FRY I HUNT HAVE STATS WAY HIGHER THAN ME...
IF I FOUGHT THEM HEAD-ON, I'D PROBABLY BE SCREWED.
HP: 148/148
SP: 96/96

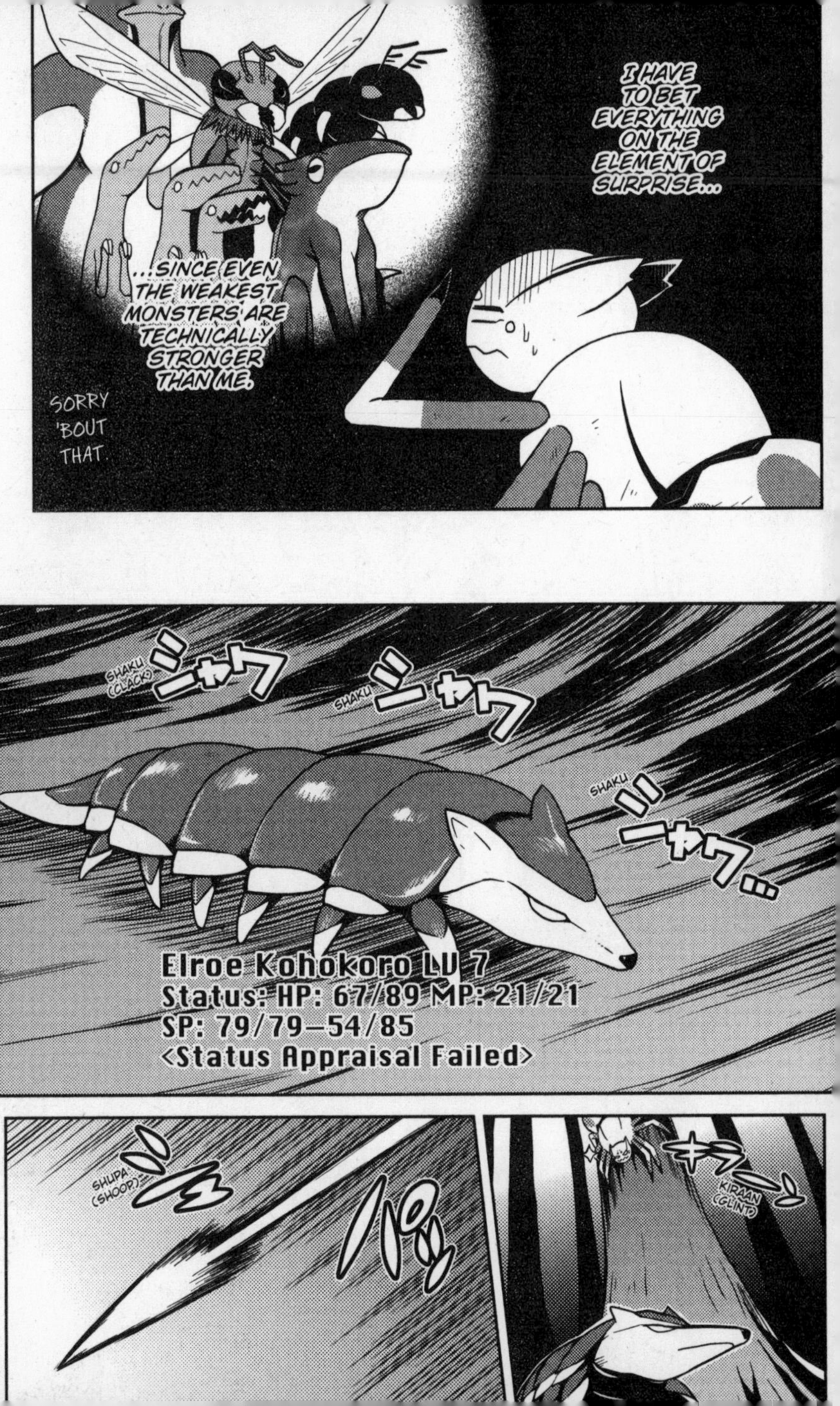
I HAVE TO BET EVERYTHING ON THE ELEMENT OF SURPRISE...
...SINCE EVEN THE WEAKEST MONSTERS ARE TECHNICALLY STRONGER THAN ME.
SORRY 'BOUT THAT.
SHAKU (CLACK)
SHAKU
SHAKU
Elroe Kohokoro LV 7
Status: HP: 67/89 MP: 21/21
SP: 79/79—54/85
<Status Appraisal Failed>
KIRAAN (GLINT)
SHUPA (SHOOP)

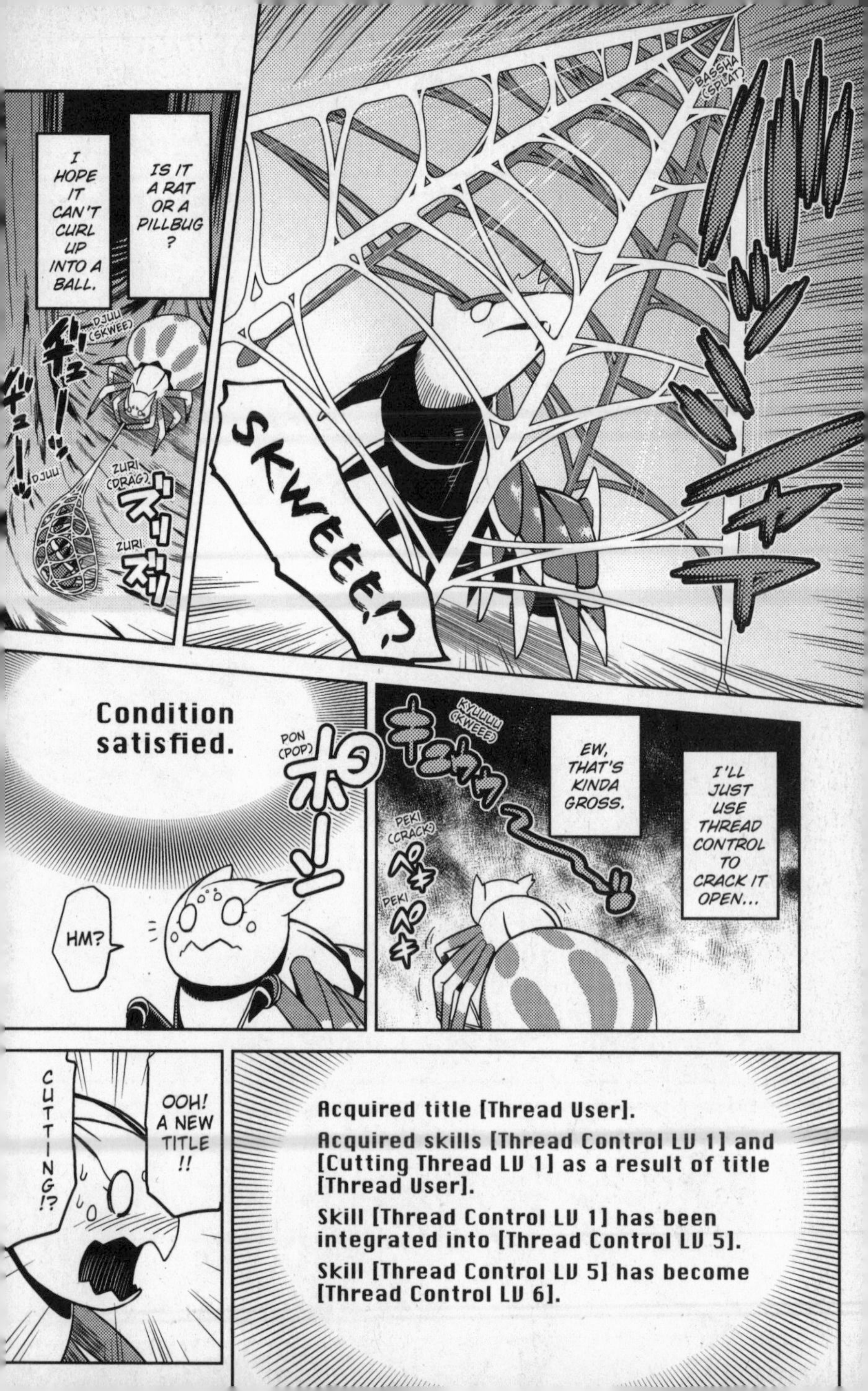
BASSHA (SPLAT)
SKWEEE!?
IS IT A RAT OR A PILLBUG?
I HOPE IT CAN'T CURL UP INTO A BALL.
DJUU (SKWEE)
DJUU
ZURI (DRAG)
ZURI
I'LL JUST USE THREAD CONTROL TO CRACK IT OPEN...
EW, THAT'S KINDA GROSS.
KYUUUU (KWEEE)
PEKI (CRACK)
PEKI
Condition satisfied.
PON (POP)
HM?
Acquired title [Thread User].
Acquired skills [Thread Control LV 1] and [Cutting Thread LV 1] as a result of title [Thread User].
Skill [Thread Control LV 1] has been integrated into [Thread Control LV 5].
Skill [Thread Control LV 5] has become [Thread Control LV 6].
OOH! A NEW TITLE!!
CUTTING!?

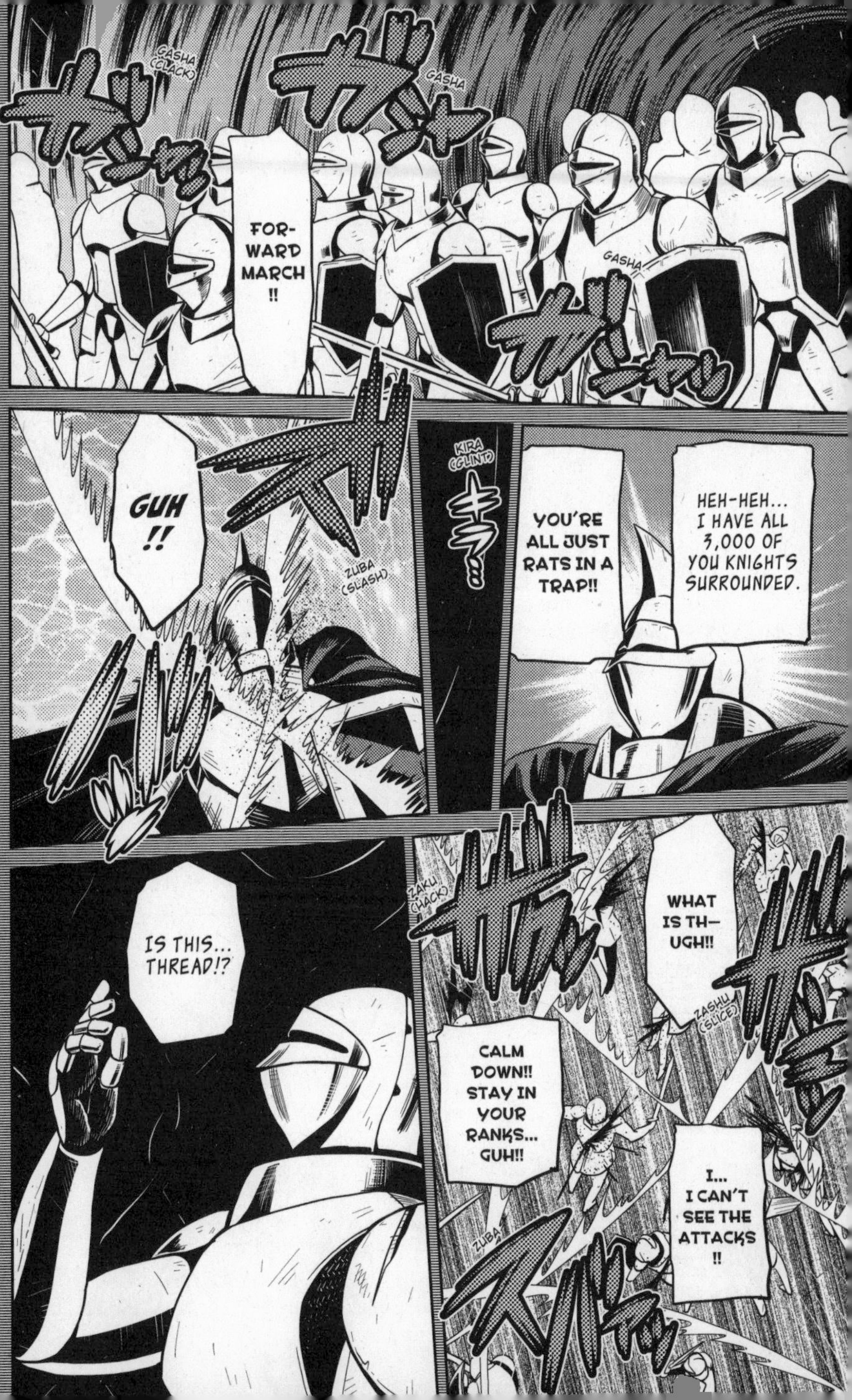
GASHA
GASHA (CLACK)
FOR-WARD MARCH !!
GASHA
HEH-HEH... I HAVE ALL 3,000 OF YOU KNIGHTS SURROUNDED.
YOU'RE ALL JUST RATS IN A TRAP!!
KIRA (GLINT)
ZUBA (SLASH)
GUH !!
WHAT IS TH— UGH!!
ZAKU (HACK)
ZASHU (SLICE)
CALM DOWN!! STAY IN YOUR RANKS... GUH!!
I... I CAN'T SEE THE ATTACKS !!
ZUBA
IS THIS... THREAD!?

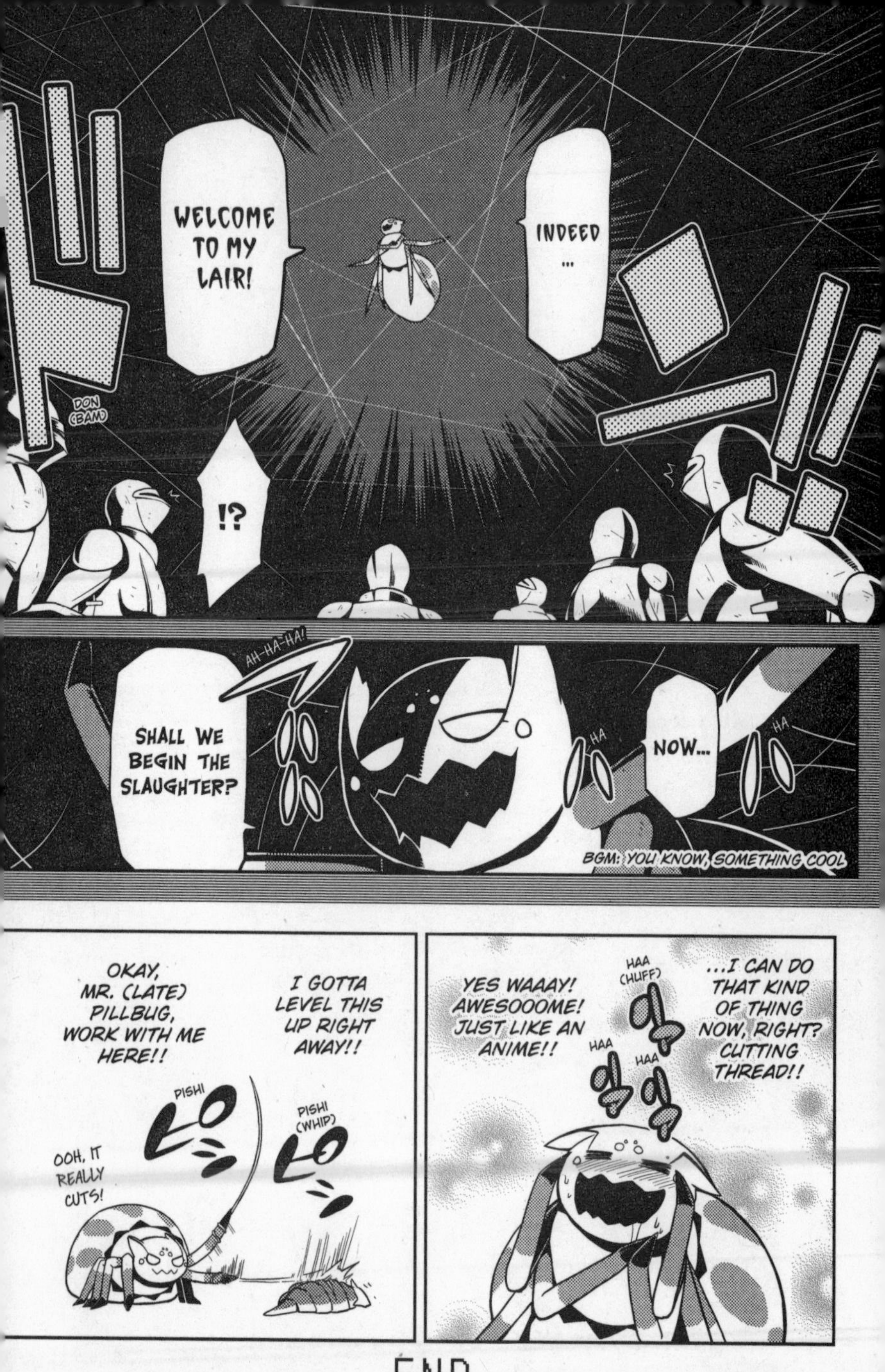
INDEED ...
WELCOME TO MY LAIR!
DON (BAM)
!?
NOW...
HA
HA
AH-HA-HA!
SHALL WE BEGIN THE SLAUGHTER?
BGM: YOU KNOW, SOMETHING COOL
...I CAN DO THAT KIND OF THING NOW, RIGHT? CUTTING THREAD!!
HAA (HUFF)
YES WAAAY! AWESOOOME! JUST LIKE AN ANIME!!
HAA
HAA
I GOTTA LEVEL THIS UP RIGHT AWAY!!
OKAY, MR. (LATE) PILLBUG, WORK WITH ME HERE!!
PISHI (WHIP)
PISHI
OOH, IT REALLY CUTS!

END

So I'm a Spider, So What?

※ WHAT'S IN A NAME? "KUMOKO" IS A SELF-REFERENTIAL NICKNAME THAT LITERALLY MEANS "SPIDER GIRL."

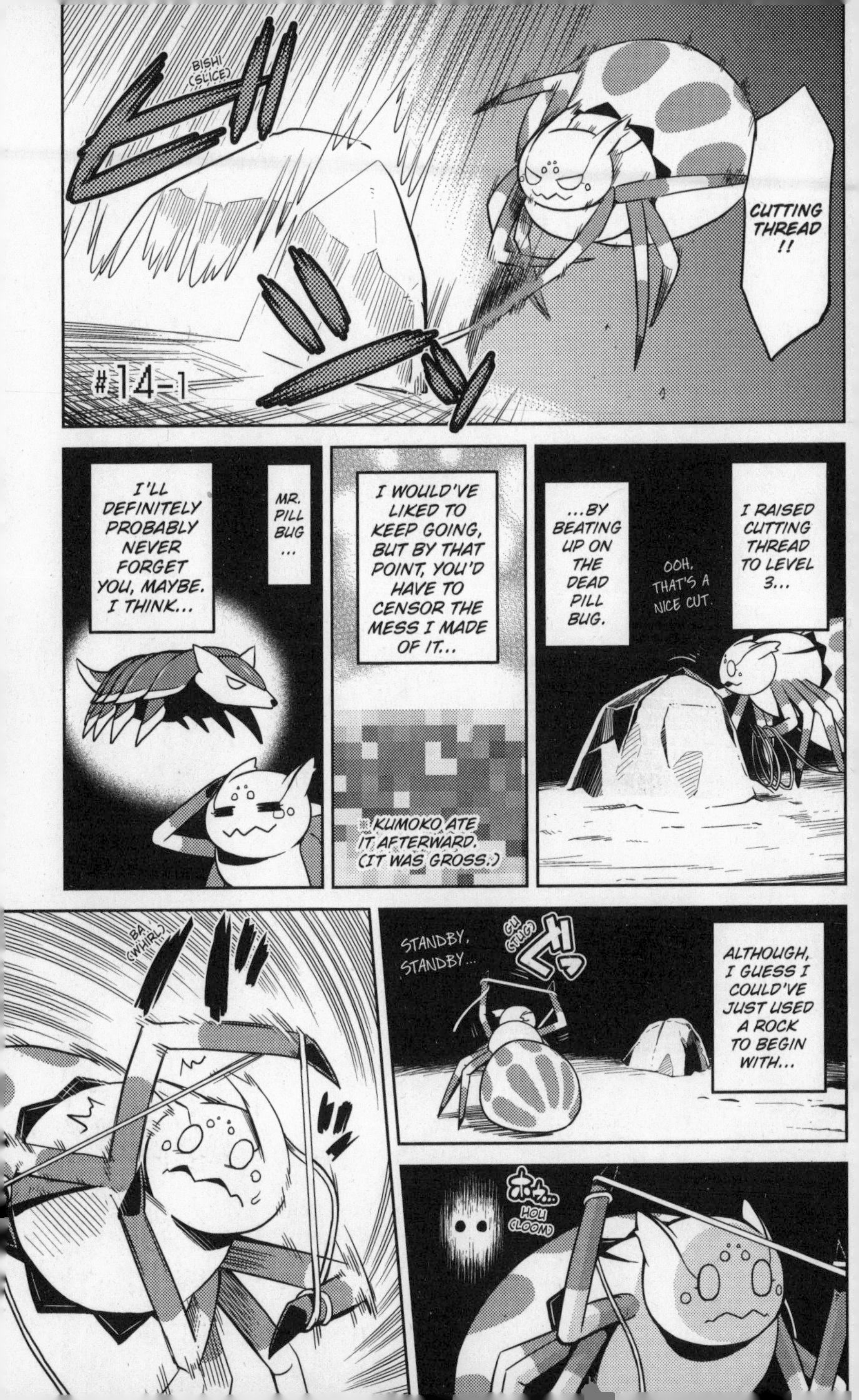
CUTTING THREAD !!
BISHI (SLICE)
#14-1
I RAISED CUTTING THREAD TO LEVEL 3...
OOH, THAT'S A NICE CUT.
...BY BEATING UP ON THE DEAD PILL BUG.
I WOULD'VE LIKED TO KEEP GOING, BUT BY THAT POINT, YOU'D HAVE TO CENSOR THE MESS I MADE OF IT...
※KUMOKO ATE IT AFTERWARD. (IT WAS GROSS.)
MR. PILL BUG...
I'LL DEFINITELY PROBABLY NEVER FORGET YOU, MAYBE. I THINK...
ALTHOUGH, I GUESS I COULD'VE JUST USED A ROCK TO BEGIN WITH...
GU (STUG)
STANDBY, STANDBY...
HOU (LOOM)
BA (WHIRL)

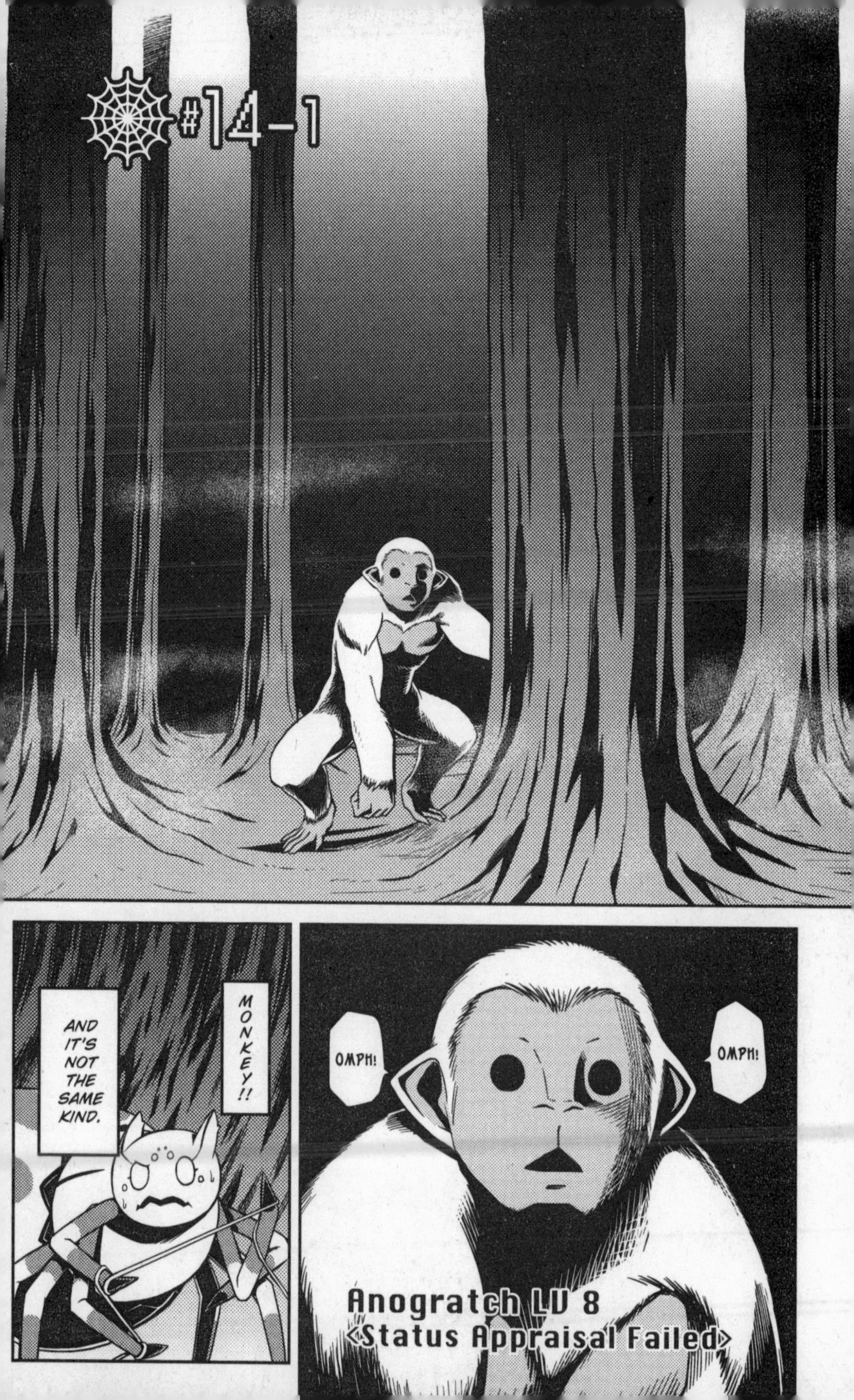
#14-1
OMPH!
OMPH!
Anogratch LV 8
〈Status Appraisal Failed〉
MONKEY!!
AND IT'S NOT THE SAME KIND.

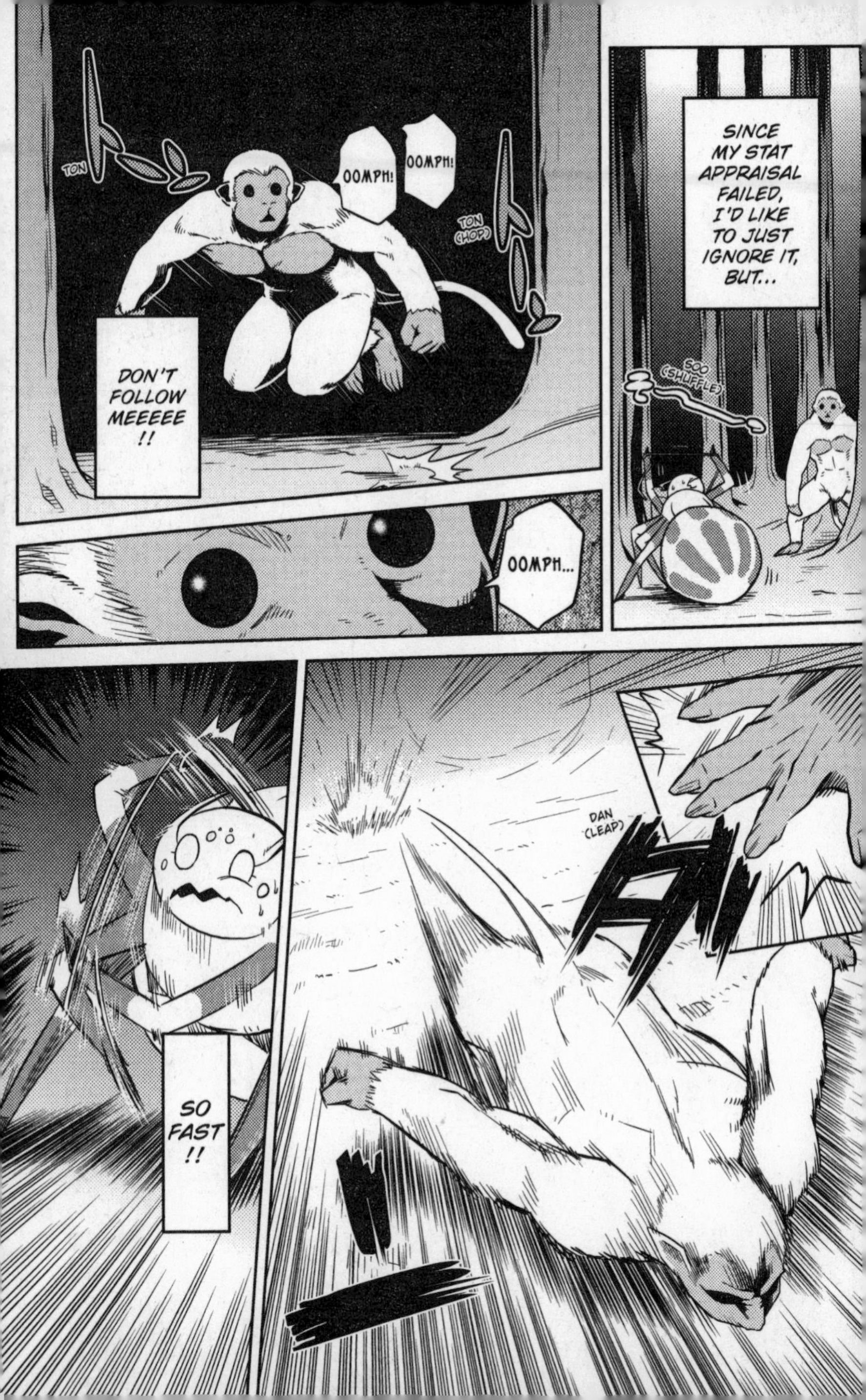

SINCE MY STAT APPRAISAL FAILED, I'D LIKE TO JUST IGNORE IT, BUT...
SOO (SHUFFLE)
TON (HOP)
OOMPH!
OOMPH!
TON
DON'T FOLLOW MEEEEE!!
OOMPH...
DAN (LEAP)
SO FAST!!

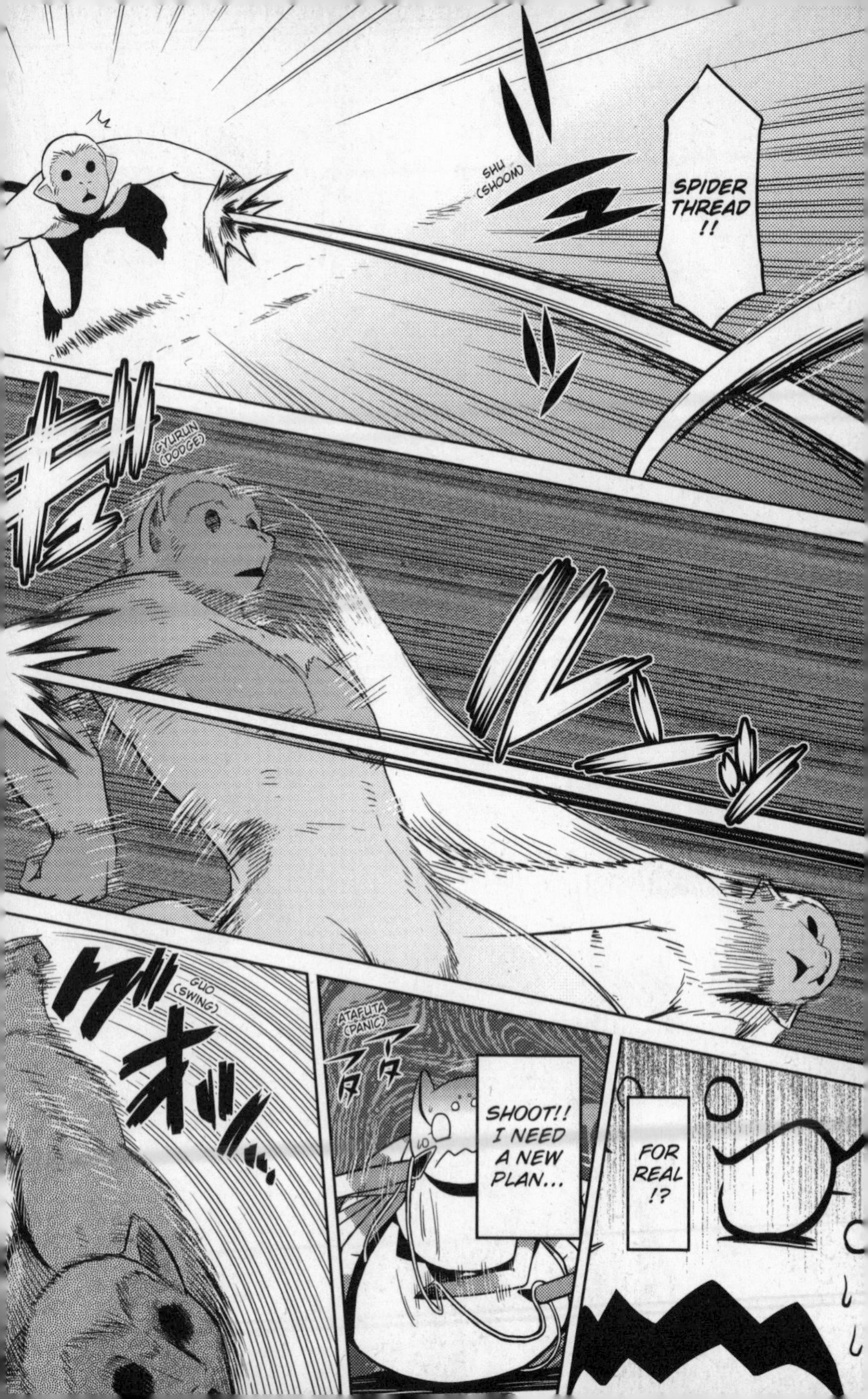
SPIDER THREAD!!
SHU (SHOOM)
GYURUN (DODGE)
FOR REAL!?
SHOOT!! I NEED A NEW PLAN...
ATAFUTA (PANIC)
GUO (SWING)

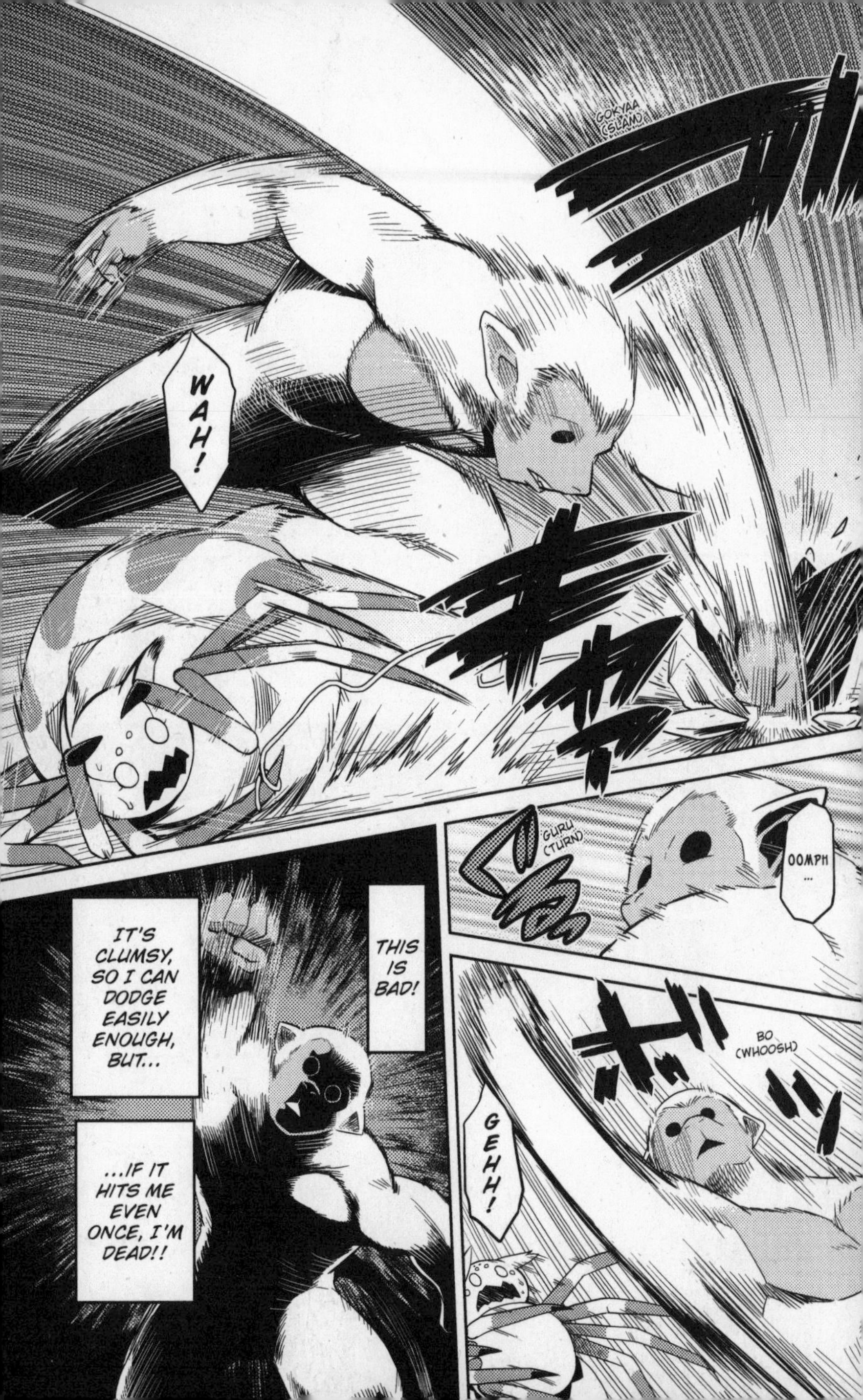
GOKYAA (SLAM)
WAH!
OOMPH ...
GURU (TURN)
BO (WHOOSH)
GEHH!
THIS IS BAD!
IT'S CLUMSY, SO I CAN DODGE EASILY ENOUGH, BUT...
...IF IT HITS ME EVEN ONCE, I'M DEAD!!

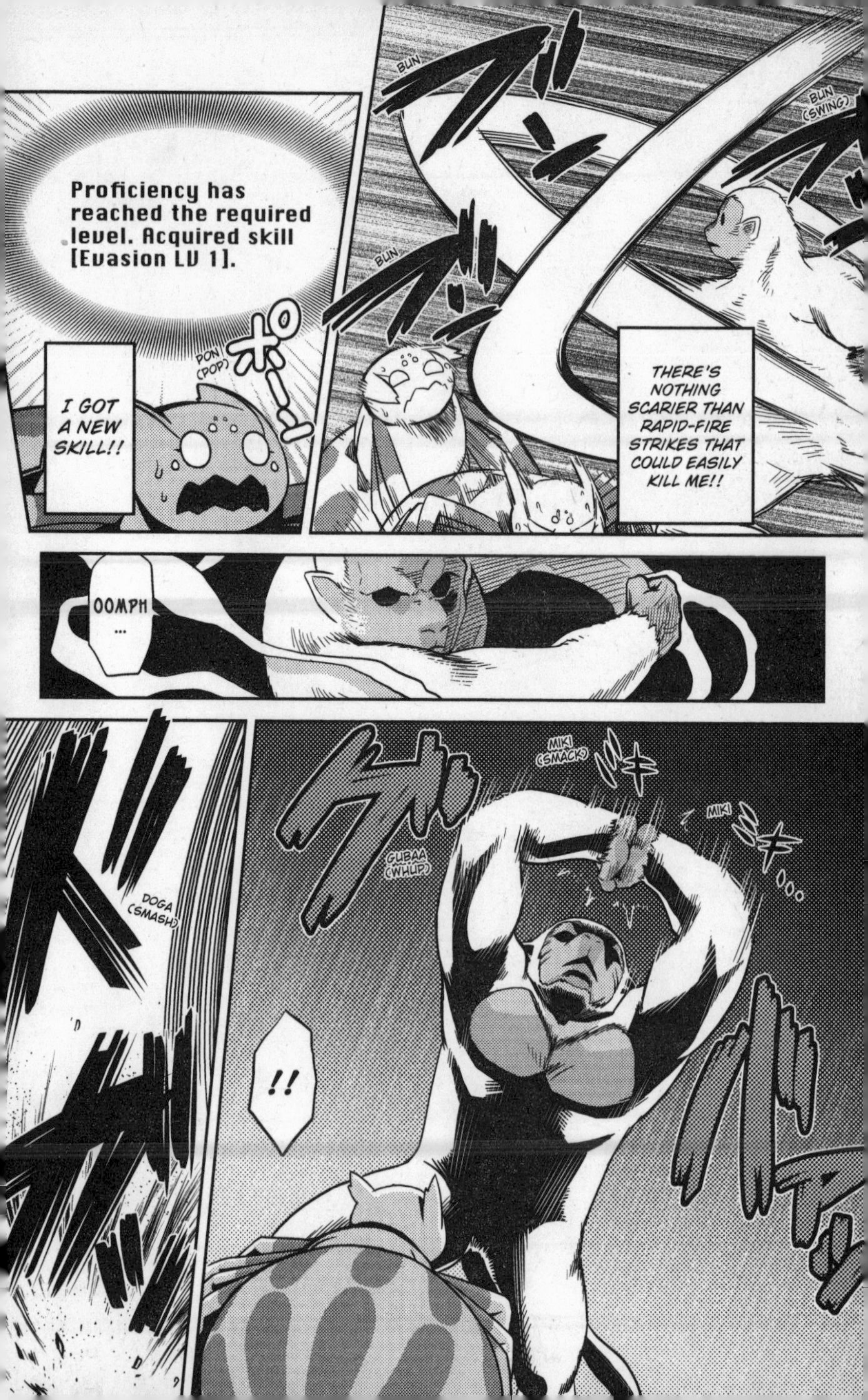
BUN
BUN (SWING)
BUN
THERE'S NOTHING SCARIER THAN RAPID-FIRE STRIKES THAT COULD EASILY KILL ME!!
Proficiency has reached the required level. Acquired skill [Evasion LV 1].
PON (POP)
I GOT A NEW SKILL!!
OOMPH ...
MIKI (SMACK)
MIKI
GUBAA (WHUP)
!!
DOGA (SMASH)

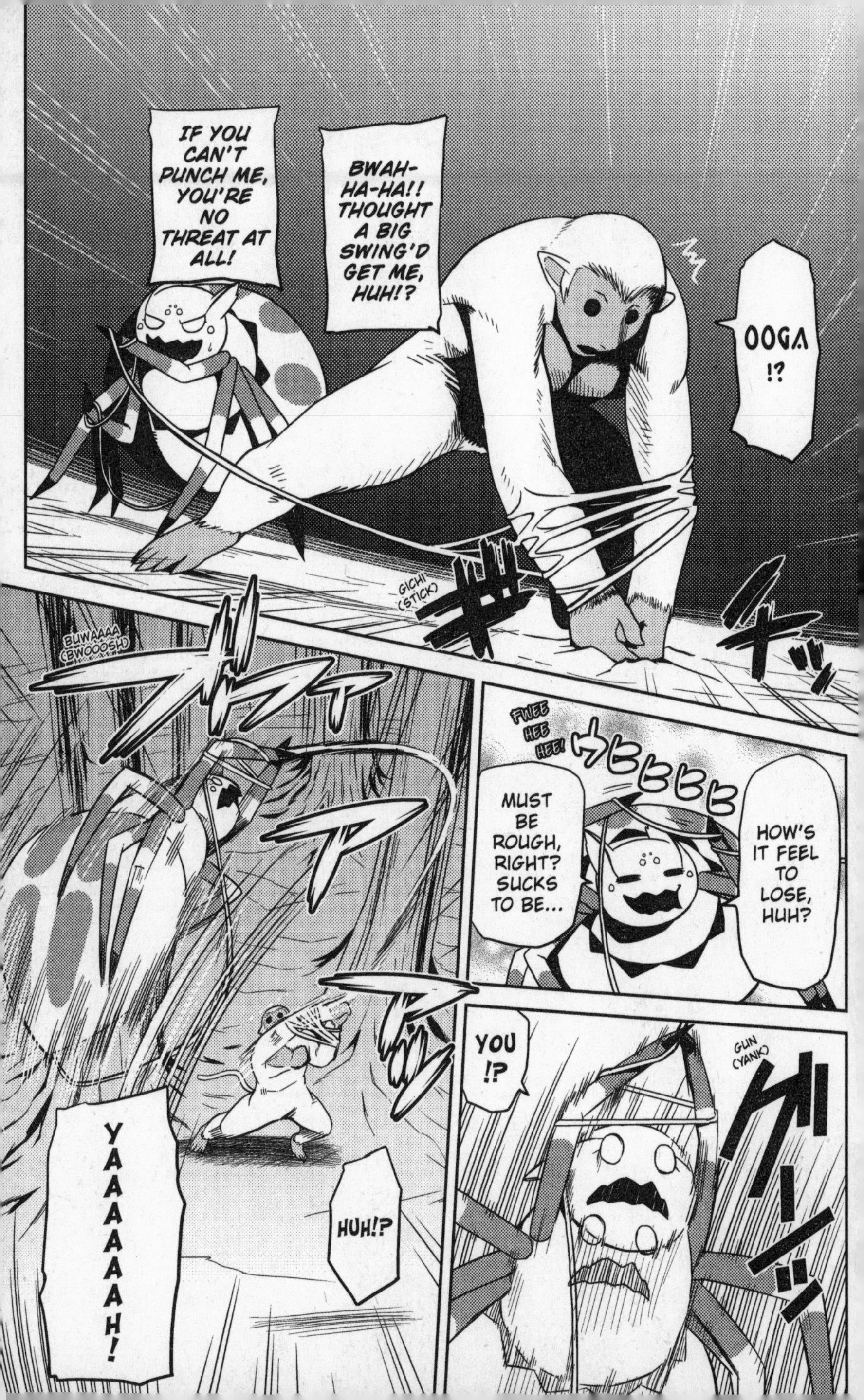
OOGA !?
BWAH-HA-HA!! THOUGHT A BIG SWING'D GET ME, HUH!?
IF YOU CAN'T PUNCH ME, YOU'RE NO THREAT AT ALL!
GICHI (STICK)
FWEE HEE HEE!
HOW'S IT FEEL TO LOSE, HUH?
MUST BE ROUGH, RIGHT? SUCKS TO BE...
YOU !?
GUN (YANK)
BUWAAA (BWOOOSH)
HUH!?
YAAAAAAAH!

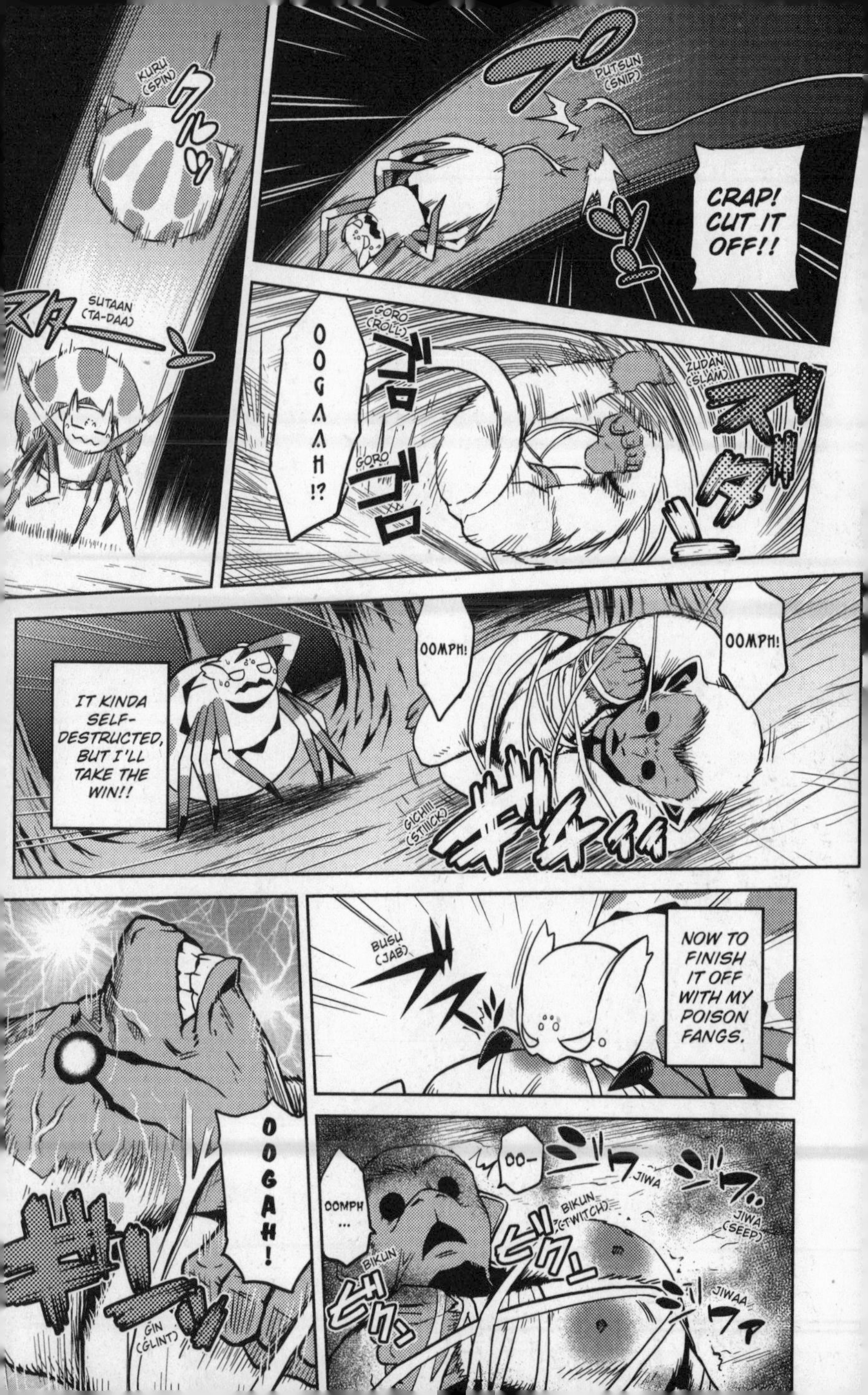
CRAP! CUT IT OFF!!
PUTSUN (SNIP)
ZUDAN (SLAM)
GORO (ROLL)
GORO
OOGAAH!?
KURU (SPIN)
SUTAAN (TA-DAA)
OOMPH!
OOMPH!
GICHIII (STIIICK)
IT KINDA SELF-DESTRUCTED, BUT I'LL TAKE THE WIN!!
NOW TO FINISH IT OFF WITH MY POISON FANGS.
BUSU (JAB)
JIWA (SEEP)
JIWA
OO-
BIKUN (TWITCH)
JIWAA
OOMPH ...
BIKUN
OOGAH!
GIN (GLINT)

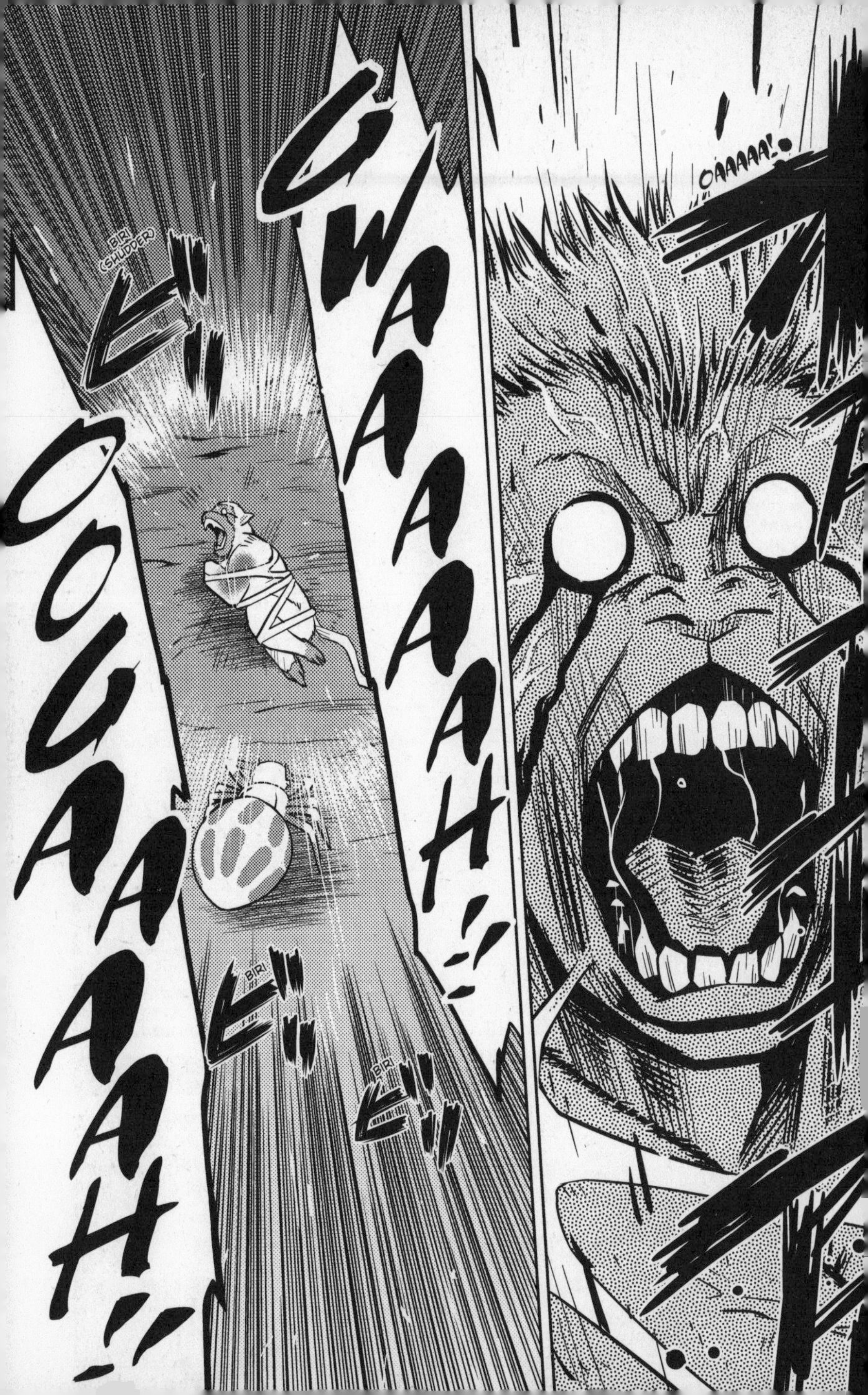
OAAAAA!
UWAAAAAAH!!
BIRI (SHUDDER)
OUAAAAAH!!
BIRI
BIRI

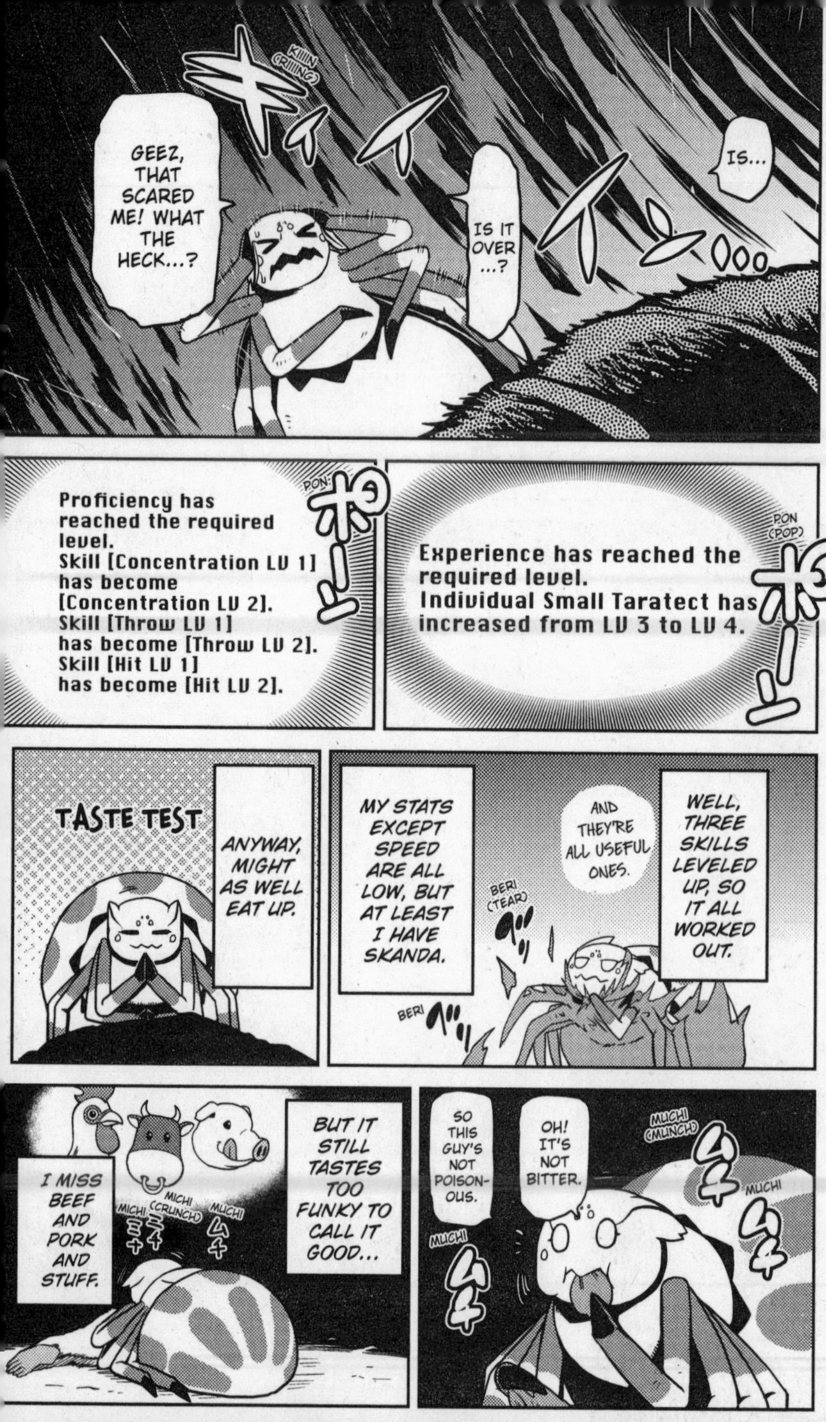
IS...
IS IT OVER...?
KIIIN (RIIING)
GEEZ, THAT SCARED ME! WHAT THE HECK...?
PON (POP)
Experience has reached the required level.
Individual Small Taratect has increased from LV 3 to LV 4.
PON
Proficiency has reached the required level.
Skill [Concentration LV 1] has become [Concentration LV 2].
Skill [Throw LV 1] has become [Throw LV 2].
Skill [Hit LV 1] has become [Hit LV 2].
WELL, THREE SKILLS LEVELED UP, SO IT ALL WORKED OUT.
AND THEY'RE ALL USEFUL ONES.
BERI (TEAR)
MY STATS EXCEPT SPEED ARE ALL LOW, BUT AT LEAST I HAVE SKANDA.
BERI
ANYWAY, MIGHT AS WELL EAT UP.
TASTE TEST
MUCHI (MUNCH)
OH! IT'S NOT BITTER.
SO THIS GUY'S NOT POISON-OUS.
MUCHI
MUCHI
BUT IT STILL TASTES TOO FUNKY TO CALL IT GOOD...
MUCHI
MICHI (CRUNCH)
MICHI
I MISS BEEF AND PORK AND STUFF.

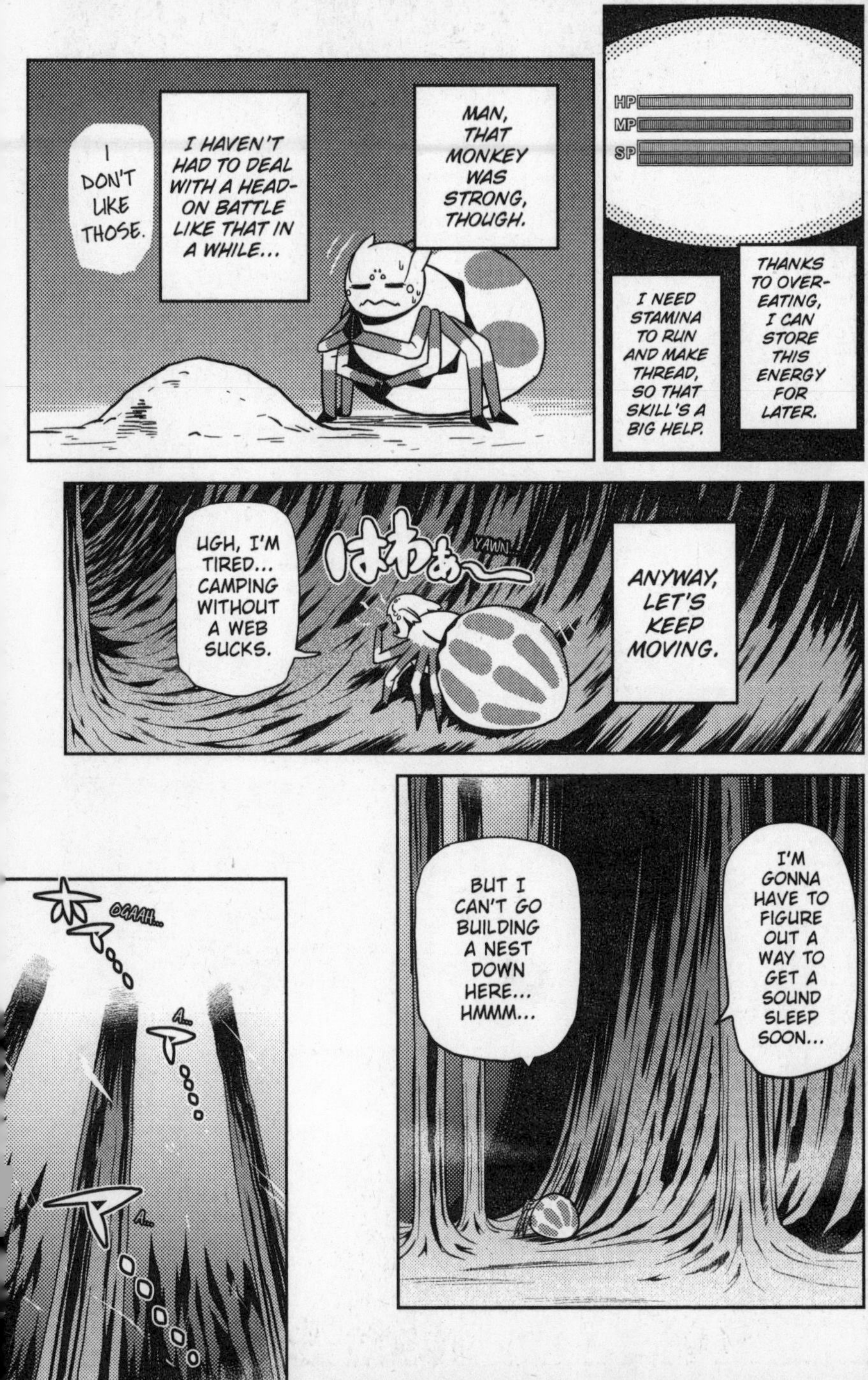
HP
MP
SP
THANKS TO OVER-EATING, I CAN STORE THIS ENERGY FOR LATER.
I NEED STAMINA TO RUN AND MAKE THREAD, SO THAT SKILL'S A BIG HELP.
MAN, THAT MONKEY WAS STRONG, THOUGH.
I HAVEN'T HAD TO DEAL WITH A HEAD-ON BATTLE LIKE THAT IN A WHILE...
I DON'T LIKE THOSE.
ANYWAY, LET'S KEEP MOVING.
はわぁ〜
YAWN...
UGH, I'M TIRED... CAMPING WITHOUT A WEB SUCKS.
I'M GONNA HAVE TO FIGURE OUT A WAY TO GET A SOUND SLEEP SOON...
BUT I CAN'T GO BUILDING A NEST DOWN HERE... HMMM...
GAAH...
A...
A...

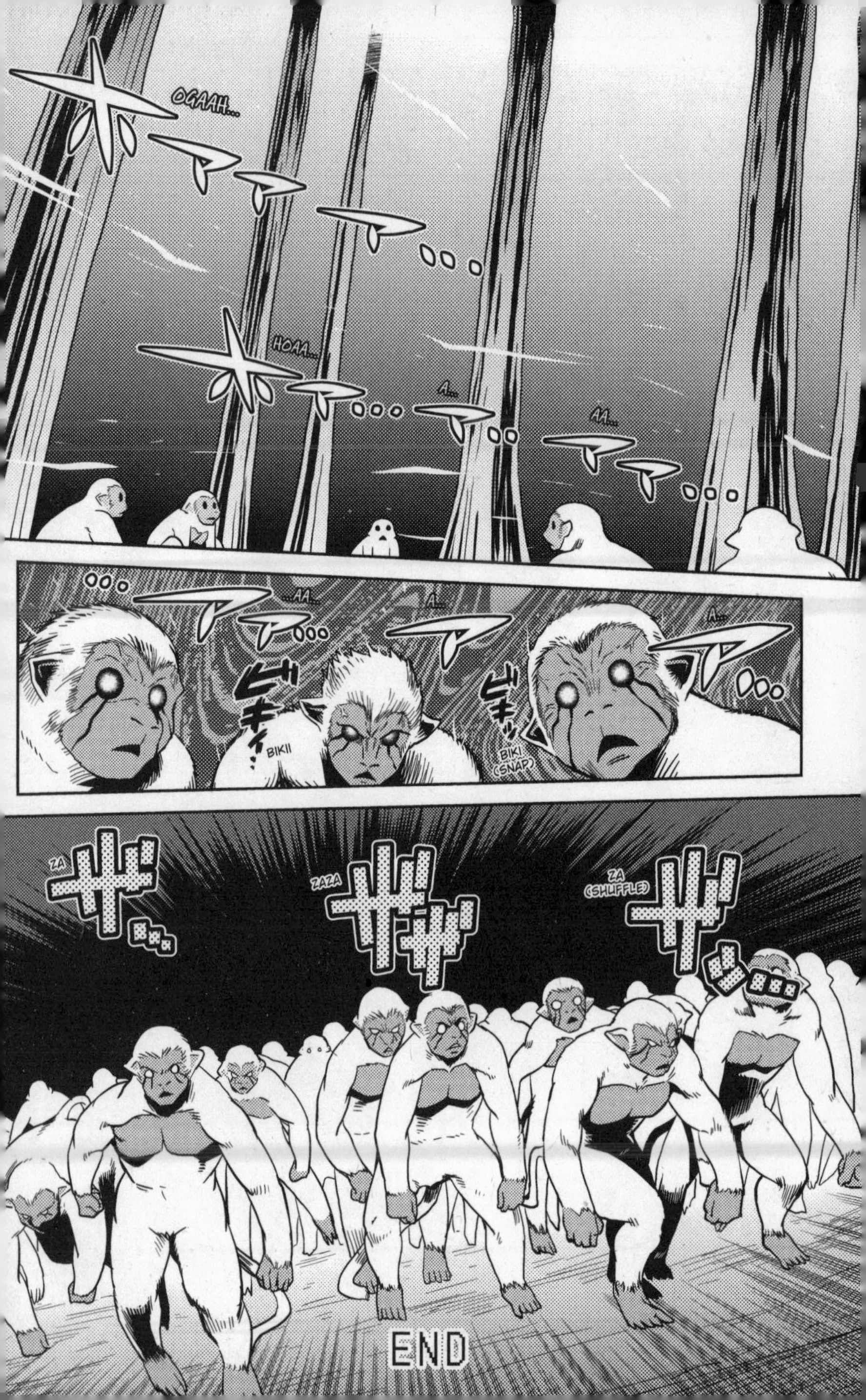
OGAAH...
HOAA...
A...
AA...
A...
BIKI (SNAP)
A...
BIKII
...AA...
ZA (SHUFFLE)
ZAZA
ZA
END

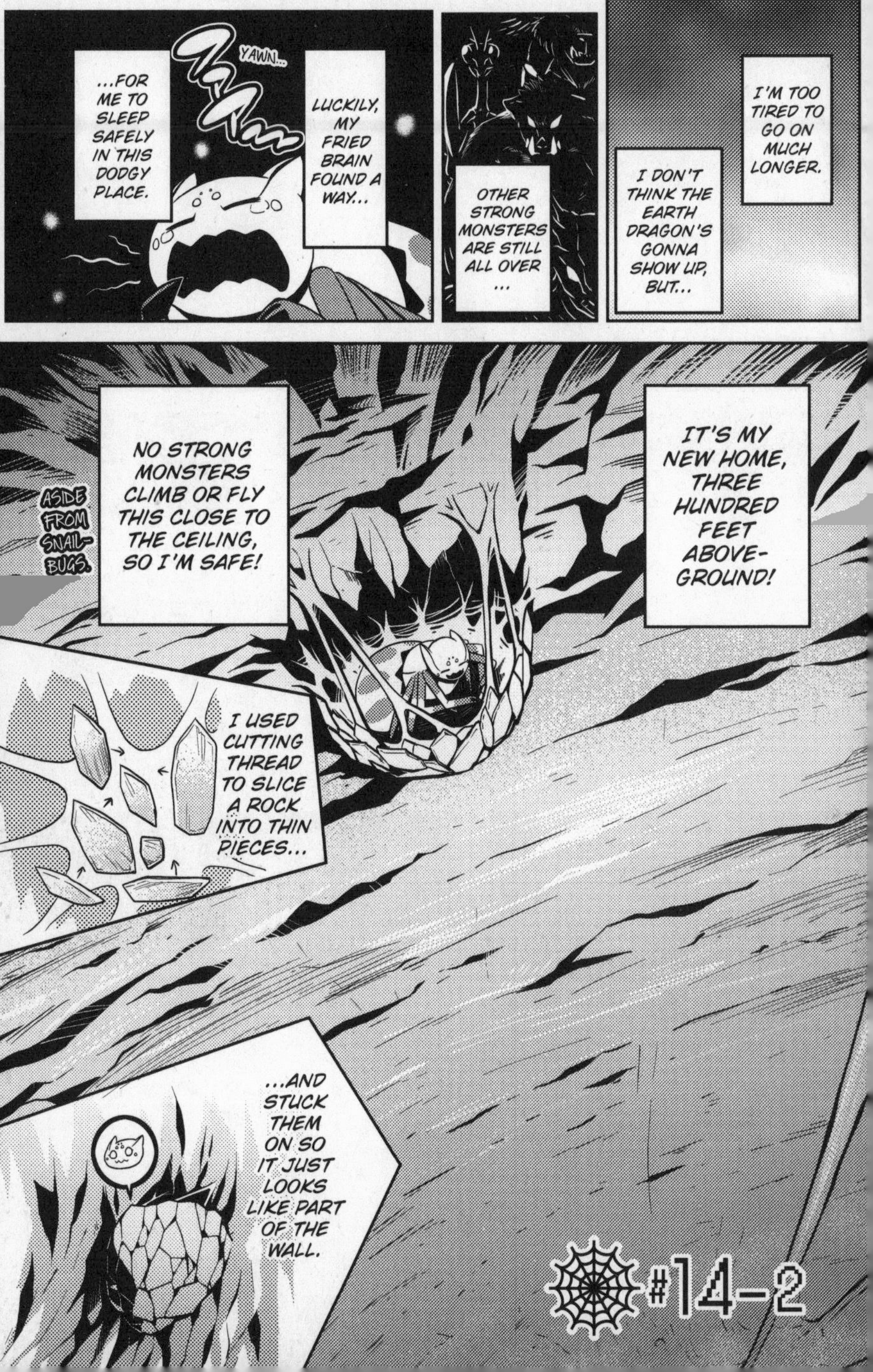
I'M TOO TIRED TO GO ON MUCH LONGER.
I DON'T THINK THE EARTH DRAGON'S GONNA SHOW UP, BUT...
OTHER STRONG MONSTERS ARE STILL ALL OVER...
LUCKILY, MY FRIED BRAIN FOUND A WAY...
YAWN...
...FOR ME TO SLEEP SAFELY IN THIS DODGY PLACE.
IT'S MY NEW HOME, THREE HUNDRED FEET ABOVE-GROUND!
NO STRONG MONSTERS CLIMB OR FLY THIS CLOSE TO THE CEILING, SO I'M SAFE!
ASIDE FROM SNAIL-BUGS.
I USED CUTTING THREAD TO SLICE A ROCK INTO THIN PIECES...
...AND STUCK THEM ON SO IT JUST LOOKS LIKE PART OF THE WALL.
#14-2

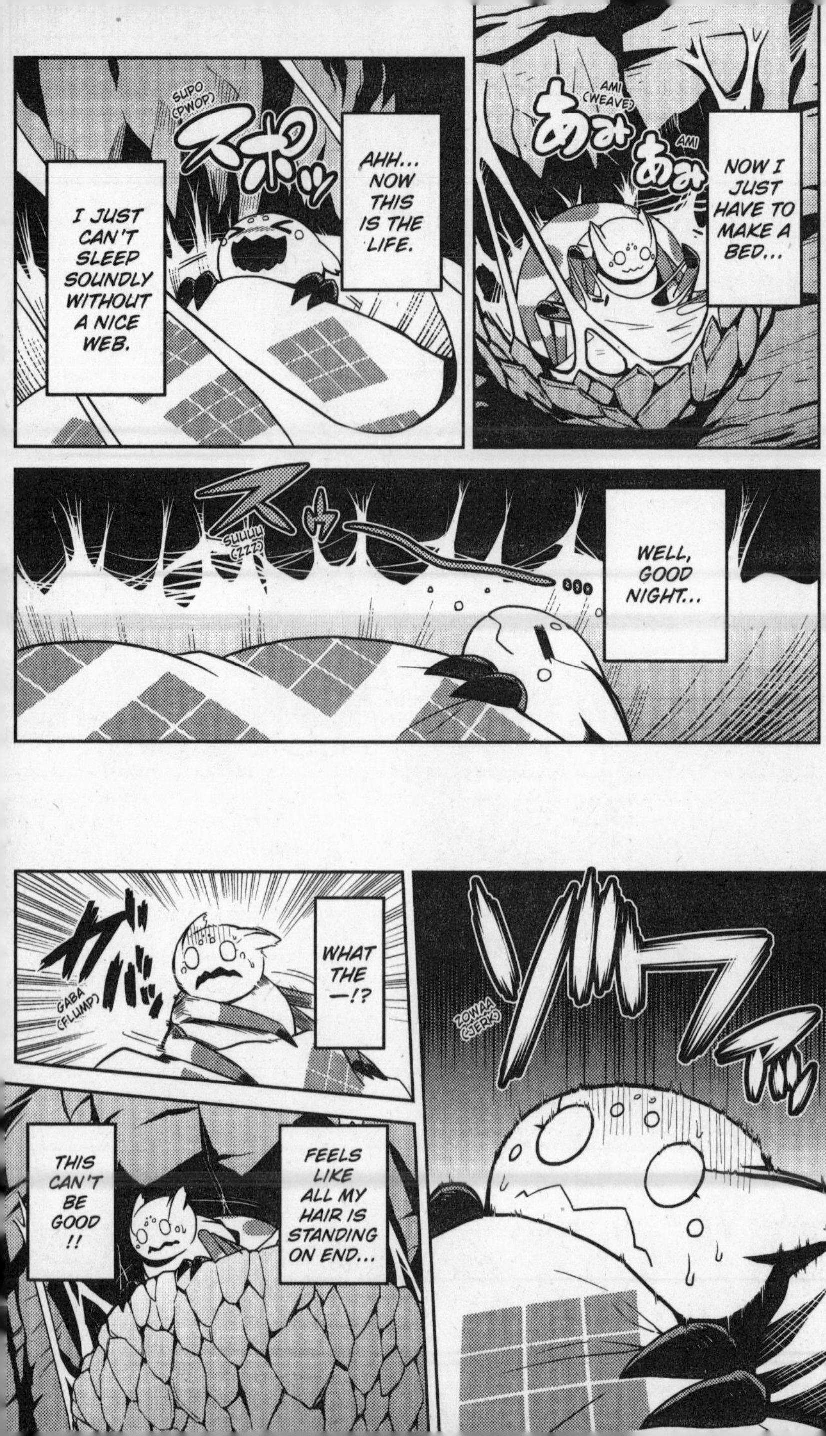
あみ
AMI (WEAVE)
あみ
AMI
NOW I JUST HAVE TO MAKE A BED...
スポッ
SUPO (PWOP)
AHH... NOW THIS IS THE LIFE.
I JUST CAN'T SLEEP SOUNDLY WITHOUT A NICE WEB.
WELL, GOOD NIGHT...
SUUUU (ZZZ)
ZOWAA (JERK)
WHAT THE—!?
GABA (FLUMP)
FEELS LIKE ALL MY HAIR IS STANDING ON END...
THIS CAN'T BE GOOD!!

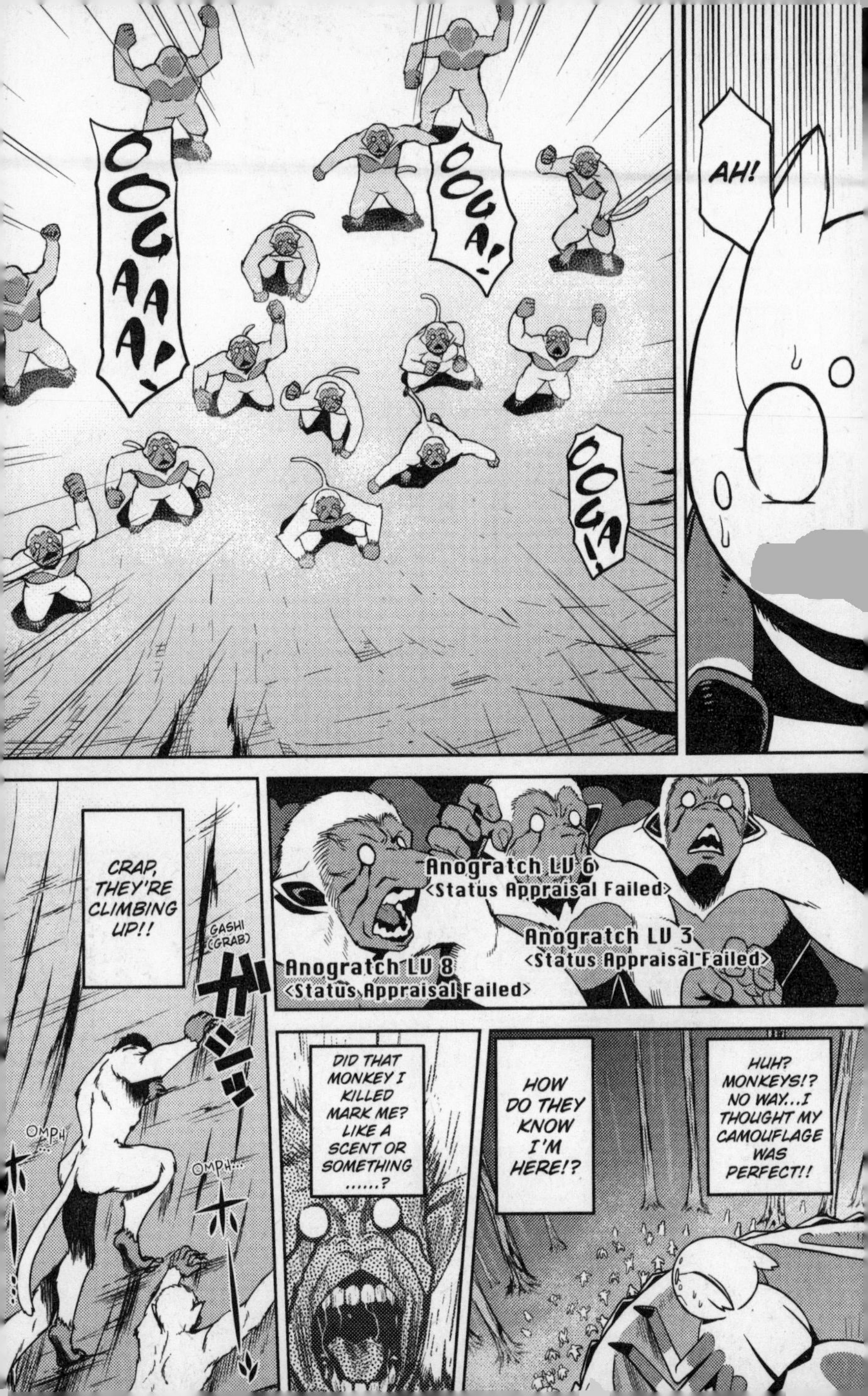
AH!
OOGA!
OOGA!!
OOGAAAA!
Anogratch LV 6
<Status Appraisal Failed>
Anogratch LV 3
<Status Appraisal Failed>
Anogratch LV 8
<Status Appraisal Failed>
HUH? MONKEYS!? NO WAY...I THOUGHT MY CAMOUFLAGE WAS PERFECT!!
HOW DO THEY KNOW I'M HERE!?
DID THAT MONKEY I KILLED MARK ME? LIKE A SCENT OR SOMETHING ......?
CRAP, THEY'RE CLIMBING UP!!
GASHI (GRAB)
OMPH...
OMPH

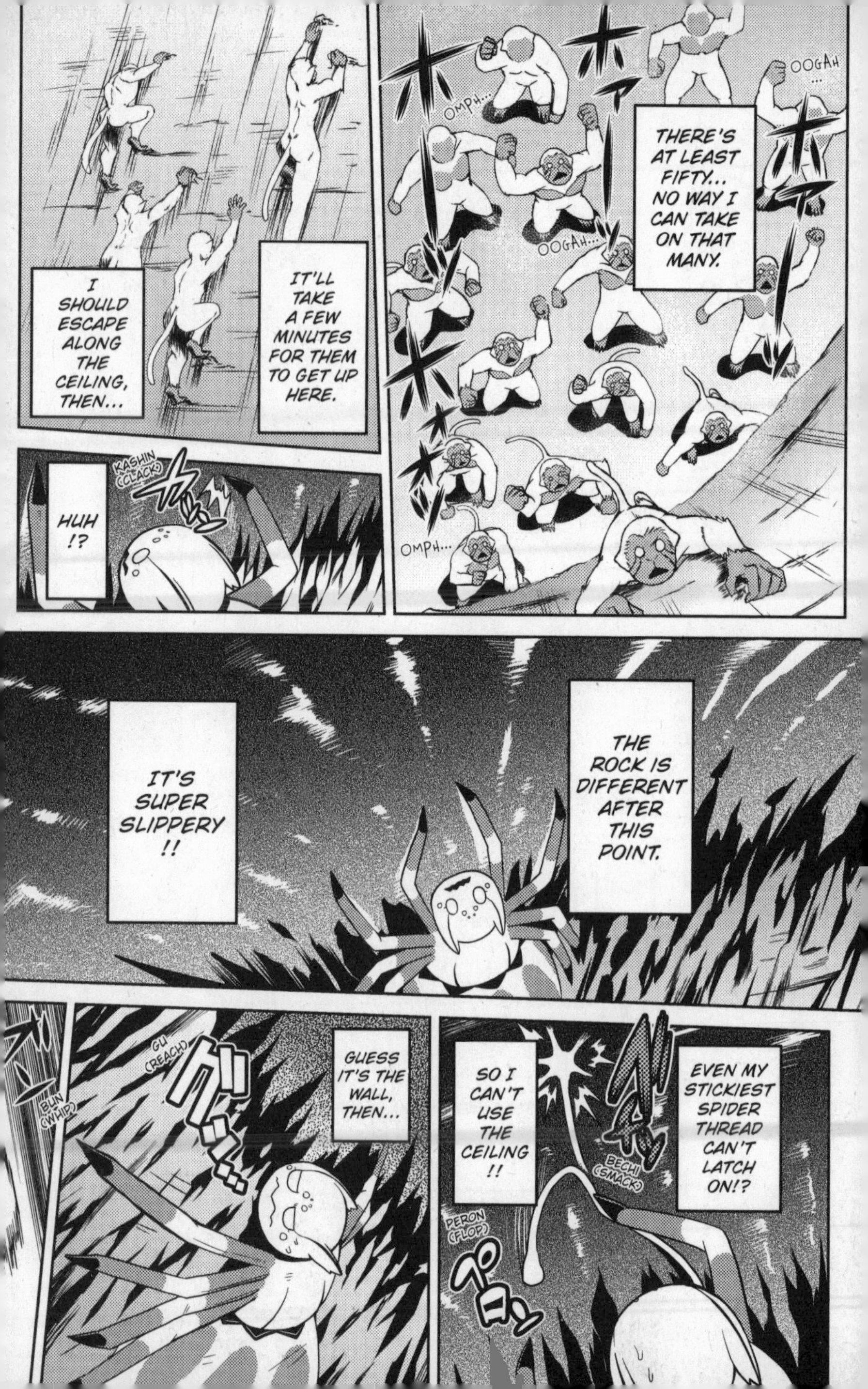
OOGAH...
THERE'S AT LEAST FIFTY... NO WAY I CAN TAKE ON THAT MANY.
OMPH...
OOGAH...
OMPH...
IT'LL TAKE A FEW MINUTES FOR THEM TO GET UP HERE.
I SHOULD ESCAPE ALONG THE CEILING, THEN...
KASHIN (CLACK)
HUH!?
THE ROCK IS DIFFERENT AFTER THIS POINT.
IT'S SUPER SLIPPERY!!
EVEN MY STICKIEST SPIDER THREAD CAN'T LATCH ON!?
BECHI (SMACK)
SO I CAN'T USE THE CEILING!!
PERON (FLOP)
GUESS IT'S THE WALL, THEN...
GU (REACH)
BUN (WHIP)

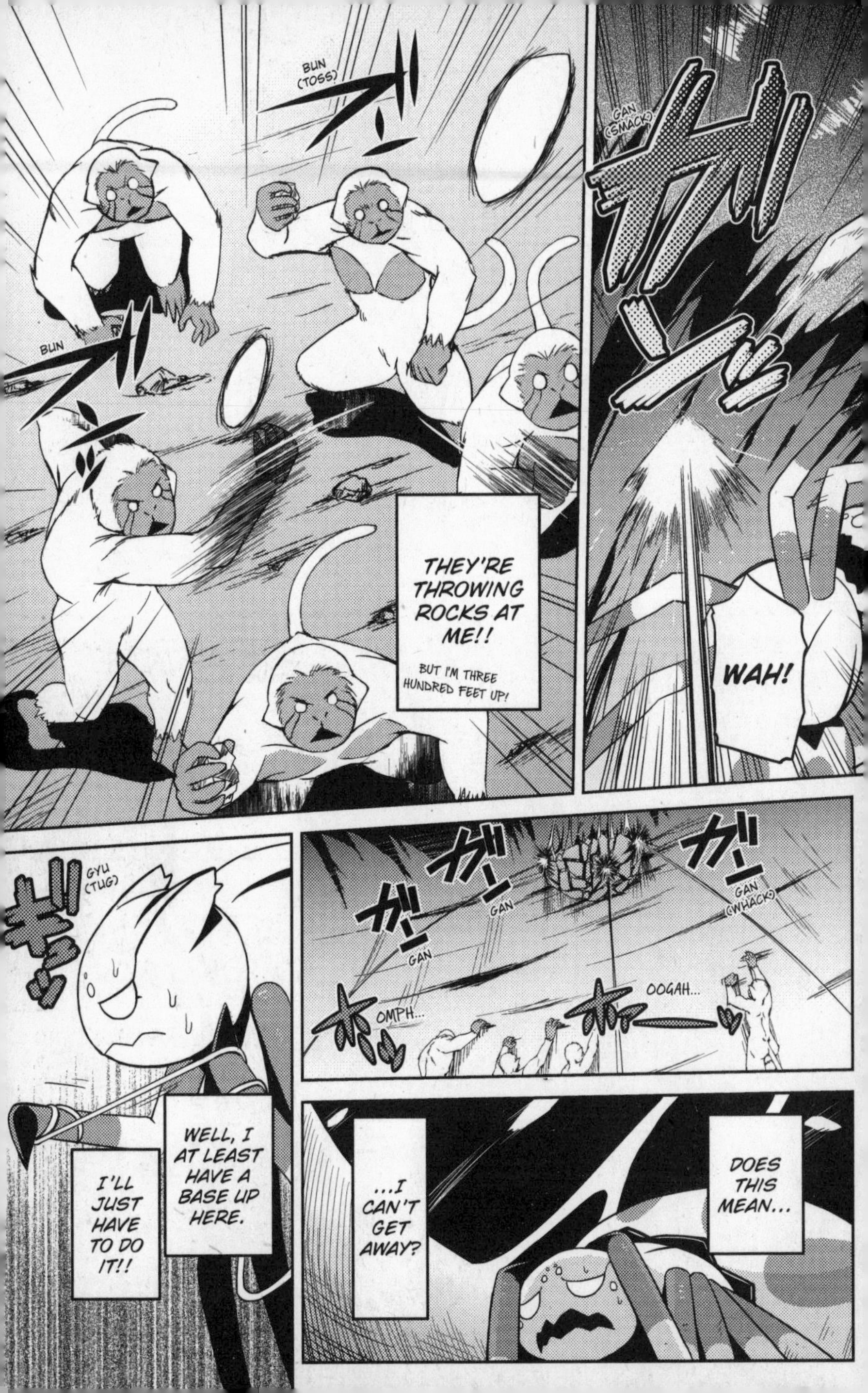
GAN (SMACK)
WAH!
BUN (TOSS)
BUN
THEY'RE THROWING ROCKS AT ME!!
BUT I'M THREE HUNDRED FEET UP!
GAN (WHACK)
GAN
GAN
OOGAH...
OMPH...
DOES THIS MEAN...
...I CAN'T GET AWAY?
GYU (TUG)
WELL, I AT LEAST HAVE A BASE UP HERE.
I'LL JUST HAVE TO DO IT!!

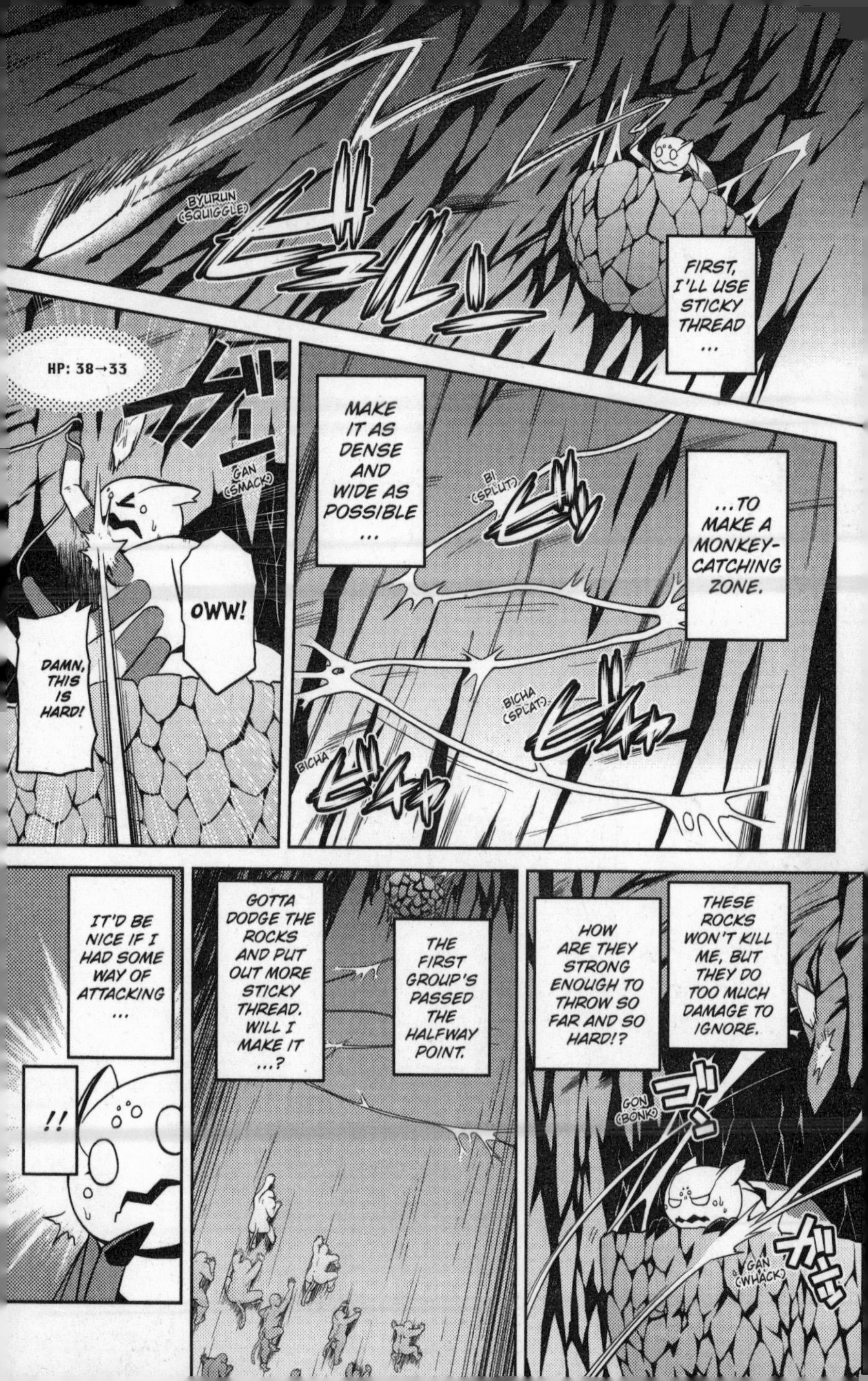
BYURUN (SQUIGGLE)
FIRST, I'LL USE STICKY THREAD...
MAKE IT AS DENSE AND WIDE AS POSSIBLE...
...TO MAKE A MONKEY-CATCHING ZONE.
BI (SPLUT)
BICHA (SPLAT)
BICHA
HP: 38→33
GAN (SMACK)
OWW!
DAMN, THIS IS HARD!
THESE ROCKS WON'T KILL ME, BUT THEY DO TOO MUCH DAMAGE TO IGNORE.
HOW ARE THEY STRONG ENOUGH TO THROW SO FAR AND SO HARD!?
GON (BONK)
GAN (WHACK)
THE FIRST GROUP'S PASSED THE HALFWAY POINT.
GOTTA DODGE THE ROCKS AND PUT OUT MORE STICKY THREAD. WILL I MAKE IT...?
IT'D BE NICE IF I HAD SOME WAY OF ATTACKING...
!!

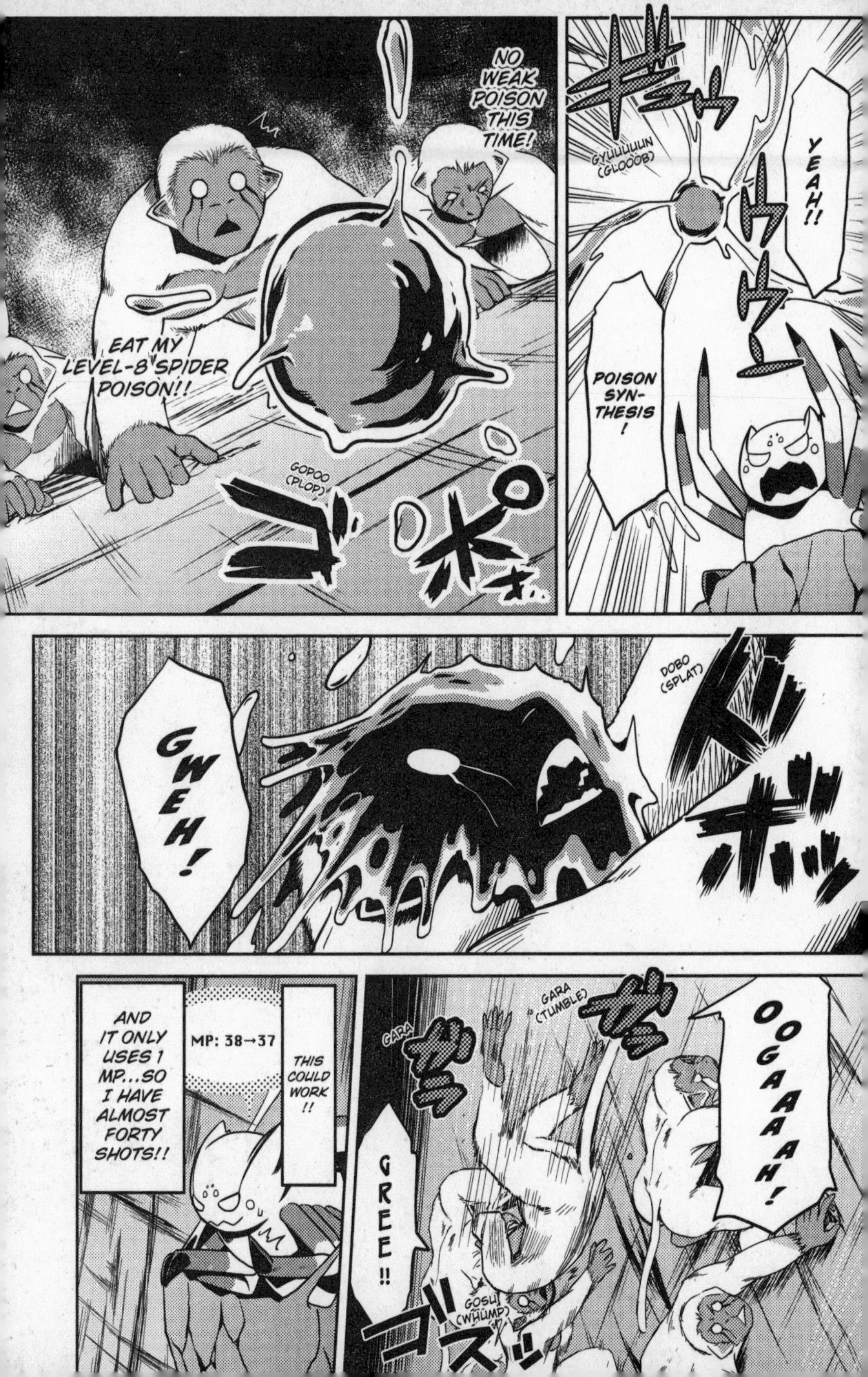
GYUUUUUN (GLOOOB)
YEAH!!
POISON SYN-THESIS!
NO WEAK POISON THIS TIME!
EAT MY LEVEL-8 SPIDER POISON!!
GOPOO (PLOP)
DOBO (SPLAT)
GWEH!
GARA (TUMBLE)
OOGAAAAH!
GARA
GREE!!
GOSU (WHUMP)
THIS COULD WORK!!
MP: 38→37
AND IT ONLY USES 1 MP...SO I HAVE ALMOST FORTY SHOTS!!

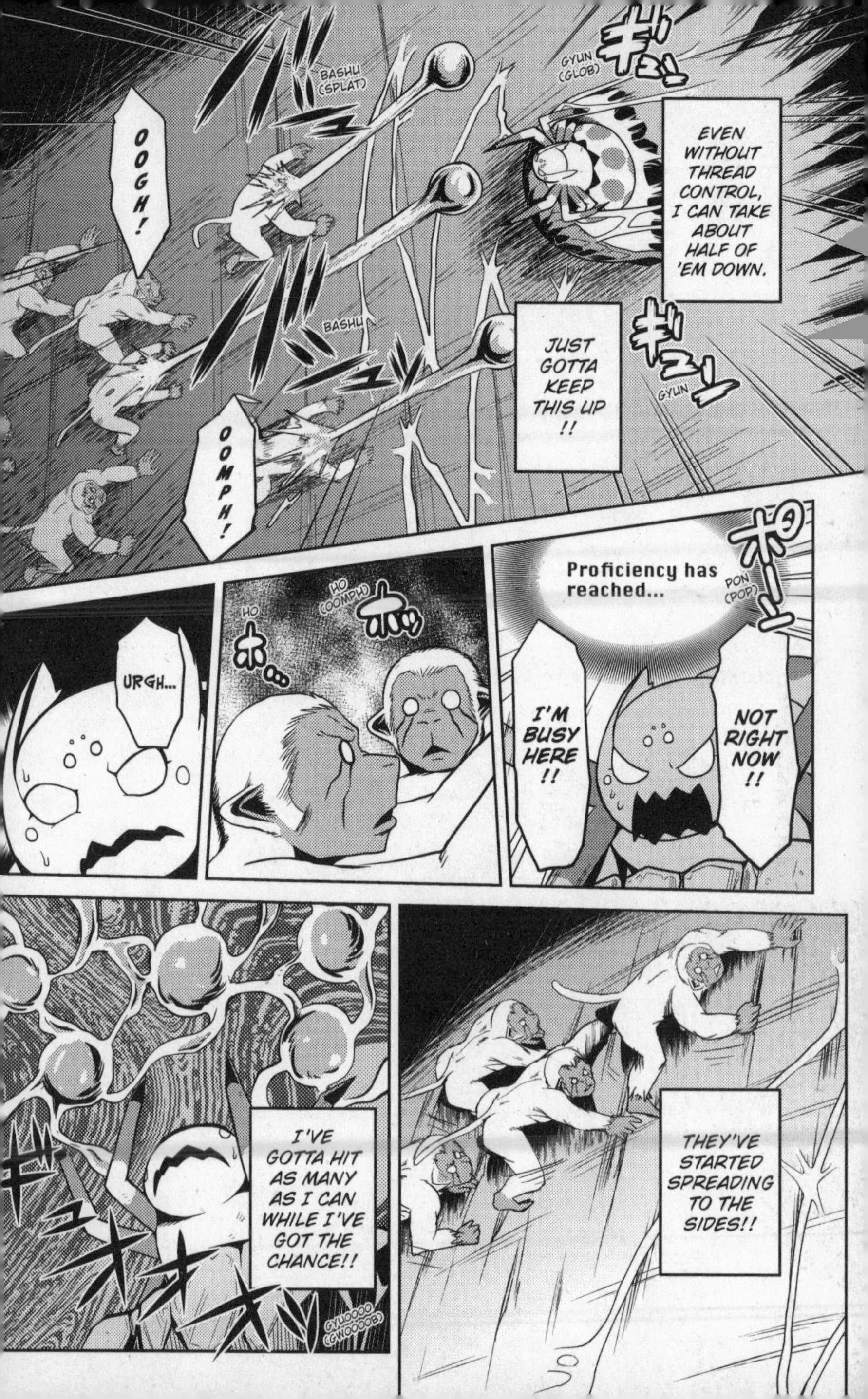
GYUN (GLOB)
EVEN WITHOUT THREAD CONTROL, I CAN TAKE ABOUT HALF OF 'EM DOWN.
GYUN
JUST GOTTA KEEP THIS UP!!
BASHU (SPLAT)
BASHU
OOGH!
OOMPH!
PON (POP)
Proficiency has reached...
NOT RIGHT NOW!!
I'M BUSY HERE!!
HO (OOMPH)
HO
URGH...
THEY'VE STARTED SPREADING TO THE SIDES!!
I'VE GOTTA HIT AS MANY AS I CAN WHILE I'VE GOT THE CHANCE!!
GYUOOOO (GWOOOOB)

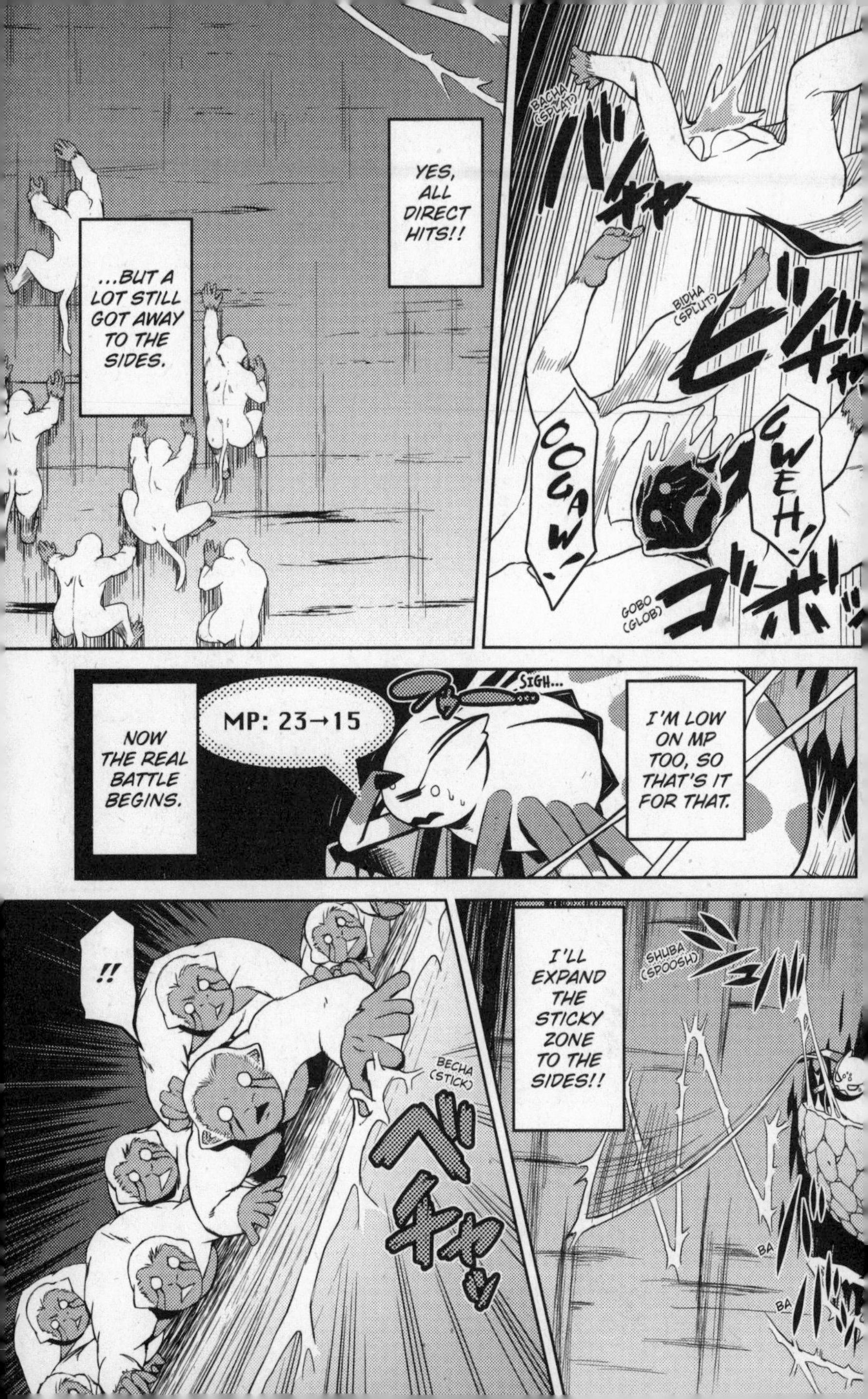
BACHA (SPLAT)
BIDHA (SPLUT)
GWEH!
OOGAW!
GOBO (GLOB)
YES, ALL DIRECT HITS!!
...BUT A LOT STILL GOT AWAY TO THE SIDES.
I'M LOW ON MP TOO, SO THAT'S IT FOR THAT.
SIGH...
MP: 23→15
NOW THE REAL BATTLE BEGINS.
I'LL EXPAND THE STICKY ZONE TO THE SIDES!!
SHUBA (SPOOSH)
BA
BA
!!
BECHA (STICK)

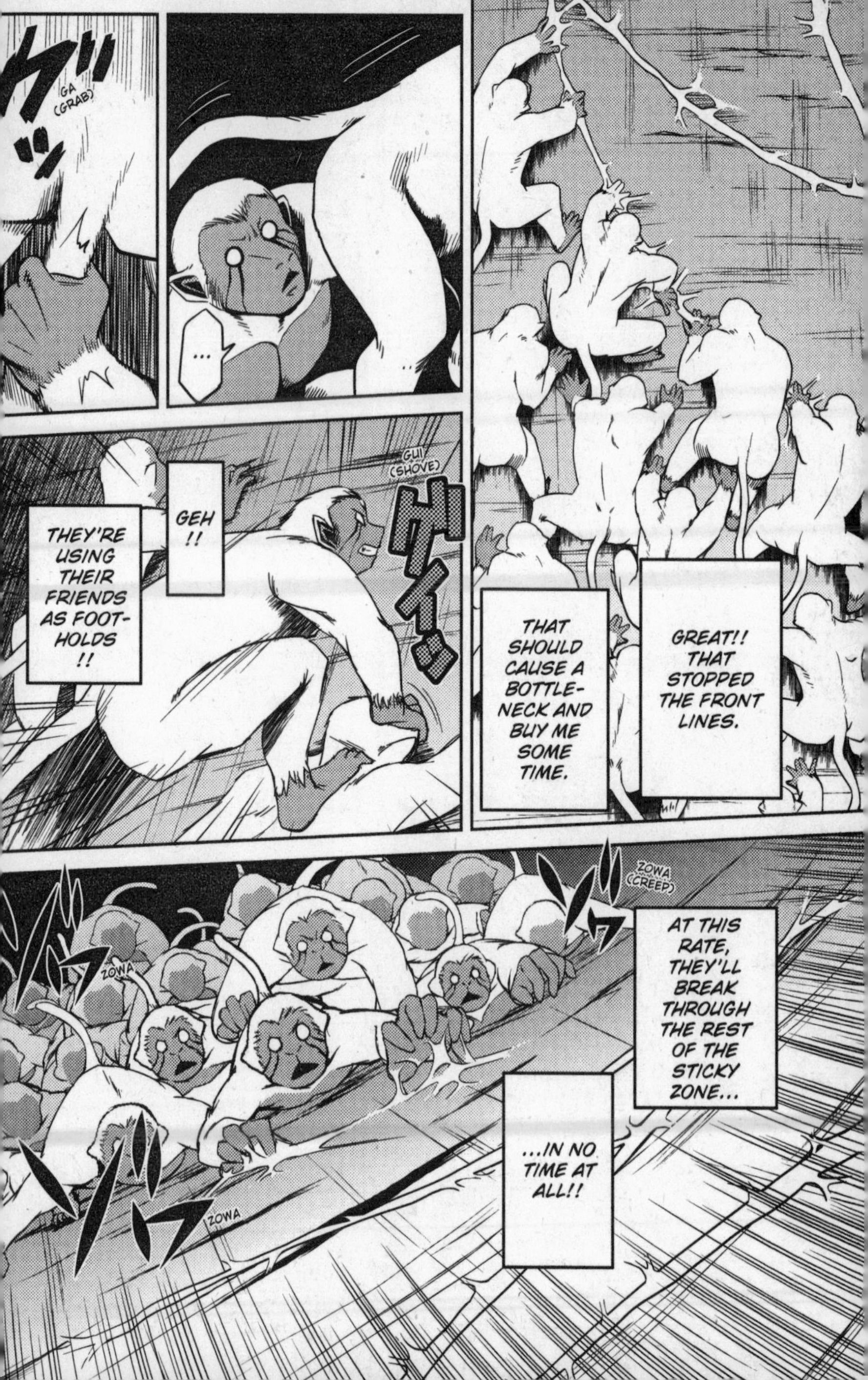
GREAT!! THAT STOPPED THE FRONT LINES.
THAT SHOULD CAUSE A BOTTLE-NECK AND BUY ME SOME TIME.
...
GA (GRAB)
GUI (SHOVE)
GEH !!
THEY'RE USING THEIR FRIENDS AS FOOT-HOLDS !!
ZOWA (CREEP)
AT THIS RATE, THEY'LL BREAK THROUGH THE REST OF THE STICKY ZONE...
...IN NO TIME AT ALL!!
ZOWA
ZOWA

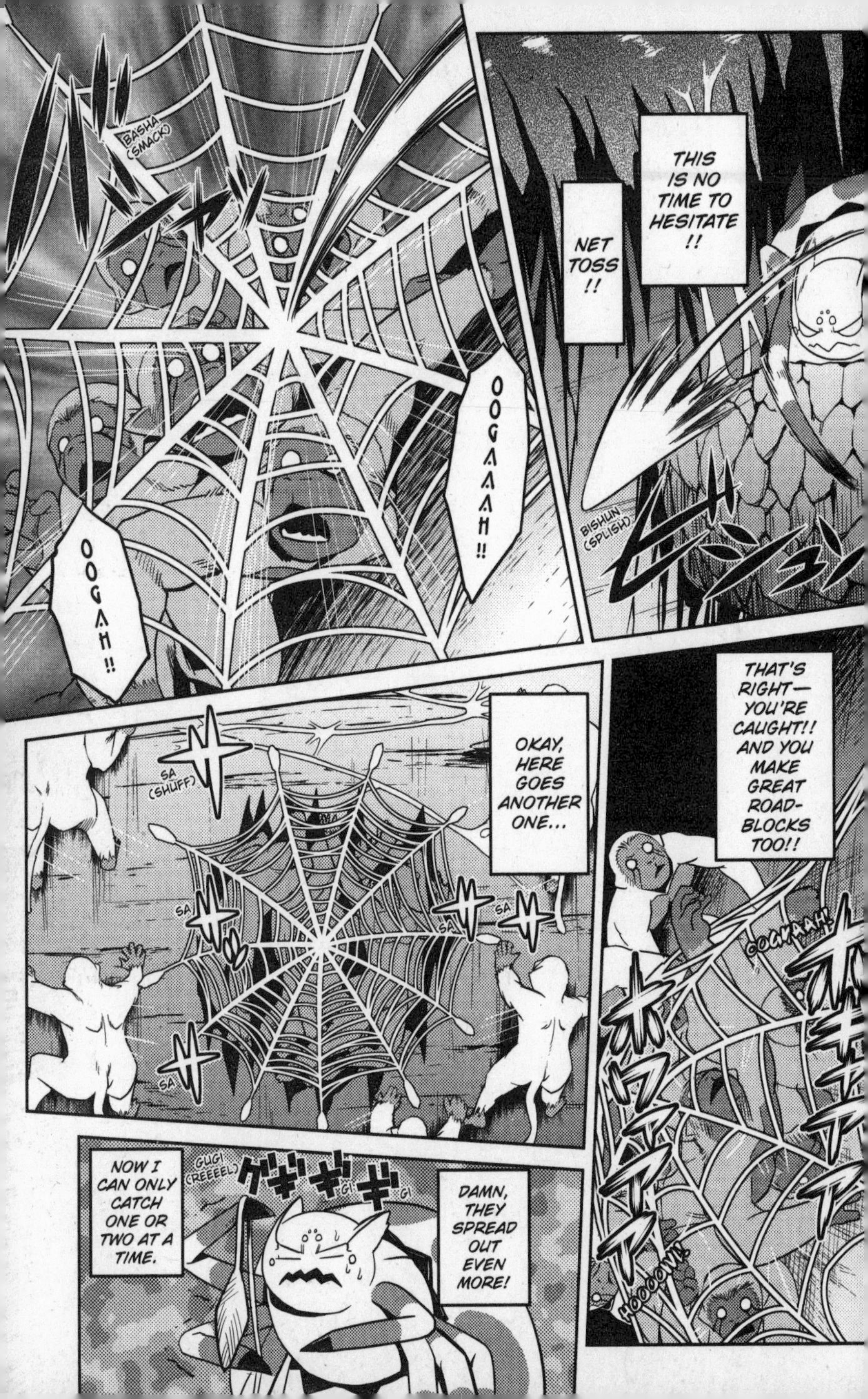
THIS IS NO TIME TO HESITATE!!
NET TOSS!!
BISHUN (SPLISH)
BASHA (SMACK)
OOGAAAAH!!
OOGAH!!
THAT'S RIGHT—YOU'RE CAUGHT!! AND YOU MAKE GREAT ROAD-BLOCKS TOO!!
OOGYAAH!
HOOOOWL!
OKAY, HERE GOES ANOTHER ONE...
SA (SHUFF)
SA
SA
SA
SA
DAMN, THEY SPREAD OUT EVEN MORE!
GUGI (REEEEL)
GI
GI
NOW I CAN ONLY CATCH ONE OR TWO AT A TIME.

THESE GUYS ARE WAY SMARTER THAN ANY MONSTERS I'VE FOUGHT BEFORE!!
IF THEY'RE THAT SMART, WHY ARE THEY WASTING THEIR TIME GOING AFTER ONE LITTLE SPIDER!?
UGH, GIMME A BREAK! THEY'RE TOO INTENSE FOR ME...
HAA (SIGH)
FOCUS THAT PASSION ON SOMETHING ELSE, LIKE [INSERT ACTIVITY HERE]!
WAIT A SEC...
ARE THERE MORE THAN BEFORE NOW!?
LIKE, SEVERAL TIMES MORE!!
ZA
ZA (SWOOSH)
ZA
AND THEIR BACKUP KEEPS COMING!
ZA

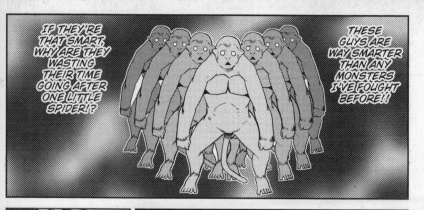

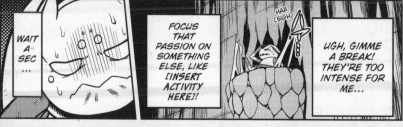

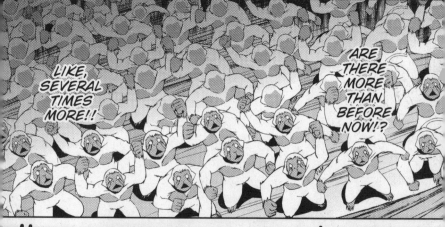

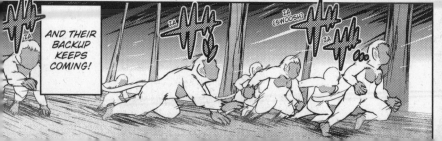

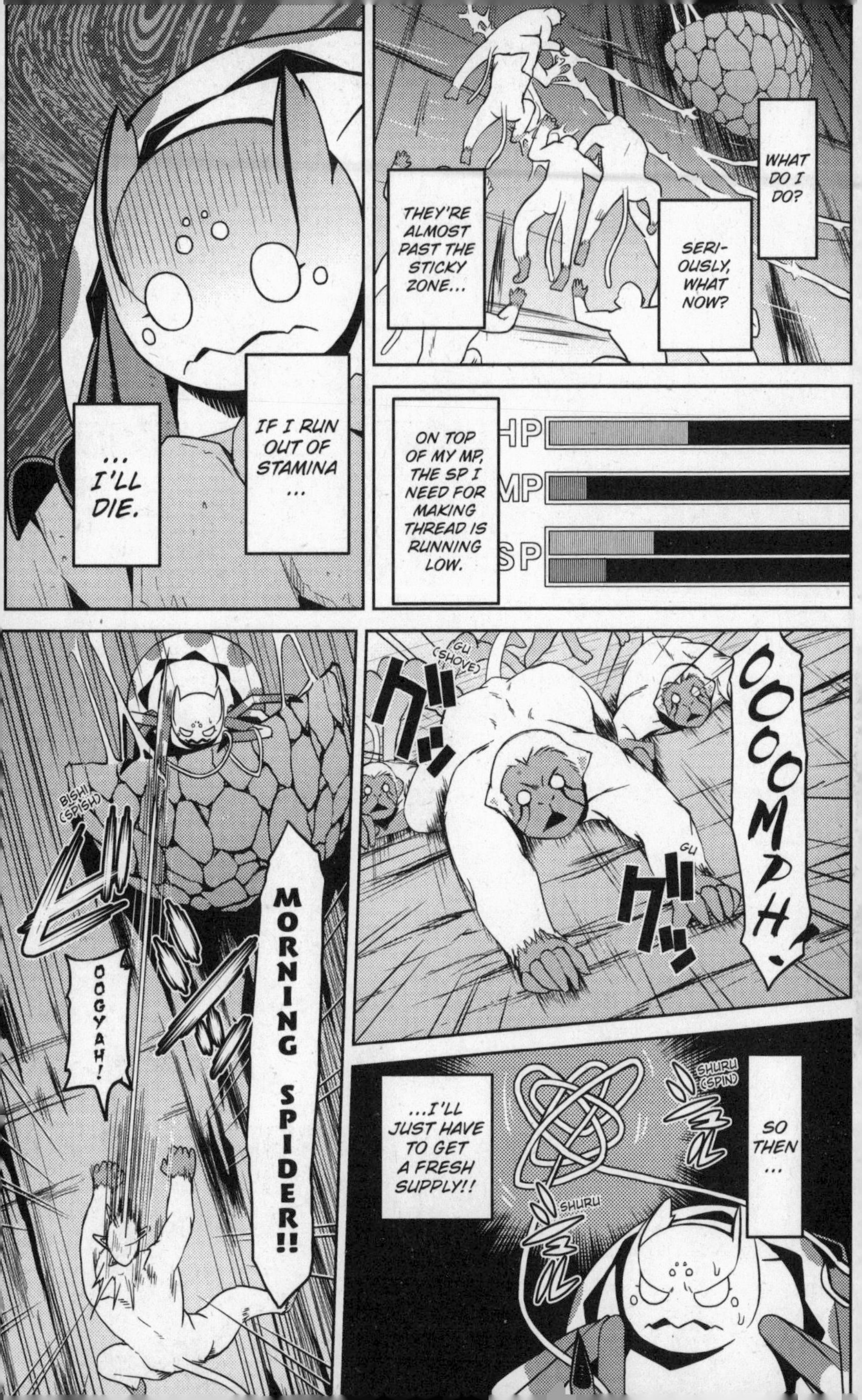
WHAT DO I DO?
SERI-OUSLY, WHAT NOW?
THEY'RE ALMOST PAST THE STICKY ZONE...
HP
MP
SP
ON TOP OF MY MP, THE SP I NEED FOR MAKING THREAD IS RUNNING LOW.
IF I RUN OUT OF STAMINA ...
... I'LL DIE.
OOOOMPH!
GU (SHOVE)
GU
SO THEN ...
SHURU (SPIN)
...I'LL JUST HAVE TO GET A FRESH SUPPLY!!
SHURU
MORNING SPIDER!!
BISHI (SPISH)
OOGYAH!

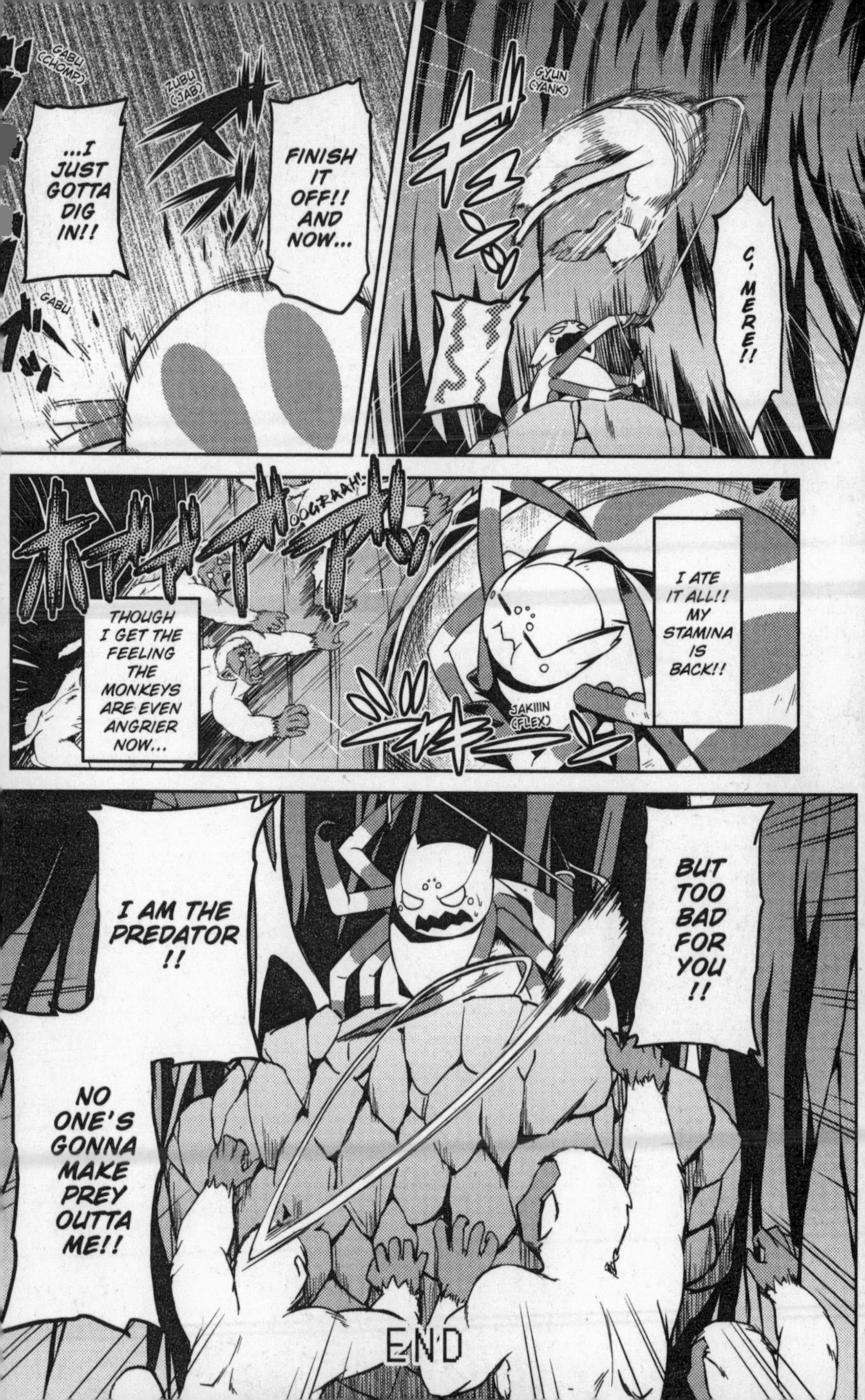
GYUN (YANK)
C'MERE!!
ZUBU (JAB)
FINISH IT OFF!! AND NOW...
GABU (CHOMP)
...I JUST GOTTA DIG IN!!
GABU
I ATE IT ALL!! MY STAMINA IS BACK!!
JAKIIIN (FLEX)
OOGRAAH!!
THOUGH I GET THE FEELING THE MONKEYS ARE EVEN ANGRIER NOW...
BUT TOO BAD FOR YOU!!
I AM THE PREDATOR!!
NO ONE'S GONNA MAKE PREY OUTTA ME!!
END

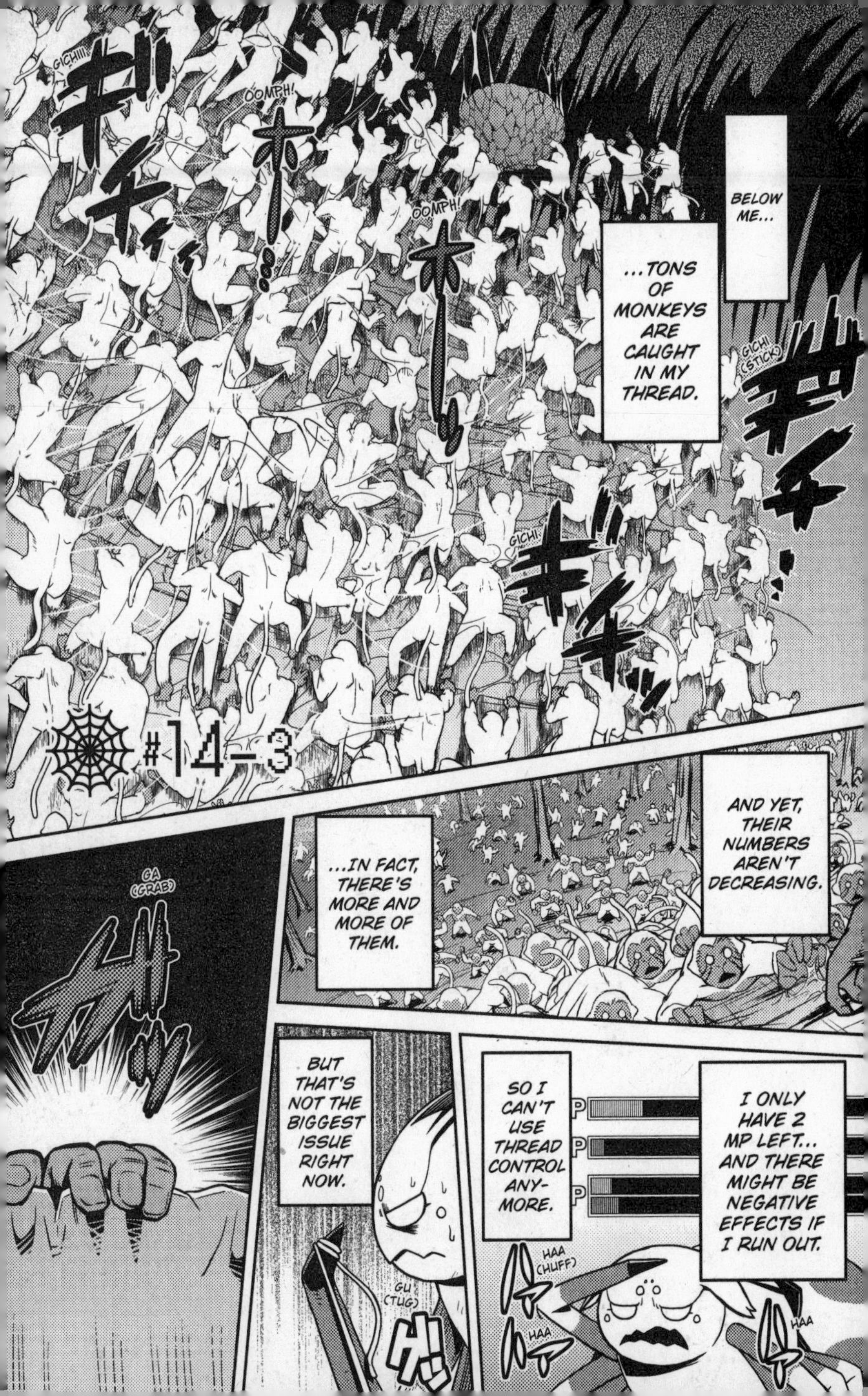
BELOW ME...
...TONS OF MONKEYS ARE CAUGHT IN MY THREAD.
GICHI (STICK)
GICHI
OOMPH!
OOMPH!
GICHIII
#14-3
AND YET, THEIR NUMBERS AREN'T DECREASING.
...IN FACT, THERE'S MORE AND MORE OF THEM.
I ONLY HAVE 2 MP LEFT... AND THERE MIGHT BE NEGATIVE EFFECTS IF I RUN OUT.
SO I CAN'T USE THREAD CONTROL ANYMORE.
HAA
HAA (HUFF)
HAA
BUT THAT'S NOT THE BIGGEST ISSUE RIGHT NOW.
GU (TUG)
GA (GRAB)

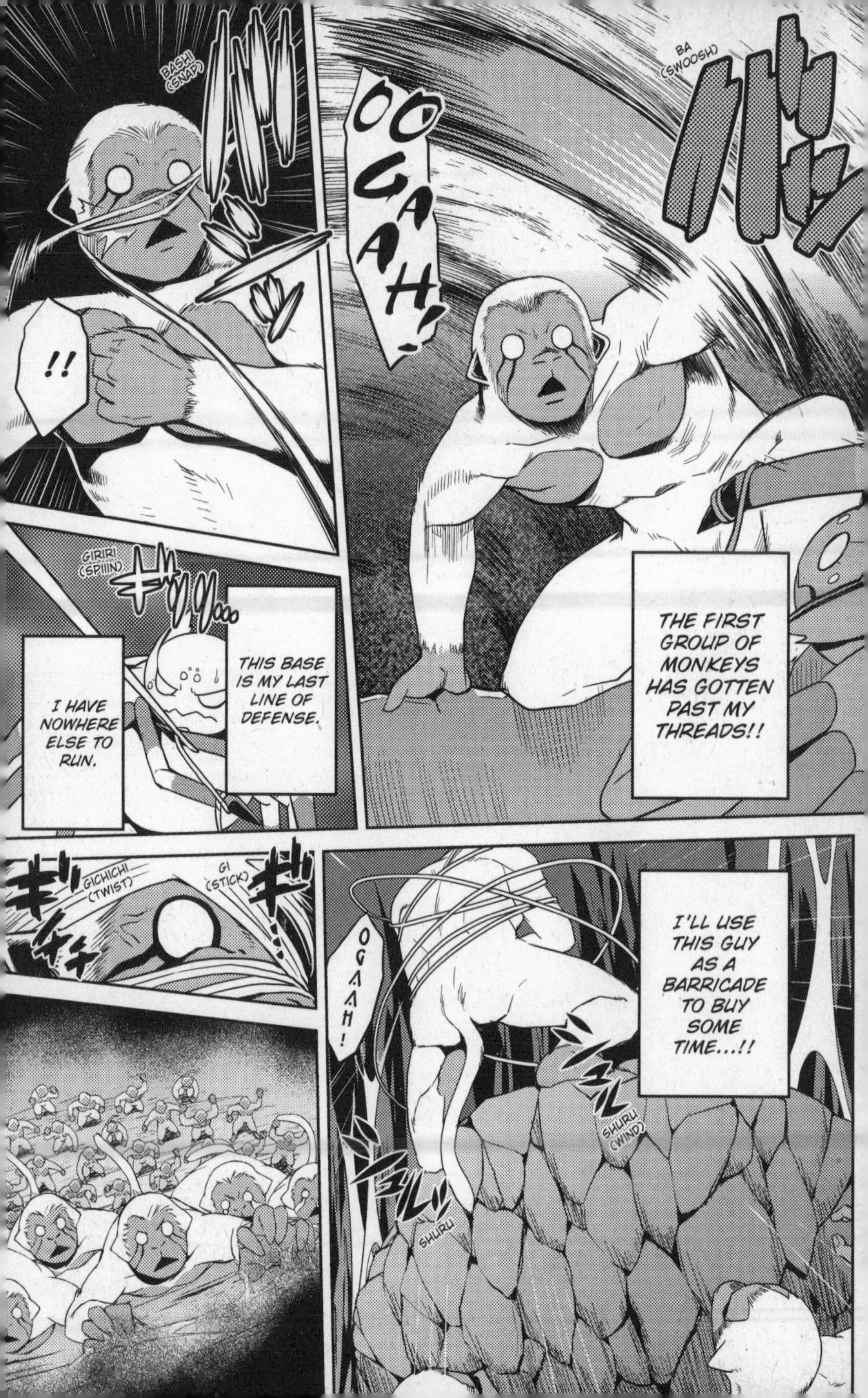
BA (SWOOSH)
OOGAAH!
THE FIRST GROUP OF MONKEYS HAS GOTTEN PAST MY THREADS!!
BASHI (SNAP)
!!
GIRIRI (SPIIIN)
THIS BASE IS MY LAST LINE OF DEFENSE.
I HAVE NOWHERE ELSE TO RUN.
I'LL USE THIS GUY AS A BARRICADE TO BUY SOME TIME...!!
OGAAH!
SHURU (WIND)
SHURU
GI (STICK)
GICHICHI (TWIST)

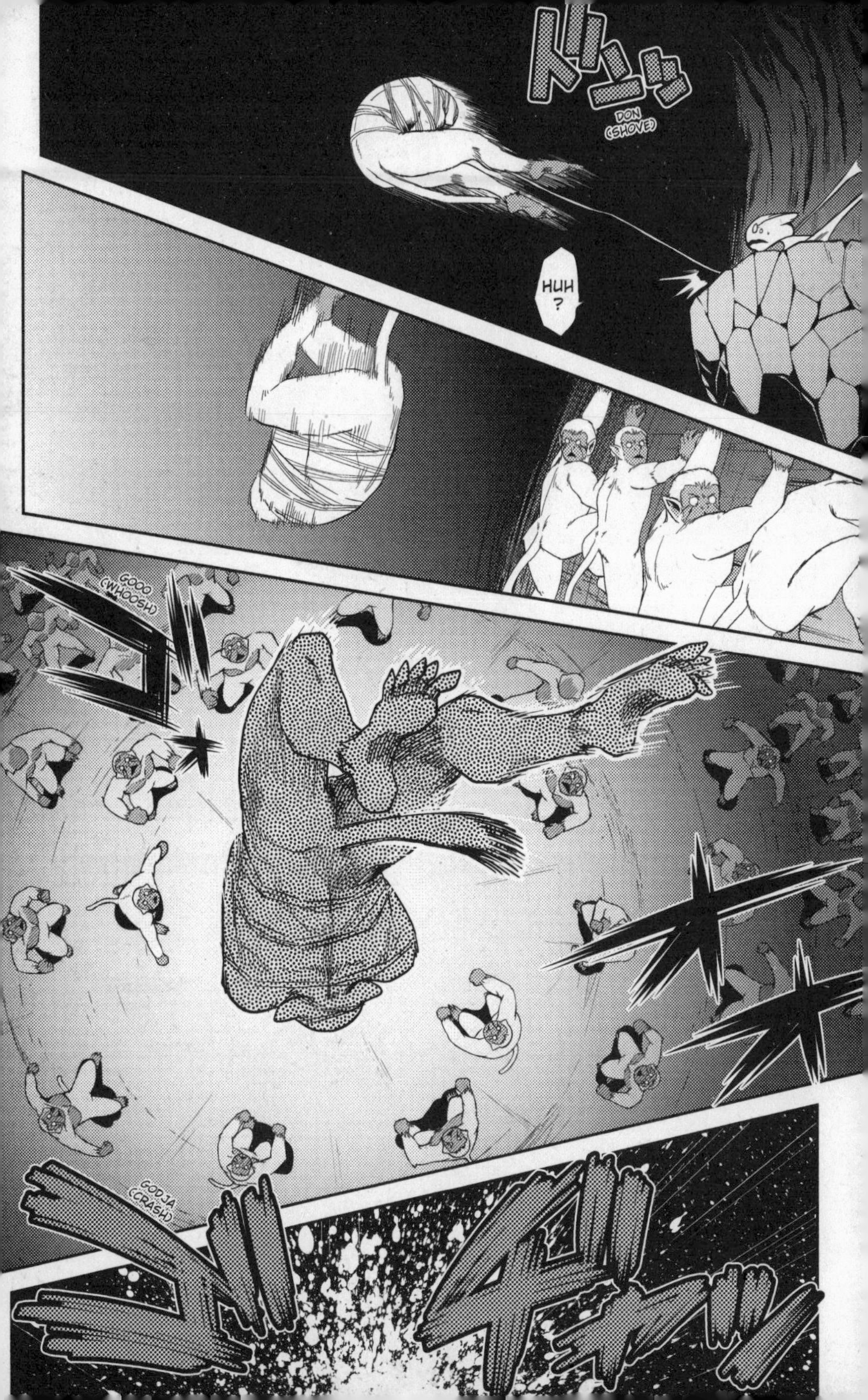
DON
(SHOVE)
HUH?
GOOO
(WHOOSH)
GODJA
(CRASH)

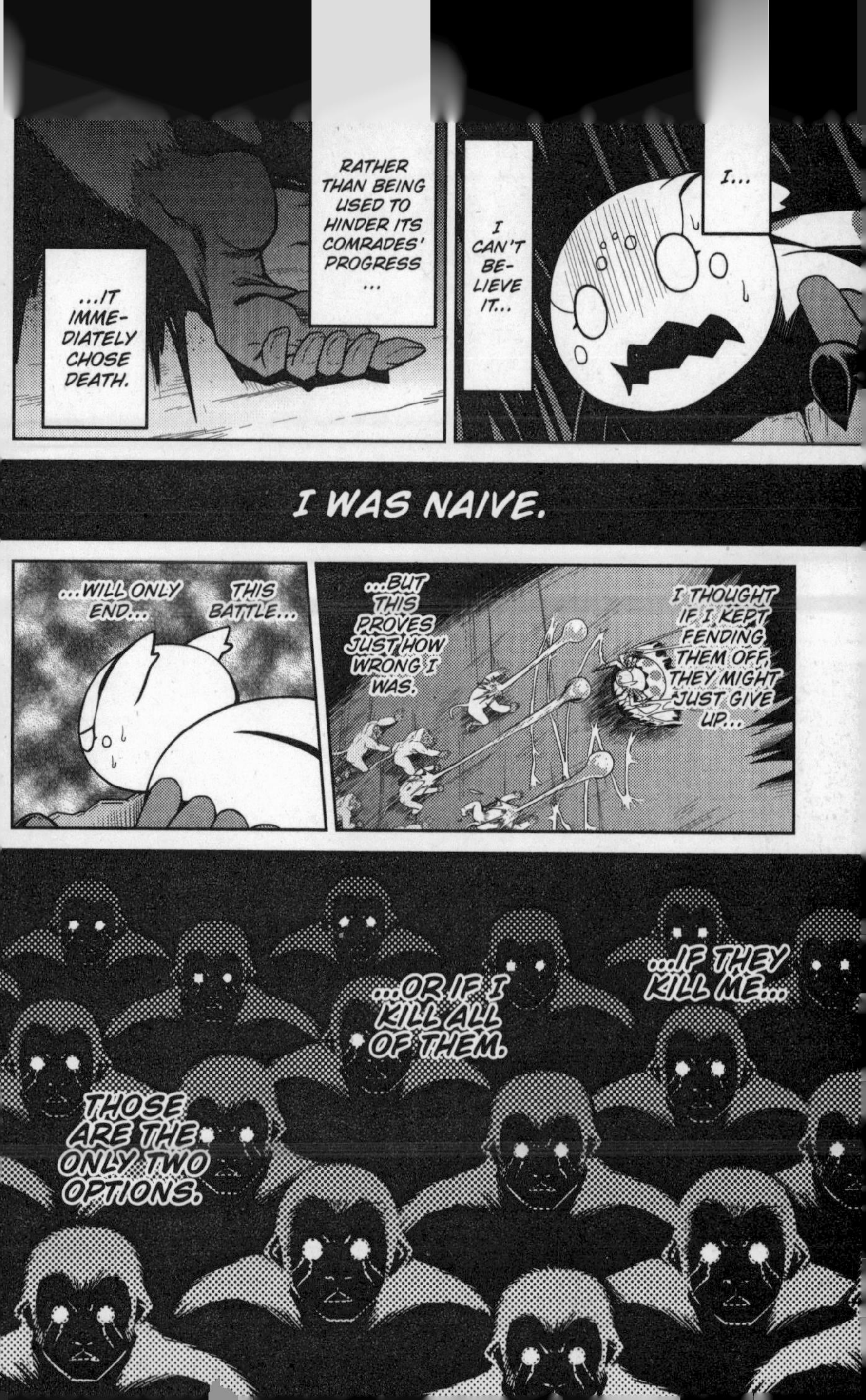
I...
I CAN'T BELIEVE IT...
RATHER THAN BEING USED TO HINDER ITS COMRADES' PROGRESS...
...IT IMMEDIATELY CHOSE DEATH.
I WAS NAIVE.
I THOUGHT IF I KEPT FENDING THEM OFF, THEY MIGHT JUST GIVE UP...
...BUT THIS PROVES JUST HOW WRONG I WAS.
THIS BATTLE...
...WILL ONLY END...
...IF THEY KILL ME...
...OR IF I KILL ALL OF THEM.
THOSE ARE THE ONLY TWO OPTIONS.

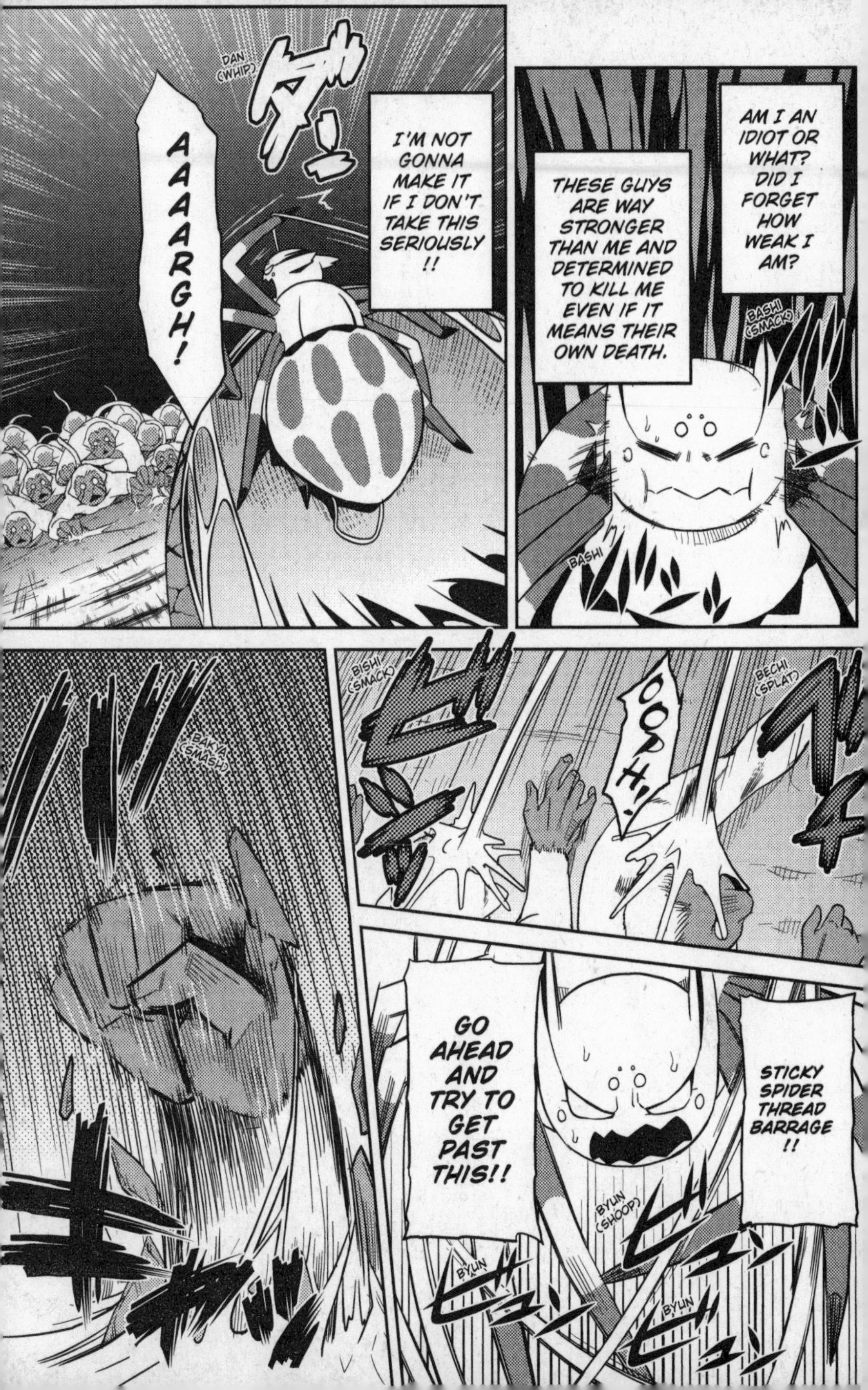
AM I AN IDIOT OR WHAT? DID I FORGET HOW WEAK I AM?
THESE GUYS ARE WAY STRONGER THAN ME AND DETERMINED TO KILL ME EVEN IF IT MEANS THEIR OWN DEATH.
BASHI (SMACK)
BASHI
I'M NOT GONNA MAKE IT IF I DON'T TAKE THIS SERIOUSLY!!
DAN (WHIP)
AAAARGH!
BECHI (SPLAT)
OOPH!!
BISHI (SMACK)
STICKY SPIDER THREAD BARRAGE!!
GO AHEAD AND TRY TO GET PAST THIS!!
BYUN (SHOOP)
BYUN
BYUN
BAKYA (SMASH)

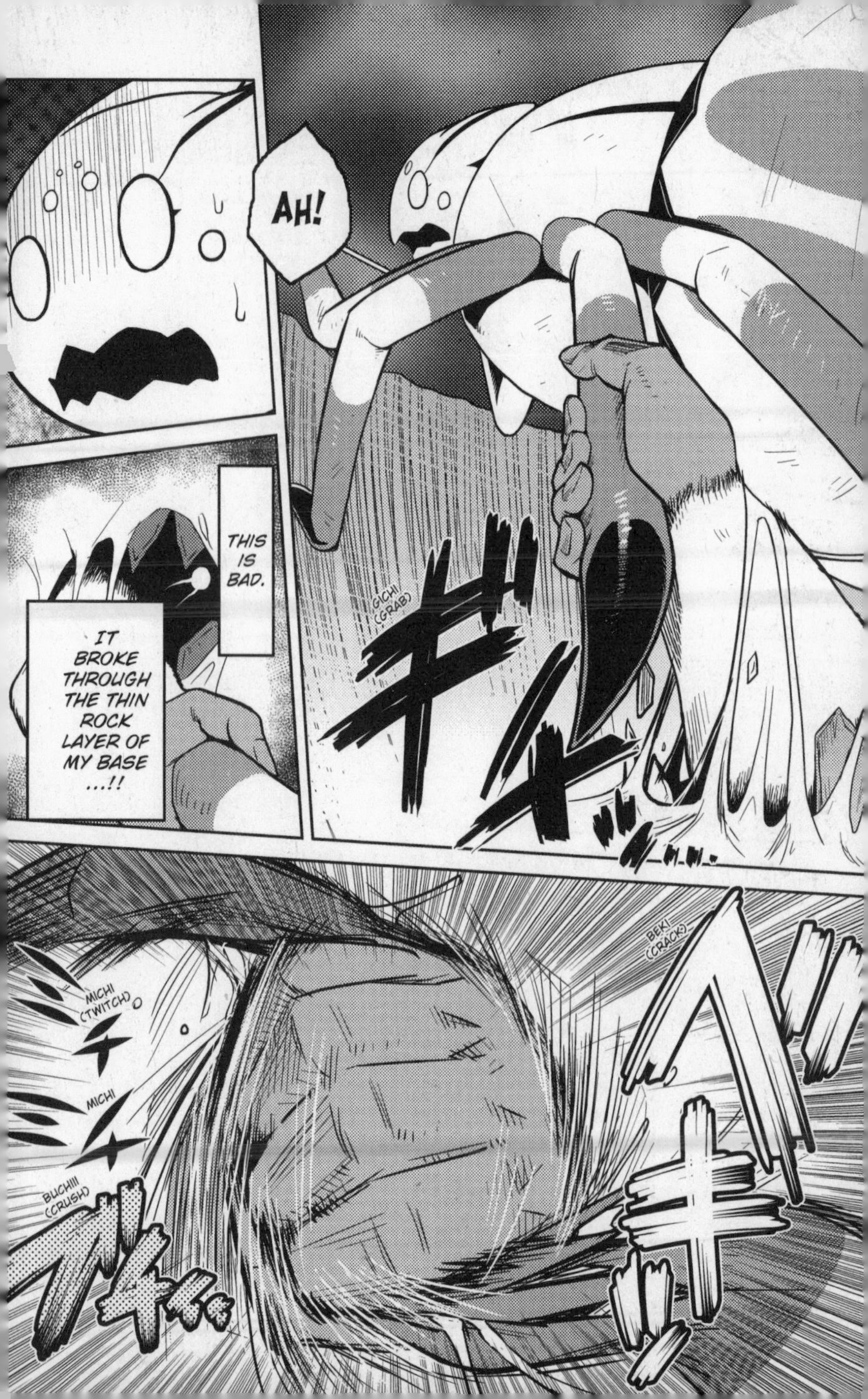
AH!
GICHI (GRAB)
THIS IS BAD.
IT BROKE THROUGH THE THIN ROCK LAYER OF MY BASE ...!!
BEKI (CRACK)
MICHI (TWITCH)
MICHI
BUCHIII (CRUSH)

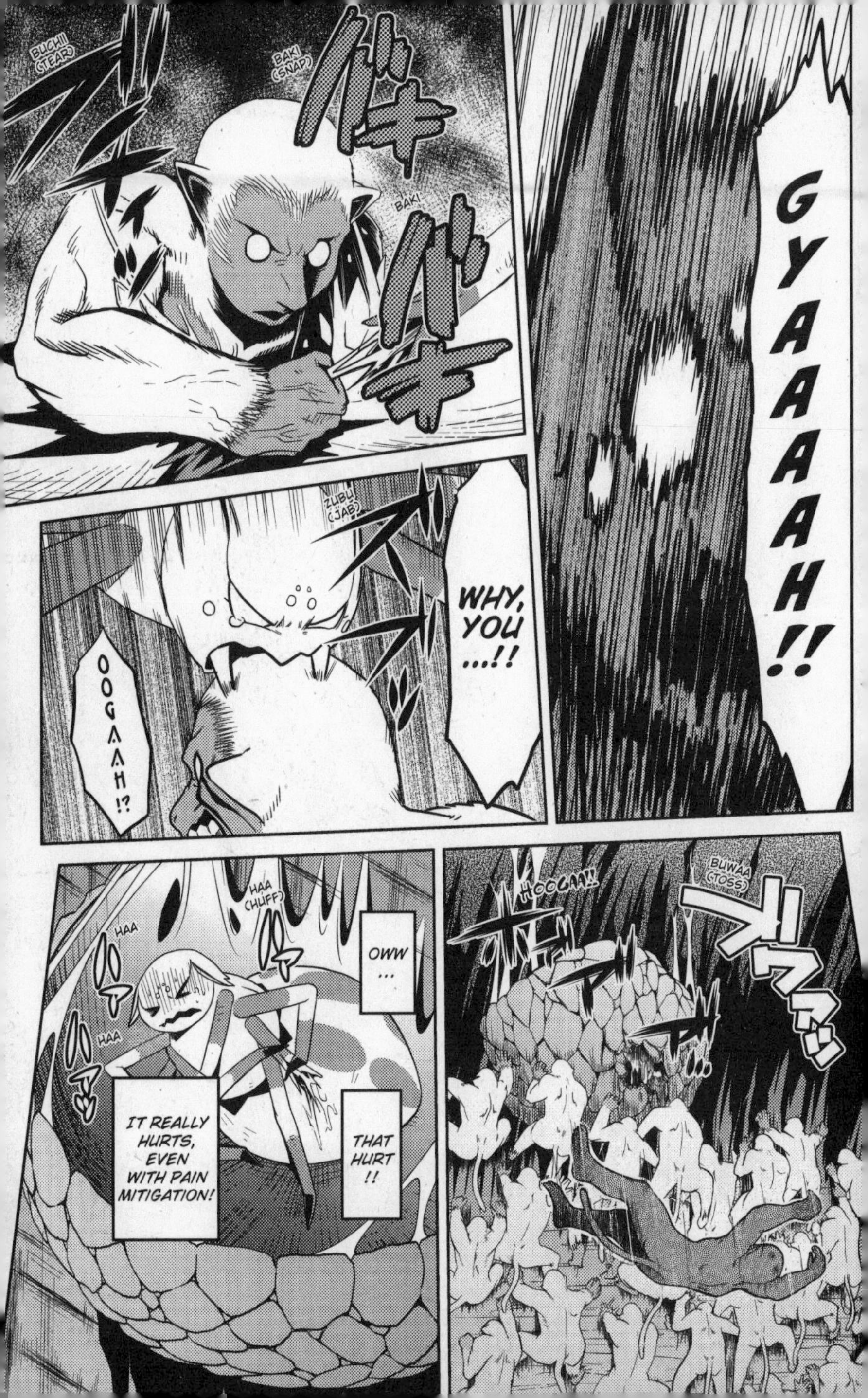
GYAAAAAH!!
BAKI (SNAP)
BUCHI (TEAR)
BAKI!
ZUBU (JAB)
WHY, YOU ...!!
OOGAAAH!?
BUWAA (TOSS)
HOOGAA!!
OWW ...
HAA (CHUFF)
HAA
HAA
THAT HURT!!
IT REALLY HURTS, EVEN WITH PAIN MITIGATION!

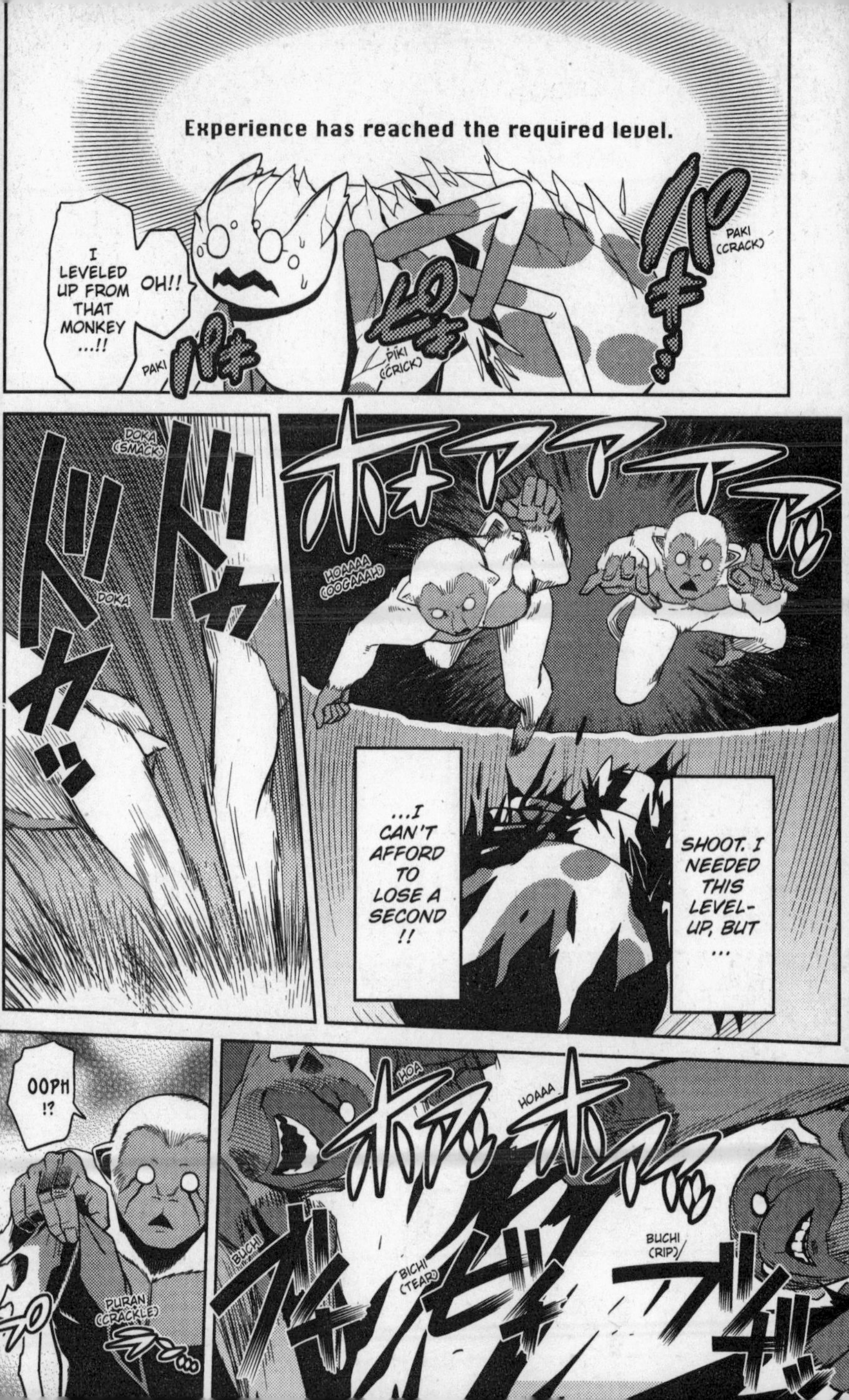
Experience has reached the required level.
PAKI (CRACK)
PIKI (CRICK)
OH!!
I LEVELED UP FROM THAT MONKEY ...!!
PAKI
HOAAAA (OOGAAAAH)
SHOOT. I NEEDED THIS LEVEL-UP, BUT ...
...I CAN'T AFFORD TO LOSE A SECOND !!
DOKA (SMACK)
DOKA
HOA
HOAAA
BUCHI (RIP)
BICHI (TEAR)
BUCHI
OOPH !?
PURAN (CRACKLE)

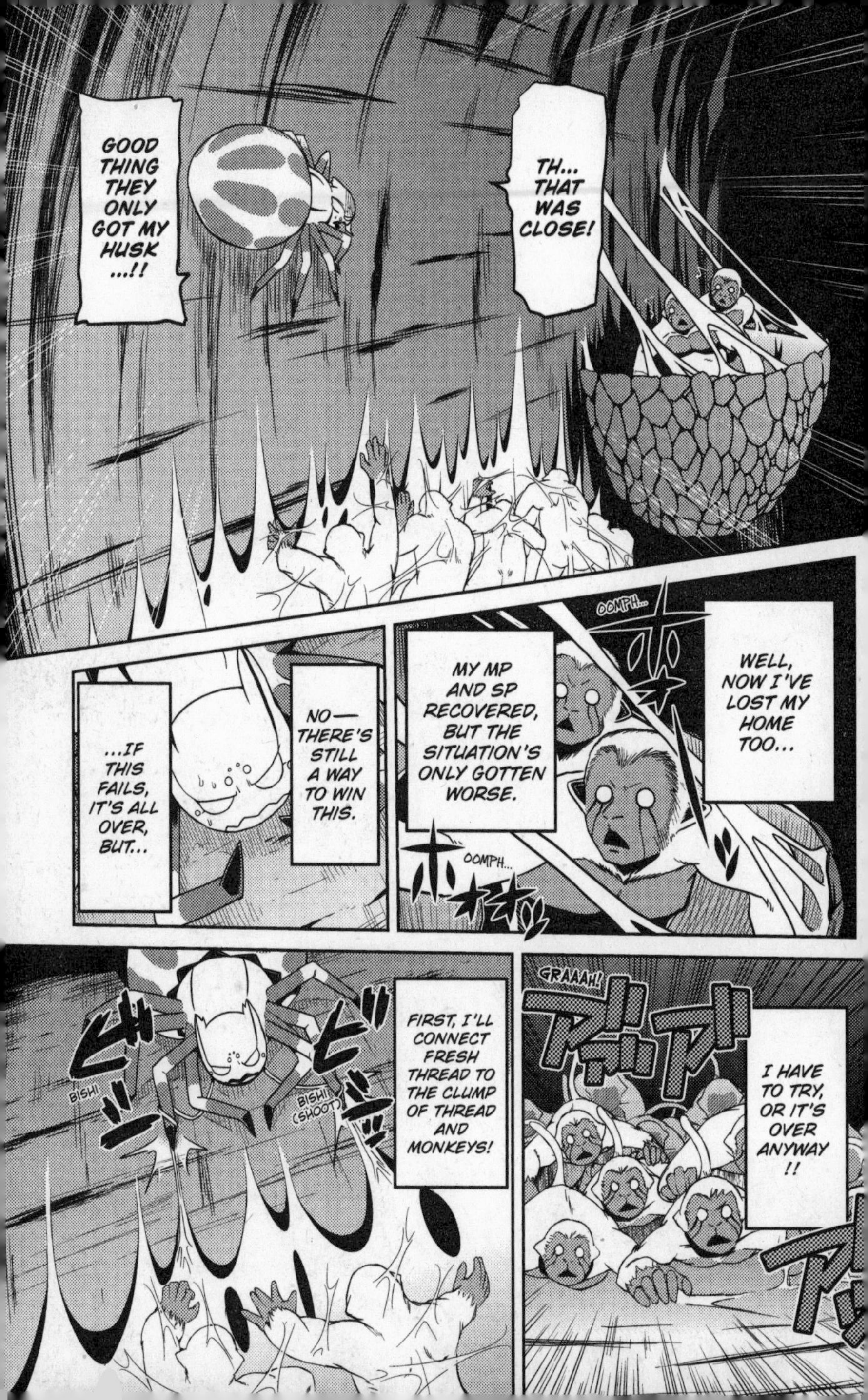
TH... THAT WAS CLOSE!
GOOD THING THEY ONLY GOT MY HUSK ...!!
OOMPH...
WELL, NOW I'VE LOST MY HOME TOO...
MY MP AND SP RECOVERED, BUT THE SITUATION'S ONLY GOTTEN WORSE.
OOMPH...
NO— THERE'S STILL A WAY TO WIN THIS.
...IF THIS FAILS, IT'S ALL OVER, BUT...
GRAAAH!
I HAVE TO TRY, OR IT'S OVER ANYWAY!!
FIRST, I'LL CONNECT FRESH THREAD TO THE CLUMP OF THREAD AND MONKEYS!
BISHI (SHOOT)
BISHI

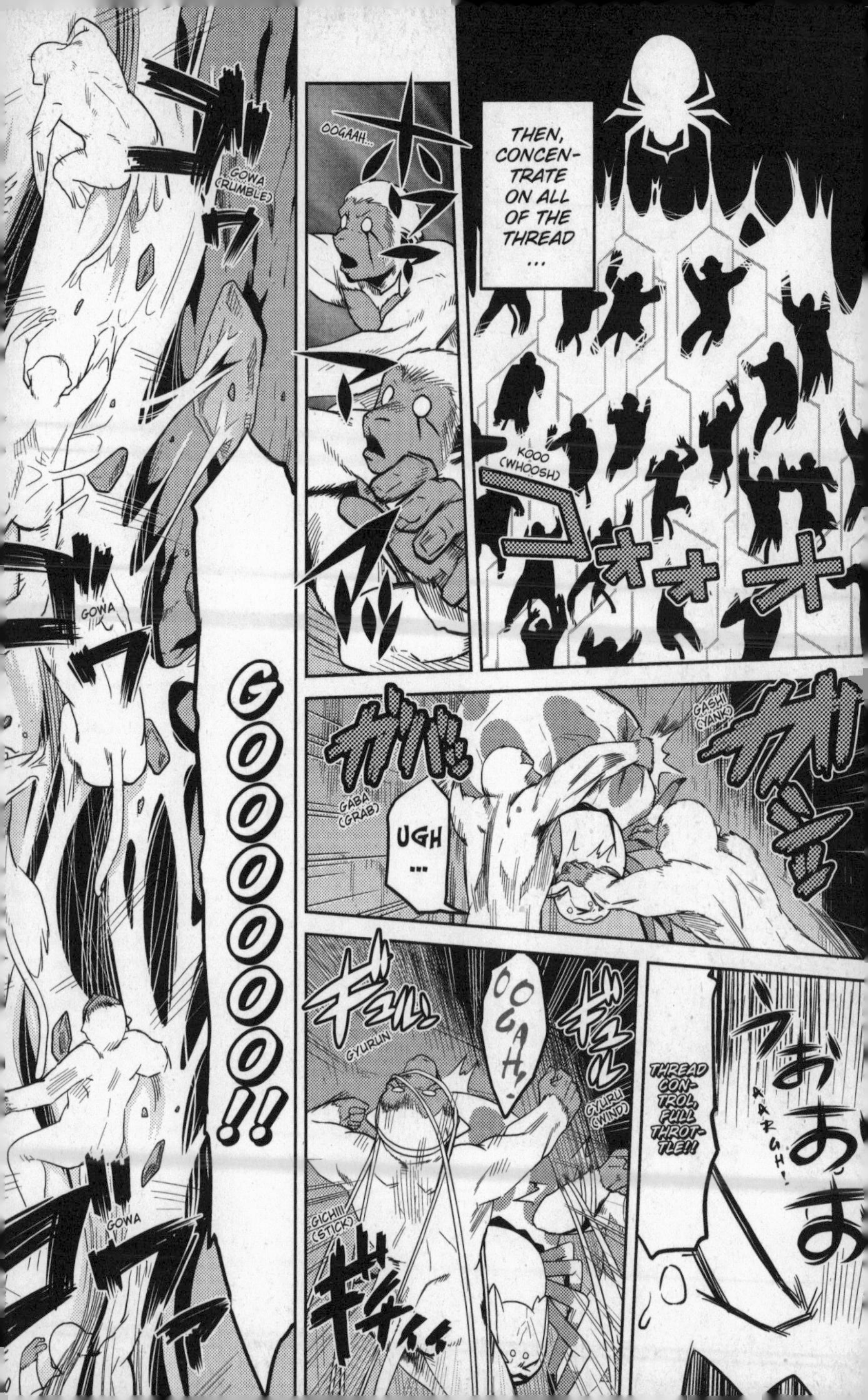
THEN, CONCENTRATE ON ALL OF THE THREAD...
KOOO (WHOOSH)
OOGAAH...
GASHI (YANK)
GABA (GRAB)
UGH...
THREAD CONTROL, FULL THROTTLE!!
AARGH!
OOGAH!
GYURU (WIND)
GYURUN
GICHIII (STICK)
GOWA (RUMBLE)
GOWA
GOOOOOOOO!!
GOWA

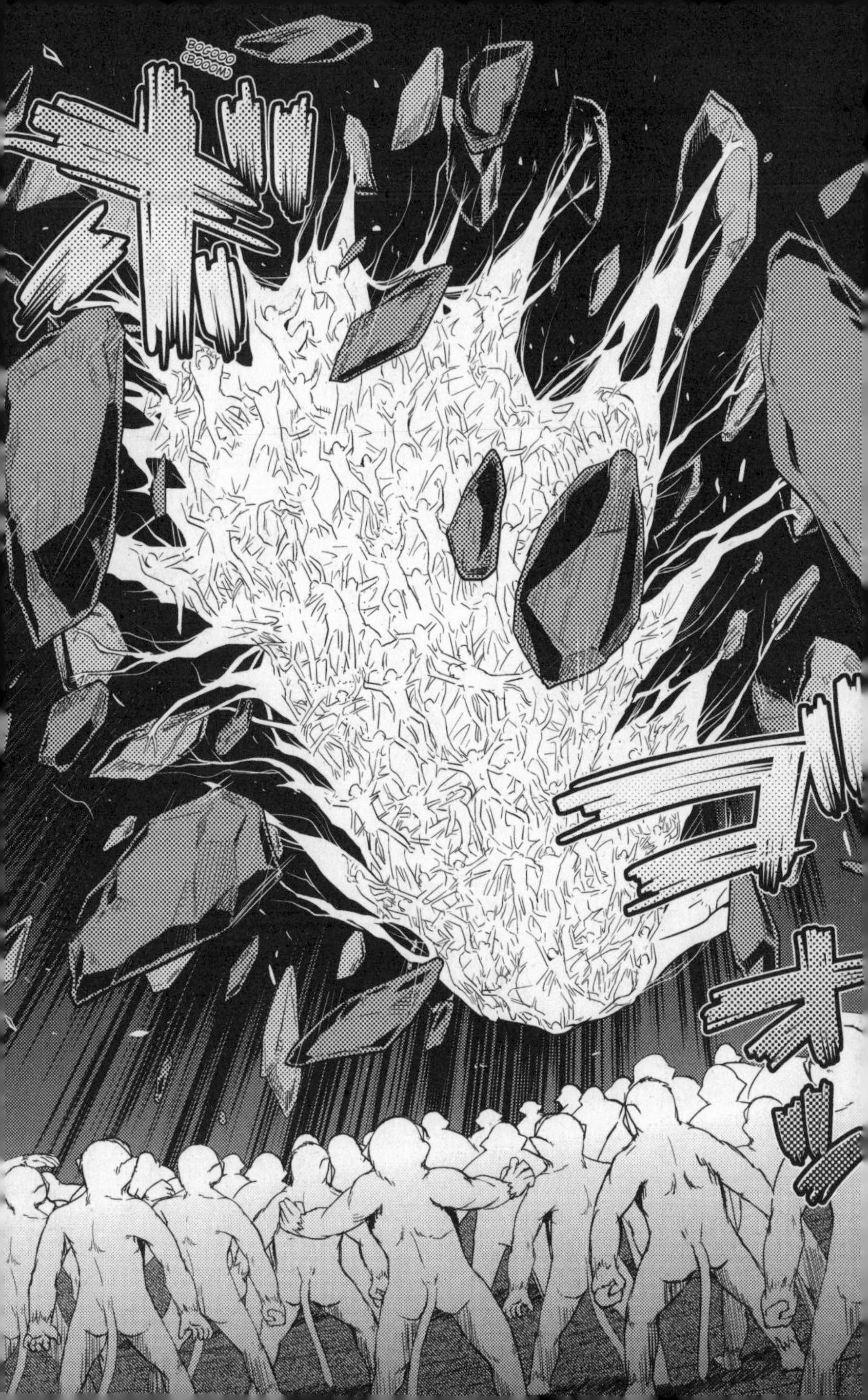
BOGOOO
(BOOOM)

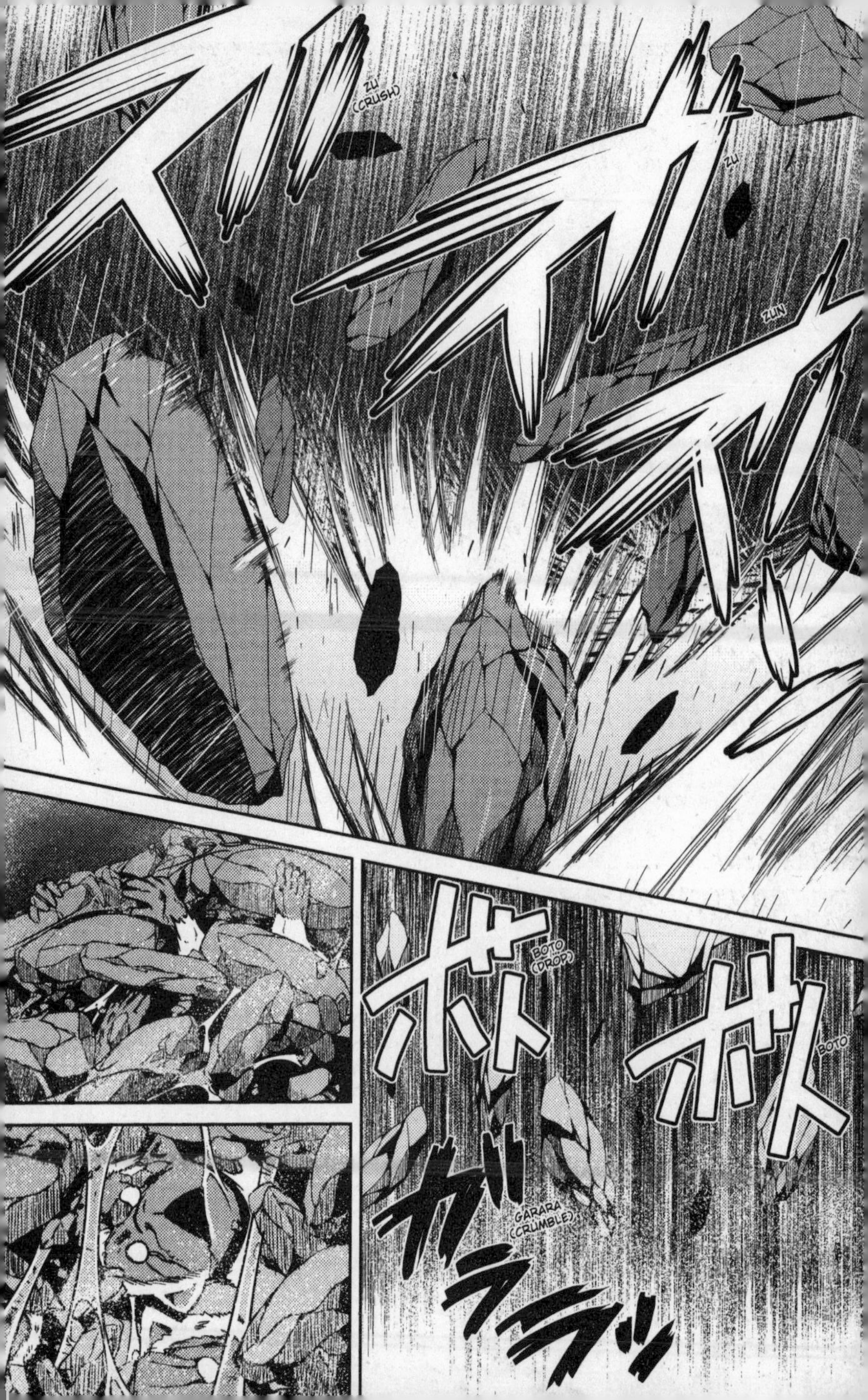
ZU (CRUSH)
ZU
ZUN
BOTO
BOTO (DROP)
GARARA (CRUMBLE)

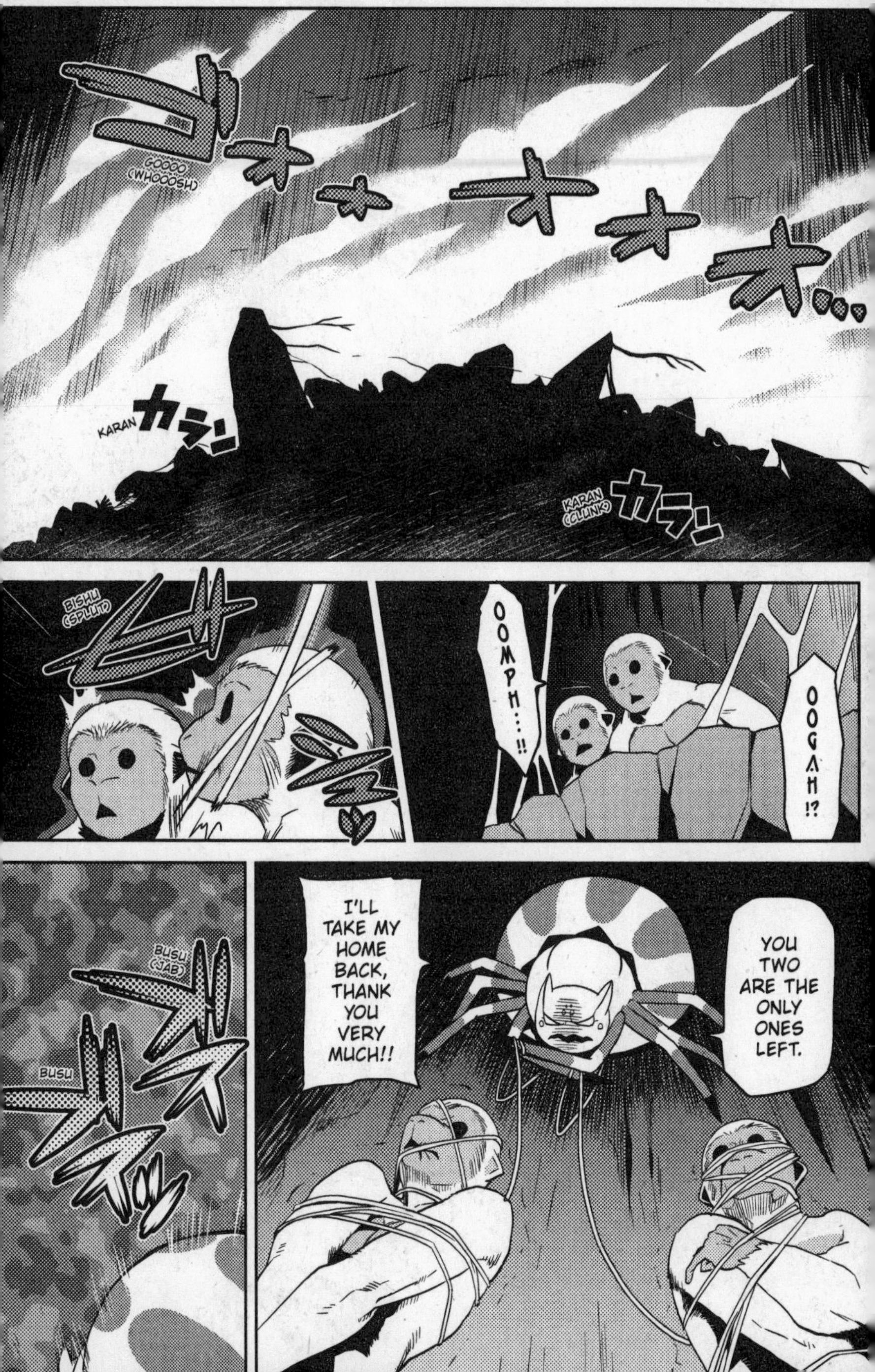
GOOOO (WHOOOSH)
KARAN
KARAN (CLUNK)
OOGAH!?
OOMPH...!!
BISHU (SPLUT)
YOU TWO ARE THE ONLY ONES LEFT.
I'LL TAKE MY HOME BACK, THANK YOU VERY MUCH!!
BUSU (JAB)
BUSU

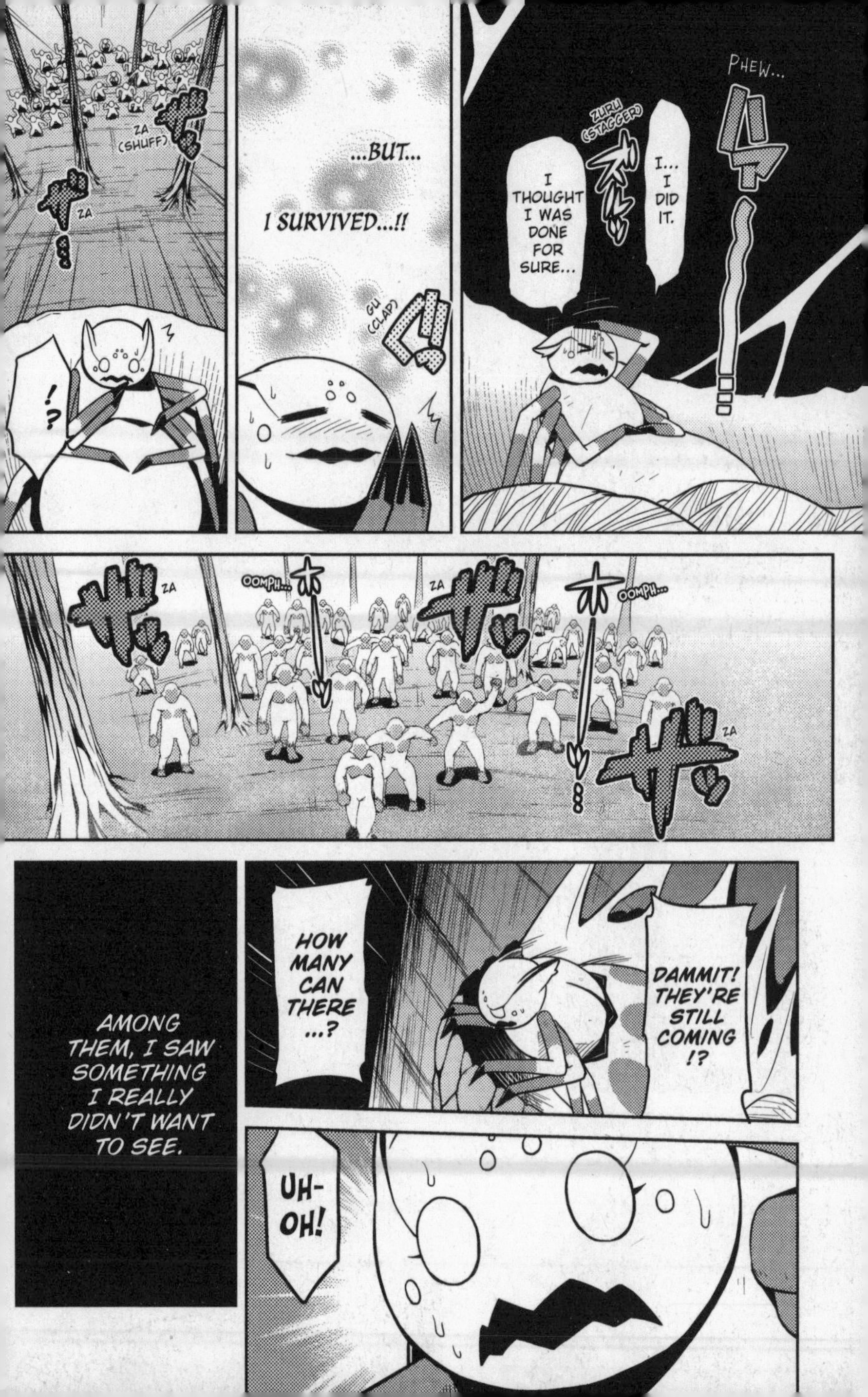
PHEW...
I... I DID IT.
ZURU (STAGGER)
I THOUGHT I WAS DONE FOR SURE...
...BUT...
I SURVIVED...!!
GU (CLAP)
ZA (SHUFF)
ZA
!?
OOMPH...
ZA
ZA
OOMPH...
ZA
DAMMIT! THEY'RE STILL COMING!?
HOW MANY CAN THERE ...?
UH-OH!
AMONG THEM, I SAW SOMETHING I REALLY DIDN'T WANT TO SEE.

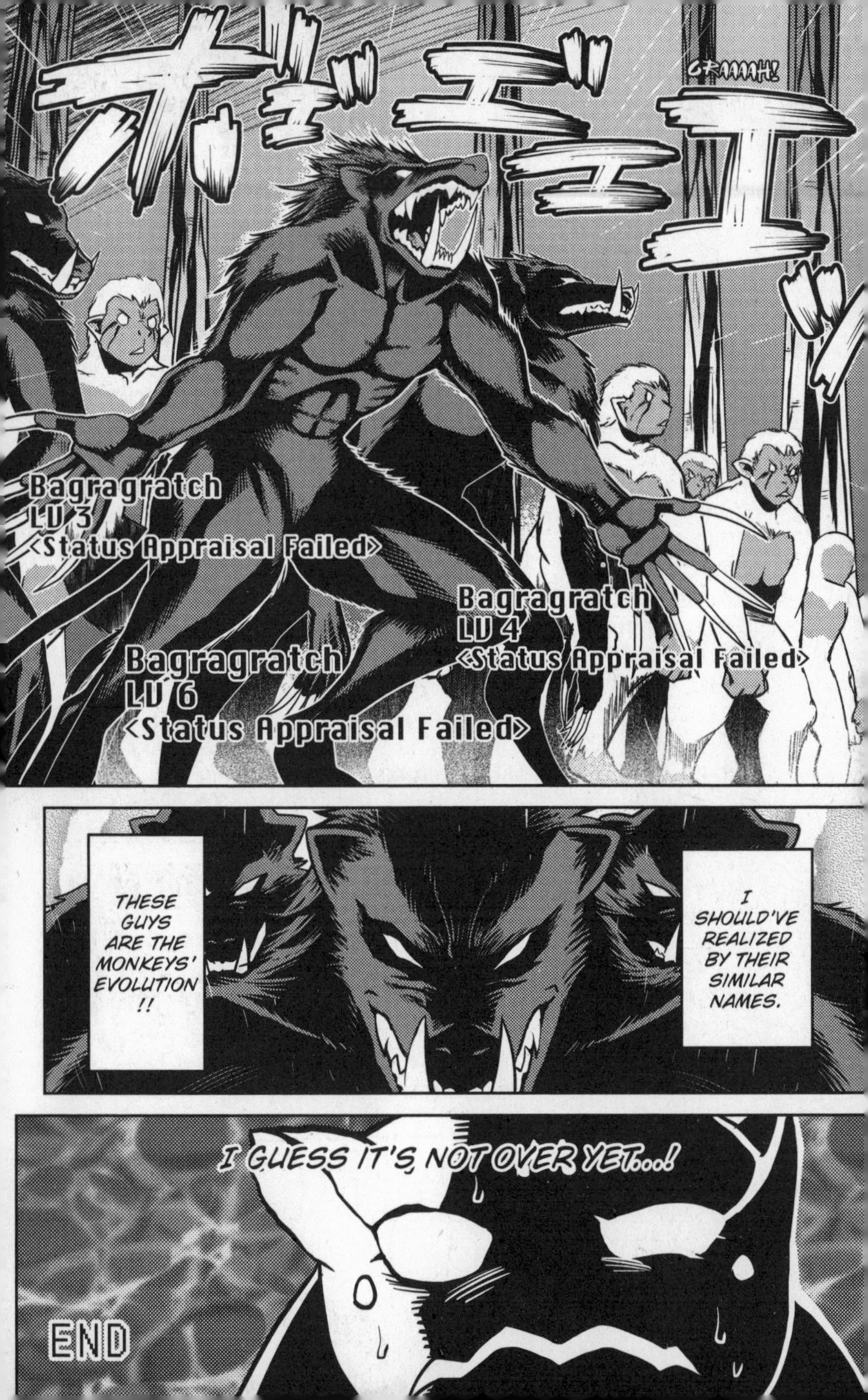
GRAAAAH!
Bagragratch
LV 3
<Status Appraisal Failed>
Bagragratch
LV 4
<Status Appraisal Failed>
Bagragratch
LV 6
<Status Appraisal Failed>
I SHOULD'VE REALIZED BY THEIR SIMILAR NAMES.
THESE GUYS ARE THE MONKEYS' EVOLUTION!!
I GUESS IT'S NOT OVER YET...!
END

AFTERWORD

ORIGINAL CREATOR: OKINA BABA

YAHOO! I'M OKINA BABA, AND I'M CURRENTLY CELEBRATING THE SUCCESSFUL RELEASE OF VOLUME 2.

IF VOLUME 1 IS ABOUT KUMOKO STARTING HER LIFE IN THE DUNGEON, VOLUME 2 IS ABOUT STARTING LIFE IN THE LOWER STRATUM.

IN THE FIRST VOLUME, SHE'S SUDDENLY REBORN AS A SPIDER, WITHOUT KNOWING WHY, AND BEGINS A BATTLE FOR SURVIVAL IN A GIANT DUNGEON.

IN THIS VOLUME, THE LEVEL OF DIFFICULTY IS AMPED UP WHEN THE STAGE IS MOVED TO THE DANGEROUS LOWER STRATUM OF THE DUNGEON, AND AN EVEN MORE INTENSE BATTLE FOR SURVIVAL BEGINS.

THERE, SHE MEETS THE EARTH DRAGON ARABA.

IT LOOKS REALLY STRONG. (SHE FEELS SMALL.)

ARABA WAS DESIGNED BY TSUKASA KIRYU-SENSEI, WHO DOES THE ILLUSTRATIONS FOR THE ORIGINAL NOVELS.

AND KAKASHI-SENSEI DOES A GREAT JOB DRAWING THAT DESIGN WITH DEVASTATING IMPACT.

IT'S SCARY. (I FEEL SMALL.)

READING THE SCENE WHERE ARABA SHOWS UP GOT ME REALLY EXCITED.

GOOD THING I PUT ALL THE MONSTER DESIGNS IN TSUKASA KIRYU-SENSEI AND KAKASHI-SENSEI'S HANDS, HUH?

AFTER ALL, MY MANTRA IS "EVERYTHING WILL BE FINE IF I LEAVE IT UP TO KAKASHI-SENSEI!"

I HOPE YOU'LL KEEP SUPPORTING KAKASHI-SENSEI'S DELIGHTFULLY DRAWN *SPIDER* ADAPTATION.

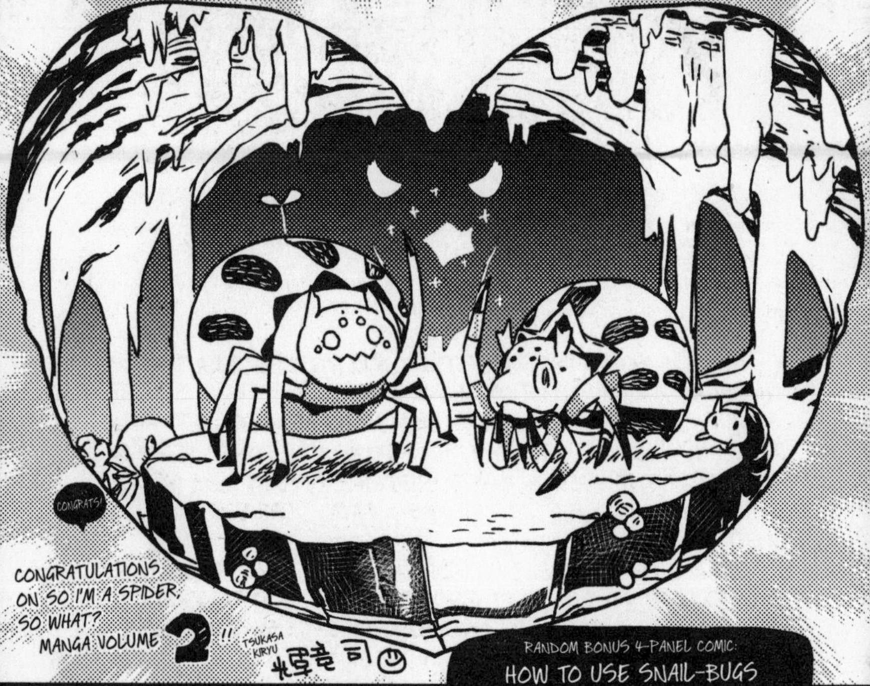
CONGRATS!
CONGRATULATIONS ON SO I'M A SPIDER, SO WHAT? MANGA VOLUME 2!!
TSUKASA KIRYU

RANDOM BONUS 4-PANEL COMIC:
HOW TO USE SNAIL-BUGS

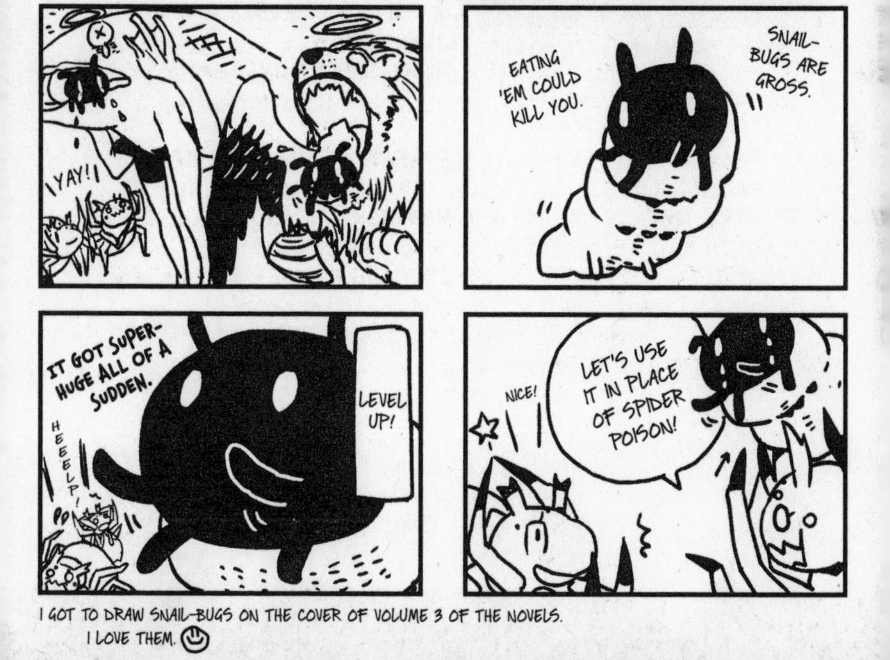
SNAIL-BUGS ARE GROSS.
EATING 'EM COULD KILL YOU.
YAY!
LET'S USE IT IN PLACE OF SPIDER POISON!
NICE!
LEVEL UP!
IT GOT SUPER-HUGE ALL OF A SUDDEN.
HEEELP!

I GOT TO DRAW SNAIL-BUGS ON THE COVER OF VOLUME 3 OF THE NOVELS. I LOVE THEM.

AFTERWORD

THANK YOU VERY MUCH FOR BUYING VOLUME 2 OF THE MANGA VERSION OF SO I'M A SPIDER, SO WHAT?

I'VE BEEN A MANGA ARTIST FOR A PRETTY LONG TIME, BUT THIS IS MY FIRST TIME DRAWING A DIRECT ADAPTATION OF SOMETHING.

MANY OF MY FRIENDS DRAW COMIC ADAPTATIONS, SO I ALREADY KIND OF KNEW THAT IT'S DIFFICULT IN A DIFFERENT WAY FROM CREATING AN ORIGINAL WORK—BUT I DIDN'T REALLY UNDERSTAND THE FEELING OF TRYING TO LIVE UP TO THE WORK IT'S BASED ON UNTIL I EXPERIENCED IT FOR MYSELF. HONESTLY, IT'S A LOT OF PRESSURE.

SINCE THE FIRST VOLUME, THE ORIGINAL CREATOR, OKINA BABA-SAN, AND THE ILLUSTRATOR, TSUKASA KIRYU-SAN, HAVE BEEN KIND ENOUGH TO CONTRIBUTE BONUS STORIES AND DRAWINGS, AND THEY EVEN PUT UP WITH ANY (ARBITRARY) CHANGES I MAKE IN MY ADAPTATION. I'M EXTREMELY GRATEFUL.

FROM THE BEGINNING, WE DECIDED THAT SINCE IT'D BE FUNDAMENTALLY IMPOSSIBLE TO REPRODUCE THE NOVEL VERSION IN THE MANGA, WE'D TREAT THE NOVEL VERSION LIKE A HI-RES 3-D GAME AND THE MANGA LIKE A PIXELATED 2-D GAME. AS SUCH, I'VE BEEN GIVEN MORE OR LESS TOTAL CONTROL OVER THE AMOUNT OF INFORMATION IN THE MANGA.

I'LL KEEP DOING MY BEST TO PRESERVE THE FEELING AND SCENERY OF THE ORIGINAL, SO I HOPE YOU'LL KEEP FOLLOWING ALONG WITH THE MANGA VERSION OF KUMOKO ON HER ADVENTURES.

11/2016 ASAHIRO KAKASHI

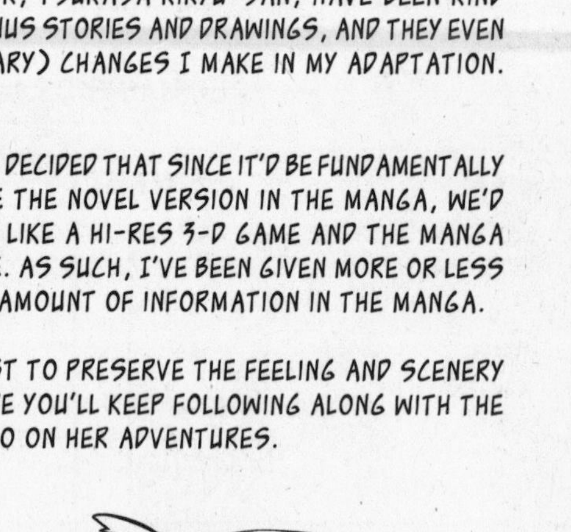

ASAHIRO KAKASHI

STAFF LIST

The author

ASAHIRO KAKASHI

Assistants

TERUO HATANAKA

REI HASEKURA

MIMASAKA

Design

R design studio

(Shinji Yamaguchi, Chie Ooshima, Sanae Kogure)

You're reading
the wrong way!
Turn the page to read
a bonus short story by
So I'm a Spider, So What?
original creator,
Okina Baba!

and the frog prince swallowed it just like that.

But in the process, some of those digestive fluids went flying toward me, even though I was hiding pretty far away. I was this close to getting hit by a stray shot.

I decided then and there that trying to learn from a Lower Stratum monster battle wasn't worth the risk.

I mean, can you imagine getting killed just by a stray shot from someone else's fight?

No waaay.

Monster battles are only fun when you're watching them from the other side of a screen.

It's not something you wanna be anywhere near in reality!

[The end]

move so quickly your eyes can't even follow it?

Ha-ha-ha. No way could I ever beat that.

But, y'know, all these freaks are constantly fighting each other.

The weak monsters get eaten by the strong monsters, the strong monsters get eaten by even stronger monsters, and so on.

The weaker monsters get by with self-defense mechanisms like poison, but even that has its limits.

Still, most monsters wouldn't knowingly eat something poisonous.

So they usually hunt monsters that aren't.

Meaning, of course, monsters that are so strong they don't need to be poisonous.

That's why eat-or-be-eaten fights between super-strong monsters break out here sometimes.

In fact, it's just part of daily life in the Great Elroe Labyrinth Lower Stratum.

No, seriously.

The second I lay eyes on a fight like that, I run away, of course.

If a weakling like me gets into the middle of such a dangerous battle, I could easily be killed in the crossfire.

There was one time when my curiosity got the better of me and I drew a little closer to try to learn from the battle, but it almost cost me my life.

The contenders in that fight were some kinda frog prince and what looked like a giant, metal pond skater.

I'm pretty sure the frog prince was a super-evolved form of the normal frogs.

As for the pond skater, I have no idea.

But its whole body looked like it was practically made of knives, so it was obviously really freaking dangerous.

But that crazy deadly monster ended up being eaten almost casually by the frog prince.

It watched the pond skater dart around for a minute. Then, when it came within close range, the frog prince spat some digestive fluids on it.

As soon as the attack landed, the pond skater started dissolving,

So I'm a Spider, So What?

Monster Battle

Okina Baba

The Great Elroe Labyrinth.

A dungeon full of powerful monsters.

For the most part, I don't even need to Appraise them to know they're out of my league.

I mean, it's obvious from their appearance that they're super strong!

First of all, they're huge.

And huge means strong.

Seriously, I'm not even joking. Of course, bigger monsters are stronger.

Think about it!

Between a kid and an adult, of course the adult is gonna be stronger, right?

It's like that.

A bigger body means more power and higher resistance, too.

Sure, you might say, but wouldn't their movements be slower? But that's not always the case.

In this world, we all have stats, and that includes a "Speed" stat.

If it has a high speed stat, even a giant, heavy-looking creature can dart around with ease.

Which leads to some really bizarre sights, let me tell you. The kinda thing you'd normally only ever see in a movie or something.

There used to be monsters in games and stuff that moved so unnaturally it made you wonder if the physics engine was broken, but compared to here, that was normal.

Seriously, why would a beast that's over ten feet long be able to

so I'm a Spider, so What?

2

Art: **Asahiro Kakashi**

Original Story: **Okina Baba**

Character Design: **Tsukasa Kiryu**

Translation: Jenny McKeon ☥ Lettering: Bianca Pistillo

Kumo desuga, nanika? Volume 2
© Asahiro KAKASHI 2016
© Okina Baba, Tsukasa Kiryu 2016
First published in Japan in 2016 by KADOKAWA CORPORATION, Tokyo.
English translation rights arranged with KADOKAWA CORPORATION, Tokyo,
through TUTTLE-MORI AGENCY, INC.

English translation © 2018 by Yen Press, LLC

Yen Press
1290 Avenue of the Americas
New York, NY 10104

Visit us at yenpress.com
facebook.com/yenpress
twitter.com/yenpress
yenpress.tumblr.com
instagram.com/yenpress

First Yen Press Edition: March 2018

Yen Press is an imprint of Yen Press, LLC.
The Yen Press name and logo are trademarks of Yen Press, LLC.

Library of Congress Control Number: 2017954138

ISBNs: 978-0-316-52109-3 (paperback)
978-0-316-52110-9 (ebook)

10 9 8 7 6 5 4 3 2 1

WOR

Printed in the United States of America